After Redress

After Redress

Japanese Canadian and Indigenous Struggles for Justice

Kirsten Emiko McAllister and Mona Oikawa
with Roy Miki

UBCPress · Vancouver · Toronto

Printed in Canada on FSC-certified ancient-forest-free paper (100% post-consumer recycled)
that is processed chlorine- and acid-free.

UBC Press is a Benetech Global Certified Accessible™ publisher. The epub version of this
book meets stringent accessibility standards, ensuring it is available to people with diverse
needs.

Library and Archives Canada Cataloguing in Publication

Title: After redress : Japanese Canadian and Indigenous struggles for justice / Kirsten
　　Emiko McAllister and Mona Oikawa ; with Roy Miki.
Names: McAllister, Kirsten Emiko, author. | Oikawa, Mona, author.
Description: Includes index.
Identifiers: Canadiana (print) 20240516095 | Canadiana (ebook) 2024051663X |
　　ISBN 9780774870658 (hardcover) | ISBN 9780774870665 (softcover) | ISBN 9780774870672
　　(PDF) | ISBN 9780774870689 (EPUB)
Subjects: LCSH: Reparations for historical injustices—Canada. | LCSH: Social
　　justice—Canada. | LCSH: Canada—Race relations—History. | LCSH: Reconciliation—
　　Canada. | LCSH: Indigenous peoples—Canada—Social conditions. | CSH: Japanese
　　Canadians—Social conditions.
Classification: LCC HM671 .M33 2025 | DDC 305.8956/071—dc23

Canadä

Canada Council　Conseil des arts
for the Arts　　du Canada

BRITISH COLUMBIA
ARTS COUNCIL

BRITISH
COLUMBIA

UBC Press gratefully acknowledges the financial support for our publishing program of the
Government of Canada, the Canada Council for the Arts, and the British Columbia Arts Council.

This book has been published with the help of a grant from the Canadian Federation for the
Humanities and Social Sciences, through the Scholarly Book Awards, using funds provided by
the Social Sciences and Humanities Research Council of Canada.

This book was also made possible with the financial support from the York University, York
Centre for Asian Research (YCAR); the Faculty of Liberal Arts and Professional Studies at
York University; and the Faculty of Art, Communication and Technology's Dean's Office at
Simon Fraser University.

*UBC Press is situated on the traditional, ancestral, and unceded territory of the xʷməθkʷəy̓əm
(Musqueam) people. This land has always been a place of learning for the xʷməθkʷəy̓əm, who have
passed on their culture, history, and traditions for millennia, from one generation to the next.*

UBC Press
The University of British Columbia
www.ubcpress.ca

For Roy Miki (1942–24) and for Grace Eiko Thomson (1933–24).

We also dedicate this volume to the generations of Indigenous and Japanese Canadian researchers, writers, and thinkers who made critical scholarship possible, especially those whose work and lives have yet to be recognized.

Contents

Acknowledgments

This volume would not have been possible without the contributors' steadfast commitment to the goals of this book and their participation in informing its vision through their dialogue and critique. Their brilliance, original contributions, and persistent support have kept us going through the years involved in producing the manuscript.

We extend sincere appreciation to UBC Press and its editorial, production, and marketing staff for their dedication to the book. Darcy Cullen encouraged us to put a manuscript together when we first proposed the book. Senior Editor Randy Schmidt guided us through the submission and review process with care and supportive advice. We are grateful for his belief in, and commitment to, this project. UBC Press's production editor, Megan Brand; assistant director of marketing and business development, Laraine Coates; along with Farhad Moghimi, Brian Lynch, Carmen Tiampo; as well as the copy editor and designer, provided the guidance, labour, and logistics required to turn our words into a finished volume that could circulate in the larger world.

We also acknowledge the time and thought the peer reviewers put into assessing the manuscript. Their comments gave us the opportunity to strengthen the volume and highlight its goals.

We are honoured that the renowned Nisei artist Takao Tanabe gave us permission to use his lithograph *Cook Channel, Nootka Sound* (1996) for our book cover. Born in 1926 in the fishing port of Prince Rupert, his long, reflective meditations on the sea and land convey their barely containable power and dynamism in the seemingly calm skies and seascapes of his work. His art reminds us that this book is made possible by the life-sustaining territories of Indigenous peoples on which each of us lives. While expressing his deep respect and intimacy with these places' moods and saturated shifting light, Tanabe's art also registers the undercurrent of turmoil and loss of the thousands of Japanese Canadians whom the government removed in the 1940s, many of whom never returned after their displacement and dispossession.

We want to also thank the director of the Art Gallery of Guelph, Shauna McCabe, for assisting us with the permission process involved in using *Cook Channel, Nootka Sound;* Anona Thorne for her correspondence regarding permissions; and Naomi Sawada of UBC's Morris and Helen Belkin Gallery for sharing her knowledge of copyright and art gallery practices.

In addition, we thank Davina Bhandar for sharing her expertise by reading and commenting on one of the chapters, Paul Tsang for arranging the use of a room at OISE/University of Toronto for our first Toronto workshop, Smaro Kamboureli for providing the use of a room and facilities at the University of Toronto for our second Toronto workshop, Tod Duncan for assisting us in setting up the first Toronto workshop, and Adjua Akinwumi, a PhD candidate in the School of Communication at Simon Fraser University, for assisting us with references.

After Redress

Introduction: Japanese Canadian and Indigenous Writings on Justice "After Redress"

Kirsten Emiko McAllister and Mona Oikawa

Over the last two decades, there has been a growing body of literature that criticizes state redress and reparations nationally and internationally (Coulthard 2014; Fujitani 2011; Henderson and Wakeham 2009, 2013; James 2006a, 2006b, 2008, 2012, 2013, 2014; Lanegran 2005; Matsunaga 2016, 2021; Oré Aguilar and Gómez Isa 2011; Paik 2016; Sarkin-Hughes 2019; Simpson 2014, 2016; Yoneyama 2016). This scholarship examines how states that accept responsibility for the violation of persecuted groups' rights, whether through redress, apologies, reparations, or reconciliation, are motivated primarily by the desire to preserve their reputations nationally and internationally in accordance with terms set by the multilateral international human rights regime that was established following the Second World War. Critics claim that states apologize and agree to reparations while avoiding the implementation of structural changes that ensure justice for survivors and ending further violations. In Canada, scholars specializing in redress and reconciliation, such as Matt James (2006a, 2006b, 2008, 2012, 2014), and Jennifer Henderson and Pauline Wakeham (2009, 2013), have critically examined state redress, starting with the first redress agreement in the country, which the National Association of Japanese Canadians (NAJC) negotiated with the government and signed in 1988.[1]

They have argued that subsequent state apologies and acknowledgments, including those for the Chinese head tax; the 1914 *Komagata Maru* incident; Indigenous residential schools; the internment of Ukrainian

Canadians during the First World War and Italian Canadians during the Second World War; the treatment of South Asian Canadian families of the victims of the 1985 Air India bombing; and, most recently, the removal of Indigenous children from their families during the Sixties Scoop, have been more about serving the political agenda of the state rather than resolving the injustices (Chakraborty, Dean and Failler 2017; Cho 2021; Coulthard 2014; Dhamoon, Bhandar and Mawani 2020; Iacovetta, Perin, Principe 2000; Li 2008; Luciuk 2006; Simpson 2016). More specifically, Wakeham (2012, 215–16) argues that these apologies have been used for the "strategic co-option of the ethical project of offering recompense for injustices by the political program of silencing resistance and manufacturing premature closure upon questions of power imbalances that continue to structure Canadian society." While this volume contributes to the critiques of state redress, reparations, and apologies in the context of the complex and often paradoxical process of seeking justice through the Canadian settler state's mechanisms for redress and reconciliation, it foregrounds the practices and perspectives of communities seeking justice and our histories of organizing.

Researchers from these communities have played a central role in producing evidence to challenge the settler state's justifications for everything from residential schools to internment and immigration bans. With the exception of research by Indigenous scholars, there are only a limited number of academic studies on redress and state apologies from the perspectives of survivors and subsequent generations who have been intergenerationally affected (see Dhamoon, Bhandar, and Mawani 2020; Kobayashi 1992; McAllister 1999, 2010; Matsunaga 2016, 2021; Miki 2004; Oikawa 2012). But in contrast to many of these earlier studies and, in particular, some written by members of our community, this volume foregrounds Indigenous scholars' critiques of the settler state, reconciliation, and the politics of recognition that make clear that non-Indigenous peoples illegally occupy Indigenous territories, which is land Indigenous peoples continue to struggle to regain (Coulthard 2014; Lawrence 2012; Matsunaga 2021; A. Simpson 2014; L. Simpson 2011; Tuck and Yang 2012). Likewise, this volume starts from the premise that the settler colonial state's redress settlements and apologies for racialized communities are fundamentally different from its redress agreements, reparations, and apologies for Indigenous peoples. As Jodi Byrd (2011), Jonathan Okamura and Candace Fujikane (2008), Eve Tuck and K. Wayne Yang (2012), and Jennifer Matsunaga (2021) have argued, demands to redress the state's violations against racialized settlers have been based on its refusal to recognize their full rights as "citizens," in other words, as settlers who benefit from colonialism. In contrast, the violations against Indigenous peoples have been based on genocidal strategies to eradicate them and gain control of their lands. Chapter 1 by Bonita Lawrence and Chapter 3 by Dorothy Christian, as described below, discuss these ontological (foundational) differences and why the colonial state has had different aims and used different strategies for racialized settlers and Indigenous peoples.

As the literature on state redress and reconciliation in Canada recognizes, there are reasons for demanding acknowledgments, apologies, and reparations from the state that are not simply about abstract concepts of justice or material compensation. This volume builds on this premise, and focuses on Indigenous and Japanese Canadians' critical interventions rather than on the mechanisms of the state. As the authors of the different chapters make clear, for movements led by survivors and the next generations, the demand for justice, in whatever form, typically starts with the aim of empowerment. They are driven by the desire for truth telling (Matsunaga 2021). As Audrey Kobayashi wrote in 1992 (3), the mobilization of Japanese Canadians to demand redress "contains an immense scope for study, in terms both of understanding the relationship between government and citizen's groups, and the process by which community groups develop the resources to achieve political ends." *Redress: Inside the Japanese Canadian Call for Justice* (Miki 2004) remains the only book-length academic study of Japanese Canadian redress from "inside the call for justice" – and lays the ground for many more in-depth studies deepened with the insights we can now garner from the passage of time in the context of today's political urgencies. The contributors in this volume write from and about the positionalities "inside the call[s] for justice" for Indigenous peoples and Japanese Canadians.

While in 1992 Kobayashi (13) was hopeful that the terms of the Japanese Canadian Redress Agreement would "strike an important blow against racism," today, along with scholars who criticize state apologies, the editors and contributors in this volume are more than aware that state redress and reconciliation aim to further extend the control and management of Indigenous peoples and racialized settlers. Yet, even if these communities' struggles for justice are co-opted, including in some cases by their community's own organizations as they compete for power and influence, that doesn't detract from the importance of struggle (Miki 2004). While some would likely disagree with the argument of Naomi Paik (2016, 13; emphasis added) regarding Japanese American redress that "rightless people have *no choice* but to resist state violence from within the state's structures," they would likely agree with her conclusion, citing Lisa Cacho, that the decision to struggle can be more important than the outcome (13). Knowing our histories of struggle, which include incidents of co-option, is essential not only for guiding our own struggles today but also for our understanding of ourselves as political subjects and the insidious ways that power can incorporate what it seeks to destroy. This book focuses on what can be learned from the struggles of Indigenous peoples and Japanese Canadians.

Genesis of the Book

The idea for this volume came from a trip to Winnipeg in 2012 when the NAJC National Office invited Roy Miki, Mona Oikawa, and Kirsten Emiko McAllister to assist in organizing its records from the period encompassing when the NAJC became involved in the redress movement to the implementation of the agreement it signed with the federal government. As Miki, Oikawa, and McAllister sifted through the many boxes of records from the early days of redress activism to the establishment of the Japanese Canadian Redress Foundation and viewed the funding applications for community projects across Canada, they discussed just how little research had been conducted on Japanese Canadians' struggles for justice and more specifically, how little research has been conducted on redress, which has been primarily analyzed by white scholars through the lens of the government, its policies and discourses (with the exception of Kobayashi 1992; McAllister 1999; Miki 2004; and Matsunaga 2016 and 2021). In their analyses, it is "the redress agreement" that stands in as a reified signifier for redress, and *the movement* has been largely forgotten in the scholarship on Japanese Canadian redress. As Japanese Canadians, we took this lacuna as the starting point for this volume.

Now over thirty-five years after the Japanese Canadian Redress Agreement, there is little critical reflection on the movement's political legacy, whether in terms of its aims, hurdles, discursive tactics, media campaign or alliances with other groups, never mind what can be learned from its limitations and possibilities, even within the community. Indeed, arguably, what Japanese Canadian community organizations have predominantly committed to our collective memory is the redress agreement – rather than the movement, its driving principles, and its methods of organizing.[2] More specifically, within the community what is now remembered, in its most conservative iteration, is how the state finally recognized Japanese Canadians as loyal citizens (i.e., how it wrongly failed to do so previously) and its provision of individual and community compensation, for which we are now (supposedly) eternally grateful.

Moreover, the insights offered by scholarship critiquing state apologies about power and the appropriation of demands for justice over the past two decades ironically now threaten to reduce these movements to some scholars' assessments of their co-option. This scholarship has been produced in a context where there has been little critical research published from the perspective of Japanese Canadian survivors, their descendants and other communities seeking redress and reparations for the violation of their rights. In addition, there has been little acknowledgment of the pedagogical and emotional work that survivors have undertaken in familial, institutional, and communal spaces (Oikawa 2012, 306). Instead, there is a growing body of publications by non-Japanese Canadian scholars who claim entitlement to write our histories and assert their authority over our experiences as Japanese Canadians who are descendants from the generations the Canadian state removed from BC's coastal settlements during the 1940s. Here, the editors are also aware of the Japanese Canadian community's fading memory of the redress movement after three decades of depoliticizing multicultural policy (see Chapter 4, this volume), which has obscured the movement's larger legacy of challenging the state's racist laws and actions. In this context, the editors want to enliven discussions about how we can analyze and organize in the "after"(math) of (as well as the ongoing) mobilizations of Indigenous and Japanese Canadian peoples in different struggles for reparations and justice. The "after" includes subsequent calls for reparations and justice, including, for example, the provincial redress settlement for Japanese Canadians that the NAJC negotiated with the Government of British Columbia in 2022 as well as goals that go beyond state formulas.

By using the word "after," we also emphasize the ongoing demands by different Indigenous nations and peoples for land and sovereignty (Alook et al. 2023; Coulthard 2014; Lawrence 2012). We also decry the lack of redress for settler colonialism itself; settlers must recognize our occupation of Indigenous territories and meet our own treaty obligations (Sehdev 2011; Truth and Reconciliation Commission of Canada 2016). Other ongoing struggles by Indigenous nations and peoples include those described by Bonita Lawrence in Chapter 1: the "thousands of individuals" who were not included in the Indian Residential Schools Settlement Agreement (IRSSA) and the "survivors needing significant help," as well as the thousands whose claims have been rejected by the Sixties Scoop Settlement. Action must be taken on the recommendations of the Truth and Reconciliation Commission (2015) and the National Inquiry into Missing and Murdered Indigenous Women and Girls (2019). As David MacDonald, Andrea Breen, and Norma Jacobs (2022) state of the latter, "Trudeau's government has failed to follow up on any of the calls to justice besides the proposed action plan, and the ongoing [COVID-19] pandemic has made life more dangerous for Indigenous women and girls." All genocidal practices, including the settler killing of Indigenous women, girls, and Two Spirit, Lesbian, Gay, Bisexual, Transgender, Queer, Questioning, Intersex, and Asexual Plus (2SLGBTQQIA+) peoples and the settler killing of Indigenous men (Razack 2015; Roach 2019) must end. These, among innumerable calls for redress, rights, and reparations, show that state apologies do not foreclose or co-opt calls for justice and the aim to build just forms of community based on principles such as mutual respect and interdependence.

As mentioned above, *how* we recall the political activism and struggles of previous generations or don't – for example, by attributing the accomplishment of redress to the work of only the Sansei generation and forgetting the activism of the Issei and the Nisei – and critically assess the significance and limitations of their pursuit of justice and what they decided to prioritize and how they pursued their aims (Miki 2004), shapes how we understand our constitution as (a)political subjects today. What is the significance of survivors and their descendants researching and critically assessing the activism of past generations instead of non-Japanese Canadian scholars and researchers (who have received the majority of the grants and contracts available to conduct studies on Japanese Canadians)? Whose frameworks do we use, and what agendas do they serve? With the exception of especially Miki's, Kobayashi's, and Matsunaga's scholarship, as indicated above, there is a dearth of critical research on Japanese Canadian redress and its aftermath from "inside" the community, never mind in dialogue with other groups who have demanded justice from the state. Without insight into, on the one hand, how we as a community have been discursively produced through (and against) state violence, and, on the other hand, in relation to the larger racist and colonial structures, it is difficult to recognize that if we truly seek to change structural injustices (Young 1991), we need to understand how we have been produced, not only in relation to other Japanese Canadians (Oikawa 2012) but also, at a foundational colonial level, in relation to Indigenous peoples (Matsunaga 2021; Oikawa 2006, 2012; Okamura and Fujikane 2008; McAllister in Chapter 6; Oikawa in Chapter 2) and other groups whom the settler state has attempted to exploit, dispossess, segregate, suppress, or eradicate within and beyond Canadian borders.

Conceptual Framework

While this book aims to highlight the importance of examining the legacy of Japanese Canadian redress activism, it more widely aims to explore critical questions about how political praxis has been conceptualized and enacted by Japanese Canadians after redress (see Chapters 1, 2, 4, 5, 6, and 7), and Indigenous peoples (Chapters 1, 3, and 5) in the context of groundbreaking Indigenous scholarship and activism. It also aims to challenge the colonial, nationalist, and ethnonationalist frameworks through which redress has been defined (Matsunaga 2021). Here, a number of the chapters examine redress in the larger context of Canadian settler colonialism (see Chapters 1, 2, 3, 5, and 6) and others focus more on these questions of justice primarily in relation to the activism and concerns of Indigenous peoples or Japanese Canadians (see Chapters 3, 4, and 7). Moreover, by framing their analyses in relation to the "after" of redress, the contributors variously reflect on the effectiveness, the possibilities, and the negative effects of both the demands for reparations and the strategies Indigenous peoples and Japanese Canadians have developed to assert self-determination. The "after," however, is not meant to suggest that redress for different types of state violence has been achieved. Indeed, the "after" signifies the survival and ongoing struggles of Indigenous peoples and of the differently positioned settler Japanese Canadians.

One of the challenges the editors faced in developing this book was how to set up a framework that avoided simply reifying redress movements as co-optation while at the same time recognizing that much more research on redress settlements is needed. Perhaps, ironically, it is in part because the majority of the research on redress, with the exception of Indigenous scholarship, has, on the one hand, focused on settlements while, on the other hand, so convincingly concluding (despite authors' qualifications that they recognize the significance of pursuing redress and reconciliation for survivors) that state apologies have succeeded in co-opting calls for justice (Wakeham 2012, 215) that there has been less impetus over the last decade to revisit the complex implications of these movements and the settlements they secure for the survivors and subsequent generations. This book is thus concerned with critical scholarship from both our community and Indigenous communities that assesses what can be learned from the strategies and practices activists have developed to mobilize members and (re)build their communities, and also challenge the hegemonic authority of the settler state. Accordingly, contributors examine the strategies and practices these communities have used to reckon with what they have learned about the complex interlocking fields of power that work as much structurally as they do at the level of our identities to silence and fragment our efforts to analyze and mobilize. They consider what subsequent generations and other communities might find informative, problematic, or inspiring, whether in terms of possibilities or in terms of approaches to avoid. For instance, some of the contributors discuss how people have exposed and eluded the machinations of the state while creating tactics that reaffirm the principles and world views that can define their peoples according to their principles (Dorothy Christian in Chapter 3, and Smaro Kamboureli in Chapter 5); tactics for reckoning with the impacts of the state's process of restitution and redress (Bonita Lawrence in Chapter 1 and Christian in Chapter 3); initiatives for cross-group alliances and collaborative research methods (Audrey Kobayashi and Jeff Masuda in Chapter 7, and Mona Oikawa in Chapter 2); approaches for examining structures that reinforce state power across different sites, from communities to cultural policy to academia (Tod Duncan in Chapter 4, and Kirsten Emiko McAllister in Chapter 6).

As pointed out above, examining redress through the critical lens that reduces it to co-optation ironically functions to impose the very closure that scholars (rightly) critique: where the responsibility of the state ends with its public apology and amends. At worst, those demanding justice are seen as co-opted and their struggles terminated. This erases how their fights against settler colonialism and racism continue, involving not just new generations of activists but also elders who have led now little-remembered calls for justice and continue to participate in recent redress movements despite the physical, material, social and emotional toll. Again, as editors we recognize the importance of critiques of redress and apologies, especially with respect to how the state has positioned us as Japanese Canadians in relation to Indigenous and other racialized peoples, and our own complicities in settler colonialism. As Matsunaga (2021, 108) argues, "setting the record straight about one historical injustice, [here] in the form of acknowledgments to Japanese Canadians, hides the parallels to injustices faced by Indigenous communities in plain sight." As she explains, the state constructed the Japanese Canadian Redress Agreement through "the simultaneous avowal of the injustices suffered by Japanese Canadians and disavowal of Indigenous land dispossession," the core of settler colonialism (109), using the redress agreement as camouflage for the state's violent colonialism and more generally "the nature of how Canada governs [through] racist strategies of elimination, exclusion, dispossession, relocation, and marginalization" (108).

But while it is important to examine the mechanisms the settler state uses to co-opt movements demanding redress, reparations, and recognition of their rights, it is also important to research the strategies that have been effective in challenging state power. As explained above, this book draws from our experiences as Japanese Canadians who have taken part in our community's movement for redress in the 1980s (Oikawa and Miki) or in its immediate aftermath (McAllister). Thus, following Matsunaga (2021), Oikawa (2012), Miki (2004), McAllister (1999), and Kobayashi (1992), we wanted this volume to highlight the perspectives and practices of communities calling for justice. This means that in addition to studying how state power is deployed through reparations and apologies and maintained through other intersecting institutional sites, including the university and cultural agencies, the authors discuss strategies that confront racist structures and settler colonial power as well as foster just, regenerative relations and forms of knowing that draw on multiple sources and inspirations that as Christian and Kamboureli explain, envision the world in life-affirming ways. As explained below, this volume also highlights the different methods of writing and analysis as well as epistemological approaches that the authors not only examine but also have developed themselves, from storytelling to community-based research.

In order to avoid discourses that reproduce both the ethnonationalist reification and the fragmentation of racialized and Indigenous calls for justice, in addition to criticizing the broader systems of racism and colonialism, the editors wanted to broaden the analysis in this book beyond Japanese Canadian concerns, recognizing our complex relations and responsibilities as racialized settlers to Indigenous peoples and their lands. Our effort to avoid the reification of redress as co-optation was further contingent on framing the volume in a way that countered the reification of the Japanese Canadian redress movement as a call for justice achieved solely by and for Japanese Canadians. Mirroring the way multiculturalism silos "ethnic communities," Matt James argues, the pursuit of redress by different communities can also potentially corrode "the solidarity [between racialized groups]" when they focus on their individual interests (James 2006a, 228). In this regard, Matsunaga (2021) has analyzed the discursive strategies the government developed to "[isolate] Japanese Canadian redress from other cases in order to manage compensation risks" (110). In contrast, as she makes clear, the success of the NAJC's call for justice depended on the mobilization of a wide coalition of rights-seeking groups, from unions and civil rights groups to Indigenous leaders and ethnocultural organizations also seeking redress at the time (also see Miki 2004; Miki and Kobayashi 1991, 112; and Oikawa in Chapter 2).

Given the recognition of the importance of working in alliance, whether through the lens of intersectional research or allyship with Indigenous and other movements (see Chapters 2, 3, 5, 6, and 7), the contributors to this volume write across the siloing enforced by state apologies and discourses like multiculturalism (James 2006a; Chapter 4), as well as the "disavowal of Indigenous land dispossession," which is central to settler colonialism (Matsunaga 2021, 109). While more work is needed to expand the scope of analysis and allyship, we hope this volume provides critical frameworks for future research and encourages groups to share their analyses and strategies in support of work that fosters solidarity.

Foregrounding the Concerns, Strategies, and Methodological Approaches of Survivor Communities

The contributors to this book discuss strategies used by community members that are adapted from their own epistemological or experiential roots. Much of the information about these communities is not published, nor can it be found in any one archive. This research requires "insider knowledge," which in turn requires building networks and ethical relations with the people about whom we write in order to establish sufficient trust and understand our obligations to the diverse individuals who possess knowledge about organizing and its effects, or the location of community records and personal archives. Contextualizing our findings requires even more research in newspapers, community bulletins and more; most of these sources remain undigitized. All of the contributors use one or more of these strategies as methodologies in their activist research projects and critiques of hegemonic power. As many of the contributors make clear, these strategies and methodologies involve not only countering the hegemonic production of knowledge that supports the authority of white settlers' versions of "Canadian" history and their studies of Indigenous and other racialized communities but also building alliances (Chapter 2) and asserting their autonomy by exploring new ways to articulate the principles and practices that define them (Chapters 3 and 5). At another level, their deployment of narrative techniques as well as research and storytelling methodologies inspired by the principles and practices of their, and other, communities contesting racist and colonial systems, can be seen as a call to explore the political legacies of their communities' pursuit of what is entailed in a just world (see Chapters 1, 2, 3, 5, 6, and 7).

The authors are concerned with not just (re)assessing the repercussions and what might (have) be(en) achieved in the aftermath of redress and reconciliation agreements (see Chapters 1, 2, 6, and 7) but also the ongoing efforts of Canadian institutions to control the narratives about Indigenous residential schools and Japanese Canadian internment, for instance (see Chapters 1, 3, and 4), which are both part of the larger genocidal system of colonization and racial management of the population. This volume also examines how, on the one hand, the mobilization of Indigenous peoples and Japanese Canadians against the state, and, on the other, their process of negotiation and the reparations they seek have been informed by a range of different ideas about political subjectivity and discourses of social justice as well as larger questions about the guiding principles of life (see Chapters 1, 3, 5, and 7). The contributors discuss how many of the ideas that have informed Indigenous peoples and Japanese Canadians predate lawsuits against, and redress agreements with, the state, and how their ideas have changed, and new understandings have emerged, following their struggles for justice (see Cajete 2016; Simpson 2011; Smith 2012; and see Chapters 2, 3, 6, and 7). A number of the chapters focus on the politics of knowledge as well as the ongoing efforts to assert both Indigenous and Japanese Canadian knowledge and systems of governance, whether through storywork and textual and narrative tactics (see Chapters 3, 4, and 5) or political strategy (see Chapters 1, 2, 3, and 7). While both Indigenous peoples and Japanese Canadians have experienced persecution by the Canadian settler state, this book makes evident the differences in the nature and scale of, on the one hand, their persecution – as Lawrence states in Chapter 1, "the historic violences of colonialism have lasted for centuries, and therefore have involved much larger numbers of people," and also Japanese Canadians benefit from settler colonialism, living on the lands of Indigenous peoples (Chapters 1, 2, and 6) – and, on the other hand, their aims, the effectiveness of their demands for reparations and recognition of their rights, and the strategies they have developed to resist and assert their right to self-determination. Questions regarding the political relations and alliances (Lawrence and Dua 2005; Mackey 2016; Regan 2010) between Indigenous peoples and Japanese Canadian groups are also critically discussed (see Chapters 1, 2, 3, and 6).

Overview of the Chapters

To foster a dialogue between contributors, Miki, Oikawa, and McAllister ran a series of workshops, and as the process unfolded, clear themes began to emerge. The chapters are organized to reflect the dialogue between the contributors. In Chapter 1, "Redress Settlements as Colonial Recognition," Bonita Lawrence (Mi'kmaw), assesses the gains and losses for Indigenous peoples when they negotiate redress settlements with settler states. To understand the limits of what can be gained through these settlements, she theorizes the relation of the settler state to Indigenous peoples wherein "the goals of settler societies are both to amalgamate Native peoples and to eliminate them so that settlers can replace them on their lands." Lawrence's chapter focuses on the largest redress settlement in Canada – the Indian Residential Schools Settlement Agreement and its implications for the struggles of survivors of the Sixties Scoop to seek redress for the thousands of Indigenous children who have been fostered or adopted into non-Indigenous homes under the child welfare system. To further illuminate limitations and possibilities of negotiating state redress, she examines the terms of the Japanese Canadian Redress Agreement, which she identifies as the first successful struggle toward restitution for past wrongs in Canada. As she points out, it "profoundly shaped the possibilities for IRSSA." Here Lawrence provides the most systematic comparative analysis between Japanese Canadian redress and the IRSSA to date, importantly, foregrounding the goals of Japanese Canadian and Indigenous leaders. She indicates that for Japanese Canadians, public support for redress was acquired through their claims to and reception as Canadian citizens, whereas for Indigenous peoples the fight for a settlement was waged in the courts, where "racialized articulations of colonial law and economy have rendered Indigenous peoples as always incommensurably Other in Canada," and successfully securing a settlement came at a great cost to Indigenous survivors. As Lawrence makes evident, for instance, redress for Japanese Canadians "enabled a larger project of redressive historiography," while in the IRSSA and the subsequent Truth and Reconciliation Commission for Indigenous residential schools, colonial violence continues as survivors are forced by the settler state "to remember and relive the atrocities they experienced as children in order to qualify for payments." Lawrence's comparative analysis of the IRSSA and Japanese Canadian redress also makes clear the foundational difference between Indigenous peoples and Japanese Canadian settlers. In sum, insofar as Japanese Canadians wanted the state to recognize their rights as Canadian citizens, and protect racialized Canadians against acts of dehumanization, their redress settlement further reinforced Canada's colonial project. Comparing the two processes reveals the different outcomes for Japanese Canadians, who were officially accepted (if only rhetorically) by the settler nation through redress, and Indigenous peoples, who were pathologized and who experienced the whitewashing of their long histories of genocide.

In Chapter 2, "Web of Recognition: The National Association of Japanese Canadians and the 1989 Task Force on First Nations Peoples," Mona Oikawa examines Japanese Canadians' inaugural efforts to organize in solidarity with Indigenous peoples, continuing their commitment to social justice following the 1988 redress settlement. Like Chapters 1, 3, and 6, this chapter is concerned with the pursuit of justice and the relations between Indigenous peoples and Japanese Canadian settlers. In particular, Oikawa examines the records of the Task Force on First Nations Peoples, which was initiated by the Greater Toronto Chapter of the NAJC and was active from the late 1980s to the early 1990s. Central to her analysis are theories of recognition. As she argues, Indigenous and other scholars have critiqued the Canadian state's politics of recognition and its processes of recognizing Indigenous and marginalized groups' demands for justice and state accountability for injustice. She points out, however, that there has been little scholarly analysis of how racialized people recognize Indigenous peoples. In terms of methodology, Chapter 2 shows the rich possibilities of in-depth archival research. Drawing on the records from the task force's meetings and correspondence, which involved approximately forty-five people from across the country and was initiated by a core group in Toronto whose work was informed by the knowledge shared with them by a number of Indigenous peoples, she makes evident that there is not one monolithic Japanese Canadian position. The records reveal a wide range of discourses and the complexity of deciding how to approach initiatives, as part of a national racialized organization, regarding Indigenous rights. Reminding readers that the task force's deliberations took place over thirty years ago, before the proliferation of research examining racialized peoples' relationships to Indigenous peoples and settler colonialism, she shows how the task force's discussions and deliberations give insights into the self-recognitive processes of Japanese Canadians in relation to Indigenous peoples. Here, in the larger context of the critiques of state recognition, Oikawa draws on the work of Yellowknives Dene scholar Glen Coulthard (2014) and Mohawk scholar Audra Simpson (2014), who critique the politics of state recognition and offer analytical and political tools that "encourage us to think about other forms of recognition that contest and 'refuse' (Simpson 2014, 11) settler state politics of recognition." Furthermore, in using their concept of "web of recognition," Oikawa illustrates how the task force and members of the NAJC were both "agent[s] and object[s] of recognition" (Williams 2014, 12). On the one hand, they are racialized subjects seeking to recognize Indigenous peoples, but, on the other hand, many of them have been the objects of state recognition through the redress settlement and have also spent years challenging how the state has constructed them as enemy aliens. Oikawa states that "the selves produced through internment and redress, and the selves recruited in both service and resistance to settler colonialism require further examination, a project to which I hope this chapter contributes."

Whereas Chapter 2 offers a framework for analyzing Japanese Canadians' relationship to settler colonialism and white supremacy as non-Indigenous racialized people, in Chapter 3, "The Reconciliation That Never Was: Political Skulduggery on Indigenous Lands," Dorothy Cucw-la7 Christian, who is Secwepemc and Syilx, uses Indigenous storytelling as her methodological approach. By making evident how integral storytelling is for Indigenous values, laws, and interrelationships with the land, she makes clear what is politically at stake for First Nations, Inuit, and Métis filmmakers and writers who have challenged successive settler governments' attempts not only to rob them of their nations' lands but also to control their narratives. Christian gives a history of the different ways these storytellers have resisted colonial control over the production and distribution of their stories and the importance of challenging the policies of settlers' cultural institutions and stopping their appropriation of First Nations, Inuit, and Métis stories and experiences. Next, she delves into what is entailed in reconciliation between Indigenous peoples and colonial Canada, including corporate Canada. With humour that deflates, she identifies the political skulduggery of colonial Canada, contrasting its seemingly progressive rhetoric with its ongoing political trickery. She then turns to the work of Ron Derrickson (Syilx) and Arthur Manuel (Secwepemc) (2015) to explain how land and its resources must be a central component of any new framework for reconciliation between Indigenous and settler peoples. She concludes that establishing a new relationship between Indigenous and settler peoples needs to recognize that "Indigenous place-based stories and settler colonial stories are competing narratives that are at the core of social and political tensions that exist in Canada's very colonial political landscape." In relation to this book's focus on movements calling for justice, Christian asks: "What is it going to take to transform the embedded national colonial narrative so that the grandchildren and great-great-grandchildren of both Indigenous and settler peoples can share a sustainable future on these lands that could be mutually beneficial to all?"

Following Christian's discussion of why it is politically necessary for Indigenous peoples to control their narratives, in Chapter 4 Tod Duncan examines how knowledge production is also a site of political struggle for Japanese Canadians. In "Whither Redress? Interrogating Liberal Multicultural Accounts of Japanese Canadian History," he examines both who is (not) granted the authority to produce research on Japanese Canadians and discursively how the resulting texts reproduce deeply entrenched multicultural discourses that continue the deracinating drive of wartime policies. Understanding the context of Duncan's critique is important. He is continuing the critical tradition of Japanese Canadian scholars, going back over fifty years to the 1960s, when the National Japanese Canadian Citizens Association leaders commissioned Ken Adachi to research what he eventually published as *The Enemy That Never Was* in 1976, which challenged the dominant historical narrative that constructed Canada as a democratic nation and upholder of the principles of equality and justice. Thirty years after the redress settlement, Duncan – as a Sansei who began his university studies post-redress, after the government acknowledged there had been no basis for treating Japanese Canadians as threats to national security and admitted that its actions had been "influenced by discriminatory attitudes" (Government of Canada, in Miki and Kobayashi 1991, 138) – decided to conduct a genealogical analysis of Japanese Canadian studies. Despite the government's admission that it was motivated by racism, which prominent white historians of the day attempted to justify, a new generation of white scholars is now specializing in Japanese Canadian internment and dispossession, dominating academic publications about the community. Thus, Duncan makes clear that the relation between power and knowledge hasn't changed and Japanese Canadian scholars still struggle against the hegemonic forces in academic and other institutions to write their histories "from inside the [continuing] calls for justice." In contrast to earlier research, now it isn't simply a matter of a battle over what is credible evidence. He explains how liberal multiculturalism, serving as a technique of liberal governance that manages "difference through processes of exclusion," structures the research and writing on the internment by "liberal-revisionist historians" (McKay 2000). In theorizing the trajectories of liberal multiculturalism as imposed by the Canadian state "from above" and as struggled over by Japanese Canadians during the redress campaign "from below," Duncan lays out the political terrain on which most of the histories of Japanese Canadians continue to be both told and read. He examines the reception of histories written from within Japanese Canadian communities by five white liberal-revisionist historians and analyzes their claims to "objectivity," which they argue the Japanese Canadians they critique lack. Duncan's chapter reveals the racialized power relations that are masked by their self-professed "objectivity" and their derogation of Japanese Canadians' work that complicates and challenges liberal multicultural notions of the internment, redress, Japanese Canadians, Canada, and the discipline of history itself. More generally, the chapter is an important contribution to the literature on theorizing liberal multiculturalism in Canada and the gatekeeping role liberal-revisionist historians have demonstrated in their investment in controlling what histories can be told, how they should be told, and by whom. Moreover, like Chapters 1, 3, and 6, Chapter 4 traces how state power continues its deracinating and genocidal drive "after redress," and, like Christian in Chapter 3, Duncan calls on anti-racist community researchers to reappropriate their histories and determine what and how to conduct research that is relevant to them.

In Chapter 5, "Narrating the After of the Moment of Redress: Fred Kelly's 'Confession of a Born Again Pagan' and Roy Miki's *Redress: Inside the Japanese Canadian Call for Justice*," Smaro Kamboureli conducts a close analysis of Roy Miki's narrativization of the moment when Parliament passed the Japanese Canadian Redress Agreement and Anishinaabe Fred Kelly's (2008) essay "Confession of a Born Again Pagan" from the Aboriginal Healing Foundation's volume on reconciliation and Indigenous residential schools. In contrast to the scholars Duncan criticizes in Chapter 4, who dismiss publications written by Japanese Canadians because of their supposed lack of objectivity, Kamboureli identifies what can be learned from texts written by Anishinaabe and Japanese Canadian writers. Both authors, she argues, redress themselves and remain undisciplined subjects. In particular, she writes about Kelly's and Miki's essays on state reconciliation and redress, respectively, and examines the tactics they use and how they position themselves in relation to the state. Kelly, for instance, contests and subverts colonial practices inculcated in residential schools and in subsequent state and public performances of reconciliation by embracing decolonizing Indigenous epistemologies. Kamboureli argues that in *Redress*, Miki's description of the moment in Parliament – when the government read its acknowledgment of its violation of Japanese Canadians' rights – acts as a "repetition" and exceeds the limits of the liberal settler state's construction of the internment as an event in the distant past (19). Like Lawrence, Kamboureli situates the Japanese Canadian Redress Agreement and the Truth and Reconciliation Commission in a larger genealogy of apologies undertaken by liberal states. She argues that these apologies turn the Christian trope of confession into a "ritual of repentance that is enacted publicly." Confessions typically function to convert, and thus promise to transform, but she argues that state apologies, in contrast, usually do not result in fundamental changes. Her nuanced micro-level analysis of Kelly's and Miki's narratives works, as she explains, as an "epistemological telescope" that provides a larger macro view of the process of redress. She argues that the temporality that both Miki's and Kelly's narratives enact push against the margins of the settler state's temporality, while revealing the differences between the state's apologies to Japanese Canadians and Indigenous peoples. As Kamboureli writes,

> The after of redress may start in the now of time, but this doesn't perforce mean that it has sublimated the particularities of what has preceded it, nor does it guarantee the beginning of an ethically re-envisioned relationship between the liberal state and the redressed subjects. The after of redress encompasses the limits of justice; it may even signal a political or ethical impasse.

In Chapter 6, "The Political Act of Defining Ourselves After Redress: Japanese Canadian Activism, Identity, and What Can Be Learned from the Principles of Indigenous Storytelling," Kirsten Emiko McAllister turns her attention to the political legacy of the redress movement for today's Japanese Canadian community. While Chapter 5 examines texts written by Kelly and Miki that tactically subvert the state's discourses of reconciliation and redress, this chapter seeks to critically assess how the community has been constituted through the discourse of redress, starting with activists' initial call for justice and then the appropriation of their call by the state. The chapter begins by reminding readers of the ongoing intergenerational impact of the state's systematically deployed plan to remove "the Japanese" from Canada in the 1940s, which has made it difficult to understand who we are as Japanese Canadians. Here the chapter recognizes the significance of the redress movement and how it affected McAllister's own understanding of identity by reasserting the political subjectivity of Japanese Canadians. Emphasizing the importance of community-based knowledge, she discusses what she learned from older generations about the movement and how it contributed to rebuilding the postwar community; but she also argues that now, more than thirty-five years after the redress agreement, it is time to critically assess how the story of redress has constituted us in the context of the settler colonial state and imperialism.

At a methodological level, to guide her analysis, McAllister draws on the ethical framework of Indigenous storytelling conceptualized by Cherokee Daniel Heath Justice (2016). Justice explains how stories teach a people how they are defined through their kinship – their relations of interdependence with humans and non-humans – and the responsibilities these relations entail. He explains that to be a good relative "is to counter [the violence of colonialism's] exploitative forces and the stories that legitimate them, while at the same time ... reaffirming – better, more generative, more generous ways to uphold our obligations and our commitment to our diverse and varied kin" (Justice 2016, 84). Thinking about how to counter exploitative stories while reaffirming more generative and generous ways of upholding our obligations, McAllister questions how the story of Japanese Canadian redress teaches us who we are as a people using (ethno)national terms that constitute us as Canadian citizens loyal to the settler colonial state. She argues that if we are to recognize our responsibilities, in particular to the Indigenous peoples whose lands we illegally occupy, we need to examine how the national terms of redress – specifically its embrace of the discourse of Canadian citizenship – reinforce colonialism. Moreover, she argues that Japanese Canadians need to face their ambivalent relation to Japan, which is also reinforced by the discourse of Canadian citizenship, and confront, for instance, the fate of 4,000 community members the government shipped there after 1945 as well as the atrocities that Imperial Japan committed throughout Asia. She concludes with an account of her family's visit to Lillooet, where her mother's family was interned in the 1940s and shares the stories told by her elderly Nisei mother and Chief Michelle Edwards of the Cayoose Creek Band of the St'át'imc Nation, which remind us of the responsibilities stories entail as well as their power.

Chapter 7, "Post-Redress Japanese Canadian Scholar Activism," by Audrey Kobayashi and Jeff Masuda, concludes the volume with the authors' intergenerational account of scholar activism as two Japanese Canadians committed to human rights. The first section provides autobiographical accounts of their politicization coming of age in two very different eras of community activism. Kobayashi describes how she first became involved in

Asian Canadian grassroots activism in the 1970s, and then in the redress movement during the 1980s. She explains how she emerged "with two commitments that have been the foundation of [her] research ever since: First, if we are to overcome oppression of all kinds, we need to understand the fundamental social, institutional processes that create it ... Second, community research involves grassroots participation in community life and an understanding from the inside out of how social change can be achieved." Kobayashi also explains that during the 1980s, universities did not welcome activism and there was little community-based research and gives a chilling account of the challenges she faced getting tenure at her university which, as other racialized and Indigenous scholars from this period and later decades know, was not an isolated incident. In contrast, Masuda explains that by the time he started graduate training, his disciplines (Geography and Health Studies) recognized activist research in no small measure because of the "boundary breaking led by feminist and anti-racist geographers" like Kobayashi. But Masuda also explains how his own identity as a Japanese Canadian as well as finding a "coherent way to articulate [his] positionality ... [took] years of training [and connections with mentors that channelled him] toward a career [focused on] ... urban social and environmental justice." The second part of the chapter describes Kobayashi's and Masuda's activist research on housing in Vancouver's Downtown Eastside. The authors provide an analysis of the changes this area has undergone as a landscape that has been formed through multiple dispossessions while recognizing that the area belongs to the traditional territories of the Indigenous First Nation of the Sḵwx̱wú7mesh (Squamish). Weaving the history of Japanese Canadians into their analysis, they tie their community's experiences to those of other communities inhabiting the area and involved in struggles for their rights. This forms the context, as they explain, for their project "Right to Remain." As a participatory action research project, it involved collaboration with local activists and residents to advocate for housing rights. Importantly, rather than romanticizing the Japanese Canadian redress movement as part of the past, they show how the struggle for Japanese Canadian rights continues to fuel their scholar activism and commitment to social change.

Conclusion

We recognize that individual redress agreements and state apologies will not change Canada's colonial, racist structures, which continue to target Indigenous peoples, Black people, Muslims, Asians, and other racialized peoples in Canada, including racialized migrants and undocumented workers as well as marginalized populations outside the settler colony state's borders. The state's effort to isolate individual cases of injustice, as if they were distinct and unrelated, as discussed above, fragments calls for justice (James 2006a; Matsunaga 2021); this is reinforced across different institutional and discursive sites, including multicultural institutions, census categories, and funding programs, and perpetuates the construction of increasingly ethno-nationalized identities (Yoneyama 2016) of Canada's racialized settler communities. This ethnonationalist construction in turn ignores differences within these communities that are based not only on power relations rooted in class, social status, political views, and gender and sexuality but also on regional and religious differences and the periods when different immigrants came to Canada and the ways in which government programs and policies have rewarded community leaders who comply with their (de)politicized terms of racial community management.

We hope this volume will encourage survivors and their communities to pursue research on their movements for liberation, reparations, reconciliation, and rights and determine what is significant for them as well as wider movements for justice. In addition, as McAllister and Oikawa have argued (1996) along with Indigenous researchers (Archibald 2006; Kovach 2009; Thomas 2005), we want to emphasize that this research is not based on distanced, objective tools for collecting data "about" victims of racism and colonialism. Research conducted by members of our communities requires relearning cultural protocols and rebuilding relations with members of our communities and the networks involved in different generations of movements. Research conducted by members is necessary if we are to continue to produce knowledge – knowledge that politically defines and guides us, as Chapter 3 makes clear regarding Indigenous peoples. It necessarily involves not only rebuilding relations but also the transmission of intergenerational knowledge within our communities and building alliances with other groups the state has tried to destroy. Thus, this book is also a testament to how the act of research and writing by community members – as they draw from what they have learned from their communities to develop new methodological approaches, decide what research needs to be prioritized, share what they see as significant events, stories, and accounts about people, and identify what needs to be critically analyzed and what is the most productive and responsible way to conduct this research – necessarily contributes to the ongoing work of (re)building these communities and a more just world.

Notes

1 "Japanese Canadian redress" refers to the 1980s movement led by the National Association of Japanese Canadians (NAJC), which mobilized Japanese Canadians across Canada to fight for justice for their community. In their negotiations with the Canadian government, they demanded an official acknowledgment of and reparations for the government's racially motivated actions during the 1940s, when Prime Minister Mackenzie King's cabinet used the War Measures Act to classify Japanese Canadians as enemy aliens who posed a threat to national security and then launched a systematically deployed plan to remove all people of Japanese ancestry from Canada, using mechanisms from internment camps, forced labour, and forced dispersal from British Columbia to expulsion to war-torn Japan (Adachi 1991; Sunahara 1981). They demanded an acknowledgment rather than an apology. "An apology – not an acknowledgement – for the violation of rights, four decades later, would then simply reproduce the 'victim' position of Japanese Canadians: they would be seen to be on the receiving end of a political gesture that released the state from further accountability" (Miki 2004, 286). On September 22, 1988, the Canadian federal government formally acknowledged that the "forced removal and internment of Japanese Canadians during World War II and their deportation and expulsion following the war, was unjust" (Prime Minister Brian Mulroney, quoted in Miki and Kobayashi 1991, 8). The redress agreement included a token payment of $21,000 to each survivor born before April 1, 1949, who was alive at the time the settlement was signed; $12 million for the rebuilding of Japanese Canadian communities; $12 million for the establishment of a Race Relations Foundation in commemoration of all those interned topped up with an additional $12 million dollars from the federal government, and an application process for citizenship for those who were deported to Japan and had their citizenship revoked between 1941 and 1949 (Miki and Kobayashi 1991, 138–39).

2 A recent exception is the symposium "An Inheritance of Activism. Celebrating 75 Years: A Tribute to the Founders of the NJCCA-NAJC," organized by the Greater Toronto chapter of the NAJC with the NAJC Human Rights Committee, held in Toronto from October 28 to 30, 2022.

References

Adachi, Ken. (1976) 1991. *The Enemy That Never Was: A History of the Japanese Canadians*. Toronto: McClelland and Stewart.

Alook, Angele, Emily Eaton, David Gray-Donald, Joël Laforest, Crystal Lameman, and Bronwen Tucker. 2023. *The End of This World: Climate Justice in So-Called Canada*. Toronto: Between the Lines.

Archibald, Jo-Anne. 2006. *Indigenous Storywork: Educating the Heart, Mind, Body, and Spirit*. Vancouver: UBC Press.

Byrd, Jodi. 2011. *The Transit Empire: Indigenous Critiques of Colonialism*. Minneapolis: University of Minnesota Press.

Cajete, Gregory. 2016. *Native Science: Natural Laws of Interdependence*. Santa Fe: Clear Light.

Chakraborty, Chandrima, Amber Dean, and Angela Failler, eds. 2017. *Remembering Air India: the Art of Public Mourning*. Edmonton, Alberta: The University of Alberta Press.

Cho, Lily. 2021. *Mass Capture: Chinese Head Tax and the Making of Non-citizens*. Montreal: McGill-Queen's University Press.

Coulthard, Glen S. 2014. *Red Skin, White Masks: Rejecting the Colonial Politics of Recognition*. Minneapolis: University of Minnesota Press.

Derrickson, Ronald, and Arthur Manuel. 2015. *Unsettling Canada: A National Wake-up Call*. Toronto: Between the Lines.

Dhamoon, Rita, Davina Bhandar, and Renisa Mawani, eds. 2020. *Unmooring the Komagata Maru: Charting Colonial Trajectories*. Vancouver: UBC Press.

Fujitani, Takashi. 2011. *Race for Empire: Koreans as Japanese and Japanese as Americans during World War II*. Berkeley: University of California Press.

Henderson, Jennifer, and Pauline Wakeham. 2009. "Colonial Reckoning, National Reconciliation? Aboriginal Peoples and the Culture of Redress in Canada." *ESC: English Studies in Canada* 35 (1): 1–26.

–, eds. 2013. *Reconciling Canada: Critical Perspectives on the Culture of Redress*. Toronto: University of Toronto Press.

Iacovetta, Franca, Roberto Perin, and Angelo Principe, eds. 2000. *Enemies Within: Italian and Other Internees in Canada and Abroad*. Toronto: University of Toronto Press.

James, Matt. 2006a. "Do Campaigns for Historical Redress Erode the Canadian Welfare State?" In *Multiculturalism and the Welfare State: Recognition and Redistribution in Contemporary Democracies*, edited by Keith Banting and Will Kymlicka, 222–46. Oxford: Oxford University Press.

– 2006b. "The Permanent-Emergency Compensation State: A 'Postsocialist' Tale of Political Dystopia." In *Critical Policy Studies*, edited by Michael Orsini and Miriam Smith, 321–46. Vancouver: UBC Press.

– 2008. "Wrestling with the Past." In *The Age of Apology: Facing Up to the Past*, edited by Mark Gibney, Rhoda E. Howard-Hassmann, Jean-Marc Coicaud, and Niklaus Steiner, 137–53. Philadelphia: University of Pennsylvania Press.

– 2012. "A Carnival of Truth? Knowledge, Ignorance and the Canadian Truth and (Re)conciliation Commission." *International Journal of Transitional Justice* 6 (2): 182–204.

– 2013. "Neoliberal Heritage Redress." In *Reconciling Canada: Critical Perspectives on the Culture of Redress*, edited by Jennifer Henderson and Pauline Wakeham, 31–46. Toronto: University of Toronto Press.

– 2014. "Degrees of Freedom in Canada's Culture of Redress." *Citizenship Studies* 19 (1): 35–52.

Justice, Daniel Heath. 2016. *Why Indigenous Literature Matters*. Waterloo, ON: Wilfrid Laurier University Press.

Kelly, Fred. 2008. "Confession of a Born Again Pagan." In *From Truth to (Re)conciliation: Transforming the Legacy of Residential Schools*, edited by Marlene Brant

Castellano, Linda Archibald, and Mike DeGagné, 13–41. Ottawa: Aboriginal Healing Foundation Research Series.

Kobayashi, Audrey. 1992. "The Japanese-Canadian Redress Settlement and Its Implications for 'Race Relations.'" *Canadian Ethnic Studies* 24 (1): 1–19.

Kovach, Margaret. 2009. *Indigenous Methodologies: Characteristics, Conversations, and Contexts*. Toronto: University of Toronto Press.

Lanegran, Kimberly. 2005. "Truth Commissions, Human Rights Trials and the Politics of Memory." *Comparative Studies of South Asia, Africa and the Middle East* 25 (1): 111–21.

Lawrence, Bonita. 2012. *Fractured Homeland: Federal Recognition and Algonquin Identity in Ontario*. Vancouver: UBC Press.

Lawrence, Bonita, and Enakshi Dua. 2005. "Decolonizing Antiracism." *Social Justice* 32 (4): 120–43.

Li, Peter. 2008. "Reconciling with History: the Chinese-Canadian Head Tax Redress." *Journal of Chinese Overseas* 4 (1): 127–40.

Luciuk, Lubomyr Y. 2006. *Without Just Cause: Canada's First National Internment Operations and the Ukrainian Canadians, 1914–1920*. Kingston, ON: Published for the Ukrainian Canadian Civil Liberties Association by Kashtan Press.

MacDonald, David, Andrea Breen, and Norma Jacobs. 2022. "'End the Genocide': Little Action on MMIWG Calls for Justice in the 3 Years since the National Inquiry Concluded." *The Conversation*, June 2. https://theconversation.com/end-the-genocide-little-action-on-mmiwg-calls-for-justice-in-the-3-years-since-the-national-inquiry-concluded-174320.

Mackey, Eva. 2016. *Unsettled Expectations: Uncertainty, Land and Settler Decolonization*. Black Point, NS: Fernwood.

Matsunaga, Jennifer. 2016. "Two Faces of Transitional Justice: Theorizing the Incommensurability of Transitional Justice and Decolonization in Canada." *Decolonization: Indigeneity, Education and Society* 5 (1): 24–44.

– 2021. "Carefully Considered Words: The Influence of Government on Truth Telling about Japanese Canadian Internment and Indian Residential Schools." *Canadian Ethnic Studies* 53 (2): 91–113.

McAllister, Kirsten Emiko. 1999. "Narrating Japanese Canadians Inside and Outside the Canadian Nation: A Critique of Realist Forms of Representation." *Canadian Journal of Communication* 24 (1): 79–103.

– 2010. *Terrain of Memory: A Japanese Canadian Memorial Project*. Vancouver: UBC Press.

McAllister, Kirsten Emiko, and Mona Oikawa. 1996. "Research: Re-search, Search, Searching, Sear-ch-ing." *Nikkei Voice* 10 (2): 1, 11.

McKay, Ian. 2000. "The Liberal Order Framework: A Prospectus for a Reconnaissance of Canadian History." *Canadian Historical Review* 81 (4): 616–45.

Miki, Roy. 2004. *Redress: Inside the Japanese Canadian Call for Justice*. Vancouver: Raincoast Books.

Miki, Roy, and Cassandra Kobayashi. 1991. *Justice in Our Time: The Japanese Canadian Redress Settlement*. Vancouver/Winnipeg: Talonbooks/National Association of Japanese Canadians.

National Inquiry into Murdered and Missing Indigenous Women and Girls. 2019. *Reclaiming Power and Place: The Final Report of the National Inquiry into Missing and Murdered Indigenous Women and Girls.* Vancouver: National Inquiry into Missing and Murdered Indigenous Women and Girls.

Oikawa, Mona. 2006. "Connecting the Internment of Japanese Canadians to the Colonization of Aboriginal Peoples." In *Aboriginal Connections to Race, Environment, and Tradition,* edited by Jill Oakes and Rick Riewe, 17–25. Winnipeg: Aboriginal Issues Press, University of Manitoba.

– 2012. *Cartographies of Violence: Japanese Canadian Women, Memory, and the Subjects of the Internment.* Toronto: University of Toronto Press.

Okamura, Jonathan Y., and Candace Fujikane, eds. 2008. *Asian Settler Colonialism: From Local Governance to the Habits of Everyday Life in Hawaii.* Honolulu: University of Hawai'i Press.

Oré Aguilar, Gaby, and Felipe Gómez Isa, eds. 2011. *Rethinking Transitions: Equality and Social Justice in Societies Emerging from Conflict.* Portland, OR: Intersentia.

Paik, Naomi A. 2016. *Internment Remains: The 1988 Civil Liberties Act and Racism Re-formed.* Chapel Hill: University of North Carolina Press.

Razack, Sherene H. 2015. *Dying from Improvement: Inquests and Inquiries into Indigenous Deaths in Custody.* Toronto: University of Toronto Press.

Regan, Paulette. 2010. *Unsettling the Settler Within: Indian Residential Schools, Truth Telling, and (Re)conciliation in Canada.* Vancouver: UBC Press.

Roach, Kent. 2019. *Canadian Justice, Indigenous Injustice: The Gerald Stanley and Colten Boushie Case.* Montreal and Kingston: McGill-Queen's University Press.

Sarkin-Hughes, Jeremy, ed. 2019. *The Global Impact and Legacy of Truth Commissions.* Cambridge, UK: Intersentia.

Sehdev, Robinder Kaur. 2011. "People of Colour in Treaty." In *Cultivating Canada Reconciliation through the Lens of Cultural Diversity,* edited by Ashok Mathur, Jonathan Dewar, and Mike DeGagné, 263–74. Ottawa: Aboriginal Healing Foundation, 2011.

Simpson, Audra. 2014. *Mohawk Interruptus: Political Life Across the Borders of Settler States.* Durham, NC: Duke University Press.

– 2016. "Reconciliation and Its Discontents: Settler Governance in an Age of Sorrow." Public lecture, Aboriginal Education Research Centre, Department of Indigenous Studies and Department of Educational Foundations, University of Saskatchewan, March 15, 2016.

Simpson, Leanne Betasamosake. 2011. *Dancing on Our Turtle's Back: Stories of Nishnaabeg Re-creation, Resurgence and a New Emergence.* Winnipeg: Arbeiter Ring.

Smith, Linda Tuhiwai. 2012. *Decolonizing Methodologies: Research and Indigenous Peoples.* London: Zed Books.

Sunahara, Ann Gomer. 1981. *The Politics of Racism: The Uprooting of Japanese Canadians during the Second World War.* Toronto: James Lorimer.

Thomas, Robina (Qwul'sih'yah'maht). 2005. "Honouring the Oral Traditions of My Ancestors through Storytelling." In *Research as Resistance: Critical, Indigenous, and Anti-Oppressive Approaches,* edited by L. Brown and S. Strega, 237–54. Toronto: Canadian Scholars.

Truth and Reconciliation Commission of Canada. 2015. *Honouring the Truth, Reconciling for the Future: Summary of the Final Report of the Truth and Reconciliation Commission of Canada*. Ottawa: Truth and Reconciliation Commission of Canada.

– 2016. "We Are All Treaty People: Canadian Society and Reconciliation." In *Canada's Residential Schools: Reconciliation; The Final Report of the Truth and Reconciliation Commission of Canada*, 6: 193–222. Montreal and Kingston: McGill-Queen's University Press.

Tuck, Eve, and K. Wayne Yang. 2012. "Decolonization is Not a Metaphor." *Decolonization: Indigeneity, Education and Society* 1 (1): 1–40.

Wakeham, Pauline. 2012. "The Cunning of Reconciliation: Reinventing White Civility in the 'Age of Apology.'" In *Shifting the Ground of Canadian Literary Studies*, edited by Smaro Kamboureli and R. Zacharias, 209–33. Waterloo: Wilfrid Laurier University Press.

Williams, Melissa S. 2014. "Introduction: On the Use and Abuse of Recognition in Politics." In *Recognition versus Self-Determination: Dilemmas of Emancipatory Politics*, edited by Avigail Eisenberg, Jeremy Webber, Glen Coulthard and Andrée Boisselle, 3–19. Vancouver: UBC Press.

Yoneyama, Lisa. 2016. *Cold War Ruins: Transpacific Critique of American Justice and Japanese War Crimes*. Durham, NC: Duke University Press.

Young, Iris Marion. 1991. *Responsibility for Justice*. Oxford: Oxford University Press.

1

Redress Settlements as Colonial Recognition

Bonita Lawrence

In this chapter, I seek to understand the implications of redress settlements for Indigenous peoples. While it is a given that redress for any of the past wrongs that have shaped the lives of Indigenous peoples is long overdue, I am wondering what is gained and lost when Indigenous peoples' organizations negotiate redress settlements with settler states. To begin to unpack this question, it is important to consider Steven Blevins's (2016, 16) conceptualization of colonial redress as always shaped "in its most reductive form, as economic calculation," and how a counter discourse that imagines the possibility of historic justice must be marshalled as a form of resistance. In examining the largest redress settlement in Canadian history – the Indian Residential Schools Settlement Agreement (IRSSA) – I have found it useful to first of all consider the Japanese Canadian struggle for redress, as it was the first successful struggle toward restitution for past wrongs that profoundly shaped the possibilities for the IRSSA, as well as the later struggles of survivors of the Sixties Scoop (the term coined by Patrick Johnston in 1983), where redress has been achieved, albeit on far too small a scale, for the thousands of Indigenous children who were fostered or adopted into non-Native homes under the child welfare system, beginning in 1951. I have found it useful to ask what the circumstances were of each struggle for redress, and the effects on the peoples in question. The Japanese Canadian redress settlement and the Indian Residential Schools Settlement Agreement were won with different tactics and with different goals. However, although there are aspects of these struggles that may be incommensurable, there are also powerful commonalities between the Japanese Canadian internment and specific instances of colonial treatment of Indigenous peoples. For that reason, I will begin by briefly addressing some aspects of what Indigenous peoples see as commonalities with racialized non-Indigenous people in general, and ultimately with Japanese Canadians in particular – as well as what they consider to be incommensurable between these communities. Subsequently I will explore differences in experiences of redress.

What Are the Commonalities, and What Is Incommensurable?

In Canada, Indigenous peoples are usually quite firm about distinguishing the differences between them and other racialized but non-Indigenous peoples; I will use the category "peoples of colour" here for the sake of simplicity. The most crucial difference relates to land – the fact that Indigenous peoples have original and present connections to lands – that is, relationships to land that predate the existence of the colonial process and the Canadian settler state – and in many cases these relationships still exist. Despite the Supreme Court of Canada's 1973 Calder decision (*Calder v Attorney-General of British Columbia* SCR 313, [1973]), which ruled that Indigenous peoples have an underlying title to the land not referenced in the Crown (Monture-Angus 1999, 76), and the subsequent enshrinement of the concept of "Aboriginal rights" in the 1982 Canadian constitution, a number of subsequent legal decisions regarding the content of Aboriginal rights and Aboriginal title, as well as the policies that Canada has adopted, have narrowed and reduced the possibility of utilizing these rights or successfully asserting Aboriginal title (Asch and Macklem 1991; Barsh and Henderson 1997; Borrows 2002). One result of these court decisions is Canada's assertion of a range of rights to infringe on existing Aboriginal rights and title which, along with the long-standing constitutional division of so-called Crown land to the provinces, continues to enable Indigenous lands to be easily appropriated for resource development, as well as being leased, or sold outright to settlers. The fact that some of this land is now owned by different peoples of colour only heightens this sense of incommensurability around the question of land.

In a related manner, the fact that peoples of colour lack this original relationship to land and as a result must rely on obtaining citizenship in the settler nation in order to survive and to obtain the right to stay in Canada represents another aspect of incommensurability, because even through

Indigenous peoples are currently also considered to be citizens of Canada, this has no real bearing on their actual relationship to the Canadian settler state.

Commonalities do exist relative to citizenship because of the white supremacist nature of Canadian society. For example, for both peoples of colour and Indigenous peoples, being citizens does not provide the same rights that citizenship affords to white people. But citizenship also represents an aspect of incommensurability between peoples of colour and Indigenous peoples, because Indigenous peoples have a much more complex relationship to Canadian citizenship than most peoples of colour do.

There are two reasons for the complexity of Indigenous peoples' relationship to citizenship. The first is that many of the rights pertaining to citizenship are rendered effectively meaningless because the Indian Act represents a separate legal regime that routinely violates any commonality with others who have Canadian citizenship.[1] This includes the lack of basic human rights such as access to clean drinking water (Swampy and Black 2021) and sufficient access to decent housing (Stastna 2011), but even more important is the fact that different forms of low-intensity warfare are waged against any Indigenous communities that resist predatory resource extraction on their territories – which can include actual military occupation (Pindara 2020), long-term military surveillance (Barrera 2016), routine attacks by provincial police combined with cutting off all food and medical supplies to communities in resistance (Pasternak 2017), and the utilization of RCMP special paramilitary police units (Forester 2022).

The other complexity relating to citizenship is that Canadian citizenship represents a way of enfolding Indigenous peoples into the national polity against their will – because Indigenous peoples are, first of all, citizens of their own nations, and the imposition of Canadian citizenship effectively weakens treaty rights. After all, what nation is required to observe the treaties it once signed with distinct people who are now its own citizens?

Whereas American citizenship was imposed on American Indians in 1924, Canadian citizenship has been considered normative for anybody born in Canada. In practice, however, Canadian citizenship has been wrapped up with the right to vote, which at different times has been withheld from both Indigenous peoples and some peoples of colour (McRae 2019). Inuit people were first legally denied the vote and then were granted it in 1950, while Status Indians were among the last to receive the right to vote – not until 1960 (McRae 2019). However, in both Canada and the United States, Indigenous peoples have been very apprehensive that claims to settler citizenship means weakening their own citizenship in their Indigenous nation. To this day, many Mohawk communities in Canada, with their long history of being allies with Canada in defending its borders rather than being subordinate peoples, refuse to vote (Bonspiel 2015; Gabriel 2021); indeed, in Kahnawake, in particular, there are people who not only refuse to vote and pay taxes but may reject old-age pensions and other so-called "gifts" of citizenship, refusing to recognize the authority of Canada since the Canada-US border was imposed across their territories (Simpson 2014, 4–7). Some from Kahnawake refuse to travel except on a passport issued by the Iroquois Confederacy, to avoid acknowledging the jurisdiction of what they see as "a competitor nation" (1). Indeed, across Canada, while individuals from other Indigenous nations may refuse to vote in defence of their sovereignty (Waabshkigaabo 2021), most First Nations, when addressing citizenship, are primarily seeking to recreate the citizenship in their own nations that Canada transformed or nullified under the Indian Act or its predecessor legislation. This inevitably means challenging the control that the Indian Act maintains over both First Nations identity and lands. As Kent McNeil (2004, 19) notes, Indigenous citizenship can truly be meaningful only when Indigenous communities have the necessary jurisdiction, which he addresses as follows:

Simply put, jurisdiction means governmental authority or political power. It is usually regarded as having two dimensions, one territorial and one personal. The territorial dimension empowers the government in which the jurisdiction is vested to exercise authority over a specific geographical area. The personal dimension involves authority over persons, who are usually either citizens of the "nation" in question or residents of the territory over which the government has jurisdiction.

These existing incommensurable differences between Indigenous peoples and peoples of colour are heightened by two sets of issues that threaten Indigenous struggles for autonomy by blurring the boundaries between Indigenous peoples and the generally larger numbers of peoples of colour. One tendency, far more common in the United States but present to some degree in Canada, is to focus on race as the primary division between white people and all others, which situates Indigenous peoples according to their

racialized bodies as "peoples of colour," rather than acknowledging autonomy and relationship to land. This is articulated most clearly by Jodi Byrd
(2011, 125):

> In many ways, then, one might argue that the idea of "Internal colonialism"
> services the construction of the United States as a multicultural nation that
> is struggling with the legacies of racism rather than as a colonialist power
> engaged in territorial expansion since its beginning ... This transformation
> of more than five hundred and sixty Indigenous nations into a single racial
> minority within the national borders of the United States is folded a priori
> into postcolonial and racial critiques of what Patrick Wolfe has identified as
> "regimes of difference" in deep settler societies.

This also speaks to Mark Rifkin's (2009, 206) notion that a critique of racial
discourse cannot address the structuring force of sovereignty in US settler
society. The same statement, of course, applies to Canada and other settler
societies.

The second issue, unique to Canada, is its multiculturalism policy, which
is roundly critiqued by many women of colour for the ways in which it trans-
lates (and therefore subordinates) questions of racism, social justice, and
socio-economic marginalization into questions of "cultural difference," in
general, reducing the political to the cultural (Bannerji 2000; Razack 1998;
Das Gupta 1999). However, the effect of multiculturalism on Indigenous
peoples is to erase Indigenous political rights through inclusion into a
multicultural mosaic of cultural difference within the settler state; Indigenous peoples are then seen as just another group struggling for inclusion (St.
Denis 2011).

Both trends threaten the ability and power of Indigenous peoples to
assert political autonomy and reclaim what is most important to them – the
land. The result is Indigenous peoples strongly asserting that Indigenous
issues are incommensurable with those of peoples of colour. Such asser-
tions tend to ignore those instances where commonalities *do* exist between
Indigenous peoples and other racialized peoples.

There are powerful connections between Black people and Indigenous
people – their unique global histories of genocide and enslavement – and
the repercussions of Black fungibility and myths of Indigenous savagery,
which continue to affect Black and Indigenous communities today. However, a massive body of literature across the Americas exists (too large to cite
here) addressing these issues. By comparison, there has been very little work

addressing connections between the Japanese Canadian internment and the experiences of Indigenous peoples, which is the focus in this chapter.

The internment represents a modern attempt at the extinguishment of a people, most of whom until the Second World War had been Canadian citizens. No other peoples of colour in Canada have been targeted to such an extent and so recently. With the internment, Japanese Canadians endured forced removal (including violent deportation to another land), the confiscation of their homes and personal property, the withdrawal of all basic human rights, the separation of families, imprisonment in camps and other carceral spaces, forced labour, and over a decade of intensive government surveillance, long after the war ended. It is this condition of being so relentlessly stripped of their humanity by the Canadian state with the internment that makes the Japanese Canadian experience unique and represents a powerful commonality with Indigenous peoples, especially in the latter's experiences with residential schools. It is therefore not surprising that these are the only two groups in Canada that have won forms of redress for the intensive experiences of state-organized violence they faced.

The Japanese Canadian Redress Settlement

In February 1942, the federal government ordered the expulsion of 22,000 Japanese Canadians residing within 100 miles of the Pacific coast. With that order, these Canadian citizens were branded as enemy aliens, on the basis of race, uprooted from their homes, confined in detention camps, stripped of their property, and forcibly dispersed across Canada or exiled to a war-torn Japan that, for most Japanese Canadian citizens, was no longer "home" (Sunahara 2000, 13–14).

The end of the war did not signify a return to the "normality" of prewar conditions. Instead, citizenship and the ability to live in the BC restricted area were withheld from the survivors of the internment until 1949, with government surveillance of Japanese Canadian families lasting into the 1950s. Nor was property returned. Indeed, the property of these Canadians had long since been confiscated by the Custodian of Enemy Alien Property and sold before and during the internment. And despite the struggles of Japanese Canadian organizations to regain citizenship and to receive full compensation for their losses, the establishment of a Royal Commission addressing financial losses resulted in initial offers of minimal levels of cash, with the condition that accepting such compensation would disqualify claimants from pursuing the larger question of justice for the devastation that was the internment (Sunahara 2000, 13–14). Compensation on such terms, without justice for the experience of the internment itself, was not considered tenable.

The reality for Japanese Canadians is that negotiations for redress became possible only when they had regained their citizenship, and only then after decades of struggle and efforts to obtain public support for their cause. Finally, in 1988, the National Association of Japanese Canadians (NAJC) was successful in negotiating a redress settlement, which included an acknowledgment of the injustice of the wartime events; individual payments of $21,000 to all eligible Japanese Canadians; the establishment of a community fund of $12 million; the expunging of all criminal records for those charged under the War Measures Act; restoration of Canadian citizenship to all of those exiled to Japan; and the creation of the Canadian Race Relations Foundation, which was established in 1997 (Sunahara 2000, 153).

When I think about the Japanese Canadian experience, it seems apparent that the long struggle for justice through redress was not only about financial restitution but also about claiming the human rights implicit in full citizenship, as a means of ensuring that the remaining survivors who experienced the camps, as well as their descendants, would never again be dehumanized in this manner. For racialized people, however, claiming what are essentially the rights of the liberal bourgeois subject – who is always white – makes such assurances impossible. This is underlined by the post-9/11 reality of security certificates that the Canadian state can use to detain Muslims indefinitely, which is part of what Sherene Razack (2008, 5) has termed the expulsion of Muslims from the West, from political community, "a casting out that takes the form of stigmatization, surveillance, incarceration, abandonment, torture, and bombs." Despite this, in seeking justice for past wrongs and their human rights as citizens, Japanese Canadians sought to ensure that other racialized groups would never experience what they had.

For example, in 1987, when the government of Brian Mulroney proposed to replace the War Measures Act with legislation that would permit different responses to different kinds of emergencies, the NAJC legal committee examined the proposed bill and challenged its weaknesses, clarifying that the new act would have the same powers to do everything that had been done to Japanese Canadians under the War Measures Act. The association fought successfully to appear on the final day of debate about the proposed new legislation; its intervention resulted in sixty-five amendments being made that expanded Parliament's ability to supervise and even revoke various aspects of emergency powers, mandated compensation for those experiencing abuse of emergency powers, and, most importantly, prohibited the detention or imprisonment on the basis of race, national or ethnic origin, colour, religion, sex, age, or mental or physical disability (Sunahara 2000, 154–55). Safety from violent dehumanization, then, for Japanese Canadians meant at least the hope of safety for all racialized peoples.

Despite the struggle for justice and the victory of winning some form of redress, the financial settlement could not alleviate the experience of the internment for Japanese Canadians. However, it represented a beachhead from which the descendants of the survivors could address the survivors' memories of loss and displacement and dehumanization and the effects on the lives of their descendants, as well as challenge Canada's – and white Canadians' – ongoing erasure of the realities of the internment. In this respect, redress, even if reduced to economic calculation, enabled a larger project of redressive historiography. These efforts against erasure have ranged from the struggles of the Greater Vancouver Japanese Canadian Citizens' Association with the Pacific National Exhibition over the establishment of a plaque to observe the site of Hastings Park, where 8,000 people were first incarcerated while waiting for further removal (Oikawa 2012, 91), to the creation of the Nikkei Internment Memorial Centre at New Denver, where 7,250 people were interned in six internment camps and where the so-called incurables – almost 1,000 people who through disease, age, or lack of surviving family members were permitted to remain in British Columbia after 1945 at the former tuberculosis sanitarium built for internees (McAllister 2010, 2–3). Both Kirsten Emiko McAllister and Mona Oikawa have explored the memories of those who were interned, and both have highlighted the multiple tensions and even contradictions in the efforts of the descendants of survivors to write about those memories. Both texts highlight the strength of survivors' employment of memory, and the pain of those memories – and the fact that the internment was a wounding that has continued to be felt not only by survivors but also by their descendants. From this experience, it appears that until Japanese Canadians obtained full citizenship, the redress settlement could not be obtained, and expressing its full meaning, both for survivors and for other Canadians, was not possible.

Both authors, however, also highlight what can be left out in remembering – or memorializing – the internment, namely, that the colonial domination of Indigenous peoples sometimes took place almost adjacent to some sites of the internment, and that the technologies of the internment process were created through a history of colonial removal of Indigenous peoples. Mona Oikawa, in addressing how 22,000 Japanese Canadians could be removed so quickly across municipal, provincial, and federal boundaries (2012, 12) involving multiple and escalating provincial and federal statutes of exclusion, references how the power and ability to do this was created by the ongoing national processes of Indigenous colonization and removal.

Oikawa has also traced, in detail, the manner in which the Canadian government, in organizing the internment, initially sought to displace the Native students at residential schools in Kamloops, Edmonton, Brandon, and Winnipeg, or the Mount Elgin school at the Munsey reserve in Ontario, in order to intern Japanese Canadians on these premises (2006, 20–21). She suggests that it is vital to examine the different spaces where racialized and colonized peoples are spatially situated, in order to address ways of challenging white dominance in Canada that begins with the colonization of Indigenous peoples and works from there (2006, 23). Indeed, when news of the graves at Kamloops and Marieval Residential Schools was broken, the NAJC circulated an open letter to Japanese Canadians and their allies to support the survivors of residential schools and to advocate for the Truth and Reconciliation Commission's "Calls to Action" (National Association of Japanese Canadians 2021).

A cursory look at the Indian Residential Schools Settlement Agreement reveals both commonality and incommensurability with the Japanese Canadian redress settlement. For example, although Indigenous peoples are nominally considered Canadian citizens, the Indian Act, as a colonial legal regime that still controls Indianness, maintains a profound separation between Indigenous peoples and other Canadian citizens. When Japanese Canadians regained Canadian citizenship, it levelled some aspects of the playing field between a public that had, after decades of civil rights, anti-apartheid, and other struggles against racism become somewhat sympathetic to the denial of human rights on the basis of race, which the internment had signified, and Japanese Canadians seeking redress. However, as I argue below, no such articulations of commonality on the basis of citizenship are possible across the biopolitical boundaries (Agamben 1998, 2005) of the Indian Act and the manner in which racialized articulations of colonial law and economy have rendered Indigenous peoples as always incommensurably Other in Canada. Because of this, unlike the Japanese Canadian redress settlement, the IRSSA was fought in the courts with little focus on gaining public support. Indeed, the efforts of Sixties Scoop survivors to obtain justice followed the same trend: seeking damages through court cases, with little focus on appealing to public opinion.

To some extent, the Japanese Canadian redress settlement has high-lighted the importance of documenting that survivors did resist and speak out about their experiences. While engaging with memory has represented a critical historiography about redress for Japanese Canadian survivors, a central problem for Indigenous peoples seeking redress for residential schools has been that the role of memory within the IRSSA has been less about resistance than about recolonization. Even as the children of sur-vivors of residential schooling struggle to make sense of their parents' and grandparents' experiences, the survivors themselves have been forced to remember and relive the atrocities they experienced as children, in order to qualify for payments.

The Indian Residential School Redress

The Indian Residential Schools Settlement Agreement represents the nego-tiated settlement of a class action launched in 2005 by the Assembly of First Nations and other Indigenous organizations representing an estimated 86,000 residential school survivors, against the federal government and the four churches (Anglican, Presbyterian, Roman Catholic, and United) that ran Canada's residential schools on behalf of the federal government. It is the largest class action settlement to date in Canada (Independent Assess-ment Process Oversight Committee 2021, 7).

The terms of the IRSSA consisted of a $2 billion compensation pack-age for survivors. The five main components of the settlement were the Common Experience Payment, for anybody who attended the schools; the Independent Assessment Process (IAP), for those who suffered abuse in the schools; the Truth and Reconciliation Commission (TRC); a Commem-oration fund; and Health and Healing Services (Government of Canada 2002a). By far the most important components have been the two payment processes and the Truth and Reconciliation Commission.

The Common Experience Payment was blanket compensation, consisting of an initial payment of $10,000 per person with an additional $3,000 for every year spent in the schools. The average lump sum payment that long-term occupants of the schools received was $20,457 (Independent Assess-ment Process Oversight Committee 2021). While 105,540 applications were received under the Common Experience Payment, $1.62 billion was paid to only 78,750 recipients. While Indigenous and Northern Affairs Canada asserts that this represented 98 percent of an estimated 80,000 survivors (Miller, J.R., 2012), nearly 26,000 survivors were turned down because the institution they attended was not included in the settlement (for example, those in Newfoundland and Labrador) or because they were unable to supply adequate proof as to which school they had attended as children (*CBC News* 2015).

The Independent Assessment Process was allotted $960 million for claims of sexual abuse, serious physical abuse, and other wrongful acts. This is where survivors were forced to relive their stories of unspeakable terror by testifying before adjudicators at hearings to qualify for restitution. The maximum payment that any claimant could receive under the terms of the settlement was $275,000, but an additional $250,000 could be awarded for proven claims of actual income loss due to debilitation from trauma. In the end, however, those who endured the process received on average only $111, 265 (Government of Canada 2002b).

Even with the burden of proof resting with survivors, the scale of costs for the Independent Assessment Process has clarified that violent abuse was rampant in the residential schools, rather than the isolated incidents that Canada had claimed.

From implementation to October 1, 2020, a total of 38,276 IAP applications were submitted, of which only 33,861 were admitted (Independent Assessment Process Oversight Committee 2021, 56). The administration of this process was extremely complex and costly; notably, while the IRSSA did allow adjudication to proceed for those who accepted the Common Experience Payment, once individuals agreed to take part in the Independent Assessment Process, they forfeited their ability to take Canada to court.

The terms under which survivors have been forced to carry the burden of proof for claims against the settlement have resulted in significant impacts on survivors, including having to contend with dishonest lawyers. The sum of $100 million was allocated by the IRSSA for the payment of plaintiffs' legal fees; however, a number of lawyers in the process have been investigated for fraud, with at least one lawyer disbarred and forced to repay survivors nearly $1 million in misappropriated funds; meanwhile, a convicted murderer on parole who had worked with some of the lawyers in threatening and extorting funds from survivors has had his parole revoked (*CBC News* 2012). It is also worth comparing the actual average payment of $111,265 for each survivor to what the non-Native survivors of the Mount Cashel orphanage in Newfoundland were offered, which averaged $223,000 per person (Antle 2016).

A study by the Aboriginal Healing Foundation found that for survivors, even the Common Experience Payment process, which did not require disclosure of abuse, was difficult; in fact, 20 percent of the people who had received their payments found the process challenging, both logistically and emotionally. Those who were more fluent or literate in English or French and under sixty years of age found the process somewhat easier; however, a quarter of the people interviewed had to reapply because of lack of proof of what school they had attended. These individuals reported they were made to feel like liars. Ten percent of those who had experienced difficulties with the Common Experience Payment said that they would not attempt to access the Independent Assessment Payments despite considerable experiences of abuse, because they could not face being questioned about their traumatic experiences. One-third of the survivors indicated that simply claiming the Common Experience Payment triggered negative emotions or traumatic flashbacks, sometimes leading to self-destructive behaviours. A common conclusion was that the decision to settle for individual monetary compensation was misguided and insufficient, compounded by a lack of planning on the part of those implementing the Common Experience Payment. They were ill-prepared for the triggering of self-destructive reactions of many survivors, and for the predatory behaviour of lawyers and others involved in the process (Aboriginal Healing Foundation 2010, xiii–xvi).

By the time the IAP was wound down in March 2019, $3.233 billion had been distributed, 26,707 claimant hearings had taken place, and 27,846 individuals had been compensated. The total cost of the Independent Assessment Process and the Common Experience Payment together was more than $4.7 billion. A total of $60 million was earmarked by the Indian Residential Schools Settlement Agreement for establishing a Truth and Reconciliation Commission and providing a space for survivors to share and document their histories (Independent Assessment Process Oversight Committee 2021, 88).

The sheer number of those involved in the IAP indicated the magnitude of physical and sexual violence that marked the residential school experience. Meanwhile, despite the trauma so many experienced in recounting their stories, many were willing to endure this trauma simply because after a lifetime of colonial impoverishment, the settlement finally provided them with money to provide for their children.

The Truth and Reconciliation Commission was formally established on June 1, 2008; however, conflicts arose with the initial appointments, so Justice Murray Sinclair was appointed the new chair of the TRC on July 1,

2009, along with commissioners Chief Wilton Littlechild and Marie Wilson (Truth and Reconciliation Commission 2015, 3).

The commission faced multiple problems related to obstruction from Canada. Over 941,000 documents were made available to the commission by 2012. However, Library and Archives Canada refused to provide the 5 million documents it had on residential schools until January 2013, after being ordered to do so twice by the Ontario Superior Court of Justice. The third time, the commission had to take Canada to court in connection with information relating to the criminal case that had been mounted at the St. Anne's Residential School. Because of these delays, the mandate of the commission was extended from 2014 to 2015 (Truth and Reconciliation Commission 2015, 28–29).

The commission also addressed multiple problems with the IRSSA. It discovered that during survivors' testimonies, the adjudicators had repeatedly failed to inform survivors of their right to have their statements delivered to the Truth and Reconciliation archive and had instead required an undertaking of strict confidentiality of all parties, including the survivors themselves. In June 2014, the chief adjudicator of the Independent Assessment Process publicly announced that he supported the immediate destruction of all documents related to the adjudication of claims by residential school survivors, which would wipe out years of painstakingly and painfully told survivors' stories. At the time of the publication of the commission's *Final Report*, efforts were still being made to preserve testimonies of the survivors that had been made at such high cost (Truth and Reconciliation Commission 2015).

Canada's haste to obliterate survivors' stories represents an attempt to erase what the TRC, even with its deliberately narrowed terms, had enabled – a national reckoning of over 100 years of residential schooling, its repercussions, and the implications for Canada's reputation. Like Brazil, whose government deliberately ordered the rounding up and destruction of all records relating to 300 years of African enslavement, to whitewash Brazil's reputation as the last nation in the Western world to abolish slavery (Aidoo 2018, 11–12), Canada has willingly sought to erase the memory of its victims in an attempt to salvage its international reputation.

The commission crossed Canada, holding seven national events, several regional events, and 238 days of local hearings in seventy-seven communities across the country. Upon closing, it issued a document with ninety-four "Calls to Action" to redress the legacy of residential schools. The six-volume *Final Report* was released in 2015.

The TRC frequently received testimonies referencing the deaths of children in the schools. It investigated and found evidence of 3,201 deaths; however, its requests to continue these investigations were denied (Smith 2015).

It is important to recognize that the IRSSA did not spring full-blown into existence. What led up to this class action suit was over a decade of multiple intensifying lawsuits by individuals or groups of survivors across the country against their abusers. While some of these individuals were, at great cost, able to see their abusers convicted of their crimes, many others were far less successful. Among the most notorious instances where individuals were denied justice were the trial of Bishop Hubert O'Connor, former head of the now-defunct St. Joseph's Residential School at Williams Lake, who was accused in 1991 of six counts of rape against five Native girls during the 1960s, involving one pregnancy; and the *Blackwater v Plint* case, a three-year trial from 1998 to 2000 involving twenty-two individuals accusing dormitory supervisor Arthur Plint of offences ranging from extremely violent anal and oral rape to loss of culture and language at the Port Alberni Residential School. For *Blackwater v Plint*, only seven cases relating to the most violent sexual abuse were accepted out of the twenty-two plaintiffs, and the seventy-seven-year-old Plint received a sentence of only eleven years (Miller 2001). However, this leniency pales compared with the treatment that Bishop O'Connor received. O'Connor, the highest-ranking member of the Catholic Church to be accused in Canada, was convicted in 1996 of only two charges of rape out of the six and sentenced to only two and a half years in prison. Indeed, he was released on $1,000 bail after only six months. He later was accused of an additional charge of rape but was acquitted after apologizing to the victim at an Indigenous healing circle in 1998. "Although he admitted wrongdoing, the Church continued to refer to him as honorific of most reverend and he retained his title of bishop emeritus" (Hawthorn 2007).

The most disturbing case of leniency, however, was that of Paul Leroux, who had already served a prison sentence for gross indecency, indecent assault, attempted indecent assault, and attempted buggery with several underage males at Grollier Hall, the residential school in Inuvik where Leroux worked as an activities supervisor and guidance counsellor between 1967 and 1969, when he was hired to become supervisor at the Beauval Indian Residential School in Saskatchewan. At Beauval, Leroux perpetrated indecent assault on at least a dozen boys throughout the 1970s. His case wound its way through the courts for years before he was convicted in 2012 and sentenced to eight years behind bars. After serving only a third of his sentence, he was released on parole in 2016, even though he is still considered dangerous because of his denial of the Saskatchewan episodes of abuse (*CBC News* 2016).

Despite these failures of justice, the significant aspect of these lawsuits was that survivors were able to ensure, despite great cost to them, that those who had abused them as children were at least prosecuted for their wrongdoing. In some instances, they were able to bring about police investigations into conditions in specific schools. In taking their abusers to court, however, each group of survivors had to fight not only the people who had abused them as children but also the Canadian government, which supported those accused of abuse. Throughout the process, the federal government had become so adept at hiding information that survivors needed to win their cases that the final term of the Truth and Reconciliation Commission had to be extended because of the need to institute legal action three times against Canada to force it to produce required documents (Alamenciak 2014).

The efforts of survivors to have their abusers charged and the extent to which they had to fight Canada in court individually must be contrasted with what took place within the Indian Residential Schools Settlement Agreement. According to Indigenous and Northern Affairs Canada (INAC), seventeen private investigation firms were hired by the federal government, at a cost of $1,576,380, to find abusers who worked at their residential schools, as part of the terms of the IRSSA. In this manner, 5,315 individuals accused of physical and sexual abuse were located. Filing criminal charges was not the goal of the search for the alleged abusers; rather, it was to solicit their testimonies as counter-evidence for the Independent Assessment Process hearings that were deliberating on compensation for the most extreme cases (Troian 2016). However, these abusers could not be forced to attend the hearings for fear of self-incrimination; indeed, 4,450 individuals refused to attend. Only 840 former abusers agreed to attend and challenge survivors' claims (Troian 2016).

The importance of a collective settlement such as the IRSSA was its potential to move beyond individual experience to address the collective nature of the harm done by residential schooling. Unfortunately, the settlement avoided any recognition of collective harm. Arguably the most flawed aspect of the IRSSA has been its treatment of language rights, one of the prime areas targeted by residential schools and of central importance for collective Indigenous survival. Rather than taking this as a basic right requiring that Indigenous languages be promoted at all levels of Canadian society, the IRSSA reduced the problem of language loss to the TRC's call to action for governments and universities to promote Indigenous languages as part of "reconciliation." It is telling that if the agreement had addressed loss of language as central, it would have highlighted the *collective* nature of Canada's deliberate colonial practices in "killing the Indian in the child" and their genocidal attacks on Indigenous collectivities by preventing the intergenerational passing down of language and tradition. Instead, individual experiences of violation, which could be reduced to individual abusers, were emphasized.

Most problematic, however, is the manner in which Canada controlled the process and therefore limited the TRC to a fact-finding mission only. The commission was not granted the power to address the perpetrators, but instead to document abuse. In this, it most closely resembled the common Canadian practice of creating Royal Commissions to study problems and then shelving their reports. Also significant is the fact that out of the TRC's report, the jargon of "reconciliation" has been adopted wholesale by the Canadian government (and the general public) while the "truth" aspect of the commission has largely been ignored in public discourse. The concept of reconciliation, which generally involves the bringing together of two equal adversaries, both of whom have done wrong, is therefore singularly inappropriate in terms of the Indian Residential Schools Settlement Agreement. As Justice Murray Sinclair has stated, for most survivors, "reconciliation means trying to reconcile with a car while it is running you over" (Sinclair 2015).

Indeed, as the settlement wound down, many Indigenous leaders increasingly asserted that the inadequacies in the implementation of the IRSSA be addressed. These leaders did not call for renegotiations but for a more accurate implementation (Barnsley and Martens 2016; Galloway 2016), noting that after the process had ended there were still survivors needing significant help, as well as thousands of individuals who were left out of the settlement.

The scale of the IRSSA is massive as compared with the Japanese Canadian redress, mainly because of the length of time that residential schools operated (for over a century) and the correspondingly larger groups of people affected, as well as the willful abuse of so many children in the schools. Both settlements involved pervasive denials of history, however. On the one hand, Canada has treated the Japanese Canadian internment as a past isolated unfortunate incident, a construction that has served to absolve Canada of its past and present institutionalized racism against peoples of colour. On the other hand, by treating residential schooling as an unfortunate mistake, Canada has been able to absolve itself not only of a violently colonial past but also of ongoing settler colonialism. Indeed, the manner in which the government of Stephen Harper issued an apology for residential schooling in 2008, followed less than a year later by his statement that "Canada has no history of colonialism" (Morgensen 2013, 67) confirms that Canada's apology for residential schooling did not acknowledge that the schools were a central disciplining apparatus of settler colonial power. Harper's apology could be construed as another apology for Canada's treatment of certain racialized groups, like the 2006 apology to Chinese Canadians for the head tax and indeed the 1988 apology to Japanese Canadians for the internment. In this view, Indigenous peoples are constructed as a racialized group only; their Indigeneity and Canadian settler colonialism are erased in such apologies.

Continuing Struggles for Colonial Redress: The Child Welfare System

Struggles surrounding redress for Indigenous peoples have been taken up in recent years by the efforts of survivors of the so-called Sixties Scoop for restitution for the losses that accompanied the widespread theft of Native children from their communities after the 1951 Indian Act enabled provincial child welfare agencies to extend their jurisdiction onto reserves for the first time.

The subsequent funding agreements that the federal government entered into with the provinces established the parameters of this massive theft of Native children, enabling child welfare workers to apprehend approximately 20,000 Status Indian children and even greater numbers of non-Status children (Alston-O'Connor 2010). Approximately 70 to 90 percent of these children grew up in non-Native homes with little to no sense of a Native identity (RCAP 1996, 26).

Patrick Johnston (1983) demonstrated the scale of the scoop, noting that particularly in Northern Ontario and Western Canada, the massive increase of numbers of children in care saw them going from less than 1 percent in 1951 to between 30 and 50 percent of all children in care by the mid-sixties – and child apprehensions only increased from that point. In British Columbia, the Spallumcheen band lost all 150 of its children to child welfare, an entire generation for this tiny community (107).

By 1978, in British Columbia 3.5 percent of the population were Status Indians but Native children made up 44 percent of all children in care; at the same time, in Saskatchewan 8.3 percent of the population had Indian status, but Native children made up 65 percent of all children in care. By 1981, in northern Ontario, where the percentage of Native people is the highest, 85 percent of the children in care in the Kenora-Patricia agency were Native (RCAP 1996, 25). Across Canada the majority of Native children in child welfare were not adopted out but spent years shuttling from family to family as well as group homes (25). Another problem was the practice of allowing the adoption of Native children out of their province of origin, or out of Canada. In 1982, 25 percent of all Manitoba children were placed outside the province, and virtually all were Native children (28).

Three things need to be highlighted to address this massive scale of child apprehensions. First is the federal government's practice of paying only for in-care costs for Native children. At the time it had already been established in the professional community that children should be removed from their families only as a last resort in protecting children from harm. However, the federal government would not pay costs to support Native families in trouble; removal of the children was all they would pay for (RCAP 1996, 27). Second is that social welfare agencies accepted this double standard – that children should be taken into care if they were Native – because of widespread colonial attitudes among welfare workers that Native mothers were inherently deficient. The third issue is the complex interplay between the residue of residential schools and colonial impoverishment. Some children needed to be apprehended – their parents, traumatized by residential school, with no experience of being parented themselves, and often struggling with addictions, ended up neglecting their children (27). But for every child removed because of neglect, dozens were removed simply because children were being cared for by extended family members while parents were away working – and most often, simply because families were poor. It was always assumed that white middle-class families would be better suited for the children.

These assumptions about the best interests of the child were generally false. Children all too often were removed to families that were indifferent to them, if not abusive. Families took in Native children just to get the money. Farmers took in Native children just to work them. Most problematically, the situation enabled abusers complete and untrammelled access to children by having them in their own homes, where they could be abused with impunity – nobody believed the word of Indigenous foster children when the foster family was considered respectable in its community. Unlike in residential school, children fostered into abusive families did not even have other children to turn to.

Even when children were placed in "good" families, they were raised in ignorance of their culture, with no knowledge of their own identity and few defences against the racism they encountered from some family members or the wider community. The practice of obscuring the Native heritage of adoptees was widespread, so that adoptees could not access the rights and services they were entitled to as Status Indians (Johnston 1983, 95).

Dealing with the problem was hampered by Canada's refusal to acknowledge any level of sovereignty to First Nations, in contrast to the situation of tribes in the United States. In the United States, it was possible to pass a National Indian Child Welfare Act because jurisdiction for children could pass from the federal government to tribes; in Canada this was not possible (Johnston 1983, 89). A further problem was that each of the ten provinces as well as the two territories (at the time) had its own system of child welfare. The only option was to create Native child welfare agencies in each province or territory– and while they were hampered by having to proceed with the same bureaucratic processes as Children's Aid, most specified that at-risk children should be placed within the extended family, if possible; if not, then within the same community or with a family of the same cultural background; and if not that, then with a Native family of another background; only if none of these options was available should non-Native families be involved (RCAP 1996, 29).

A major role that Native child welfare agencies have played (despite being massively underfunded relative to provincial child welfare organizations [Chaarani, 2022]) is related to repatriation, namely, helping adoptees to trace their families and communities. When adoptees reached the age of eighteen and could access information about their families, it generally did not involve what communities their parent(s) came from. Native child welfare agencies networked with each other to find out what possible communities individuals came from and helped them reconnect with existing family (Native Child and Family Services et al. 1999). Meanwhile, the majority of adoptions tended to break down, so large numbers of Indigenous children ended up on the street as adolescents. These homeless girls and boys made up the majority of adolescent sex workers and trafficked youth (Johnson 2019).

Redress for the survivors of the Sixties Scoop became possible with the 2013 Ontario Superior Court of Justice decision in *Brown v Canada Attorney General* (2013 ONSC 5637) where the plaintiffs were successful in defining Indian child welfare survivors as a "class" who could sue for damages. Despite appeals organized by the federal government, the Ontario Superior Court upheld earlier court rulings in February 2017 (Mandell Pinder LLP 2017). In August 2018, the settlement was approved by the Ontario Superior Court and the Federal Court.

It's important to note that the settlement was solely for loss of access to cultural knowledge. Despite the numbers of individuals severely damaged by their abuse in foster care and the racism so many faced in foster homes, loss of cultural knowledge was the one commonality that every adoptee had faced, and it was an important one. In any case, the severely restricted records of the child welfare system made it impossible to access any other kinds of collective experience of the sort that was possible with the IRSSA.

The terms of the Sixties Scoop Settlement restricted beneficiaries to those who were either registered Indians under the Indian Act or who were eligible to be registered as Indians, and who were removed from their homes in Canada between January 1, 1951, and December 31, 1991, and placed in the care of non-Indigenous foster or adoptive parents (Class Action: Sixties Scoop Settlement 2024). There was a complex system of awards, depending on how many eligible survivors applied. If fewer than 20,000 individuals applied, the amount would be $50,000; if between 20,000 and 30,000 individuals applied, the compensation would be $25,000 per person. Given the numbers of eligible respondents, the final settlement was for $25,000 per person (Class Action: Sixties Scoop Settlement 2024).

The requirement to be eligible for Indian status was particularly difficult for survivors, given that many children in the foster care system were told nothing about their community of origin and did not know where they came from or whether they were eligible for Indian status. Normally, individuals who found out their parent(s)' names from child welfare would go to Native child welfare agencies, who would network to see where such individuals might come from. This process quickly became overloaded, especially during the COVID-19 pandemic and given the tight deadlines for application for a settlement. After finding out who they were, these individuals still had to apply to see whether they were eligible for Indian status.

Another issue is that many survivors of the Sixties Scoop experienced significant physical, sexual, and emotional abuse in their foster homes, leading to profound low self-esteem and high-risk behaviours, including drug and alcohol abuse, mental health issues, and suicide attempts (Carriere 2005). Far too many of these youths ended up in prison (Lamirande, Nation to Nation, 2020). As a result, too many survivors have lacked the skills to pursue the complex demands of finding their communities and families and proving their eligibility for Indian status – certainly not within a finite time frame. And finally, even recalling the past could be triggering for many of the adoptees who experienced profound abuse in their foster homes (K. Rae and J. Usher, personal communication, April 2019).

As of June 2022, 34,785 individuals had applied to the class action settlement; of these, 12,068 claims were rejected, and an additional 650 people were given the right to either reapply or provide more information to an existing claim; however, the deadlines in each case were a mere thirty days. Failure to provide missing information by the deadline would result in these claims being rejected as well (Class Action: Sixties Scoop Settlement 2024). Given that over a third of all applicants were rejected, the inability of adoptees to access sufficient information within the time frames of the settlement clearly meant that many of them were denied justice.

A total of 20,495 claims were approved. Since this number exceeded the limit for a $50,000 settlement that had been set at 20,000 claimants, successful claimants were eligible for only $25,000 each. Because of COVID, $21,000 was initially sent to each claimant, with the final $4,000 being sent out subsequently.

The settlement has established a short-term Aboriginal Healing Foundation to bridge the generations and give meaning to their suffering as well as to promote "healing and reconciliation" (Class Action: Sixties Scoop Settlement 2024). The Healing Foundation for Sixties Scoop survivors hosted ten engagement sessions in different locations across Canada between September 2019 and February 2020 to hear voices and recommendations from many affected individuals to best serve them in recovery. The Healing Foundation sought to provide support for survivors and document their voices.

In Manitoba, where the province has apologized for the Sixties Scoop, two survivors filed a motion in 2016 with the Court of Queen's Bench in Winnipeg, seeking $50 million in punitive damages and $200 million in damages for breach of fiduciary duty and negligence (Taylor 2016). In October 2017, the federal government announced it had reached a $750 million agreement with about 20,000 people who were placed in non-Indigenous foster homes as far away as New Zealand between 1951 and 1991. The agreement was subsequently harmonized with the Sixties Scoop class action. A national Indigenous Survivors Group had urged survivors to get out of the deal, which would conceivably preclude them from claiming damages for physical and sexual abuse, and because of concerns about lack of transparency; a clause in the agreement states that if 2,000 people agree to opt out, it can be declared null and void (Malone 2018).

On October 6, 2017, however, a settlement in principle was reached to resolve the Sixties Scoop class actions in different provinces across Canada, with the same settlements of $25,000 to $30,000, paid only to individuals (Klein Lawyers LLP, n.d.). Meanwhile, a movement is growing in Saskatchewan for a national inquiry into the Sixties Scoop – to find out the scope of the scoop, how many were taken, how many died while in foster care – the kind of information that a class action suit with a short timeline could not uncover. With this in mind, the Sixties Scoop Network is beginning a mapping process based on peoples' volunteered experiences (Southern Chiefs' Organization, n.d.).

There are two significant differences between the IRSSA and the Sixties Scoop class action. First, because of the nature of the Sixties Scoop, where culpability for abuse can too easily be deflected onto the individual family while ignoring the conditions under which the child was first taken away and then placed, and where different conditions existed broadly in different contexts and in different provinces, Native organizations did not add their voices to the class action. The fact that so many parents blame themselves for the loss of their children made support from communities more difficult. And the fact that each adoption was a "private" matter made it harder for the Assembly of First Nations (AFN) to back the settlement: with residential schools, it was clear that Canada was the culprit, but the government's role in organizing the Sixties Scoop was hidden behind the personal issues of each individual who had been taken. And without the backing of Native organizations, settlements were abysmally low, at $25,000 per person. Given the huge numbers of Indigenous people from foster care who died by suicide because of abuse, or ended up on the street as adolescents or were trafficked, or otherwise ended up serving years in prison, $25,000 for lives so terribly marked by loss and tragedy is a travesty.

Second, unlike residential schooling, which had a definitive end point in Canada, the Sixties Scoop has not, in fact, ended. Class action lawsuits have, for the most part, included adoptions into the 1990s as part of the Sixties Scoop – and yet the ongoing loss of children with the so-called "millennial scoop" is not addressed. In 2005, at least 27,500 children were in the care of child welfare agencies – three times the number during the Sixties Scoop, and the number has risen since then. Most tellingly, there are more children taken from their families today than at the height of the residential school era (Canadian Press 2011).

If the struggles around the Sixties Scoop reveal that First Nations children continue to be displaced from their homes as wards of the state, the connections and disjunctures with the Indian Residential Schools Settlement Agreement become clearer, while the connection between the Sixties Scoop settlement and the Japanese Canadian redress becomes less clear. To make sense of these connections and disjunctures, it is important to theorize redress, beginning with settler colonialism.

Theorizing Settler Colonialism

Lorenzo Veracini has focused specifically on the internal dynamics of settler colonialism. He theorizes that for the settler, the presence of both Indigenous Others and Exogenous Others represents a problem that must be managed. Accordingly, Indigenous Others are divided into two groups – those more manageable individuals that are to be "uplifted" through assimilation into settler society through their willingness to engage in negotiations with governments regardless of the cost to their communities, and those who resist the colonial state, particularly in their struggles to resist resource depredation on their lands and are therefore criminalized and permanently segregated as "abject Others." Veracini suggests that peoples of colour, as "exogenous Others," are also divided into those who are manageable, as virtuous Others, who can be viewed as potential settlers, or at least as "model minorities," and those "abject Others" who are viewed as unruly, who are criminalized and are to be segregated and controlled. As Veracini theorizes it, the settler needs to constantly empty the categories of "uplifted" potentially assimilated Indigenous Others and virtuous Exogenous Others by finding discrete and minoritized sites for them within the settler population – in order to alleviate the problem of difference, while maintaining firm controls on "abject Others" (Veracini 2010, 24–28). The politics of multiculturalism, in many respects, is how the settler accomplishes this feat of managing the "diversity" of these discrete and minoritized peoples who collectively are used to represent the essence of Canada as non-racist and non-colonial. Meanwhile, Indigenous peoples who resist colonial power and those racialized groups who are considered unassimilable continue to be categorized as "abject Others" to be permanently segregated and suppressed.

While Veracini's model highlights how the "difference" of both Indigenous peoples and "exogenous Others" is managed by white settlers through a process of absorption or subordination, which highlights the commonalities of experience between these groups, Patrick Wolfe reminds us that the goals of settler societies are both to amalgamate Native peoples and to eliminate them so that settlers can replace them on their lands; as he cogently sums it up: "Settler colonialism destroys in order to replace" (Wolfe 2006, 3). The central problem for settler colonialism, then, is that Native peoples have known the land for millennia and created whole worlds that must be destroyed for the settler society to assert its claims. Other "externalities" – peoples of colour deemed unassimilable – must also be dealt with, but the "problem" of Indigenous presence is the primary obstacle for the settler society to be able to establish itself.

Another way of understanding both the commonalities and the incommensurable aspects of the IRSSA and the Sixties Scoop Settlement, as compared with the Japanese Canadian redress settlements, is to utilize Giorgio Agamben's (1998, 108) theorizing of the camp as a site of "bare life" – a condition of being abandoned by the juridical order, stripped of political rights yet subjected to its violent power, enabled by the "states of exception" (Agamben 2005, 5) that lie at the heart of modern nation-states, that establish the rule of law precisely by placing it in abeyance within spaces of exception. In examining these concepts, it is necessary to first take into account the critique of Sunera Thobani – that the camp is always a racialized space (Thobani, 2012, 3).

Agamben's theorizing, of course, addressed the concentration camp as the state of exception at the heart of state sovereignty; however, racialized internment camps as one of the "states of exception" of Canadian sovereignty certainly follows this model. Moreover, it becomes useful in seeing the racialized internment camp as a predecessor to the modern detention centre and the current racialized "war on terror," where Muslims are being "cast out" from Western civilization (Razack 2008). It is also important to bear in mind Paul Gilroy's recognition of the plantation as camp, as a state of exception lived by enslaved Black people, where normal juridical rules were set aside (2013, 5), and the ways in which Black Canadian bodies continue to be subject to the racialized disciplining power of the police.

However, Steven Blevins suggests that Agamben's notion of the camp is inadequate to address the rendering of African lives into bio-cargo. He suggests that the Atlantic slave trade marks the moment when the enslaved, as human bio-cargo, were established as a mobile "thing" in law, and that the legal and systematic appropriation of human life into economic exchange as bio-cargo continues to be encoded in the present condition of postcolonial migrants (Blevins 2016, 25), as well as shaping the irremediability of Blackness in Western modernity. Within this context, however, Scott Lauria

Morgensen (2013, 58) theorizes that the space-outside-law that shaped slave societies could take place only to the extent that the lands placed in exception to terminate Indigenous tenure became available to new biopolitical violences. Indeed, Jane Landers describes how the conditions of slavery changed from those under the medieval slave codes of Spain – where slaves were able to buy their freedom and marry and to have Black representation in courts while Black officials administered the funds and responsibilities of Black churches, hospitals, and social welfare systems – to chattel slavery with the establishment of Spanish and Portuguese colonies in the Americas (Landers 2006, 2). Only as stolen Indigenous lands became available for European profit did the reduction of African life to bio-cargo become a central aspect of European economies, enshrined in law. The colonization of Indigenous lands, then, is the site of origin for all other spaces of exception in the Americas.

Indeed, Morgensen warns us that to see the states of exception that create the reserve, the plantation, the internment camp, and the detention centre as anything other than the primary exercise of biopower, which originates and continues to be maintained globally by settler colonialism, is to naturalize the power of settler colonialism and thus make it invisible. For Morgensen, settler colonialism represents the regimes that currently universalize Western law and maintain global systems of dominance. He asserts unequivocally that theories of the biopolitical state, regimes of global governance, and the war on terror will be insufficient unless they critically theorize settler colonialism as a historical and present condition and method of all such power (Morgensen 2013, 53–54). Asserting the centrality of settler colonialism in our theorizing creates spaces for comprehending specific "states of exception," including internment camps and plantations, in relation to the lands on which they were built. However, it is also important to address Jodi Byrd's acknowledgement that while the colonization of Indigenous land represents the source of other spaces of exception within settler colonialism (2011, 205), Indigenous epistemologies must be seen as capable of reframing recognition in ways that do not depend on Agamben's theorizing (211, 144).

Redress on Indigenous Land

A crucial question, then, in the body of work addressing Agamben's theories is the question of Indigenous peoples' relationships to their land. Juanita Sundberg, in a focus on states of exception in the United States–Mexico borderlands, addresses how the human and "other than human" nexus has become a primary site through which politically qualified life and belonging are being rearticulated. She notes that how sovereign governments organize intimate connections with non-human entities – land, plants, animals – as well as the crucial separations from them in the form of flooding rivers or creating toxic waste – is entangled with other embodied processes constituting states of exception (Sundberg 2015, 216). The fact that states of exception generally involve the stripping away of relations with the natural world through resource rape is uniquely central to the condition of "bare life" that settler colonialism creates for Indigenous peoples.

Agamben's concepts enable us to address a significant incommensurability between the Japanese Canadian redress on the one hand, and the IRSSA and the Sixties Scoop settlement on the other, concerning the role of citizenship relating to redress in colonial contexts. Sundberg (2015), addressing Agamben's notion that modern citizenship in liberal democracies is constituted in and through (ongoing) processes to purify, classify, or produce politically qualified life, suggests that strategies that uphold citizenship as a means of demanding rights will leave intact structures of abandonment (223). Seen in this light, while activists for the Japanese Canadian redress settlement actively supported the struggle for the IRSSA in critical ways, ultimately any redress settlement based on citizenship further reinforces the structures of abandonment and bare life premised on the biopolitics of the Indian Act (Lawrence 2004) and indeed risks blurring the distinction between the anti-racist struggle of peoples of colour and Indigenous resistance to colonization.

And yet struggles for recognition based on negotiations with state power can also involve a compromised notion of Indigenous empowerment that can be premised on the abandonment of racialized others. Jodi Byrd, addressing the US context and acknowledging that the colonization of Indigenous peoples provided both the bureaucratic and physical framework for the Japanese American internment, has explored the involvement of John Collier with the Japanese American internment, including his address to the first group of Japanese Americans interned at Poston in the Gila River Indian Reservation in 1941. She points out that Collier was the author of the Indian Reorganization Act (IRA), the legislation that many Native American tribes currently rely on to address their rights as Indigenous people. Byrd (2011,193) writes:

With only eight years separating the Indian Reorganization Act from Roosevelt's Executive Order 9066 (which began the Japanese American

Internment), Collier expanded his vision of colonial administration to include Indigenous and racial minorities alike as he advocated for reconsideration of self-government as a tool for assimilative incorporation. Collier's vision for the IRA which provides the cornerstone for federal recognition and nation-to-nation status of Indigenous nations colonized by the United States reveals the syllogistic fallacy at the heart of such policies – that because the IRA reestablished the language of self-governance, the act recognized Indigenous nations as sovereign entities rather than as racial, ethnic communities who would one day be assimilated into the US body politic. The implications for American Indian Studies and our reliance on the Indian Reorganization Act to provide the language of government-to-government sovereignty and self-determination are profoundly eclipsed by the intersection of colonial and racist agendas that collude to oppress, on one hand and offer the seductive recognitions that maintain state hegemony on the other.

Canada's Indian Act does not allow for making the kinds of sovereign claims to power that Byrd addresses; however, Canada has created multiple options for land-based communities to opt out of the Indian Act by forever surrendering their claims to their traditional lands, utilizing similarly compromised notions of "self-government." Such actions collude with colonial power; the cost involves impoverishing their own community members who traditionally depended on lands traded away in the process.

Denials of Colonization

What does it mean to have redress for residential schooling through the IRSSA, deflecting the reality of past and ongoing settler colonialism? First, it means that the long and multiple processes of initial colonial land acquisition – whether in the sixteenth and seventeenth centuries in eastern Canada, the eighteenth and nineteenth centuries in the west, and the twentieth century in the north – and the long resistance of Indigenous peoples across the continent to this land theft – are denied, while settler occupation is naturalized as acceptable and indeed normal. Through this denial, Indigenous lands are rewritten as "Canada."

Second, the normalization of settler colonization means the ignoring of the range of genocidal policies and processes that have enabled the Canadian government to consolidate its power and its ongoing determination to continually extend its control over the land. These policies and processes include the past and present theft of resources, which has vastly enriched Canada and devastated the communities that depended on those resources for their livelihoods (Neu and Therrien 2003; Shewell 2004), through the sequestering of people on reserves with the imposition of the Indian Act (Lawrence 2004), through the outlawing of spirituality (Pettipas 1994), and finally through the removal of children – first to residential schools and subsequently with the child welfare system. Meanwhile, the deliberate impoverishment of Indigenous communities remains at the root of many of the difficulties that Indigenous people have faced in obtaining true redress. As Hugh Shewell (2004, 23) has stated, this impoverishment is both normalized and meant to be permanent:

> Indian welfare dependency has been a manifestation of the loss of First Nations' political and economic autonomy, and of the impact of the processes of state legitimation on their communities. Thus, Indian dependency on welfare is not simply an episode in the history of their dispossession; it is an integral aspect of the continuing history of relations between First Nations and Europeans.

Finally, this denial of past and present settler colonialism enables struggles over recognition to intensify, as Canada's relentless efforts to acquire whatever Indigenous lands that still remain in Indigenous hands are maintained through policies such as the comprehensive claims process, which pits nations against nations, communities against communities, and even families against families, in a struggle over relationships to land – whether it will remain sacred or will ultimately be viewed as real estate (Lawrence 2012).

It is clear, then, that with the Indian Residential Schools Settlement Agreement, Canada has been able to sidestep addressing the root of the problem – the violent histories of colonization and ongoing process of land appropriation that have naturalized settler colonialism. The question remains as to whether the process of negotiating a redress settlement automatically demands both the intensification of colonial relations and their simultaneous denial.

Redress and the Politics of Recognition

If the Indian Residential Schools Settlement Agreement has brought residential school survivors into a complex process of what is now called "reconciliation" (a term survivors never would have chosen) with Canada through

Canada's denial of past and ongoing colonization, it may well be that it is the process of negotiating redress itself in the context of settler colonialism that co-opts and changes what is possible.

Negotiations with Canada have always been fraught with danger and loss, beginning with treaties that, from 1873 onward, were always accompanied by policies of force – reorganizing family life and land tenure, and eventually outlawing spiritual practices and taking children away. And yet Canada's practices of repressive violence – which mandated residential schooling and the Sixties Scoop – began to change after 1969. According to Glen Coulthard (2014, 25), the way colonial power relations operated in Canada historically – with "unconcealed structure[s] of domination and force" – gradually became transformed, in the face of Indigenous resistance, into "a form of colonial governance that works through the medium of state recognition and accommodation."

Coulthard, in adapting Fanon's writing in *Black Skin, White Masks* to settler colonialism in Canada, has theorized that negotiations for recognition of any kind that are not accompanied by significant social mobilization – so that both the objective and subjective aspects of colonial control are taken on – can be too easily domesticated and constrained by the state, the courts, and corporate interests into negotiations that leave the foundation of the colonial relationship relatively undisturbed (2014, 33–34, 40).

With this in mind, it is important to consider that the Japanese Canadian struggle for redress involved grassroots organizing. Not only were large numbers of the children and grandchildren of internees involved in mobilizing to bring about negotiations on their families' behalf, but they also engaged the Canadian public in the process. As a result, the settlement they achieved was comprehensive in its scope, and while actual monies that were paid out to survivors were not extensive, the range of demands they put forward – to repatriate people exiled to Japan, to expunge the criminal records of those charged under the War Measures Act, and to set up what became the Race Relations Foundation – were achieved. Moreover, the long history of activism that finally led to the redress process enabled it to fundamentally change how Japanese Canadians were viewed within Canada, from abject bodies branded as enemy aliens to rights-bearing citizens of Canada. In that respect, the Japanese Canadians redress addressed both the objective and subjective aspects of racist domination.

The conditions facing Indigenous peoples in Canada struggling for redress are, of course, on a different scale in two ways. The first is longevity: the historic violence of colonialism has gone on for centuries, and therefore has involved much larger numbers of people. The second is far more structural, however – namely, that to fundamentally change how Indigenous peoples are seen in Canada means to challenge the colonialism at the heart of Canada. As Coulthard indicates, such changes cannot be won solely through negotiation. From Fanon, he suggests that first of all what is needed is popular mobilization, and the strong cultural awareness that ultimately informs all grassroots movements of resistance; without such resistances, negotiations cannot challenge colonialism. Indeed, he is clear that it is only through prior grassroots mobilization that any form of substantive change has ever been negotiated between Canada and Indigenous peoples (Coulthard 2014, 165–68).

However, the IRSSA was negotiated by those whom Canada, for the most part, positions as Indigenous leaders or elites: lawyers and other professionals. In Coulthard's (2014, 168–69) terms, these forms of leadership generally frown on direct action as either disruptive, irrelevant, and harmful to relations with Canada, or, in terms of an individual's mental health, "backward-looking." The result is a leadership composed of professionals, who, while fighting for redress for survivors, positioned them as essentially deserving but powerless.

This is not to distract from the real need for redress from the experiences of residential school. During the negotiations, however, survivors in general were positioned by much of the leadership negotiating on their behalf as people far too traumatized by the schools to be involved in the process. Not only has this enabled Canada to continue to replicate concepts of profound Indigenous dysfunction but the anger of survivors that has had no place to be expressed could have carried them into mobilization during the negotiations. Indeed, Coulthard (2014) has challenged the constant assumption that expressing anger at the many wrongdoings that Indigenous people have experienced is "dwelling in the past, refusing to 'move on,' unhealthy for the psyche." Without denying that sometimes anger can cause individuals to function in unhealthy and disempowering ways, he asserts that for many individuals, anger at injustice can also represent ceasing to direct anger at oneself and beginning to express it outward at those who are responsible for wrongdoing (110–14). When the IRSSA was being negotiated, survivors might have had the opportunity to use their anger constructively, in mobilizing to ensure that their voices were listened to, and to assert that their abusers should be punished. They could conceivably have been a source of grassroots struggle that could have strengthened the negotiations to address the inclusion of collective realities, particularly language loss. Had Indigenous survivors of residential schooling been involved as activists in the struggle for redress, in the same manner as they courageously took their abusers to court, the terms of the settlement might have been different.

The IRSSA has irrevocably tied the jargon of reconciliation to the entire subject of residential schools. It's important to recognize, however, that no matter how redress settlements have been discursively appropriated by the state for its own ends, it does not detract from the importance of the long struggle of survivors to be heard – whether we speak of the Japanese Canadian struggle to force the government to negotiate, or the countless brave residential school survivors who stood up in court and faced the monsters who had abused them in childhood in lawsuit after lawsuit that culminated in the class action and the settlement – as well as those adoptees who stood up despite the unspeakable circumstances of those who have experienced the child welfare system, to force a Sixties Scoop settlement, however small.

In critiquing redress when it involves negotiations without mobilization, it is still extremely important to salute those grassroots people from each settlement process whose struggles won redress.

Note

1 *Indian Act*, RSC, 1985, c I-5.

References

Aboriginal Healing Foundation. 2010. *The* Indian Residential Schools Settlement Agreement's *Common Experience Payment and Healing: A Qualitative Study Exploring Impacts on Recipients*. Ottawa: Aboriginal Healing Foundation. https://www.ahf.ca/files/cep-2010-healing.pdf.

Agamben, Giorgio. 1998. *Homo Sacer: Sovereign Power and Bare Life*. Translated by Daniel Heller-Roazen. Palo Alto, CA: Stanford University Press.

– 2005. *State of Exception*. Translated by Kevin Attell. Chicago: University of Chicago Press.

Aidoo, Lamonte. 2018. *Slavery Unseen: Sex, Power and Violence in Brazilian History*. Durham, NC: Duke University Press.

Alamenciak, Tim. 2014. "Fighting for History: Uncovering the Truth of Residential Schools." *Toronto Star*, August 20. https://www.thestar.com/news/canada/fighting-for-history-uncovering-the-truth-of-residential-schools/article_53066e1e-d6c2-5362-88ff-7aa75a5a2bca.html.

Alston-O'Connor, E. 2010. "The Sixties Scoop: Implications for Social Workers and Social Work Education." *Critical Social Work* 11 (1): 53–63.

Antle, Rob. 2016. "N.L. Settles Mount Cashel Abuse Claim for $750K." *CBC News*, November 16. http://www.cbc.ca/news/canada/newfoundland-labrador/john -doe-mount-cashel-christian-brothers-suit-settled-1.3843286.

Asch, Michael, and Patrick Macklem. 1991. "Aboriginal Rights and Canadian Sovereignty: An Essay on *R. v. Sparrow.*" *Alberta Law Review* 29 (2): 498–517.

Bannerji, Himani. 2000. *The Dark Side of the Nation: Essays on Multiculturalism, Nationalism and Gender.* Toronto: Canadian Scholars.

Barnsley, Paul, and Kathleen Martens. 2016. "Residential Schools Settlement Agreement under Fire." *APTN National News*, May 19. https://www.aptnnews.ca/ national-news/residential-schools-settlement-agreement-under-fire/.

Barrera, Jorge. 2016. "Akwesasne under Surveillance by Military Counter-Intelligence Unit: Documents." *APTN National News*, February 19. https://www.aptnnews. ca/national-news/akwesasne-under-surveillance-by-military-counter-intelligence-unit-documents/#:~:text=Canadian%20military%20has%20kept% 20eye%20on%20Akwesasne%20since%201990.&text=The%20Canadian%20 military's%20counter%2Dintelligence,released%20to%20APTN%20 National%20News.

Barsh, Russell, and James Youngblood Henderson. 1997. "The Supreme Court's *Van der Peet* Trilogy: Naïve Colonialism and Ropes of Sand." *McGill Law Journal* 42: 993–1009.

Blevins, Steven. 2016. *Living Cargo: How Black Britain Performs Its Past.* Minneapolis: University of Minnesota Press.

Bonspiel, Steve. 2015. "Why Mohawks Don't Vote in Federal Elections." *Toronto Star,* August 17. https://www.thestar.com/opinion/contributors/why-mohawks-don't -vote-in-federal-elections/article_2ccf21f4–96a5–5456-b7d2–1828d89feeba. html.

Borrows, John. 2002. *Recovering Canada: The Resurgence of Indigenous Law.* Toronto: University of Toronto Press.

Byrd, Jodi. 2011. *The Transit of Empire: Indigenous Critiques of Colonialism.* Minneapolis: University of Minnesota Press.

Canadian Encyclopedia: The Indian Residential Settlement Agreement – Common Experience Payment. Accessed at: https://www.thecanadianencyclopedia.ca/ en/article/indian-residential-schools-settlement-agreement#:~:text=the%20 federal%20government.-,Common%20Experience%20Payment%20 (CEP),%243%2C000%20for%20each%20subsequent%20year.

Canadian Press. 2011. "First Nations Children Still Taken from Their Parents." *CBC News*, August 2. https://www.cbc.ca/news/politics/first-nations-children-still -taken-from-parents-1.1065255.

Carriere, Jeannine. 2005. "Connectedness and Health for First Nation Adoptees." *Paediatrics and Child Health* 10 (9): 545–48. https://doi.org/10.1093/ pch/10.9.545.

CBC News. 2012. "Lawyers Exploiting Native School Survivors, Says Group." February 2. http://www.cbc.ca/news/canada/manitoba/lawyers-exploiting-native -school-survivors-says-group-1.1196883.

– 2015. "Liberal Government Should Settle Residential Schools Suit, Says Ches Crosby." October 27. http://www.cbc.ca/news/canada/newfoundland-labrador/liberal-government-should-settle-residential-schools-suit-says-ches-crosbie-1.3290109.

– 2016. "Sex Offender Paul Leroux Allowed to Serve Rest of Sentence Out of Prison." June 6. http://www.cbc.ca/news/canada/north/paul-leroux-sex-offender-sentence-serve-prison-1.3616858.

Chaarani, James. 2022. "How Underfunding of First Nations Child Welfare Has Harmed Local Kids, Parents, Caregivers." CBC News, January 25. https://www.cbc.ca/news/canada/london/how-underfunding-of-first-nations-child-welfare-has-harmed-local-kids-parents-caregivers-1.6305027.

Class Action: Sixties Scoop Settlement. 2024. "Sixties Scoop Settlement." https://sixtiesscoopsettlement.info/.

Coulthard, Glen Sean. 2014. *Red Skin, White Masks: Rejecting the Colonial Politics of Recognition*. Minneapolis: University of Minnesota Press.

Das Gupta, Tania. 1999. "The Politics of Multiculturalism: 'Immigrant' Women and the Canadian State." In *Scratching the Surface: Canadian Anti-Racist Feminist Thought*, edited by Enakshi Dua and Angela Robertson, 187–206. Toronto: Women's Press.

Forester, Brett. 2022. "'Unrestrained' B.C. RCMP Unit Should Be Reined In or Phased Out, Opponents Say." *APTN News*, June 18. https://www.aptnnews.ca/national-news/unrestrained-c-irg-unit-should-be-reined-in-or-phased-out-opponents-say/.

Fanon, Frantz. 1952. *Black Skin, White Masks*, Rev. ed. New York: Grove Press, 2008.

Gabriel, Katsi'tsakwas Ellen. 2021. "Respect My Right to Not Vote: For Indigenous Peoples, Voting in a Colonial System Comes at a Cost to Our Sovereignty." *Ricochet*, September 14. https://ricochet.media/en/3776/respect-my-right-to-not-vote.

Galloway, Gloria. 2016. "First Nations Leaders Want to Rethink Residential Schools Agreement." *Globe and Mail*, May 9. https://www.theglobeandmail.com/news/politics/first-nations-leaders-want-to-rethink-residential-schools-agreement/article29948063/.

Gilroy, Paul. 2013. *Between Camps: Nations, Cultures and the Allure of Race*. London and New York: Routledge.

Government of Canada. 2002a. "Indian Residential Schools Settlement Agreement." https://www.rcaanc-cirnac.gc.ca/eng/1100100015576/1571581687074.

– 2002b. "Statistics on the Indian Residential Schools Settlement Agreement." https://www.rcaanc-cirnac.gc.ca/eng/1315320539682/1571590489978.

Hawthorn, Tom. 2007. "Disgraced B.C. Bishop Dead of Heart Attack." *Globe and Mail*, July 27. https://www.bishop-accountability.org/news2007/07_08/2007_07_27_Hawthorn_DisgracedBC.htm.

Independent Assessment Process Oversight Committee. 2021. *Independent Assessment Process: Final Report*. https://www.residentialschoolsettlement.ca/IAP_Final_Report_English.pdf.

Johnson, Rhiannon, 2019. "Human Trafficking Survivor Says Indigenous Women and Girls Especially at Risk." *CBC News*, June 27. https://www.cbc.ca/news/indigenous/bridget-perrier-human-trafficking-mmiwg-1.5189625.

Johnston, Patrick. 1983. *Native Children and the Child Welfare System*. Toronto: Native Council on Social Development in association with James Lorimer.

Klein Lawyers LLP. n.d. "Sixties Scoop Class Action." https://www.callkleinlawyers. com/class-actions/settled/sixties-scoop-class-action/.

Lamirande, Todd. Nation to Nation, 2020. "'Child Welfare to Prison Pipeline' Feeding Rising Indigenous Incarceration Rates." *APTN National News*, January 23. https://www.aptnnews.ca/nation-to-nation/child-welfare-to-prison-pipeline -feeding-rising-indigenous-incarceration-rates/.

Landers, Jane G. 2006. "Introduction." in *Slaves, Subjects, and Subversives: Blacks in Colonial Latin America*, edited by Jane G. Landers and Barry M. Robinson, 1–8. Albuquerque: University of New Mexico Press.

Lawrence, Bonita. 2004. *"Real" Indians and Others: Mixed-Blood Urban Native People and Indigenous Nationhood*. Lincoln: University of Nebraska Press.

– 2012. *Fractured Homeland: Federal Recognition and Algonquin Identity in Ontario*. Vancouver: UBC Press.

Malone, Kelly Geraldine. 2018. "Manitoba Survivors Opting Out of '60s Scoop Settlement with Federal Government." *CityNews*, February 16. https://toronto. citynews.ca/2018/02/16/manitoba-survivors-opting-out-of-60s-scoop -settlement-with-federal-government/.

Mandell Pinder LLP. 2017. "Brown v. Canada, 2017 ONSC 251 – Case Summary." https://www.mandellpinder.com/brown-v-canada-attorney-general-2017 -onsc-251-case-summary/.

McAllister, Kirsten Emiko. 2010. *Terrain of Memory: A Japanese Canadian Memorial Project*. Vancouver: UBC Press.

McNeil, Kent. 2004. "The Inherent Right of Self-Government: Emerging Directions for Legal Research." A research report prepared for the First Nations Governance Centre, Chilliwack, BC.

– 2013. "Editorial Opinion: Idle No More Deserves our Thanks." *The Star*. January 27. https://www.thestar.com/opinion/editorialopinion/2013/01/27/idle_no_ more_deserves_our_thanks.html.

McRae, Matthew. 2019. "The Chaotic Story of the Right to Vote in Canada." Canadian Museum for Human Rights, https://humanrights.ca/story/the-chaotic -story-of-the-right-to-vote-in-canada.

Miller, J.R., 2012. *The Canadian Encyclopedia: Residential Schools in Canada*, October 12. Updated January 11, 2024, by Tabitha De Bruin, David Gallant, Michelle Filice. https://www.thecanadianencyclopedia.ca/en/article/residential -schools.

Miller, Jim. 2001. "The Alberni Residential School Case: Blackwater v Plint." *Indigenous Law Bulletin* 5 (12): 20. http://www.austlii.edu.au/au/journals/IndigLawB/ 2001/73.html.

Monture-Angus, Patricia. 1999. *Journeying Forward: Dreaming First Nations Independence*. Halifax: Fernwood.

Morgensen, Scott Lauria. 2013. "The Biopolitics of Settler Colonialism: Right Here, Right Now." *Settler Colonial Studies* 1 (1): 52–76. https://doi.org/10.1080/220 1473X.2011.10648801.

National Association of Japanese Canadians. 2021. "Open Letter to Japanese Canadians and Their Allies in Canada to Support Indian Residential School Survivors." https://torontonajc.ca/residential-school-open-letter/.

Native Child and Family Services of Toronto, Janet Budgell, and Sevenato and Associates. 1999. *Our Way Home: A Report to the Aboriginal Healing and Wellness Strategy on the Repatriation of Aboriginal People Removed from the Child Welfare System.* Joint Management Committee of the Aboriginal Healing and Wellness Strategy.

Neu, Dean, and Richard Therrien. 2003. *Accounting for Genocide: Canada's Bureaucratic Assault on Aboriginal People.* Black Point, NS/London: Fernwood/Zed Books.

Oikawa, Mona. 2006. "Connecting the Internment of Japanese Canadians to the Colonization of Aboriginal Peoples." In *Aboriginal Connections to Race, Environment, and Tradition,* edited by Jill Oakes and Rick Riewe, 17–25. Winnipeg: Aboriginal Issues Press, University of Manitoba.

– 2012. *Cartographies of Violence: Japanese Canadian Women, Memory, and the Subjects of the Internment.* Toronto: University of Toronto Press.

Pasternak, Shiri. 2017. *Grounded Authority: The Algonquins of Barriere Lake against the State.* Minneapolis: University of Minnesota Press.

Pettipas, Katherine. 1994. *Severing the Ties That Bind: Government Repression of Indigenous Religious Ceremonies on the Prairies.* Winnipeg: University of Manitoba Press.

Pindara, Loreen. 2020. "78 Days of Unrest and an Unresolved Land Claim Hundreds of Years in the Making." *CBC News,* July 11. https://www.cbc.ca/news/canada/montreal/oka-crisis-timeline-summer-1990–1.5631229.

Razack, Sherene. 1998. *Looking White People in the Eye: Gender, Race and Culture in Courtrooms and Classrooms.* Toronto: University of Toronto Press.

– 2008. *Casting Out: The Eviction of Muslims from Western Law and Politics.* Toronto: University of Toronto Press.

RCAP (Royal Commission on Aboriginal Peoples). 1996. *Report of the Royal Commission on Aboriginal Peoples.* Vol. 3, *Gathering Strength.* https://caid.ca/RRCAP3.0.pdf.

Rifkin, Mark. 2009. "Indigenizing Agamben: Rethinking Sovereignty in Light of the 'Peculiar' Status of Native Peoples." *Cultural Critique* 73 (Fall): 88–124.

Shewell, Hugh. 2004. *"Enough to Keep Them Alive": Indian Welfare in Canada, 1873–1965.* Toronto: University of Toronto Press.

Simpson, Audra. 2014. *Mohawk Interruptus: Political Life across the Borders of Settler States.* Durham, NC: Duke University Press.

Sinclair, Justice Murray. 2015. Presentation at the Assembly of First Nations Challenge to University, Truth and Reconciliation Forum, University of Saskatchewan, Saskatoon, November 18–19.

Smith, Joanna. 2015. "Truth and Reconciliation Commission's Report Details Deaths of 3,201 Children in Residential Schools." *Toronto Star,* December 15. https://www.thestar.com/news/canada/truth-and-reconciliation-commissions-report-details-deaths-of-3-201-children-in-residential-schools/article_693fcb93-b6e3-5b93-869c-8c0fbdd57b7f.html.

Southern Chiefs' Organization. n.d. "Sixties Scoop Survivors." https://scoinc.mb.ca/sixties-scoop-survivors/.

St. Denis, Verna. 2011. "Silencing Aboriginal Curricular Content and Perspectives through Multiculturalism: 'There Are Other Children Here.'" *Review of Education, Pedagogy, and Cultural Studies* 33 (4): 306–17.

Stastna, Kazi. 2011. "First Nations Housing in Dire Need of Overhaul." *CBC News,* November 28. https://www.cbc.ca/news/canada/first-nations-housing-in-dire-need-of-overhaul-1.981227.

Sunahara, Ann Gomer. 2000. *The Politics of Racism: The Uprooting of Japanese Canadians during the Second World War.* 2nd ed. Ottawa: Ann Sunahara.

Sundberg, Juanita. 2015. "The State of Exception and the Imperial Ways of Life in the United States–Mexico Borderlands." *Environment and Planning D: Society and Space* 33: 209–28.

Swampy, Mario, and Kerry Black. 2021. "Tip of the Iceberg: The True State of Drinking Water Advisories in First Nations." *University of Calgary News,* May 7. https://ucalgary.ca/news/tip-iceberg-true-state-drinking-water-advisories-first-nations.

Taylor, Jillian. 2016. "Two Manitobans Hope to Launch Class-Action Lawsuit over Sixties Scoop." *CBC News,* April 22. https://www.cbc.ca/news/canada/manitoba/manitobans-hope-launch-class-action-lawsuit-sixties-scoop-1.3548764.

Thobani, Sunera. 2012. "Empire, Bare Life and the Constitution of Whiteness: Sovereignty in the Age of Terror." *Borderlands* 11 (1). *Gale Academic OneFile,* link. https://go.gale.com/ps/anonymous?id=GALE|A325496364.

Troian, Martha. 2016. "Indian Residential Schools: 5,300 Alleged Abusers Located by Ottawa." *CBC News,* February 2. https://www.cbc.ca/news/indigenous/residential-school-alleged-abusers-iap-1.3422770.

Truth and Reconciliation Commission. 2015. *Honouring the Truth, Reconciling for the Future: Summary of the Final Report of the Truth and Reconciliation Commission of Canada.* Winnipeg: Truth and Reconciliation Commission of Canada. https://ehprnh2mwo3.exactdn.com/wp-content/uploads/2021/01/Executive_Summary_English_Web.pdf.

Veracini, Lorenzo. 2010. *Settler Colonialism: A Theoretical Overview.* Houndmills, Basingstoke, UK: Palgrave Macmillan.

Waabshkigaabo. 2021. "As an Anishinaabe Citizen, I Can't Vote in Good Conscience in Federal Elections." *CBC News,* September 17. https://www.cbc.ca/news/canada/first-person-anishinaabe-vote-federal-election-1.6178236.

Wolfe, Patrick. 2006. "Settler Colonialism and the Elimination of the Native" *Journal of Genocide Research* 8 (4): 387–409.

2

Web of Recognition: The National Association of Japanese Canadians and the 1989 Task Force on First Nations Peoples

Mona Oikawa

In the critical Indigenous and political science literature, there has been much discussion about the politics of recognition. Indigenous and racialized scholars, in particular, have pointed out the limitations of and problems with the Canadian settler state's politics of recognition, the state processes of recognizing Indigenous and marginalized groups' demands for justice and state accountability for injustice. While there is a critical literature examining Black and other racialized groups' relationships to Indigenous peoples and settler colonialism (Byrd 2011; Dhamoon 2005; Fujikane and Okamura 2008; Jafri 2020; King 2017, 2019; King, Navarro, and Smith 2020; Lawrence and Dua 2005; and others), analyses of the internment of Japanese Canadians in relation to settler colonialism (Day 2016; Oikawa 2006, 2012; Yakashiro 2021), and Canadian settler state practices in negotiating Japanese Canadian redress that erased "the appropriation of Indigenous lands by settler governments and practices that attempt to eliminate Indigenous peoples from their lands" (Matsunaga 2021, 91), there has been little analysis in the scholarly literature of the role redress has played in informing Japanese Canadians' recognition of their relationship to Indigenous peoples. Moreover, how Japanese Canadians represent themselves in relation to Indigenous peoples requires further analysis. This chapter contributes to addressing this lacuna by analyzing examples from the Greater Toronto Chapter of the National Association of Japanese Canadian (NAJC) Task Force on First Nations Peoples' preliminary efforts in 1989 to recognize

Indigenous peoples.[1] In so doing, it also complexifies our understanding of Japanese Canadian histories by adding to our knowledge of their past political organizing. Using documents authored by the National Council of the NAJC and the task force, I argue that Japanese Canadians' recognition of Indigenous peoples was a process of self-constitution simultaneous to their representation of Indigenous peoples and their calls for justice. I hope that my work may contribute to understanding "how we come to know who we are" (Razack 1999, 167) as we engage in building relations among Japanese Canadians and with Indigenous peoples and others, and may assist us in identifying and contesting our complicities with settler colonialism.

This chapter is drawn from a larger project that examines the relationship of the NAJC to the Indigenous peoples with whom it worked in the 1990s. It comprises two sections. The first is a discussion of the "politics of recognition" and some of its critiques. The second provides examples from the NAJC Task Force on First Nations Peoples' preliminary work undertaken before initiating or supporting specific projects or actions with Indigenous peoples. Analytical tools discussed in the first section are then applied to a discussion of documents authored by the task force and the National Council of the NAJC.

Politics of Recognition

Janice McLaughlin, Peter Phillimore, and Diane Richardson (2011, 1) describe the concept of recognition as lying "at the heart of multiple contests around citizenship rights, identity politics, claims for material redistribution and demands for past harms to be acknowledged and redressed." In his seminal article "Subjects of Empire: Indigenous Peoples and the 'Politics of Recognition' in Canada" and his book *Red Skin, White Masks: Rejecting the Colonial Politics of Recognition*, Yellowknives Dene scholar Glen Coulthard analyzes and critiques the politics of recognition. He defines the "politics of recognition" in relation to Indigenous peoples as the "now expansive range of recognition-based models of liberal pluralism that seek to reconcile Indigenous claims to nationhood with Crown sovereignty via the accommodation of Indigenous identities in some form of renewed relationship with the Canadian state" (Coulthard 2007, 438).

The term "politics of recognition" gained currency with the publication of Charles Taylor's 1994 essay titled with the term. While I do not discuss the essay in detail here, in brief, Taylor's text begins by analyzing some of the philosophical ideas underpinning Western notions of democracy, individual identity, and equality. He follows his survey of ideas with an examination of the tensions between a liberalism positing equal rights and what he describes as "the politics of difference" (Taylor 1994, 37), where collectivities, like "indigenous and colonized people" (25), people with "different cultures" (64), and "women" (64) demand "equal status" (27). Taylor dismisses critiques of power mobilized by such groups and attributes their analyses to "subjectivist, half-baked neo-Nietzschean theories" (69) of scholars such as Michel Foucault and Jacques Derrida. Sidestepping the issue of power, including how it informs his own position as an academic, Taylor divorces political struggle from power and concludes, "the driving force of this kind of politics is the search for recognition and respect" (69). Amy Gutmann (1994, 6) describes Taylor's essay as revealing "what is at stake in the demand made by many people for recognition of their particular identities by public institutions."

As noted by Himani Bannerji (2000) and Coulthard (2007, 2014), however, it is what is at stake for the white settler hegemonic group that is of concern to Taylor. Both Bannerji and Coulthard provide important critiques of Taylor's essay and indicate that Taylor's analysis is bereft of an acknowledgment of the power relations between the "recognizer" and the "recognized," and the material histories of colonialism that are formative in social and political positionalities.

In the essay, Taylor (1994) discusses whether "different cultures" should be considered as of equal value to "our" culture (64) and concludes that "we are very far away from that ultimate horizon from which the relative worth of different cultures might be evident" (73). As Bannerji (2000, 135) astutely comments, his "tone of hospitality notwithstanding, the element of mutuality that is signalled by the philosophical level and necessary for a real situation of recognition is absent from Taylor's development of its premises and practicalities." Coulthard (2007, 440) underlines that Taylor's (1994, 41; 1994, 148) notion of "'recognition' is conceived as something that is ultimately 'granted' or 'accorded' to a subaltern group or entity by a dominant group or entity," and will thus be unable "to significantly modify, let alone transcend, the breadth of power at play in colonial relationships." He elaborates: "The 'master' – that is, the colonial state and state society – does not require recognition from the previously self-determining communities upon which its territorial, economic, and social infrastructure is constituted. What it needs is land, labor and resources" (Coulthard 2007, 451). This lack of mutuality is in fact illustrated by Taylor's support of state recognitive processes that discursively enunciate a normative Canadian subject as the recognizer of marginalized others, for example, in his statement, "The challenge is to deal with *their* sense of marginalization without compromising *our* basic political principles" (Taylor 1994, 63; emphasis added).

Bannerji (2000, 135) identifies the "recognizer" as the "anglo-European, so-called Canadian 'us'" on whom Taylor bestows "voluntary recognition" (143), the power to recognize or not, the Other. In her assessment of Taylor as a "conservative liberal," she critiques his lack of historical analysis of social, economic, and political contexts that produce "us" in relation to "them." As she states (139):

> It is a historical tale of physical and cultural genocides, of colonial robbery of history and resources, of silences and marginalization. This narrative has as its context the very foundation of Canada, its methods of acquiring economic resources, of populating this colony, modes and regulations of labour importation and labour market, existence of these others in a racially ethnicized and legally constructed hierarchical form of citizenship.

Hence, the power relations that produce the "hegemonic recognizer's" own dominant identity and the use of the politics of recognition to "entrench ... the mastery of the master and the enslavement of the slave" (Bannerji 2000, 148) are not acknowledged by Taylor. Bannerji asks a pivotal question of the recognizer: "Does this voluntary recognition hold as its foundational principle an element of self-recognition as well?" (143). Lacking in Taylor's formulation of the politics of recognition – outside of the self-aggrandizement of the recognizers – is their self-recognition of their social and economic positions forged historically through "their colonies, colonized and enslaved others, and their civilizational discourses" (Bannerji 2000, 148).

The cultural assessment that occurs in Taylor's formulation of the politics of recognition reflects his own and the Canadian settler state's reification of culture and identity. As Michael Seymour (2010, 4) suggests, recognition can be "constitutive of the institutional identity of peoples." Conflating numerous cultures and nations into one "Aboriginal" culture and usurping Indigenous peoples' rights and territories through the use of settler definitions of Indigenous culture and the identity categories in, for example, laws such as those inscribed by the Indian Act,[2] are tools the settler nation uses to continue its occupation and confiscation of Indigenous territories.

The notion of the politics of recognition has taken on a more expansive definition than the recognition of cultures suggested in Taylor's essay. This is demonstrated by McLaughlin, Phillimore, and Richardson's (2011) definition cited above, and by Roy Miki (2004, 169), who uses Taylor's essay to describe "the public spheres" into which the NAJC moved in 1984 as the "politics of recognition." These notions of recognition cannot be reduced to struggles for recognition of different cultures, but, as noted by Bannerji (2000, 147) in her critique of Taylor's essay, many subordinated groups "struggle to end exploitation and injustice"; they "struggle at many levels, including that of culture" (149) and "the identity of their politics need not only be the politics of identity" (148).

Importantly, in contrast to proving their cultural difference, during the campaign for redress for the internment, Japanese Canadians had to prove themselves as culturally Canadian and as having been deprived of the rights of Canadian citizens in the 1940s. Japanese Canadian activists sought to have the cultural and political identity of those interned acknowledged as "Japanese *Canadian*" and different from the "Japanese," an identity co-constructed by both Japanese Canadians and the Canadian state, in order to emphasize that their past construction as Japanese, alien, and enemy was used by the federal government in the 1940s to justify their removal and incarceration. Furthermore, Miki (1998, 11) reminds us that "the redress movement depended ... on the identity formation, 'Japanese Canadian' ('JC')." This identity construction was a discursive method for, as Kirsten Emiko McAllister (1999, 84) describes it, "narrating Japanese Canadians into the nation." Admittedly, this binarized identity still marks Japanese Canadians as Other to the normalized, unmarked white Anglo Canadian, but the recognition of their Canadian – albeit hyphenated or qualified – identity was paramount in the campaign for redress and in the federal government's recognition of the internment.

Notwithstanding the differences in identity construction through recognitive processes, the thrust of state recognition is to homogenize the group recognized, in this case as *Japanese Canadians*. Such homogenization discursively enables the racialized group's assimilation as a distinct totality into the Canadian multicultural settler nation. Moreover, this recognitive assimilative process furthers the goal of former prime minister William Lyon Mackenzie King's 1945 dispersal policy – launched simultaneously with his effort to deport as many Japanese Canadians as possible – to assimilate any person of Japanese ancestry whom he was unable to deport and who remained in Canada (Oikawa 2012; Sunahara 1981). As I have argued in past work (2012) and I argue below, Japanese Canadians are not a homogeneous group. Nonetheless, as Bonita Lawrence (Mi'kmaw) underlines in Chapter 1, "ultimately any redress settlement based on citizenship further reinforces the structures of abandonment and bare life [of Indigenous peoples] premised on the biopolitics of the Indian Act." Our recognition as Canadian citizens, therefore, legitimizes the structures of Canada as a nation, a nation that is founded on the dispossession of Indigenous peoples.

Self-Recognition and Social Recognition

Using the work of Frantz Fanon ([1952] 2008), Coulthard (2014, 48) theorizes and defines self-recognition for Indigenous peoples as a "self-affirmative and self-transformative ethics of desubjectification ... [that] must be cautiously directed away from the assimilative lure of the statist politics of recognition, and instead be fashioned toward our own on-the-ground struggles for freedom." Furthermore, Mohawk scholar Audra Simpson (2014, 189) describes "social recognition," within and between Indigenous communities, and "forms of social belonging, forms of social recognition, and recognition that does not necessarily entail a juridical or state form of recognition." While Simpson does not further define the concept of social recognition, she gives examples of "a complex of social belonging, of family, of intracommunity recognition" (188). However, she also points out that "forms of recognition (and processes) are in dialectical tension with each other" (189), and settler recognitive processes affect intra-community social recognition. For example, settler law changed the social and economic conditions for women who lost their "Indian" status through the Indian Act and were unable to live in their reserve communities (Lawrence 2004). When changes were made to the Indian Act through Bill C-31, reinstating the status of some women, some of whom then wished to return to their reserves – as was indicated by a woman Simpson interviewed – they were not always welcomed by all community members into what Simpson (2014, 189) calls the "social web of recognition."

Coulthard's and Simpson's analyses encourage us to think about other forms of recognition that contest and "refuse" (Simpson 2014, 11) state politics of recognition.[3] As settlers on Indigenous territories, Japanese Canadians are differently materially and socially located from Indigenous peoples and cannot appropriate the Indigenous and anti-colonial self-recognitive processes as described by Fanon and Coulthard. Nevertheless, if recognizing Indigenous peoples is a relational recognitive process for non-Indigenous peoples, how did Japanese Canadians construct themselves in their efforts to work with Indigenous peoples in the 1990s, and how might knowledge of their past political organizing inform a process of self-recognition for Japanese Canadians that deepens our analysis of who we are and our relationship to settler colonialism, white supremacy, hetero-patriarchy, and capitalism as non-Indigenous racialized people?

As I have argued elsewhere, the subjugating processes of the intern-ment produced different and relational Japanese Canadian subjects. Using Michel Foucault's notion of discourse as "not only language, but also the rules that govern their practice" (Oikawa 2012, 7) and understanding that discourse is always forged through relations of power, I offered the following analysis: "The federal government and its administrators used discourses of race, gender, class, ability, nationality, and others in determining who went where. Each discourse affected and enabled the other and their interlock-ing insinuated power relations in a complex way producing hierarchies of relational subjects in relational places" (12). Hence, our subjection by and negotiation with the Canadian settler state before, during, and after redress similarly produces heterogeneous subjects despite the singular "redressed" and "Japanese Canadian" identities that have been promulgated through the acquisition of the official state acknowledgment.

While I would argue that much more work must be done in under-standing how those of us with histories of internment by Canada were differently affected by these histories and how we have been subjected to white supremacy, heteropatriarchy and capitalism, and the effects of that subjection, our processes of recognizing our historical subject formations and our self-recognition must attend to the systems of power articulated by Bannerji (2000). A critical race feminist interlocking analysis (Crenshaw 1991; Hill Collins 2014; Razack 1998) of discourses of colonialism, gender, racialization, class, sexuality, and other valences of power as they construct each of us in relation to others might assist us in this process. How have we been produced and constructed ourselves under Canadian settler colonial-ism, white supremacy, heteropatriarchy, and capitalism, relationally to each other as Japanese Canadians and to Indigenous, Black, and other racialized peoples?

Simpson's concepts of social recognition and refusal of state recognition inspire us to examine our own relationships with other Japanese Canadians and our situatedness in relation to structures and discourses of power, including the internment, slavery, colonialism, and our "own ontological situation" (Markell 2003, 34) and complicities in relation to Indigenous peoples, Black peoples, Japanese Canadians, other racialized peoples, and other marginalized peoples. The selves produced through internment and redress, and the selves recruited in both service and resistance to settler colonialism require further examination, a project to which I hope this chapter contributes. While this chapter focuses on the self-recognitive processes of Japanese Canadians in relation to Indigenous peoples, critiques of the politics of recognition invite us to consider how state politics of recognition and redress have shaped and continue to shape Japanese Canadians in relation to the Canadian nation, Indigenous, Black, and racialized peoples, and the implications of refusing state recognition.

Web of Recognition

Coulthard's work has been used by Indigenous scholars in their critiques of settler states' politics of recognition (Byrd 2011; Lawrence 2012; Simpson 2014). For the most part, these critiques of the politics of recognition have focused on the relationship between the white settler state and/or white settlers and Indigenous peoples. While Coulthard (2014, 173) is clearly setting forth a theorization and politics of action for Indigenous peoples, he adds:

> This reality [the small size of Indigenous populations] demands that we continue to remain open to, if not actively seek out and establish, relations of solidarity and networks of trade and mutual aid with national and transnational communities and organizations ... including ... racial and ethnic communities that find themselves subject to their own distinct forms of economic, social, and cultural marginalization.

As James Tully (2008, 293) suggests, recognition is not simply "two-member struggles" but is "multiple rather than dyadic." It is, therefore, necessary to explore the construction of what Coulthard (2007, 454) describes as the "multifarious web of recognition relations that are at work in constructing identities and establishing (or undermining) the conditions necessary for human freedom and flourishing."

In the next section, I examine the formative stage of a particular web of recognition by focusing on the Greater Toronto Chapter of the NAJC Task Force on First Nations Peoples, processes that informed its work with Indigenous groups and individuals with whom it collaborated in the 1990s. Critical to this analysis is the understanding that Japanese Canadians are both "agent and object of recognition" (Williams 2014, 12). As recipients of redress, Japanese Canadians were and are the subjects of state recognition; members of the task force were also, as I will discuss, subject to the recognition of members of the NAJC National Council. At the same time, task force members were agents of recognition in attempting to acknowledge the position of Indigenous peoples. It is with the analyses thus presented in mind that I examine documents authored by members of the NAJC National Council and the Task Force on First Nations Peoples, documents that are, in part, revelatory of the self and selves recognized by their members in relation to Indigenous peoples and Canada, selves that undertook to recognize Indigenous peoples.

Methodology

A lesser-known aspect of Japanese Canadian organizing occurred under the umbrella of the NAJC in the years "after redress," namely, the organization of the Task Force on First Nations Peoples by the Greater Toronto Chapter of the NAJC.[4] My goal in this section is not to criticize the NAJC or the important work it did during and after the redress struggle; rather, I seek to contribute to the conversations and scholarship examining Black and racialized peoples' relationships to Indigenous peoples and settler colonialism by examining the work of the task force and the NAJC. This preliminary analysis of the work of the task force aims to examine Japanese Canadian relational subject constitution – in this case, in relation to the Indigenous peoples that it describes and with whom it aspired to work – and is an extension of my earlier work where I examined Japanese Canadians' subject constitution in relation to each other during and after the internment, and in relation to the white enactors and administrators of the internment (Oikawa 2012).

Using Foucault's (1990) formulation of discourse analysis, I examine the language used in documents authored by members of the Task Force on First Nations Peoples and the NAJC National Council, held in personal collections and in the UBC Library Rare Books and Special Collections,[5] and some of the social practices and power relations that the language describes and in which it is embedded. As Katherine Bischoping and Amber Gazso (2016, 2) explain "language is but one instance of power relations. Foucault studied discourses (which involve language) as bodies of knowledge and asked what power relations underpin them." A Foucauldian notion of discourse therefore involves "both texts and the rules and structures that account for their production" (Bischoping and Gazso 2016, 6). Moreover, the documents I examine are mediated texts, authored by people from various subject positions, and are not undisputed sources of truth or knowledge. Nevertheless, through discourse analysis we can examine the "multiplicity of discursive elements that come into play in various strategies" (and how "discourse can be both an instrument and an effect of power" (Foucault 1990, 100, 101). Indeed, as Erin C. Tarver (2011, 807) argues, Foucault's "account of power's effects (including meaning, normativity, and subjectivity) enables us to think the relational constitution of differentially oppressed or privileged subjects in a way that allows for greater complexity."

Using the method of discourse analysis, therefore, assists us in analyzing the language used by the NAJC in preparing for its work with Indigenous peoples, language still used by some Canadians as they describe their relationships to Indigenous peoples. This analysis more broadly supports the chapter's goal of preliminarily investigating the process through which we recognize Indigenous peoples as a relational recognitive process and how Japanese Canadians constructed themselves in relation to Indigenous peoples in their efforts to work with them in the 1990s.

While my work seeks to critically analyze efforts on the part of the task force and the NAJC to work with Indigenous peoples and the Japanese Canadian subjects produced discursively through their initiatives, I also wish to document and acknowledge their efforts and underline that their organizing took place over thirty years ago, before the Canadian settler state discourse of reconciliation with Indigenous peoples gained currency.[6] The task force's work also preceded the current, burgeoning critical literature analyzing Black and other non-Indigenous racialized peoples' relationship to settler colonialism.[7] While participating in making discourses about Indigenous peoples and themselves, the task force's language also reflects the time of its work and who they were at that time. The documents discussed here were produced in the months immediately following the redress settlement, a time when the NAJC was attempting to bring together Japanese Canadians divided through federal government processes of internment and dispersal, some of whom were working together for the first time in a national organization. It is my hope that this documentation and analysis will be useful not only to Japanese Canadians but also to others seeking to examine their relationships to Indigenous peoples and settler colonialism.

Inauguration of the Task Force on First Nations Peoples

In 1988, the NAJC negotiated an acknowledgment from the Canadian federal government for the injustice of the 1940s expulsion, detention, internment, dispossession, forced labour, dispersal, and deportation of Japanese Canadians. During the years of organizing for redress, the NAJC received support from Indigenous individuals, hailing from different nations. For example, George Erasmus (Dene), National Chief of the Assembly of First Nations from 1985 to 1991, was listed among those who joined the National Coalition for Japanese Canadian Redress, a group that endorsed "the NAJC's call for a negotiated settlement" (Miki and Kobayashi 1991, 113). The NAJC also received support from differently racialized and ethnicized organizations, such as the Canadian Arab Federation, the Chinese Canadian National Council, and the National Council of Jamaicans and Supportive Organizations in Canada, all of whom became members of the National Coalition for Japanese Canadian Redress (Miki and Kobayashi 1991, 115).[8] In addition to the perhaps better-known support of redress by some prominent white Canadians, the support of Indigenous nations, groups, and individuals, and racialized and ethnicized groups and individuals, was invaluable to the development of NAJC strategy and the public presentation of solidarity and numerical strength, which contributed to the ultimate fulfillment of its goal of obtaining acknowledgment of the injustice of the internment from the Canadian federal government. Michiomi Abe Kabayama, chair of the Task Force on First Nations Peoples, reflected on the support of Indigenous peoples in stating: "The Assembly of First Nations was one of our earliest, and strongest supporters. George Erasmus, Gord Peters and many others worked unstintingly with us."[9]

During and after the redress movement, the Greater Toronto Chapter of the NAJC made a commitment to work in support of Indigenous peoples' struggles for justice. As Kabayama explained, "some of us felt that we could not stop our work for civil and human rights. If we did, all our rhetoric about the necessity of Redress, based on our concern for human dignity for all Canadians, would ring hollow."[10] Four months after the signing of the redress acknowledgment, the Task Force on First Nations Peoples was formed in Toronto in January 1989 by members of the Greater Toronto Chapter.[11] Its first formal meeting was held on January 28, 1989. By October that year, there were forty-five individual members of the task force in different areas of Canada, including Winnipeg, Toronto, and Halifax.[12] The centre of organizing, however, remained in Toronto for the duration of the task force's existence. Some of the people who attended meetings during this first year were task force chair Michiomi Abe Kabayama, Joy Kogawa, Monica McKay (Nisga'a), Roger Obata,[13] John Flanders, Shirley Yamada, and Tak Ariga.

Scientist, journalist, broadcaster, and activist Dr. David Suzuki is credited by a founding member of the task force for inspiring their decision to organize. This founding member, writer Joy Kogawa, noted that she saw Suzuki on television announcing that he intended to use his $21,000 from the redress settlement for "native concerns." As Kogawa states: "He urged other redress recipients to donate at least $100.00" toward "native concerns."[14] At a meeting of the task force in Toronto on January 28, 1989, Kogawa described Suzuki's suggestion in these words: "Canadians of Japanese origin should express their concern for justice and fairness by working with oppressed Canadians everywhere, specifically, he suggested that we should begin networking with Native Indians, who have a sad, long and continuing history of neglect, oppression and injustice in Canada."[15] Hence both Suzuki and, through her witnessing of his statement, Kogawa connected their receipt of redress to the position of Indigenous peoples and their non-receipt of justice. Suzuki's comments were used to support Kogawa's own efforts to garner support for the task force.

Kogawa's recognition of Suzuki and his recognition of Indigenous peoples were therefore a generative part of the web of recognition in which the task force was formed. This recognitive process is also evidence of what Simpson has called "social recognition" in that Kogawa and Suzuki turned to each other and to other Japanese Canadians, particularly those who had been interned and had thus been recognized by the Canadian state for their internment, to organize in support of Indigenous peoples. Further to this web of recognition, the 1988 president of the Greater Toronto Chapter, Bill Kobayashi, was reported as placing "the highest priority on this concern."[16]

Social recognition of interned Japanese Canadians is also apparent in Kogawa's invitation to her friend Kabayama to chair the task force in Toronto, where she was a member of the Greater Toronto Chapter. As Kabayama explained, Kogawa approached him because they were good friends who had met "in church work [and she] knew of my commitment to civil rights."[17] In advocating for the work of the task force and setting up a "fund to assist in joint JC and Native ventures," Kogawa stated, "I'd like to believe that Redress was not wasted on us. That we are not a selfish bunch. That justice empowers people. That our community is capable of doing something significant."[18] In this statement, Kogawa constructs herself as empowered by the state recognition of redress. In her social recognition of other Japanese Canadians who were also recognized by the state, she extends the aspiration to demonstrate their lack of selfishness and to use the recognition bestowed on them to do "significant work" by supporting the task force.

In May 1989, Kabayama reported to the National Council of the NAJC[19] that monthly meetings of the task force were held in Toronto, where half of the task force members lived at that time. He described the task force as wanting "to focus the concerns of Japanese Canadians on the long-standing plight; [and] injustices of Native Canadians. It was hoped that with the dissemination of information, issues, and challenges, that a network of concerned, dedicated JC's would form across Canada."[20] The reports from the meetings were sent to all forty-two members of the task force and "comments and advice" were solicited from them.

When the task force was publicized through the *Nikkei Voice*, the Japanese Canadian newspaper established by the NAJC during the redress movement and instrumental in community organizing for redress, Indigenous individuals contacted the Greater Toronto Chapter in support of the task force. For example, on April 11, 1989, the task force reported A.J. Scow (Kwakwaka'wakw), a judge of the Provincial Court of British Columbia, as being "much interested in your task force activities, particularly on the legal side." In the same report, it was noted that Art Solomon (Anishinaabe), elder, teacher, and writer, "welcomes us to join in the fight against the beast."[21] Solomon had earlier extended support to the task force, described in the report of February 19, 1989 as: "Art Solomon, of K.K. Kanada, wrote to express appreciation and hope that the promise of the kind of work hinted in the first report would blossom."[22]

Kabayama set up a meeting with Solomon on April 24, 1989, and invited him to attend the next task force meeting. On April 26, Solomon was present at the meeting and was reported as "express[ing] his support for a considered approach to a selection of worthwhile projects. He also gave a solid, realistic view of politics within the Native community."[23] Also in attendance at this meeting was Viola Thomas (Tk'emlúps te Secwépemc), executive director of the Association for Native Development in the Performing and Visual Arts. Monica McKay also attended, and provided a list of groups and contacts, including "Assembly of First Nations," "Chiefs of Ontario," "Inuit Tapirisat of Canada," "National Association of Friendship Centres," and "Native Women's Association of Canada." Because interest was expressed regarding the "Lubicon Lake people," Solomon offered to send the task force information about the issues facing them.[24]

Self-Education

The work of the task force involved a commitment to a process of self-education. In a progress report, Kabayama described the inaugural process of working together as members of the task force: "Initially, we were appalled by the problem, the number of issues and our lack of knowledge. Moreover, coming together from our different backgrounds, experience and motivations it took a while to establish some sense of understanding and a sense of direction."[25] Disclosing their "lack of knowledge" and their "different backgrounds" to other members was a gesture of situating themselves in relation to each other and to the issues facing Indigenous peoples.

After their third meeting, there was general agreement among the members that "intimate co-operation with native peoples in identifying and fashioning of appropriate projects was crucial."[26] Kabayama stated that building "a common knowledge base" could be used "to forge action plans."[27] He acknowledged the knowledge Indigenous peoples provided to the task force: "Dialogue with native peoples has begun to educate us with the breadth and depth of their problems and some understanding of their frustrations, not dissimilar to our dealings with the government on Redress."[28] Indigenous peoples who attended the task force meetings, read its reports, and gave critical feedback and support were continuing a long and generous process whereby Indigenous peoples share their knowledge with settlers. The task force's goal of self-education could not have been achieved without the knowledge provided by Indigenous elders, teachers, writers, artists, organizers, scholars, speakers, and participants.

The self-education process included activities such as attending political, literary, artistic, and educational events, and demonstrations organized by Indigenous peoples. The task force members in Toronto invited Indigenous and non-Indigenous guests, and read reports and calls for action, viewed videos, and authored reports and calls for action. One example of self-education occurred when the task force discussed the report of the Aboriginal Rights Coalition (Project North) on August 18, 1989.[29] Kabayama prepared a six-page summary of the report for task force members. He stated that he was impressed with the coalition's thesis that "the quest for 'fiscal restraint' [by the federal government] has become – and will continue to be – the predominant factor shaping native policies in Canada," and the report's recommendation that "informing the middle class (read NAJC) that the business-oriented agenda of the Tory government ... must be opposed. Otherwise long-term sympathy/support for Native issues cannot be sustained."[30] While Kabayama's description of the NAJC in its entirety as middle class is homogenizing, it speaks to his awareness of class divisions and his willingness to challenge the business interests of the federal Conservative government.

At the September 1989 task force meeting in Toronto, Kabayama stated that he was preparing a report for the October NAJC National Council annual general meeting, whose "major requirement must be to challenge at least some members of NAJC to develop not only concern, but commitment to the cause." He added that, "compared to Redress, Native affairs is complex and enduring, and without a long-term commitment, NAJC will not be able to accomplish anything."[31]

Kabayama's report stated that the "core group of the Task Force has met monthly in Toronto, to define and study the issues."[32] It also emphasized that "although we may have honest differences of opinion about what the real figures are, or which priority should be supported, we must believe that there is no question that the Native People have been terribly discriminated against historically. Regrettably, this discrimination and injustice is continuing today."[33] Some of the figures to which the report referred were compiled in a document titled "Comparisons: Native Peoples (NP's) and Japanese Canadians (JC's)," which was accompanied by a vision statement in the minutes of the task force meeting of September 19, 1989.[34] Kabayama credited the findings he had summarized in the document to "some of the things we have learned in the past few months."[35] The comparisons document was included in Kabayama's report that was sent to the NAJC National Office in Winnipeg from the Greater Toronto Chapter on September 19.[36]

The identity construction in the comparisons document is clearly "Japanese Canadian," as well as the abbreviated "JC's" constructed in relation to "Native Peoples" or "NP's." While it is not known how Kabayama defined himself and others before the redress settlement, this appellation confirms Roy Miki's (1998, 111) contention that "Japanese Canadian" and "JC" were hegemonic identities post-redress, identities that were remade in this document and in relation to Indigenous peoples.

The comparisons document contrasts "Native Peoples" to "Japanese Canadians" in categories such as "population," "language," "education," "employment," "discrimination," "incarceration," "suicide rate," "assimilation." While these comparisons are reductive and some, like "suicide rate," arguably pathologize Indigenous peoples,[37] the document provides an interesting example of self-identification simultaneous to the social recognition of Indigenous peoples. While their use of the term "Native Peoples" erases specific national groupings, the pluralization that is consistent through the task force documents recognizes that they are peoples in the plural, and not a singular group. The use of the concept of peoplehood is also an important discursive and recognitive choice. As Jeff Corntassel (2003) indicates, the concept of peoplehood is useful in clarifying and asserting the legal, social, cultural, and historical position of Indigenous peoples in relation to the settler nation. The peoples, however, are also often described in the task force documents as "Native peoples *of Canada*," as in the October 8 meeting report described below, rather than being situated as nations unto themselves, despite Canadian occupation of their lands. Indeed, as will be shown, Canadian nationalism informed the task force's construction of both themselves and Indigenous peoples as Canadians.

Importantly, the document moves beyond a "commonality" approach that focuses on the so-called shared oppression of a racialized group (in this case, Japanese Canadians) with Indigenous peoples.[38] This discursive shift from emphasizing commonalities to acknowledging positions of social difference may also be deduced from the change from the initial name of the task force in January 1989 – NAJC Task Force on Mutual Native Indian/ Japanese Concerns – to NAJC Task Force on Native Peoples in April 1989. Rather than emphasizing the mutuality of their positions, the task force appeared to change its focus to the social position of Indigenous peoples as different from Japanese Canadians. It also dropped the problematic colonial term "Indian" and the unmodified term "Japanese," the latter highly contested by many survivors of the internment due to its use during the 1940s in constructing Japanese Canadians as foreign nationals who were the enemy. The members of the task force eventually decided on the name "Task Force on First Nations Peoples" in February 1990, explaining its decision to change "Native Peoples" to "First Nations Peoples" as "conform[ing] to official Province of Ontario usage."[39] Settler state government discourse and its recognitive category for some Indigenous peoples hence informed the naming of the NAJC group.[40]

Other examples of the task force's self-recognitive process are found in its description in each category. Under employment, Japanese Canadians are described as "many in white-collar, professional occupations: unemployment is about half of national average," compared with "Native Peoples," who are described as "many unskilled: high and chronic unemployment." Under discrimination, it is stated of Japanese Canadians that they "have suffered legal, social, economic discrimination, but this is disappearing," whereas "Native Peoples ... have suffered and continue to suffer legal, social and economic discrimination."[41]

The generalizations about the occupations of Japanese Canadians as white collar may have been informed by the middle-class position of some of the members of the task force; for example, Kabayama, its chair, had a PhD in chemistry and worked for the company Tetra Pak Incorporated. Furthermore, the analysis of Indigenous peoples as "unskilled" is class- and settler-bound, constructing skill in a modernist and colonial framework of progress. In addition, an interlocking analysis that includes an analysis of gender, not only in relation to Indigenous peoples but also in relation to Japanese Canadians, would have rendered their comparisons more complex. Nonetheless, what is also of note in this document are the attempts of Japanese Canadians to recognize their own social and economic positions, including class, based on conducting research on their own demographic and in relation to the social, economic, and demographic information on Indigenous peoples.[42] Importantly, it describes the "discrimination" faced historically by Indigenous peoples as "ongoing" and as "legal, social and economic," which implies its long duration and a critique of the social and economic structure of Canada, and the hierarchical arrangement of Japanese Canadians in relation to Indigenous peoples. This relational recognitive process, I would argue, resists what I have discussed elsewhere as the liberal notion of the autonomous self that constructs the self as separate from the histories that produce the self and other selves differently and relationally (Oikawa 2012, 218–23). After the forced separations of Japanese Canadians from families and communities during the internment and the dispersal, their effort to work together in the task force and to analyze their social and economic relationality to Indigenous peoples is notable.

Furthermore, it is significant that in the task force document there is little attention to cultural differences between Japanese Canadians and Indigenous peoples, in contrast to the liberal politics of recognition debated by Taylor. As Simpson (2014, 20) reminds us, "fixation on cultural difference and its purity occludes Indigenous sovereignty." Analyzing the social and economic conditions of Indigenous peoples compels us to ask questions about the causes of those conditions, something that a focus on cultural differences does not always enable.

Nonetheless, the process of comparison of racialized groups with Indigenous peoples is potentially effacing of the complexities of the production of both colonialism and racism. Such quantitative comparisons that construct all Japanese Canadians and Indigenous peoples as homogeneous entities mirrors the homogenizing processes of racialization and ethnicization, a feature found in processes of state politics of recognition like multiculturalism. Such comparisons may also inevitably enhance the position of persons who announce that they are privileged in relation to Indigenous and racialized peoples. As Beenash Jafri (March 21, 2012; Complicity vs. Privilege) states, "declarations of privilege can just as easily re-inscribe dominant subject positions, by centering the focus on the unlearning process of the dominant subject."

Although the task force members do not mention the word "privilege" (as in, "we are privileged") in this document, it is clear that Japanese Canadians were producing knowledge about themselves simultaneous to their knowledge of Indigenous peoples, and in a sense they became the subjects who know, and Indigenous subjects those who are known by them. As Jafri suggests, self-reflection can reassert the dominance of the knower even as we appear to demonstrate recognition of the other.[43]

The work of the task force was often compared to the work of the redress movement, as in the following statement authored by the task force after its fourth meeting in 1989: "There was a strong element that the skills and experience that NAJC had developed during its redress period should be the forces which this task force should be sharing with the native peoples."[44] While members of the NAJC did acquire skills and political contacts due to their negotiations with the federal government during redress, their self-construction as skilled ran the risk of constructing Indigenous peoples as less skillful, despite the latter's negotiations with settlers and resisting settler domination for centuries. Importantly, the state recognition of Japanese Canadians *did* position them as successfully "redressed" (Miki 1998, 323) subjects, a particular subject position from which they could impart knowledge of the Canadian state. In this way, they demonstrated how as subjects of recognition by the state, they then became agents who recognized Indigenous peoples. Through successfully achieving redress from the federal government, Japanese Canadians were positioned to extend "voluntary recognition" (Bannerji 2000, 143) in their decisions to share their knowledge with others who struggled for recognition by the state and/or by social justice organizations.

The October 1989 NAJC National Council Annual General Meeting

The NAJC National Council annual general meeting (AGM) in Calgary, which ran from October 7 to 9, 1989, was attended by delegates from member groups (or what the NAJC called Centres) across Canada, specifically, the Vancouver Island, Kamloops, Vernon, Thunder Bay, Toronto, Winnipeg,

Lethbridge, Vancouver, Kelowna, Calgary, Quebec, Ottawa, Hamilton, and Edmonton Centres.[45]

The task force's report, presented by Abe Kabayama, to the AGM indicated that there were approximately fifty people on the task force mailing list and that most of the task force members were in Toronto. They had met monthly and gathered information to present to the council. Summarizing their work to the delegates, Kabayama described the "discrimination and injustices" faced by Indigenous peoples in Canada: "We believe that these injustices constitute an open wound in our society which must be addressed and corrected." A footnote to this section in the written report added: "Redress for Japanese Canadians was a relatively simple issue in comparison to the deep and complex issues of deprivation, subjugation, land and treaty issues facing the Native Peoples of Canada."[46] The task force report ended with the statement: "If we do not have, or do not develop this conviction, we will not have the stamina to continue to work at the issues, and to help work out solutions, lasting solutions which will make us proud to be Canadians. This is the challenge that we throw out to you."[47]

Calling for immediate and sustained action, the task force members identified several goals for themselves. The goal of being proud to be Canadian reflects their self-identification as Canadians; their objective of enhancing themselves and others by becoming "proud Canadians" is linked to the goal of addressing and correcting the injustices facing Indigenous peoples. Discursively tied to nationalism and identification with the Canadian nation – where the identity of Canadian, without an ethnicized qualifier, is articulated – their self-identification was constructed here relationally to their social recognition of Indigenous peoples. While Japanese Canadians fought for inclusion in the Canadian citizenry before, during, and after the internment, this assertion of their citizenship demonstrated that it was also important to the members of the task force in 1989. As Eva Mackey (2005) argues, moments where Canadian citizenship is publicly asserted are not only reflective of Canadian nationalist discourses of the time but are moments of nation building where the notion of a singular unifying national identity and nation are reiterated and remade. Since Canadian citizenship is based on settler occupation of Indigenous territories and settler claims of sovereignty, such moments also reify the Canadian settler project.

The report concluded with two proposed motions.[48] The first motion read: "The National Association of Japanese Canadians (NAJC) hereby go on record that, in continuing efforts of the Native Peoples in Canada to obtain their aboriginal and/or treaty rights, NAJC recognizes the justice of their claims, and wholeheartedly support their efforts to achieve just and lasting solutions."[49] In the AGM minutes issued by the National Office, it was noted that after the motion was presented to the council, there were questions about the task force, its membership, and its officers. Kabayama reiterated that it was a task force (implying there were no officers) and he then invited council delegates to join the task force. After some discussion, the motion was amended by the council and the final motion read: "Moved that the NAJC support the continuing efforts of the Native Peoples in Canada to obtain just and lasting solutions in their social, economic and legal struggles."[50]

While the motion was an important step in the national organization's support for the task force, the deletion of the clause "in continuing efforts of the Native Peoples in Canada to obtain their aboriginal and/or treaty rights, NAJC recognizes the justice of their claims" arguably weakened the motion and the social recognition of Indigenous peoples. The original wording, "aboriginal and/or treaty rights," recognized that all Indigenous peoples were entitled to rights inherent to being Indigenous, even those not included in treaties with the settler nation, and asserted their very specific position of having collective and historical "rights" linked to their position as "aboriginal and/or [having] treaty rights." In contrast to the motion that was passed, the original motion's specificity also suggests the different historical formation of "social, economic and legal struggles" for Indigenous peoples and the fact that Canadians, including Japanese Canadians, are in treaty with Indigenous peoples or are living on land occupied without treaty. This original wording also implies a source of "aboriginal, and/or treaty rights," namely, the land and territories that were taken from them and their continued fight for them. The understanding of the connection between the "deprivation [and] subjugation" of Indigenous peoples and "land and treaty issues" was also articulated in the task force's written report, quoted above, to the council. Importantly, the original motion asked the NAJC National Council, representing all of its member centres, to support Indigenous and/or treaty rights

Kabayama later noted in a report to a meeting of the task force in Toronto, with eleven people in attendance,[51] that in discussing the motion, the wording "aboriginal and/or treaty rights" was changed to "human rights."[52] While the term "human rights" does not appear in the approved motion recorded in the AGM minutes, Kabayama's comment reflects the task force's commitment to ideas and language that conveyed their self-education and social recognitive process and its dissatisfaction, as I discuss below, with the change to its motion. The context for Kabayama's recollection may also be explained by what was noted in the summary of the discussion of the original task force motion in the AGM minutes: one centre was reported to have said that "it could support human rights issues," while another centre stated that "it seemed like a 'motherhood' statement."[53]

Nevertheless, the discussion offered the task force the opportunity to share its analysis and its method of self-education. When its first motion was discussed, the Toronto delegates proposed that "there could be a research group in each centre to study different problems,"[54] and underscored the need for "core groups across the country to respond to specific Native issues in their local areas."[55] They therefore proposed both a method (research) and methodology emphasizing the importance of place (Tuck and McKenzie 2015) and acknowledging each centre's and its members' relationship to Indigenous peoples in the regions in which they lived.

The second motion presented by the task force, which was eventually withdrawn, read:

> The National Association of Japanese Canadians (NAJC) hereby go on re-cord that, continuing efforts to publicize/educate Canadians to the human rights problems/plight of the Native Peoples, and to enrich our Canadian culture by enhanced exposure of Native art such as paintings, writings, songs, and dance of Native artists, NAJC will support/underwrite appro-priate activities.[56]

The motion articulated the major goals of the task force and appears to reflect a course for its future action that would include education and arts projects. It sought to convince the NAJC national organization to take on the role of publicizing the "plight" of Indigenous peoples in order to edu-cate Canadians. Commendably, the task force did not see its role as edu-cating Indigenous peoples but as educating non-Indigenous Canadians. As discussed above, however, such a role can still secure one's power as the Japanese Canadian "knower" in relation to the Indigenous subject who is known by the former.

In addition to entailing a recognitive process that might suggest an ethnographic or multicultural notion of cultural difference, such as "songs and dance" of "Native Peoples," the second motion articulates the task force's goal of enhancing "our Canadian culture." This is also a discursive moment of nationalist self-constitution as the task force members again emphasize that the NAJC National Council members are Canadians who possess a Canadian culture in relation to Indigenous Peoples and Indigenous cultures. Furthermore, as with the first motion, one of its goals – this time in funding Canadians' exposure to Indigenous cultural production – was to enhance "Canadian culture" and Canadians. Mackey (2005) has raised questions about the uses of Indigenous culture by non-Indigenous peoples. She asks how "narratives of nationhood appropriate Aboriginality and cultural difference to make *'native land'* into what settler Canadians, like myself, can think of as *'our home'*" (emphasis in original) (90). During the discussion of the motion, one centre questioned the task force's construction of Canadian culture and warned the council "to be sensitive to patronizing" and suggested that "it would be a very racist approach to put this into those terms." Indeed, by suggesting that the language was patronizing, this centre's criticism conveyed its analysis of the power relations between the NAJC members and Indigenous peoples. Additionally, these delegates mobilized their analysis of racism by describing the motion as racist. In its critical feedback, the centre was encouraging the task force to critically analyze its own motion. Hence, the National Council meetings also provided opportunities to develop critical analyses. While the delegates of the centre importantly pointed out the unequal power dynamics conveyed by the motion, they added that the "first Canadian culture is native culture," thereby using a Canadian nationalist framework to describe the culture of Indigenous peoples. This settler framework also erased the fact that Indigenous cultures predated the existence of Canada. Another centre, which had wanted human rights to be emphasized in the first motion, recommended in its discussion of the second motion that "human rights be showcased and this be confined to human rights."[57]

In discussing the response of some members of the National Council and their rejection of this motion at a meeting of the task force on October 24, Toronto delegates reported that there was a "great deal of questioning of why performing arts should be mixed up with human rights concerns. The tone of the questioning led the Toronto delegation to withdraw the motion."[58] The discussion suggested that there was no consensus among council members regarding what support for human rights involved, and despite global examples of the contestatory possibilities of the arts in anti-oppression movements and the NAJC's own use of "performing arts," such as taiko, butoh, and others during the redress movement (Miki and Kobayashi 1991, 109, 118–19), there was some resistance to the task force's motion.

The task force itself used the term "human rights" in its second motion, terminology that it had avoided using in its first motion. By adding "plight," however, it was perhaps signalling again that the term "human rights" did not entirely address Indigenous rights, or their relationships as non-Indigenous people to them.

As the task force developed language to communicate its work and lobby for support, it was situated within a settler nation where Indigenous peoples were asserting their rights as different from and even threatened by the use of the term "human rights." The task force's wording may indeed have reflected and attempted to implement its understanding of Indigenous peoples' struggles to assert their own self-recognitive processes at that time. For instance, Peter Kulchyski (2013, 22) describes the example of the attempt of Pierre Trudeau's Liberal government in 1969 to implement its white paper, "which would have done away with all the aboriginal and eventually treaty rights" of Indigenous peoples. Kulchyski demonstrates that the federal government argued that such a policy would make Indigenous peoples "equal" to Canadians, and states that "a human right to equality became the battering ram that threatened to destroy any aboriginal rights" (22). This federal government effort, defeated by Indigenous peoples organizing across the country, informed Indigenous peoples' 1980s fight for language in the Canadian constitution that enshrined Indigenous rights. Indigenous peoples fought to ensure that the language "existing aboriginal and treaty rights are hereby recognized and affirmed" was written into the constitution, and they also fought to ensure that the Canadian Charter of Rights and Freedoms could not be used to "'abrogate or derogate' ... aboriginal rights." Kulchyski concludes that the Charter "makes it clear that aboriginal rights have equal legal force with human rights, that human rights will not be used to override aboriginal rights" (22).

Indeed, the term "human rights" and the international legal apparatus that has structured its meaning have been and are utilized by marginalized people, including Indigenous peoples. However, some Indigenous and other scholars and activists question and challenge the use of the term and its politics of recognition framework. For example, Eve Tuck (Unangax̂) and K. Wayne Yang (2012, 2) argue that assertion of the specific position of Indigenous peoples and their goal of decolonization "is a distinct project from other civil and human right-based social justice projects, [and] is far too often subsumed into the directives of these projects, with no regard for how decolonization wants something different than those forms of justice." In their critique of some meetings bringing together scholars concerned with social justice, Tuck and Yang (2012, 3) remark that "there is often little recognition given to the immediate context of settler colonialism on the

North American lands where many of these conferences take place" and "struggles for the recognition of [Indigenous] ... sovereignty" are ignored. Peter Kulchyski (2013, 20–21) clarifies that "aboriginal rights ... are rights that only certain people and peoples, indigenous peoples, have by virtue of being indigenous ... we [non-Indigenous peoples] do not have aboriginal rights, nor should we. Aboriginal rights stem from the struggles of indigenous peoples." He contrasts this to the notion of "human rights," "abstract rights that reflect a notion of how all people are 'the same.'" Moreover, Dian Million (2014) (Tanana Athabascan) reminds us that the mobilization of notions of human rights through institutional, political, and "extra-state" spaces "wherein Indigenous peoples seek protections can never be perceived as any neutral, objective, or safer legal space" (9), and "these are spaces where there are multiple agendas performed, none of them totally neutral and never merely allied with the 'powerless'" (12). Furthermore, as Robyn Linde and Mikaila Mariel Lemonik Arthur (2015, 33) argue, the Western-informed and -controlled "human rights regime" can "reproduce relations of colonialism" where the West and its financial and legal institutions are dominant.

Using the term "human rights" to conflate all Indigenous peoples into an amorphous contingent that includes all marginalized peoples can serve to erase the historical and legal relationship of non-Indigenous peoples, including Japanese Canadians, to Indigenous peoples and our different locations on Indigenous territories. This can therefore enable differently socially positioned Japanese Canadians to avoid examining how our own differently accrued privileges are connected to settler colonialism.

The task force published a report on its work in the *Nikkei Voice* in June 1989; the Greater Toronto Chapter delegates were therefore surprised to learn at the October AGM that it was the "first time that many (most ?) members of Council had heard of the NAJC Task Force on Native Peoples, let alone what we were trying to do." The task force further summarized these reactions from the National Council when it met to evaluate its own actions: "only a report was expected, proposed motions were unexpected ... East-West divisions present; money should not have been mentioned; specific projects should have [been] proposed."[59]

The NAJC AGM discussions speak to the heterogeneity of views and analyses of the membership of the 1989 NAJC National Council, and more broadly demonstrates heterogeneity within so-called unitarily similar racialized people. The responses to its motions led the task force to attribute them, in part, to the geographical divisions among the delegates. Elsewhere I have written about the geographical and social divisions inculcated through the processes of the internment and the federal government's dispersal of Japanese Canadians across Canada (Oikawa 1986, 2012). These divisions were not necessarily alleviated or repaired by redress.

Despite disagreement voiced at the AGM by some delegates, one of the centres commended the work of the task force and two other centres "expressed appreciation of the work done by the Task Force to date."[60] The task force was invited by the National Council to submit a proposal for a project for consideration that would be partially funded from the sale of greeting cards, designed by artists who had donated their artwork in support of redress during the redress campaign.[61] Hence, despite their differences in views, the National Council was receptive to a funding proposal from the task force.

Criticism of the reception of the task force report and its motions by some of the delegates at the AGM, however, was later articulated by Kabayama in a letter to then NAJC president Arthur K. Miki. In his letter, Kabayama expressed his "disappointment at the events of the NAJC AGM."[62] He informed Miki that he considered resigning from the position of chair of the task force. As he articulates in the letter, however, he decided to continue to chair the task force after receiving "unsolicited letters from Winnipeg and Halifax, appreciative of the work of the Task Force and strengthened by the efforts we were making."[63] He added: "The network that we have built up over the past year (the membership has grown from the initial 25 to 49) is concerned and supportive."[64] Nonetheless, the task force decided in August 1990 to become an independent committee, associated with the Greater Toronto Chapter of the NAJC, because "proposals to undertake actions could be presented and discussed in person, and decisions arrived at quickly."[65]

Conclusion

My objective in this chapter is to begin an analysis of the role redress played in informing Japanese Canadians' recognition of their relationship to Indigenous peoples. Moreover, I seek to analyze how Japanese Canadians represented themselves in relation to Indigenous peoples in documents authored by the Greater Toronto Chapter's Task Force on First Nations Peoples during its preliminary efforts in 1989 to recognize the injustices experienced by Indigenous peoples. It is important to acknowledge that the archival documents used in this chapter are taken out of a larger context and that the work of the task force and the NAJC cannot be assessed by these documents alone. Nevertheless, the documents provide insight into how a group prepared to work with Indigenous peoples, and into the process of working in a local organization within a national organizational structure. Securing funding through the national organization, funding established through the redress settlement, entailed convincing other members of the importance of its work. Hence the task force members depended on the social recognition of other NAJC members, and in being recognized, benefited from access to the financial resources acquired through the federal government's 1988 recognition of Japanese Canadians.

Reading the task force and NAJC documents over thirty years after they were written, I acknowledge that I did not participate in the conceptualization of their initiatives or the work undertaken in their meetings. My aim is not to criticize their words or actions, but to begin to document this little-known aspect of NAJC local and national organizing and to analyze how a web of recognition produces our selves in relation to the settler state and the Indigenous peoples whose territories Japanese Canadians live on. I hope that the work of the NAJC and, specifically, the task force, as well as my own work may inform current efforts to analyze the relationships between Indigenous peoples and racialized peoples living under conditions established by a white settler system of governance and property ownership.

I acknowledge that I too am implicated in the web of recognition, attempting to recognize the work of the task force as a distant witness to its work while I identify as a Sansei (third-generation Japanese Canadian) who participated in the redress movement and continues to benefit from the Canadian state's recognition of the injustices done to Japanese Canadians. Moreover, while I attempt to trace the discursive moves to establish alliances with Indigenous peoples and I attempt to recognize Indigenous peoples, I am also complicit in Canadian settler colonialism by living on Indigenous peoples' territories and acquiring class privileges that are based, in part, on a Canadian capitalist economy that extracts resources from Indigenous territories (see, for example, Chapter 3, as well as Alook, Hussey, and Hill 2021; Carroll 2021; Altamirano-Jiménez 2020), among other complicities.

At the time of the 1989 AGM, the NAJC was in the process of reinventing itself and its objectives after securing the redress agreement. The initiative of the Task Force on First Nations Peoples was part of the recognitive process of NAJC members who were reimagining themselves and each other. The task force's immediate goal was self-education. Its larger goal is expressed in this statement: "Education, however, is not enough. Backed with the facts we must then proceed to devise policies, launch programmes and harness resources that will lead to the adoption of measures that will herald a new era for the Native Peoples of Canada."[66] Beyond the hyperbole of the language used in some of the task force documents, there is a sense of Japanese Canadians assuming a position of power where they participate in heralding "a new era" for Indigenous peoples. Their reiteration of their selves and Indigenous peoples as Canadian involved a nationalist-informed vision of their identities and aspirations. While critiquing the Canadian state for its history and present of subjugating Indigenous peoples, work that was commendable, the task force's construction of the future for Indigenous peoples appeared to be informed, in part, by state recognition of Japanese Canadians' histories of internment through redress and its recognition of them as Canadians, an identity for which many had fought and which they wanted to proudly hold by changing conditions for Indigenous peoples. In 1989, their recognition of Indigenous peoples was therefore shaped by their own goal of inclusion in the nation and was demonstrated by their arguments for the inclusion of Indigenous peoples within the national fold, rather than advocacy for their sovereignty and their autonomy from the settler nation.

The work of the Task Force has inspired me to ask the following questions, which I will continue to consider as I develop my research: Who do we choose to recognize, and why? Whose recognition matters most to us, and why? What are the implications of being included in the settler nation? While some Japanese Canadians may be rewarded through qualified inclusion – especially if they are able to acquire property, money, and gender and class privilege – how do these inclusions support the settler state and ongoing dispossession of Indigenous peoples? In the case of the federal government's 1969 white paper, as described above, purported "inclusion" in Canada was destined to complete the dispossession of Indigenous peoples. How did and does the state's recognition of Japanese Canadians as "redressed" subjects inform our processes of recognizing Indigenous peoples, and are we able to think and work outside of a state politics of recognition in devising strategies to contest settler claims of entitlement to Indigenous land and resources and the ongoing violence waged against Indigenous peoples that serve to secure settlers' power?

While this chapter does not focus on how redress itself shaped the subject constitution of Japanese Canadians[67] – and it calls for more research to be done in this area – it analyzes how some members of the task force, in particular, constructed themselves in relation to redress and the Indigenous peoples with whom they sought to work. Further examination of the work of the Greater Toronto Chapter's task force and the NAJC may illuminate these processes.

Notes

Acknowledgments: The author would like to thank the Social Sciences and Humanities Research Council and York University for funding in support of the research used in this chapter.

1 The goals of the Task Force and some of the people involved in organizing it are described in the section "Inauguration of the Task Force on First Nations Peoples."
2 *Indian Act*, RSC, 1985, c I-5. For an analysis of the Indian Act and its regulation of Indigenous peoples, see Lawrence (2004).
3 Simpson (2014, 112) elaborates on the concept of refusal, "there is a political alternative to "recognition' ... This alternative is 'refusal' ... Refusal comes with the requirement of having one's political sovereignty acknowledged and upheld, and raises the question of legitimacy for those who are usually in the position of recognizing."
4 I was a member of the Greater Toronto Chapter in 1989, but was not involved in the Task Force on First Nations Peoples.
5 I would like to thank the past president of the NAJC national organization, Arthur K. Miki, for permission to view his personal papers; Lucy Yamashita for her assistance in accessing the papers of the NAJC National Office in Winnipeg; the Japanese Cultural Association of Manitoba (JCAM) for allowing me to conduct my research in the JCAM Centre; David Fujino and Ken Noma, past presidents of the Greater Toronto Chapter of the NAJC, for permission to view the chapter records and for allowing me to conduct research in the chapter office, and Joy Kogawa for her fonds at UBC Library Rare Books and Special Collections.
6 According to Coulthard (2014, 108), "the state's approach to reconciliation ... began to explicitly inform government policy following the release of the Report of the Royal Commission on Aboriginal Peoples (RCAP) in 1996."
7 See references in the first paragraph of this chapter for some examples.
8 The support for redress of non-Indigenous ethnicized and racialized individuals and groups requires further research and analysis that are beyond the scope of this chapter.
9 Resumé of Progress to Date, April 11, 1989, UBC Library Rare Books and Special Collections (hereafter UBC Library RBSC), Joy Kogawa fonds, Box 63, folder 63–4, NAJC Task Force on First Nations Peoples.
10 M.A. Kabayama, no date (1991?). UBC Library RBSC, Joy Kogawa fonds, folder 96–9, Earth Spirit Festival 1989–1991 (7 of 7).
11 The task force had several names over the course of its existence, including: NAJC Task Force on Mutual Native Indian/Japanese Concerns (February 1989), NAJC Task Force on Native Peoples (April 1989); NAJC Task Force on Native Concerns (1989),

NAJC Task Force on First Nations Peoples (February 1990). For the purposes of this chapter, I use the last iteration of the task force's name.

12 Letter from Abe Kabayama to Art Miki, October 11, 1989, Greater Toronto Chapter of the NAJC (hereafter Toronto NAJC), File NAJC Task Force–Native Peoples Minutes.

13 Roger Obata served on the NAJC Strategy Committee during the negotiations for redress with the federal government.

14 Letter from Joy Kogawa to Tom and David, November 29, 1989, UBC Library RBSC, Joy Kogawa fonds, Box 63, folder 63–4, NAJC Task Force on First Nations Peoples.

15 Summary Report: NAJC Task Force on Mutual Native/Japanese Concerns, January 28, 1989, UBC Library RBSC, Joy Kogawa fonds, Box 63, folder 63–4, NAJC Task Force on First Nations Peoples.

16 Ibid.

17 Letter from Michiomi A. (Abe) Kabayama to Art Miki, November 1, 1989, UBC Library RBSC, Joy Kogawa fonds, Box 63, folder 63–4, NAJC Task Force on First Nations Peoples. Kabayama reported that he was approached by Kogawa in 1988 to chair the task force. (See Letter from M.A. Kabayama to Art Miki, October 11, 1989, Toronto NAJC, File NAJC Task Force–Native Peoples Minutes, 1.)

18 Letter from Joy Kogawa to Tom and David, November 29, 1989, UBC Library RBSC, Joy Kogawa fonds, Box 63, folder 63–4, NAJC Task Force on First Nations Peoples.

19 "The National Council is the governing body of the NAJC." It is made up of "member organizations and supporting member organizations" (National Association of Japanese Canadians). For a history of the establishment of the NAJC and its regional chapters, see Miki (2004).

20 Letter from M.A. Kabayama to NAJC Toronto Chapter, August 20, 1990, Toronto NAJC, file NAJC Task Force–Native Peoples Minutes, 1.

21 Resumé of Progress to Date, April 11, 1989, UBC Library RBSC, Joy Kogawa fonds, Box 63, folder 63–4, NAJC Task Force on First Nations Peoples. [Note: Task force reports were written by Kabayama and other members. Their reports of comments made by other people may not be verbatim.]

22 Summary Report of Second Meeting, February 19, 1989, UBC Library RBSC, Joy Kogawa fonds, Box 63, folder 63–4, NAJC Task Force on First Nations Peoples.

23 Report of Meeting, April 26, 1989, UBC Library RBSC, Joy Kogawa fonds, Box 63, folder 63–4, NAJC Task Force on First Nations Peoples.

24 Ibid.

25 Progress Report from M.A. Kabayama (Chair of NAJC Task Force on Native Peoples) to NAJC National Council, May 16, 1989, National Association of Japanese Canadians National Office (hereafter NAJC National), Box 11, "Implementation 1990–1992," file NAJC Task Force on Native Peoples.

26 Summary Report of Third Meeting, March 6, 1989, UBC Library RBSC, Joy Kogawa fonds, Box 63, folder 63–4, NAJC Task Force on First Nations Peoples.

27 NAJC Task Force on Native Peoples Report of Meeting, August 18, 1989, UBC Library RBSC, Joy Kogawa fonds, Box 63, folder 63–4, NAJC Task Force on First Nations Peoples.

28 Progress Report from M.A. Kabayama (Chair NAJC Task Force on Native Peoples) to NAJC Council, May 16, 1989, NAJC National, Box 11, "Implementation 1990–1992," file NAJC Task Force on Native Peoples.

29 The Aboriginal Rights Coalition (Project North) was a coalition of Canadian churches and included representatives from "the Roman Catholic, Anglican, United, Presbyterian, Evangelical Lutheran, Mennonite, and Christian Reformed churches, along with the Religious Society of Friends (Quakers), the Oblates of Mary Immaculate and the Society of Jesus (Jesuits)" (Aboriginal Rights Coalition 1993, 2).

30 NAJC Task Force on Native Peoples Report of Meeting, August 18, 1989, UBC Library RBSC, Joy Kogawa fonds, Box 63, folder 63–4, NAJC Task Force on First Nations Peoples.

31 NAJC Task Force on Native Peoples Report of Meeting, September 19, 1989, UBC Library RBSC, Joy Kogawa fonds, Box 63, folder 63–4, NAJC Task Force on First Nations Peoples.

32 NAJC Task Force on Native Peoples Report to the AGM, October 8, 1989, NAJC National, Box 11, "Implementation 1990–1992," File NAJC Task Force on Native Peoples, 1. Note omitted.

33 Ibid.

34 NAJC Task Force on Native Peoples Report of Meeting, September 19, 1989, UBC Library RBSC, Joy Kogawa fonds, Box 63, folder 63–4, NAJC Task Force on First Nations Peoples, 3.

35 NAJC Task Force on Native Peoples Report of Meeting, September 19, 1989, UBC Library RBSC, Joy Kogawa fonds, Box 63, folder 63–4, NAJC Task Force on First Nations Peoples.

36 "Comparisons: Native Peoples (NP's) and Japanese Canadians (JC's)," enclosed with Summary Report of Meeting, September 19, 1989, NAJC National, Box 11, "Implementation 1990–1992," File NAJC Task Force on Native Peoples.

37 See Simpson's (2014, 178) analysis of how "knowledge can be complicit with the imperatives of settler colonialism by giving us a particular sense of Indigenous people: if not 'vanishing,' then certainly pathological, illiberal, or acting in a racist way."

38 See Bonita Lawrence and Enakshi Dua's (2005) critique of some anti-racist analyses.

39 NAJC Task Force on First Nations Peoples Report of Meeting, February 14, 1990, UBC Library RBSC, Joy Kogawa fonds, Box 63, folder 63–4, NAJC Task Force on First Nations Peoples.

40 According to the Crown–Indigenous Relations and Northern Affairs Canada (2024) website, the term "First Nations" does not include Inuit or Métis peoples.

41 "Comparisons: Native Peoples (NP's) and Japanese Canadians (JC's)," enclosed with Summary Report of Meeting, September 19, 1989, NAJC National, Box 11, "Implementation 1990–1992," File NAJC Task Force on Native Peoples.

42 According to the Aboriginal Justice Implementation Commission, whose report was issued shortly after the task force drafted its comparisons report, "the Indian unemployment rate is four times the non-Indian rate. According to the 1986 census, the labour force participation rate for Indians on reserves (those employed or included in unemployment statistics) averaged 53%, compared to 66.6% for non-Indian persons" (Aboriginal Justice Implementation Commission 1989).

43 See also Paulette Regan's (2010, 45) analysis that settlers' "seemingly benign ways of 'knowing the Other' ... are highly problematic in their own right."

44 Summary Report of Third Meeting, 6 March 1989, UBC Library RBSC, Joy Kogawa fonds, Box 63, folder 63–4, NAJC Task Force on First Nations Peoples.

45 Annual General Meeting Minutes, October 7–9, 1989, Calgary, NAJC National, Box 2, Redress Box: 1984–1988, Art Miki, President of the NAJC, Binder of Council Meetings: October 8 and 9, 1989, Calgary; April 13 and 15, 1990, Hamilton. Arthur K. Miki was then president of the NAJC National Council, a position he held until 1992.

46 NAJC Task Force on Native Peoples Report, October 8, 1989, UBC Library RBSC, Joy Kogawa fonds, Box 63, folder 63–4, NAJC Task Force on First Nations Peoples.

47 Ibid.

48 A third motion was written in their report but was not presented to the council.

49 NAJC Task Force on Native Peoples Report, October 8, 1989, UBC Library RBSC, Joy Kogawa fonds, Box 63, Folder 63–4, NAJC Task Force on First Nations Peoples.

50 Annual General Meeting Minutes, October 7–9, 1989, Calgary, NAJC National, Box 2, Redress Box: 1984–1988, Art Miki, President of the NAJC, Binder of Council Meetings: October 8 and 9, 1989, Calgary; April 13 and 15, 1990, Hamilton.

51 Some of the people in attendance were Joy Kogawa, Shirley Yamada, Roger Obata, and Shin Imai.

52 NAJC Task Force on Native Peoples Report of Meeting, October 24, 1989, UBC Library RBSC, Joy Kogawa fonds, Box 63, folder 63–4, NAJC Task Force on First Nations Peoples.

53 Annual General Meeting Minutes, October 7–9, 1989, Calgary, NAJC National, Box 2, Redress Box: 1984–1988, Art Miki, President of the NAJC, Binder of Council Meetings: October 8 and 9, 1989, Calgary; April 13 and 15, 1990, Hamilton. I have chosen not to identify specific delegates or centres.

54 Annual General Meeting Minutes, October 7–9, 1989, Calgary, NAJC National, Box 2, Redress Box: 1984–1988, Art Miki, President of the NAJC, Binder of Council Meetings: October 8 and 9, 1989, Calgary; April 13 and 15, 1990, Hamilton. More research and documentation of other centres' work with Indigenous peoples, in support of the latters' struggles, during and/or after redress is needed.

55 Letter from Michiomi A. (Abe) Kabayama to Art Miki, November 1, 1989, UBC Library RBSC, Joy Kogawa fonds, Box 63, folder 63–4, NAJC Task Force on First Nations Peoples.

56 NAJC Task Force on Native Peoples Report, October 8, 1989, UBC Library RBSC, Joy Kogawa fonds, Box 63, folder 63–4, NAJC Task Force on First Nations Peoples, 3.

57 Annual General Meeting Minutes, October 7–9, 1989, Calgary, NAJC National, Box 2, Redress Box: 1984–1988, Art Miki, President of the NAJC, Binder of Council Meetings: October 8 and 9, 1989, Calgary; April 13 and 15, 1990, Hamilton.

58 NAJC Task Force on Native Peoples Report of Meeting, October 24, 1989, UBC Library RBSC, Joy Kogawa fonds, Box 63, folder 63–4, NAJC Task Force on First Nations Peoples.

59 Ibid.

60 Annual General Meeting Minutes, October 7–9, 1989, Calgary, NAJC National, Box 2, Redress Box: 1984–1988, Art Miki, President of the NAJC, Binder of Council Meetings: October 8 and 9, 1989, Calgary; April 13 and 15, 1990, Hamilton.

61 Ibid. Interestingly, this is an example of how art is an activist tool and can be used in organizing for social justice.

62 Letter from Michiomi A. (Abe) Kabayama to Art Miki, November 1, 1989, UBC Library RBSC, Joy Kogawa fonds, Box 63, folder 63–4, NAJC Task Force on First Nations Peoples.

63 Ibid.

64 Ibid.

65 NAJC Toronto Chapter Task Force on First Nations Peoples Report of Meeting, August 17, 1990, Arthur K. Miki Private Collection, Art Miki Papers, Box 3, NAJC Redress Files, loose papers, file NAJC Task Force on First Nations Peoples.

66 NAJC Task Force on Native Peoples Report, October 8, 1989, UBC Library RBSC, Joy Kogawa fonds, Box 63, folder 63–4, NAJC Task Force on First Nations Peoples.

67 See Roy Miki's (2004, 253) analysis of "redress identity."

References

Archival Sources

Arthur K. Miki Private Collection, Winnipeg

Greater Toronto Chapter of the National Association of Japanese Canadians, Toronto

National Association of Japanese Canadians National Office, Winnipeg

University of British Columbia Library Rare Books and Special Collections, Vancouver

Books and Articles

Aboriginal Justice Implementation Commission. 1989. "Chapter Four: Aboriginal Over-Representation." In *Report of the Aboriginal Justice Inquiry of Manitoba*, n.p. Winnipeg: Aboriginal Justice Inquiry of Manitoba. http://www.ajic.mb.ca/volumel/chapter4.html#6.

Aboriginal Rights Coalition (Project North). 1993. *Submission to the Royal Commission on Aboriginal Peoples*. Ottawa: Aboriginal Rights Coalition.

Alook, Angele, Ian Hussey, and Nicole Hill. 2021. "Indigenous Gendered Experiences of Work in an Oil-Dependent Rural Alberta Community." In *Regime of Obstruction: How Corporate Power Blocks Energy Democracy*, edited by William K. Carroll, 331–53. Athabasca, AB: Athabasca University Press.

Altamirano-Jiménez, Isabel. 2020. "Free Mining, Body Land, and the Reproduction of Indigenous Life." In *Turbulent Times, Transformational Possibilities? Gender and Politics Today and Tomorrow*, edited by Fiona MacDonald and Alexandra Z. Dobrowolsky, 159–76. Toronto: University of Toronto Press.

Bannerji, Himani. 2000. *The Dark Side of the Nation: Essays on Multiculturalism, Nationalism and Gender*. Toronto: Canadian Scholars.

Bischoping, Katherine, and Amber Gazso. 2016. "Foucauldian Discourse Analysis." In *Analyzing Talk in the Social Sciences: Narrative, Conversation and Discourse Strategies*. London: Sage.

Byrd, Jodi A. 2011. *The Transit of Empire: Indigenous Critiques of Colonialism.* Minneapolis: University of Minnesota Press.

Carroll, William K., ed. 2021. *Regime of Obstruction: How Corporate Power Blocks Energy Democracy.* Athabasca, AB: Athabasca University Press.

Corntassel, Jeff J. 2003. "Who Is Indigenous? Peoplehood and Ethnonationalist Approaches to Rearticulating Indigenous Identities." *Nationalism and Ethnic Politics* 9 (1): 75–100.

Coulthard, Glen S. 2007. "Subjects of Empire: Indigenous Peoples and the 'Politics of Recognition' in Canada." *Contemporary Political Theory* 6 (4): 437–60.

– 2014. *Red Skin, White Masks: Rejecting the Colonial Politics of Recognition.* Minneapolis: University of Minnesota Press.

Crenshaw, Kimberlé. 1991. "Mapping the Margins: Intersectionality, Identity Politics, and Violence against Women of Color." *Stanford Law Review* 43 (6): 1241–99.

Crown–Indigenous Relations and Northern Affairs Canada. 2024. "Indigenous Peoples and Communities." https://www.rcaanc-cirnac.gc.ca/eng/1100100013785/1529102490303.

Day, Iyko. 2016. *Alien Capital: Asian Racialization and the Logic of Settler Colonial Capitalism.* Durham, NC: Duke University Press.

Dhamoon, Rita. 2005. "A Feminist Approach to Decolonizing Anti-Racism: Rethinking Transnationalism, Intersectionality, and Settler Colonialism." *Feral Feminisms* 4: 20–37.

Fanon, Frantz. (1952) 2008. *Black Skin, White Masks.* Translated by Richard Philcox. New York: Grove Press.

Foucault, Michel. 1990. *The History of Sexuality,* vol. 1. Translated by Robert Hurley. New York: Vintage Books.

Fujikane, Candace, and Jonathan Y. Okamura. 2008. *Asian Settler Colonialism: From Local Governance to the Habits of Everyday Life in Hawai'i.* Honolulu: University of Hawai'i Press.

Gutmann, Amy. 1994. "Introduction." In *Multiculturalism: Examining the Politics of Recognition,* edited by Amy Gutmann, 3–24. Princeton, NJ: Princeton University Press.

Hill Collins, Patricia. 2014. *Black Feminist Thought: Knowledge, Consciousness, and the Politics of Empowerment.* 2nd ed. London: Routledge.

Jafri, Beenash. 2012. "Privilege vs. Complicity: People of Colour and Settler Colonialism." *Equity Matters* (blog), Federation for the Humanities and Social Sciences. https://www.federationhss.ca/en/blog/privilege-vs-complicity-people-colour-and-settler-colonialism.

– 2020. "Refusal/Film: Diasporic-Indigenous Relationalities." *Settler Colonial Studies* 10 (1): 110–25.

King, Tiffany Lethabo. 2017. "Humans Involved: Lurking in the Lines of Posthumanist Flight." *Critical Ethnic Studies* 3 (1): 162–85.

– 2019. *The Black Shoals: Offshore Formations of Black and Native Studies.* Durham, NC: Duke University Press.

King, Tiffany Lethabo, Jenell Navarro, and Andrea Smith, eds. 2020. *Otherwise Worlds: Against Settler Colonialism and Anti-Blackness.* Durham, NC: Duke University Press.

Kulchyski, Peter. 2013. *Aboriginal Rights Are Not Human Rights*. Winnipeg: ARP Books.

Lawrence, Bonita. 2004. *"Real" Indians and Others: Mixed-Blood Urban Native Peoples and Indigenous Nationhood*. Vancouver: UBC Press.

– 2012. *Fractured Homeland: Federal Recognition and Algonquin Identity in Ontario*. Vancouver: UBC Press.

Lawrence, Bonita, and Enakshi Dua. 2005. "Decolonizing Antiracism." *Social Justice* 32: 120–43.

Linde, Robyn, and Mikaila Mariel Lemonik Arthur. 2015. "Teaching Progress: A Critique of the Grand Narrative of Human Rights as Pedagogy for Marginalized Students." *Radical Teacher* 103 (Fall): 26–37.

Mackey, Eva. 2005. *The House of Difference: Cultural Politics and National Identity in Canada*. Toronto: University of Toronto Press.

Markell, Patchen. 2003. *Bound by Recognition*. Princeton, NJ: Princeton University Press.

Matsunaga, Jennifer. 2021. "Carefully Considered Words: The Influence of Government on Truth Telling about Japanese Canadian Internment and Indian Residential Schools." *Canadian Ethnic Studies* 53 (2): 91–113.

McAllister, Kirsten Emiko. 1999. "Narrating Japanese Canadians In and Out of the Canadian Nation: A Critique of Realist Forms of Representation." *Canadian Journal of Communication* 24 (1): 79–103.

McLaughlin, Janice, Peter Phillimore, and Diane Richardson. 2011. "Introduction: Why Contesting Recognition?" In *Contesting Recognition: Culture, Identity and Citizenship*, edited by Janice McLaughlin, Peter Phillimore, and Diane Richardson, 1–19. Houndmills, Basingstoke, UK: Palgrave Macmillan.

Miki, Roy. 1998. *Broken Entries: Race, Subjectivity, Writing*. Toronto: Mercury Press.

– 2004. *Redress: Inside the Japanese Canadian Call for Justice*. Vancouver: Raincoast Books.

Miki, Roy, and Cassandra Kobayashi. 1991. *Justice in Our Time: The Japanese Canadian Redress Settlement*. Vancouver/Winnipeg: Talonbooks/National Association of Japanese Canadians.

Million, Dian. 2014. *Therapeutic Nations: Healing in an Age of Indigenous Human Rights*. Tucson: University of Arizona Press.

National Association of Japanese Canadians. 2019. "National Council." Accessed 7 September 2019. http://najc.ca/wp/national-council/.

Oikawa, Mona. 1986. "'Driven to Scatter Far and Wide': The Forced Resettlement of Japanese Canadians to Southern Ontario, 1944–1949." MA thesis, University of Toronto.

– 2006. "Connecting the Internment of Japanese Canadians to the Colonization of Aboriginal Peoples." In *Aboriginal Connections to Race, Environment and Traditions*, edited by Jill Oakes and Rick Riewe, 17–25. Winnipeg: Aboriginal Issues Press, University of Manitoba.

– 2012. *Cartographies of Violence: Japanese Canadian Women, Memory and the Subjects of the Internment*. Toronto: University of Toronto Press.

Razack, Sherene H. 1998. *Looking White People in the Eye: Gender, Race, and Culture in Courtrooms and Classrooms*. Toronto: University of Toronto Press.

– 1999. "Making Canada White: Law and the Policing of Bodies of Colour in the 1990s." *Canadian Journal of Law and Society* 14 (1): 159–84.

Regan, Paulette. 2010. *Unsettling the Settler Within: Indian Residential Schools, Truth Telling and Reconciliation in Canada*. Vancouver: UBC Press.

Seymour, Michael. 2010 "Introduction." In *The Plural States of Recognition*, edited by M. Seymour, 1–19. Houndmills, Basingstoke, UK: Palgrave Macmillan.

Simpson, Audra. 2014. *Mohawk Interruptus: Political Life across the Borders of Settler States*. Durham, NC: Duke University Press.

Sunahara, Ann Gomer. 1981. *The Politics of Racism: The Uprooting of Japanese Canadians during the Second World War*. Toronto: James Lorimer.

Tarver, Erin C. 2011. "New Forms of Subjectivity: Theorizing the Relational Self with Foucault and Alcoff." *Hypatia* 26 (4): 804–25.

Taylor, Charles. 1994. "The Politics of Recognition." In *Multiculturalism: Examining the Politics of Recognition*, edited by Amy Gutmann, 25–74. Princeton, NJ: Princeton University Press.

Tuck, Eve, and Marcia McKenzie. 2015. "Relational Validity and the 'Where' of Inquiry: Place and Land in Qualitative Research." *Qualitative Inquiry* 21 (7): 1–6.

Tuck, Eve, and K. Wayne Yang. 2012. "Decolonization is not a metaphor." *Decolonization: Indigeneity, Education & Society* 1 (1): 1–40.

Tully, James. 2008. *Public Philosophy in a New Key*. Vol. 1, *Democracy and Civic Freedom*. Cambridge: Cambridge University Press.

Williams, Melissa S. 2014. "On the Use and Abuse of Recognition in Politics." In *Recognition versus Self-Determination: Dilemmas of Emancipatory Politics*, edited by Avigail Eisenberg, Jeremy Webber, Glen Coulthard, and Andrée Boisselle, 3–18. Vancouver: UBC Press.

Yakashiro, Nicole. 2021. "'Powell Street Is Dead': Nikkei Loss, Commemoration, and Representations of Place in the Settler Colonial City." *Urban History Review* 48 (2): 32–55.

3

The Reconciliation That Never Was: Political Skulduggery on Indigenous Lands

Dorothy Cucw-la7 Christian

> *Land is at the root of any issue or conflict you could care to name involving Indigenous and Settler peoples in Canada.*
>
> – Barker and Battell-Lowman, 2015

A Coast Salish teaching, "Hands Back, Hands Forward," that Tsimilano, Musqueam Elder Dr. Vince Stogan shared (Archibald 2008, 50–52) speaks to a number of interrelated concepts that are pertinent to this chapter. My interpretation of this teaching is that we, as Indigenous peoples, have a responsibility to ensure that our cultures continue in perpetuity, and implicit in upholding that responsibility is to know our history. Thus, intergenerational transmission of knowledge is necessary, which includes looking at historical events to understand our current experience so that we may formulate viable strategies for generations to come. This teaching of looking back to move forward is the overall theme of this chapter.

Throughout centuries of political skulduggery, settler colonial governments have enacted laws and put in place policies, practices, and procedures that reinforce the beliefs they hold about land. Land for settlers means occupying it, owning it, and extracting from it natural resources for financial profits, while hectares are set aside as recreation sites for the privileged or deemed as conservation areas or Crown lands, which can be redesignated through an agreement, licence, or permit issued by the provincial government to serve corporate interests.

On the flip side of the proverbial colonial coin, land means something completely different for Indigenous peoples. Land is something we do not own, and we carry a spiritual responsibility to uphold all the life that exists within its ecological systems. Stories of the land inextricably tie the place-based Indigenous peoples to the lands they are born to, and through the stories they are taught how to coexist with other beings on their ancestral homelands. Each Indigenous nation has a body of stories that begins with their Creation story, which tells them how they came to be on their lands. Some of the stories contain the laws on how the people are to interrelate with each other and with all the seen and unseen beings with whom they share the land. Those bodies of stories are integral to the pedagogy of how people are taught to live sustainably on the land to perpetuate the existence of life.

Given these diametrically opposed world views, it follows that the two different ways of knowing and doing also treat story/narrative differently. For Indigenous peoples, stories are a pedagogical tool that guides them in their way of knowing, way of doing, way of seeing, way of acting, and way of listening. Some stories are shared with outsiders, while some are kept for private, internal use only. On the other hand, settler peoples treat Indigenous stories as mythology or as quaint little folkloric stories for their amusement. With this attitude, successive settler governments have eroded and have made every effort to erase the Indigenous narratives of the original peoples of these lands. Today, the Indigenous and colonial narratives of these lands are interfacing under the guise of reconciliation; however, until settler peoples acknowledge the rightful place of Indigenous stories, any meaningful Indigenous-settler relations will be elusive.

Since the time of first contact, the colonial narrative has been superimposed on the Indigenous narrative on these lands known as Canada. In the arrogant and ethnocentric way of settler peoples, the French and British empires established themselves by placing their flags on Turtle Island[1] as if Indigenous peoples did not exist on these lands prior to their arrival. Under the oppressive control of the settler colonists, Indigenous peoples responded with hundreds of years of resistance to the settler colonial narrative and, through socio-political actions, have countered the politics of genocide toward generations of diverse Indigenous nations. And, as Adam Barker and Emma Battell-Lowman state in the epigraph, land is the root cause of all issues and conflicts between the two populations. It is therefore critical that settler peoples understand the role of story in Indigenous families, communities, and nations, and how integral they are to the lands.

This chapter illustrates the expansive divide between colonial and Indigenous narratives and examines how the policies and practices in the arts sector of settler governments have been an instrument of erasure of Indigenous stories and understandings of land. It provides an analytical overview of colonial Canada's political actions that enable corporate Canada's economic policies that give settlers the right to access the land and extract resources for profits, showing why both land and stories that give meaning to it are sites of resistance. In this time of so-called reconciliation, is it possible for settler peoples' colonial stories to move over and make room for the stories of Indigenous peoples? Are the settler colonists ready to make things right with the original peoples by hearing the Indigenous stories of these lands?

As an Indigenous visual storyteller myself, with years of experience in visual media, the critical question I ask is this: "What is it going to take to transform the embedded national colonial narrative so that the grandchildren and great-great-grandchildren of both Indigenous and settler peoples can share a sustainable future on these lands that could be mutually beneficial to all?" The first step is to examine and deconstruct the falsehoods of the colonial narrative with an open mind.

Resisting the Colonial Narrative

With a colonial history full of consistent political skulduggery on the part of successive settler governments since the time of first contact, it is challenging to grow and develop a sustainable future for Indigenous peoples and settler allies in Canada. Since their arrival, these hegemonic forces have assumed control of and an entitlement to Indigenous lands and resources by applying the precepts of the Doctrine of Discovery, an internationally recognized set of legal principles that Arthur Manuel and Ronald Derrickson (2015, 3) call the "legal fig leaf they could use to cover naked thievery." This is the legal instrument used to claim our lands without the consent of the Indigenous peoples, an instrument deeply buried in the twenty-first century colonial narrative with its application of the rule of colonial law in Canadian courts. Central to any resistance against colonial laws are Indigenous stories and land. Leanne Simpson (2014) calls cultural stories our "theoretical anchor," and I would say that land and stories embody the spiritual anchor that Indigenous peoples steadfastly hold on to in any resistance actions that we undertake.

Significant Indigenous-settler history in Canada[2] was made in the last decade of the twentieth century when Indigenous peoples across Turtle Island resisted this thievery by taking up arms to stand up for their ancestral homelands. The 1990 Oka Crisis on Mohawk/Haudenosaunee territories was triggered by political action by the Canadian government when it mobilized its military to intimidate the Mohawk and other Indigenous peoples standing in solidarity with the Iroquois Confederacy to protect an ancient burial site. This land resistance action was supported by many Indigenous nations throughout Turtle Island and into Mexico. The seventy-eight-day standoff started on July 11 and ended on September 26. One life was lost – Corporal Marcel Lemay of the Sûreté du Québec, the provincial police force.

The 1995 Gustafsen Lake standoff was also an armed resistance that occurred on ceremonial Sundance grounds on unceded Secwepemc territories. It started on August 18 and ended on September 17. The Canadian military and special forces were mobilized. No lives were lost. This was also a land issue (Welch 2019).

Also in September 1995, there was an act of unarmed resistance at Ipperwash Provincial Park in Ontario. The Indigenous/Chippewa peoples of Kettle and Stony Point stood up for and reclaimed lands that had been expropriated from their communities during the Second World War. The Emergency Task Force of the Ontario Provincial Police killed an unarmed Indigenous man, Dudley George. The Indigenous/Chippewa peoples of Kettle and Stony Point had grown tired of the promises made by the federal government to return their lands. It would take the federal government until 2015 to settle the land dispute with these First Nations communities (de Bruin 2019).

Another group of colonized Indigenous peoples, the Zapatistas in Chiapas, Mexico, took up arms on January 1, 1994, to express their objection to the North American Free Trade Agreement because it made it possible for multinational corporations to take over their agricultural lands and grow cash crops, pushing aside the local farmers, who had traditionally grown their crops and traded their harvests in their own local economies. They could not compete with this level of capitalism (Godelmann 2014). Indigenous populations drew their lines in the metaphorical sand in these modern-day "Indian-settler" wars during the 1990s. We were telling the dominant colonial world that we would no longer tolerate the cumulative injustices of the colonial nation-states. The social political actions of the 1990s are as notable as the civil rights movement of the 1960s and 1970s that gave rise to the Red Power Movement in Canada and the American Indian Movement in the United States, which elevated the Indigenous voice to the international sphere.

In the first decade of the twenty-first century, the political skulduggery continued at the international level with political skirmishes at the United Nations. In 2007, Australia, Canada, New Zealand, and the United States refused to become signatories to the United Nations Declaration on the Rights of Indigenous Peoples (UNDRIP). When political pressure was applied, these colonial nation-states eventually signed the declaration; however, it is important to know that "the primary obstacles for the nation-state[s] were land rights and self-determination, including the principle of free, prior, and informed consent" (Lightfoot 2016, 1–2). In 2009 and 2010, Canada, New Zealand, Australia and the United States reversed their positions and signed the UNDRIP. Even though Canada made UNDRIP a law in its legislature in June 2021,[3] it is clear that the nation-state has no intention of respecting the terms of UNDRIP because its thievery of land and resources continues with its pattern of behaviour filled with political trickery.

In recent history, on June 11, 2008, the Government of Canada issued a "hollow" apology to survivors of residential schools. It completely ignored the roles of church and state in attempting to destroy Indigenous peoples' relations to one another and to the land, as well as replacing Indigenous stories with colonial stories. Seven years later, the Truth and Reconciliation Commission (TRC) was established (Barrera 2015) to bear witness to and to document the Indian residential school experience of Indigenous peoples in Canada so that this dark history is never forgotten. The final report of the TRC (2015, 277–95) has ninety-four "Calls to Action" based on the synthesis of the experiences reported by Indigenous individuals and communities taking part in the process.

These stories are not new. Most recommendations were already found among the recommendations of the Royal Commission on Aboriginal Peoples (RCAP), which were released two decades earlier, in 1996, after which there was no real follow-up and no substantive changes in the policies and practices of Canada's colonial institutions. The absence of action on the RCAP report is a clear indication of the usual approach of the Canadian government, which appears to respond to immediate concerns and crises but only for the sake of optics. The RCAP was established in 1992, in the last decade of the twentieth century, in response to what I refer to above as modern-day "Indian-settler" wars (Oka, Gustafsen Lake, and Ipperwash), where land was the central issue – an issue that, despite the ongoing war, the TRC stories spoke more directly to the intergenerational traumas caused by these wars.

Further illustrating settler colonial states' political skulduggery, in 2009 the Canadian government contradicted itself when the same prime minister who apologized to residential school survivors a year earlier made a shocking statement at a G20 meeting in Pittsburgh: "We also have no history of colonialism" – which showed the ignorance of the highest political office in this country (O'Keefe 2009). Three years later, in November 2012, social media became a site for political action with the Idle No More movement. Led by Indigenous women, it started "among Treaty People in Manitoba, Saskatchewan, and Alberta protesting the Canadian government's dismantling of environmental protection laws, endangering First Nations who live on the land" (Idle No More, n.d.).

Idle No More garnered support from Indigenous and non-Indigenous peoples around the world to oppose the government's Bill C-45, which further revealed the deviousness of a settler government that claimed that colonialism did not exist in Canada (Idle No More, n.d.). Bill C-45 became law on December 14, 2012, and its name, "Jobs, Growth and Long-term Prosperity Act, 2012"[4] (McNeil 2013), obscured its real purpose. Although it was enacted as a budget bill, the new law amended other existing statutes, such as "the Indian Act, the Fisheries Act, the Canadian Environmental Assessment Act and the Navigable Waters Protection Act." All of these embedded amendments adversely affect Indigenous peoples in Canada because they infringe on Indigenous land and treaty rights. In addition, this law interferes with the Indigenous relationship to land and natural resources, which directly impacts food- and medicine-gathering practices on unceded territories. Many settler Canadians stood with Indigenous peoples during the winter of 2012 because they recognized the underhandedness of how Bill C-45 was rammed through Parliament and, most importantly, that this law would also affect the quality of their lives and that of future generations.

The Indigenous Narrative: Reclaiming Our Stories

It is essential to examine how Indigenous peoples have challenged the way successive settler governments have attempted to marginalize and discredit Indigenous narratives that tie us to the land. The invisible war continues in the board rooms of the arts sector of these lands now known as Canada. Our resistance to settler colonialism in the arts sector is yet another way Indigenous peoples have battled to maintain control over our lands by affirming the central role stories play in our interrelated relationships, even at a political level. As a result of political pressure from the Red Power Movement and the American Indian Movement in the late 1960s, the National Film Board (NFB) of Canada's Challenge for Change program provided opportunities for Indigenous people to direct and produce their own stories (NFB 2017). However, the non-Indigenous NFB producers and directors still had the power and privilege of maintaining creative control over the Indigenous stories (Hassannia 2017). This program ran from 1967 to 1980. Certainly, the arts, like the land, became another important site for resistance to colonialism.

The Inuit are rarely recognized for the contributions they have made to ensure that the Indigenous/Inuit story of the land is primary. In the mid-1970s, however, they were taking a strong political stance to keep their stories at the forefront. Through their consistent determination in maintaining their language and cultural values and by taking a strong political stance on resisting the television programming that was parachuted into their communities from the south, they have been a substantive force in the Indigenous storytelling world. Zacharias Kunuk and Puhipau (2005, 46) discussed some of their community's actions on Inuit and Hawaiian lands, in the 1970s. Kunuk says,

> We had voted to keep television out of the community in the mid-1970s. We didn't want it because there were no Inuktitut programs. It was all in English ... our elders were afraid of the impact it would have if there were nothing in our language on the TV. So we kept TV out for a number of years.

The foresight of the Elders in Kunuk's community of Igloolik in Nunavut is why Inuit language retention is strong, and their cultural values and aesthetics strongly inform their visual storytelling voice on national and international screens. As with all Indigenous languages, the Inuit language holds their Indigenous knowledge(s); it conceptualizes their laws and ways of interrelating with each other and with the land, including all the beings with which they share the land and waters. While the Inuit were refusing mainstream settler Canada's images and languages, many other Indigenous communities were in the process of archiving their own images, for their own purposes, in the 1970s. My own community of the Splatsin/Secwepemc Nation has an invaluable archive of stories and historical accounts from our Elders and historians collected in the 1970s. In informal conversations, other people from other Indigenous nations have shared with me that this was the period when they also started collecting pertinent historical and cultural information.

In the late 1980s, Indigenous writers, like generations before them, drew their own line in the metaphorical sand and reclaimed the right to tell our own stories, because up to this point non-Indigenous Canadian writers were freely appropriating Indigenous stories, without acknowledging the origins of the stories. This aspect of how white settler privilege controlled Indigenous narratives had not been challenged up to this point. This is when the cultural appropriation issue became a hotbed of political action. The white colonial feminist community was challenged by Lee Maracle (Tseil-wau-tulth/Stó:lō) in 1988 when she asked them to "move over" and stop appropriating and profiting from Indigenous stories – to make space for Indigenous peoples to write our stories (Greenhill and Tye 1997, 68). A formal request was made by Lenore Keeshig-Tobias (Anishinaabe) to non-Indigenous writers at the 1989 annual general meeting of the Writers' Union of Canada (n.d.) to stop appropriating stories of Indigenous writers and writers of colour (Tator, Henry, and Mattis 1998). This was a very vibrant and exciting time to be part of creating a new approach to Indigenous stories; in fact, for the first time in Canadian history, Indigenous and writers of colour were claiming a space in the national arts sector within a nation-state that claimed to be a successful multicultural democratic society.

It is important to emphasize that it was not until the 1990s when modern-day "Indian-settler" wars took place that the arts sector paid serious attention and moved beyond the existing programs, which up until that time had in fact been window-dressing exercises. The bureaucrats started changing their policies and practices regarding Indigenous artists. Before this, many Indigenous peoples were objectified in films produced by non-Indigenous filmmakers, and non-Indigenous writers wrote the scripts and non-Indigenous actors portrayed us in Indigenous specific stories (Barclay 1990, 1999, 2003a, 2003b; Christian 2017; Columpar 2010; Raheja 2010).

In 1991, Métis activist Marjorie Beaucage, a community-based visual storyteller, who was the "runner"[5] for a collective of Indigenous writers and visual storytellers/filmmakers took the lead in bringing about substantive changes by challenging the colonial practices of the cultural industries in Canada. She met with two of the major cultural institutions for artistic production in Canada, the Banff Centre for the Arts and the Canada Council for the Arts. Up to this point, these institutions had very little money allocated to Indigenous programming (M. Beaucage, personal communication, January 2017). The actions of Beaucage and the collective she was a part of transformed some of the existing arts policies and practices for Indigenous artists across these lands. For example, the Canada Council now has dedicated funding for Indigenous writers, artists, collectives, and organizations.

Other necessary changes were precipitated by the 1994 historical and revolutionary "Writing Thru Race" (Sehdev 2001) national conference in

Vancouver, spearheaded by Dr. Roy Miki and supported by Indigenous and other writers of colour who challenged the assumed entitlement of some members of the Writers' Union of Canada. During this contentious conference, a number of important relationships were developed and solidified among Indigenous writers and the Japanese Canadian, Chinese Canadian, African Canadian, and South and East Asian communities because of their shared racist and oppressive histories vis-à-vis the nation-state of Canada. They stood together against the institutionalized racism embedded in the "White supremacy [that] has been a feature of Canada since its inception" (Barker and Battell-Lowman 2015, 70) and still exists in the publishing industry today. With these political actions, Indigenous writers and visual storytellers altered the assumed dominant settler narrative.

The Inuit are leaders in challenging the settler colonial narratives by maintaining the integrity of their stories; it was therefore a natural progression for an Inuit to be the first Indigenous person from Canada to catch the attention of the global visual culture. Inuit filmmaker Zacharias Kunuk presented his award-winning 2002 film *Atanarjuat: The Fast Runner* to the world screen culture at the Cannes Film Festival. Kunuk directed and co-produced this film with his creative partner, Norm Cohn.

The Inuit's vision of their own world, coupled with their political approach, made them major players in lobbying for the licensing of the Aboriginal Peoples Television Network (APTN). Abraham Tagalik worked tirelessly with Indigenous groups in the southern regions of Canada to achieve this goal. On February 22, 1999, APTN was licensed to broadcast nationally, a first in the global Indigenous media/communications world. "Canada's aboriginal broadcasting system is, to date, the most advanced such system in the world" (Roth 2005, 10). It is important to note that these transformations took place in the last decade of the twentieth century and the first decade of the twenty-first, a time when Indigenous artistic expressions in film and communications/media exploded onto national and international screens.

Indigenous writers in Canada, too numerous to give recognition to here, have written books that now grace the shelves of many literary classrooms and provide the true stories of Indigenous peoples, not some distorted interpretation through a colonial lens. Collectively, these writers project the Indigenous stories of their culturally specific lands that are within the borders of what is known as Canada. From the time in 1988 when Lee Maracle (Tseil-wau-tulth/Stó:lō) asked non-Indigenous feminist writers to move over, she became the most prolific Indigenous writer in Canada.[6] Not only has she moved over for other Indigenous writers to join her but she also mentored many of the writers who are gaining fame in popular culture. Thirty years later, one of Maracle's mentees, Métis writer Cherie Dimaline, saw her 2017 book *Marrow Thieves* become the number one bestselling Canadian book of 2018.

At the same time, visual storytellers/filmmakers were also elevating the place of Indigenous stories at global Indigenous film festivals. The ImagineNative Film Festival based in Toronto has blossomed into the largest global Indigenous film festival in the world. It has actively brought Indigenous visual stories to the international screen culture for the past twenty years. I was invited to curate a program for the October 2018 festival, and was privileged to screen many Indigenous stories from around the world. It was exhilarating to see stories coming from within the cultures and from the lands of those stories. Unapologetically, our visual storytelling is no longer focused on who we are as Indigenous peoples in relation to our colonizers; we are telling our own stories without the colonial gaze.

One film that received national attention was *Edge of the Knife,* which was co-produced and co-directed by Helen Haig-Brown (Tsilhqot'in) and Gwaii Edenshaw (Haida) in 2018. This visual story dramatizes a Haida cultural story and is presented entirely in the Haida language. Zacharias Kunuk was the film's executive producer. In choosing him, the directors made the decision to learn from a master whose films are steeped in Inuit knowledge. Kunuk spoke to me about filming cultural stories (cited in Christian 2017, 214):

> I try to record these and sometimes I have them acted out and filming is the best tool that I found. When we are making re-enactments the costumes have to be right, I am very lucky to have elders that can still stitch the traditional way of our region; every region has different style of clothing. Even up in the Arctic, you go from the east to the west, the clothing changes and you can even come up here – you can tell by the traditional clothes, you know their traditional dialects, their language.

Kunuk's influence is apparent in the Haida story because the film exudes cultural congruency, meaning that the entire film is in the Haida language and is permeated throughout by Haida aesthetics. Most importantly, the story is told on the land where the story occurs. Increasingly in Indigenous films, visual narratives are strongly positioned within the cultural knowledge of the creative teams, not in response to how they are located within the colonial narrative, and they are not reacting to colonialism.

The written stories still have some challenges, however. In August 2017, I participated in an Indigenous Editors Circle at a conference in Toronto that demonstrated the institutional power relations between the publishing industry and Indigenous peoples. After almost a quarter of a century (twenty-three years) following the Writing Thru Race conference, Indigenous writers and editors still have to deal with the assumption that whiteness is at the pinnacle of the decision-making pyramid. It is clear to me that some settler Canadians in the publishing industry are still assuming the superiority of Euro-Western ways of knowing. The most difficult aspect for me as an Indigenous writer and editor has been the expectation that we are there to educate settler Canadians and to give them access to Indigenous knowledge. For instance, the basic colonial writing practice is to have a storytelling arc that presupposes a beginning, middle, and end, with a conflict to be resolved in the denouement. This practice is not congruent with Indigenous storytelling styles.

In contrast it appears that the visual storytelling funding bodies are beginning to understand the distinct and unique place of Indigenous knowledge(s) in telling the stories of the land. In May 2018, I was on the first-ever Indigenous jury for Telefilm that disbursed $3 million to Indigenous filmmakers across the country. On March 14, 2024, Kerry Swanson, CEO of the Indigenous Screen Office[7] (ISO) stated in a press release that Canadian Heritage had approved permanent funding of $65M over 5 years ($13M a year) for the Indigenous film industry in Canada. I sit on the Board of the ISO. It is evident that the major funding agencies are making changes to how arts sector monies are distributed in Canada. These experiences in visual and written storytelling illustrate to me how complicated the issues are because Indigenous writers and visual storytellers/filmmakers are at the mercy of the policy makers in the arts sector who appear to be awakening to the systemic barriers caused by colonial structures. This has a direct impact on how the two competing Indigenous and settler narratives coexist on these lands in contemporary times, and whether the settler narrative will be decolonized.

Decolonizing the Settler Colonial Narrative

Storytelling is a critical medium for determining how people(s) and lands are perceived, whether in written form or visual form, because the stories told are internalized and embedded in the foundation of how relationships are constructed. Thus, in this time of reconciling the Indigenous-settler stories in Canada it is vital that the existing narratives be transformed to reflect unacknowledged truths; otherwise any semblance of social or political change will not take place. Canada's colonial story is in dire need of reassessment. As a number of Indigenous and non-Indigenous scholars have argued, it is important to clarify that the ways in which Indigenous and non-Indigenous peoples engage in the process of decolonization mean very different things to each side of the colonial divide, especially in terms of the nuances in understanding what decolonization means.

Decolonizing means having uncomfortable conversations. I touch on those uncomfortable feelings in some of my classrooms. In the spring of 2017, I co-instructed a fourth-year course at Simon Fraser University for the Semester in Dialogue program titled "Decolonizing Dialogues, Solidarities and Activism." The majority of the class were settler Canadians from various cultures, and two students self-identified as Indigenous. In one of our conversations, I explained that being uncomfortable is implicit in the healing process, especially when we are naming the details and the consequences of the brutality of colonization. I also explained that this may involve unexpected emotional reactions. However, I assured the mostly settler Canadian students that Indigenous peoples were just as uncomfortable as they were.[8]

Furthermore, I explained to the students that grappling with discomfort is an indication that you are sincerely looking at where and how you and your family are implicated in perpetuating the dominant colonial story. Experiencing and acknowledging discomfort also illustrates that you as a settler are at least engaged in taking the first steps toward taking responsibility for educating yourself. I asserted that real reconciliation will not occur until the settler side of the divide sees and understands that they are the problem. Settlers' place of privilege allows them to be selective in their hearing when Indigenous lands and resources are discussed, and corporate Canada has assumed entitlement to Indigenous lands since first contact and sought only financial gain. For reconciliation, settlers need to hear about and understand the uniqueness of each Indigenous nation, which holds a body of stories from its ancestral lands, which places it there with spiritual responsibilities toward all living things. When the diverse Indigenous nation's knowledge(s) about responsibility to the land and all living things is grasped, then there are possibilities for decolonizing, reconciliation, and finding an equitable social, political, and economic resolution, thus making it possible to live together on these lands in a peaceful way.

For me as a Secwepemc-Syilx woman, decolonizing is a verb. It is about the actions that one embodies in one's day-to-day activities to counter the pervasive colonial narrative that is deeply entrenched in layers and layers of policies and practices in Canada. It is an action word, not to be frozen in theoretical frameworks or to be used as a symbolic metaphor (Tuck and Yang 2012) to ease the conscience of settler Canadians (Mackey 2016) who are complicit in perpetuating the colonial story. I have said in public oratory and in classrooms that, at a deeply personal level, decolonizing for me is about "putting the Indian back in the child," a purposeful way to counter the well-known phrase of "killing the Indian in the child."[9] I was engaged in the process of re-Indigenizing myself long before the buzzword "decolonization" entered the academic discourse. For many, including Indigenous peoples, healing the child within is a necessary first step to becoming a fully functional, whole, and healthy adult. As the Truth and Reconciliation Commission shared with mainstream Canada, generations of Indigenous children have been harmed by the white supremacist colonial policies and practices that created complex intergenerational trauma in many Indigenous families and communities.

Settler Canadian audiences are seemingly willing to hear the stories that are filled with atrocities, but I wonder what they do with those stories. Are the stories taken and integrated into their consciousness to shift their beliefs about who we are as the original peoples of these lands? Or is there something else at play here? Over the years, I have observed a display of disturbing voyeuristic behaviour in some settler audiences when Indigenous people are at their most vulnerable, while talking about their most brutal, horrific experiences. Witnessing this caused a knot in my stomach that has taken years to untangle. This kind of settler behaviour causes a confusing, harsh, and dehumanizing environment for Indigenous peoples in the reconciliation process.

In this never-before-achieved place in the history of these lands, some are striving to reconcile Indigenous and settler relations in Canada. Some Indigenous and non-Indigenous academics are deconstructing and critically analyzing Canada's colonial story in a truthful way, thus creating a small crack in the Canadian landscape that may acknowledge the rightful place of Indigenous peoples and our stories on these lands. Nevertheless, this shift reveals that the colonial narrative still dominates the current neocolonial practices, though buried in current conciliatory language. Indigenous thinkers challenge the much-touted and highly publicized efforts of the so-called reconciliation of the provincial and federal governments. Manuel and Derrickson (2017, 201) agree with Taiaiake Alfred (2016a), who voices the misgivings of many Indigenous peoples that the reconciliation plans of provincial and federal governments are a form of re-colonization (Alfred

2016b). With the TRC's Calls to Action, many institutions are trying to take constructive steps toward addressing the concerns of the commission. However, the provincial and federal governments of the day have recently turned the path to reconciliation back to the Dark Ages.

The Settler Problem

In the current environment of reconciliation, it is critical to understand what the settler colonial narrative is and what its fundamental beliefs are. Accordingly, I turn to film critic Katherine Monk (2001, 4), who says with tongue-in-cheek humour:

> We're all children of a dysfunctional family. Born together in the wilderness when two European cultures squatted in dense underbrush and gave birth to fledgling colonies on the shores of the St. Lawrence. Canada's twin identities have been at each other since the day they were born. For more than 200 years, they've been threatening to break up – not realizing that while you can leave the house, change your name and cut off all ties, you can never escape your own twin. He's always there – an amniotic consciousness to remind us of our other half. No wonder we're a bit screwed up. We deny we're even related. Neglect begets neglect. Abuse breeds abuse. Ignorance spawns ignorance and so we have developed this bizarre love-hate relationship with our own reflection as it's communicated through our cultural industries.

In decades past, this bipolar condition was called "the Canadian identity crisis." Today, it's called everything from "the unity question" to "Western alienation" to "The Ministry of Canadian Heritage." No matter what you call it, the underlying message remains the same: we are broken; we need to be fixed.

Interestingly, nowhere in Monk's description of "the Canadian identity crisis" does she include Indigenous peoples or our relationship to the settler peoples who are struggling with their identity on Indigenous lands. Although, in her version of the Canadian landscape she does include two Indigenous filmmakers, Alanis Obomsawin (Abenaki) and Zacharias Kunuk (Inuit), albeit very awkwardly, and possibly as an afterthought. Moreover, the issue of race is completely ignored. The mindset that projects this Canada includes only white English Canada and white French Canada. With the looking-back-to-move-forward theme, I maintain that although Monk's attitudes and opinions were published in 2001, they are still relevant today because she represents and reflects a dominant settler conception of Canada through a popular culture lens. This thinking is deeply embedded in the settler Canadian psyche.

Nevertheless, there are other settlers who have put forward a more realistic portrayal of the landscape of Canada. Paulette Regan started a whole new discourse with her book *Unsettling the Settler Within: Indian Residential Schools, Truth Telling, and Reconciliation in Canada* (2010). Her strategy to write as a settler woman for a settler audience transformed the positioning of the Canadian colonial narrative. It opened the door to seeing without the rose-coloured glasses of centuries of political shenanigans that privilege white settler peoples and corporate Canada, revealing truths that many Canadians find difficult to absorb. Regan's work is instrumental in shifting the academic discourse in terms of the colonial story on these lands.

From the next generation of scholars, Adam Barker and Emma Battell-Lowman (2015) take the discussion of Indigenous-settler relations to a much deeper level by conducting a critical, in-depth analysis of the colonial relationship in Canada. They begin by discussing why it is important that non-Indigenous peoples use the word "settler," and by examining the many different aspects of what it means to be a settler/occupier of Indigenous land. Without a recognition by non-Indigenous peoples that they are "settlers," they will be unable to recognize and start changing how they perpetuate the colonial system. At the outset, they say that the twentieth-century view of an "Indian problem," which continues to be perpetuated in the twenty-first century, needs to be shifted. Barker and Battell-Lowman (2015) turn the Canadian gaze back onto themselves and their settler ancestors, saying that it is a "settler" problem, not an "Indian" problem (6).

A significant part of their analysis is centred on the land. They probe the multi-faceted issue of Indigenous land and how it is the "root" of centuries of conflict between Indigenous and settler peoples (Barker and Battell-Lowman 2015, 48–68). Essentially, they expose how the power relations are structured between Indigenous and settler peoples in Canada, which reveals many Indigenous truths that many settler peoples are not open to hearing. They provide astute observations about the lands in Canada. They delve deep into the land issue by stating that both Indigenous and settler people's identities are governed by their relationship to the lands, which is a point of view not commonly considered (2):

> Our construction of "Settler" as an identity mirrors the construction of "Indigenous" in contemporary terms: a broad collective of peoples with commonalities through particular connections to land and place. For

Settler people, however, those connections are forged through violence and displacement of Indigenous communities and nations. We examine what it means to be a Settler person in Canada, how we constitute our national narratives and social structures, why Settler Canadians react as we do to Indigenous communities in resistance, and how we can begin finding more ethical, just ways of being together on the lands we call home.

This perspective is rare in any commentary on Indigenous and settler relationships. My interpretation of what these scholars are saying is that it is necessary for settlers to engage in their own decolonizing process to fully understand what their identity is on the lands they occupy in Canada. When settlers can critically analyze how they came to be on the lands they call home, then there is a possibility of moving toward a true reconciliation. This level of a deep internal examination opens up a space of shared stories on these lands we all call home and may provide possibilities for transforming the dynamics in Indigenous-settler relations to the point where we can actually build a relationship.

Although Barker and Battell-Lowman's entire text is important, their examination of the grave issue of race moves the discussion to a much higher level because they recognize that Canada was built on a white supremacist ideology (2015, 71). This stance propels their analysis into an honest and realistic space for an authentic conversation to occur. Many settler Canadians refuse to grapple with the race issue because in the historical treatment of Indigenous peoples, the policies and practices of their governments are fundamentally rooted in the effort to eradicate Indigenous peoples and their cultures. Some cannot accept their complicity in how this ideology is the foundation of the divisiveness in Indigenous-settler relations, never mind truly look at how the immigration and multicultural policies of this country have marginalized all people of colour.

In this place of denial, there are many superficial conversations and analyses that stultify constructive relationship building. This is where discomfort overwhelms the conversation between Indigenous and settler peoples because it reveals the racist and classist policies of the nation-state. Barker and Battell-Lowman (2015) critique the race issue, layer by layer, including how the superiority of whiteness affects the so-called multicultural or diversity policies that falsely create the sense of a successful multicultural nation-state in Canada. The next two sections present some of the critiques and complexities of how multicultural and diversity policies remain racist and continue to structure the settler colonial narrative, including by people of colour settlers. The critiques presented are those developed by both non-Indigenous and Indigenous scholars.

"Are People of Colour Settlers Too?"

Given the state of affairs in the nation-state of Canada, what stories will Indigenous peoples and non-Indigenous settlers write together?[10] The decolonizing discourse is ever evolving and complicated because up to this time, the narrative is still framed in the dominant story of settler colonial history. The socio-political movements of Indigenous peoples reclaiming their place on these lands defy that history. The catch-all concept of decolonization encompasses the multi-dimensional and very problematic relationship between Indigenous and settler peoples in Canada, which I contend focuses on whose story prevails on these lands. By looking at the competing colonial narrative of the privileged white settlers and the cultural stories of Indigenous peoples that are derived directly from our diverse land/place-based locations, I want to draw attention to aspects of what Eva Mackey has termed "fantasies of possession" and "fantasies of entitlement," which she says are illogically conceived though "extensively rationalized" (2016, 10) by successive settler colonial governments and settler scholars in a spectrum of disciplines. There are Indigenous and scholars of colour who are examining how these fantasies directly impact the quality of the relationships they build with their Indigenous allies.

The notion of home is a tender, fragile issue for all peoples on these lands. Malissa Phung asked a critical question – "Are People of Colour Settlers Too?" (2011, 289–98) and she deconstructs the monolithic term "settler" by addressing the complexities of what that word means to Canadians whose histories on these lands are unique to their own experiences. There are some communities within the larger diverse groups, including African Canadian, Chinese Canadian, Japanese Canadian, and South Asian and Middle Eastern communities. Some individuals from these racialized communities choose to ally with the original peoples of Canada. Each has specific histories that relate to when it encountered the Indigenous peoples of Canada.

A specific example is documented in the novel *The Book of Negroes* (Hill 2007), which recounts the history of African Canadians in the Atlantic provinces during the 1700s, when Africans escaped the slave trade of America via Mi'kmaq/Maliseet territories to return to their homelands in Africa.[11] Some of these families remained and are the longest-standing settlers on Indigenous lands. In addition, in the oral histories of the west coast of Vancouver Island, there are accounts of a Chinese artisan ship that arrived in the 1770s.[12] These are only two settler of colour stories showing the varied experiences that provide a very different picture of the settler colonial story on the traditional homelands of Indigenous peoples. Thus, it is logical that each community of colour has a unique decolonizing experience determined by when in the colonization process, they immigrated to these lands and when they started to consciously engage in decolonizing their relationships with the original peoples of the lands they occupy. An element of this process is examining how they fit into the Canadian landscape and its so-called identity crisis. Again, it is important to clarify that Indigenous decolonization is different from settler – specifically, settler of colour – decolonization.

The Diversity Narrative on Turtle Island: Is It Masking Intolerance?

In 2016, the Trump administration perpetuated a white supremacist ideology when the president made rash off-the-cuff statements that elevated racial tensions throughout his time in office. These beliefs are evident north of the forty-ninth parallel as well. For example, a Canadian Broadcasting Corporation story on August 28, 2017, revealed the horrific ordeal of an Eritrean family in Winnipeg (Barghout and Hoye 2017).[13] This family was subjected to unbelievable hatred by one neighbour who threatened them on a daily basis. Even as this level of hatred was being perpetuated, the current settler colonial government of Canada purported to welcome refugees from war-torn countries. But when war broke out between Russia and Ukraine in early 2022, racist practices became obvious as the government provided safety for Ukrainian refugees but failed to honour its agreements with Afghan refugees (Fong and Saar 2022). To say that levels of racial intolerance in both the United States and Canada are at an all-time high is an understatement.

Again, looking back to move forward, US scholar Wendy Brown examines racial intolerance in her 2006 book *Regulating Aversion: Tolerance in an Age of Identity and Empire,* and I assert that her analysis is still viable in 2022. Although Brown's original critique is of the United States as a liberal democracy, her work shifted to include a global analysis of liberal democracies and their anti-Muslim sentiments following the 9/11 attacks in 2001. Her analysis also applies to Canada, as the stated intent of her work is to "track the social and political work of tolerance discourse" and to look at the positionality of "subjects, cultures and regimes" and how, in that process, peoples and cultures are made invisible (Brown 2006, 4).

In Canada, the normalized practice that renders Indigenous peoples invisible occurs when we are wrongly included as part of the "problems" of liberal democratic citizenship, along with the multi-ethnic immigrants, women, and gay, lesbian, and transgender communities. We were all reduced to "interest groups" when equity, diversity, and inclusion policies and practices were formalized in this country. Policy makers must understand that Indigenous peoples stand alone in their location as the original peoples of these lands. When examined closely, it is clear that the white privileged decision-makers are not comfortable with having a truly equitable relationship with any of the marginalized groups. Since the publication in 2015 of the Truth and Reconciliation Commission's final report with its Calls to Action, the language of the spin doctors has become conciliatory, and the academic and political discourse in Canada now includes "decolonization and indigenization." It remains to be seen whether there will be any effective change in policies and practices, or whether, as Brown (2006) observes, "within [decolonization and anti-racist] discourses the aim of learning tolerance [will continue not to be] to arrive at equality or solidarity with others but, rather, to learn how to put up with others" (184), thus continuing the power dynamics of the status quo.

Through a systematic "legislated genocide" (W. Christian, personal communication, April 2014) that is buried in devious political acts, Canada continues to decimate Indigenous cultures. In the twenty-first century reality, however, Indigenous peoples have proven their resilience by surviving the many attempts to destroy our cultures. In this time of truth and reconciliation, a first in Canada's history, the complex Indigenous-settler relationship is under scrutiny, and the processes of decolonization and Indigenization are forcing settler colonial governments to examine their white privilege and entitlement. These same governments have also imposed their racist policies and practices on communities of colour, who are also treated as bothersome citizenry who do not fit with the values of a white supremacist ideology.

Recently in the race discourse, there are challenges to the white supremacist ideology that deconstruct the dynamics of racism while at the same time exposing the fragility of whiteness (DiAngelo 2018). Significant questions are addressed that illustrate how white privilege shifts the conversation to nullify the power dynamics of the race issue (78–79).

The analysis of power thus again extends not just to Indigenous communities but also to communities of colour. I will not delve into the details of how the settler colonial Canadian governments have inflicted state "violence and displacement" on communities of colour because they have documented their own injustices (Barker and Battell-Lowman 2015, 2). However, I will highlight the experiences of three communities of colour to illustrate the legislated state violence of Canada's racist and xenophobic immigration policies. The Japanese Canadian population were interned in camps throughout British Columbia and incarcerated in other provinces during the Second World War. They were literally robbed of all their assets. Chinese Canadian immigrants were used as cheap labour during the creation of the coast-to-coast railroad, and when the railroad was completed, a Chinese head tax was implemented in 1885 to discourage further immigration to Canada. The South Asian community bore the brunt of these mean-spirited policies when the SS *Komagata Maru* was not allowed entry into the country in 1914. These racist and xenophobic policies were designed to exclude these communities from equal standing as citizens in this so-called liberal democratic society.

Clearly, a new approach to developing and implementing multicultural and diversity policies and practices is needed in Canada because these racist and xenophobic practices still exist today. The stark reality of the normalized power and race relations in Canada is that white supremacist ideology is at the core of the Euro-Western system of knowledge(s) (EWK), which is given epistemic privilege in settler colonial institutions. Thus, it dominates the lived realities of Indigenous and settler communities of colour with its EWK ways of doing and knowing.

In the current environment of reconciliation in Canada, Indigenous systems of knowledge (IK) have gained ground in some academic disciplines. When Indigenous philosophies, epistemologies, and pedagogies are fully understood, then the source of the conflict/clash zones between the privileged EWK and IK comes into clear focus. Putting these two ways of knowing side by side brings a clearer understanding of how Indigenous-settler relationships are affected, particularly when land and resources are central to the cultural interface. Is it possible to create a new model of relating by co-creating a revised narrative on these lands?

After the Reconciliation That Never Was: Does Reconciliation Come at the Barrel of a Gun?

There was some hope when Justin Trudeau's Liberals defeated the Conservatives in the 2015 national election. With Trudeau's political rhetoric about reconciliation, it appeared that he was moving toward fixing the broken

Canadian identity and its fractured relationship with Indigenous peoples. However, the Liberals' true colours were revealed a week before Trudeau's cabinet shuffle on January 14, 2019. On January 7, he mobilized Canada's military, including special forces tactical units and the RCMP, against the Indigenous community of Unist'ot'en and the Wet'suwet'en peoples in northern British Columbia who were protecting their ancestral lands and waters (Unist'ot'en Camp 2019).

Almost thirty years after the Oka Crisis, Canada is still prepared to mobilize its military and police forces against Indigenous peoples when it comes to lands, resources, and profit and loss statements. In an interview with Democracy Now! (2019), Member of Parliament Nathan Cullen reveals the contradiction in the government's actions during the military incursions:

> The main concern that I came up here today was to see the RCMP checkpoint denying Wet'suwet'en access to their own territory. Denying the press access to what is happening further up this road here also seemed to me not in the interest of public safety or peace. The Parliament, just a few months ago, stood and voted and passed the U.N. Declaration on the Rights of Indigenous Peoples. If the current government thinks they can just do something in Parliament but not actually enforce it on the land, then I don't know what that vote means.

The history of the Indigenous community of Unist'ot'en and the Wet'suwet'en is complex, as it is for any Indigenous nation that asserts its laws on its unceded territories, which means the majority of Indigenous lands in what is geopolitically known as British Columbia. The laws of the Unist'ot'en and Wet'suwet'en peoples, given to them through their cultural knowledge, contextualizes how they are to maintain sustainable, healthy relationship to the lands, waters, and all living beings on those lands.

In 1997, the Supreme Court of Canada ruled in its precedent-setting *Delgamuukw* decision that the Wet'suwet'en and Gitxsan have never ceded their Aboriginal rights and title to their traditional territories, and most importantly that their oral histories legitimize their place on their ancestral lands.[14] The Hereditary Chiefs have taken a stance of not allowing any pipelines through their traditional territories, which is in opposition to some elected Chiefs who function under the imposed Indian Act regulations of governance.[15] This internal skirmish over who controls the lands was exacerbated by industry pushing forward with the pipeline. A *National Post* article by

Tyler Dawson dated January 10, 2019, deconstructs some of the intricacies and confusion between the two systems of governance:

> Coastal GasLink says it has signed deals with all First Nations along the pipeline route. But it's not quite so simple, because there are 13 hereditary leaders within the five clans that comprise the Wet'suwet'en nation, as well as six elected band councils. Along the routes to the pipeline, clans have set up two checkpoints and have cut off access to the pipeline. On Dec. 14, the British Columbia Supreme Court issued an injunction to allow workers access to the site. And on Jan. 7, the RCMP moved in, arresting 14 people.

The actions of the provincial and federal governments prompted support for the Unist'ot'en and Wet'suwet'en people from Indigenous and non-Indigenous peoples in thirty cities across Canada, and some in the United States rallied to demonstrate their support (Lupick 2019). On the social media platform Facebook statements of support came in from international points such as Mexico, Aoetearoa (New Zealand), and South America. A Facebook post from the Gidimt'en Checkpoint dated Nov 23, 2021, CALL TO ACTION starts with the statement, "Reconciliation Does Not Come At The Barrel of a Gun."[16] This calls attention to the hypocrisy of Canada's actions, which render talk of reconciliation meaningless. Colonial Canada revealed its true colours by totally disregarding its own high court decisions (*CBC News* 2014) that Aboriginal rights and title do exist on lands that were never ceded to any colonial force.

Indigenous Economic Rights

The core issue at the centre of this political debacle is the economics of Indigenous lands. Arthur Manuel (Secwepemc) and Ron Derrickson (Syilx) (2015, 7–8) from the interior plateau regions of British Columbia present the hard facts surrounding the economic reality of who controls the land, which is difficult information for many Canadians to process or digest for a variety of reasons. From my personal experience, I have seen white Canadians balk at the notion that "Indians" can actually live outside of the "poor Indian" stereotypes that prevail in the collective consciousness of many Canadians. For instance, when I first moved back to BC in the mid-1990s, I was still working in television production, and I drove a Toyota 4Runner out of necessity. I was pulled over by the local RCMP, and he asked: "Who owns this vehicle?". When I showed him my ownership and insurance documents, he displayed emotions that I cannot describe here. I truly believe, many racist Canadians would prefer we stay on the measly land bases that we have been assigned and that we remain invisible and poor. As Manuel and Derrickson point out, those "measly land bases" are indeed very small:

> Indigenous lands today account for only 0.36 per cent of British Columbian territory. The settler share is the remaining 99.64 per cent. In Canada overall, the percentage is even worse, with Indigenous peoples controlling only 0.2 per cent of the land and the settlers 99.8 per cent. With this distribution of the land, you don't have to have a doctorate in economics to understand who will be poor and who will be rich. (Manuel and Derrickson, 2017, 25)

With these statistical facts, surely any critical thinking person has to question why corporate Canada is so averse to revenue sharing arrangements with Indigenous peoples and communities. Confronting the current colonial economic and political reality that, on the one hand, continues to enhance the lives of settlers, while, on the other hand, continues to restrict and maintain below poverty levels in the lives and futures of Indigenous peoples and nations, one has to ask: Why does this power dynamic continue to be perpetuated? Manuel and Derrickson (2015) propose financial strategies that could shape the settlement of the long-standing debt that settler Canadians owe Indigenous peoples for the centuries of profits that corporate Canada has accumulated by exploiting Indigenous peoples, lands, and resources. It is necessary to note that colonial and Indigenous epistemologies of how to create a sustainable existence on the land belong to two different paradigms. However, because the colonial political and economic calculus currently dominates and controls who has the right to access and occupy the land and decide how the land is treated, an illogical justification of corporate Canada's privilege prevails as the narrative of the land. This illogical approach has the privileged elite of settler corporate Canada constructing a problematic narrative that Indigenous peoples are asking for charity rather than telling the truth that the colonial state illegally claims the rights to their vast territories and resources and refuses to recognize the theft of their land. As Manuel and Derrickson (2015; 2017) propose, there needs to be a financial solution for the wealth appropriated by corporate Canada to be at the very least shared with Indigenous peoples to lift them out of the cycle of poverty created by the generations of settler colonial governments.

Dealing with the hard issue of Indigenous economic rights would be a form of true reconciliation with Indigenous peoples for the cumulative theft of Indigenous lands (Manuel and Derrickson 155–66; 2017, 293–96). Settler colonizers are not accustomed to Indigenous peoples speaking to them in their own language of profits, losses, and return on investments.

Throughout colonial history, government spin doctors have counted on the general population's lack of understanding of economic principles when it comes to the financial relationship between Indigenous people and settler governments. The manipulation of public opinion has convinced Canadians that Indigenous peoples are a financial burden to taxpayers – a repeated refrain made by the settler government – when in fact Indigenous lands and resources finance the wealth and power of settler peoples and corporations. This is more of the political skulduggery that inserts a wedge between Indigenous and settler peoples and freezes the discussion in a place of stagnation. Promoting this racist settler point of view embeds incorrect assumptions and contributes to a very superficial financial analysis. I have never read an analysis that speaks to how much of our Indigenous dollars go toward funding the salaries of the fat-cat bureaucrats in large urban centres who in fact do not uphold their fiduciary responsibilities to Indigenous peoples but rather continue to perpetuate racist colonial practices while they line their own pockets with Indigenous dollars.

Colonial land appropriation is not part of the past. On May 29, 2018, Canada bought the Kinder Morgan pipeline for $4.5 billion (Morgan 2018), which indirectly lays responsibility for this project on the shoulders of Canadian taxpayers. The topic of money requires serious consideration for any reconciliation to occur between Indigenous peoples and the colonial governments that assume the privilege and entitlement to their ancestral lands. Canadians and corporate Canada have benefited for centuries from the expropriation of Indigenous lands and the extraction of natural resources, without any revenue flow back into Indigenous communities. In that scenario of David-and-Goliath economics, Indigenous peoples and communities have suffered in poverty because of the lack of revenue sharing from profits made from their lands and resources. Is it not time for Canada to change that skewed relationship? Some Indigenous thinkers have put forward concrete solutions to the problem of settler exploitation of Indigenous peoples and their ancestral lands.

Manuel and Derrickson (2015) bring clarity to the Indigenous perspective on the economics of land, resource, and revenue sharing issues. The brilliance of their work is that not only do they deliver a financial analysis from an Indigenous perspective but they also relate it in terms that are understandable to laypeople while at the same time bringing the discussion to a domain that settler Canadian governments and corporations understand – the realm of dollars and cents.

In the chapter "Taking It to the Bank: Accounting for Unpaid Debt," Manuel and Derrickson (2015, 155) say that "the new reality [is] that Indigenous rights are not simply human rights, they are economic rights as well." They go on to ask some critical questions (155):

> Given the evidence, international economic institutions were recognizing what Canadian government refused – that we indeed have economic rights on our territories. The question then was: What does Aboriginal title mean for the larger Canadian economy, and what are the real implications to Canada's refusal to recognize it?

Political and economic certainty is what Canadian governments want to project to the international domain of economics. Manuel brings some stark reality to the situation. In New York City he met with Standard and Poor's, the agency that determines the credit rating of countries in the international capitalist system. Manuel was also a lawyer, and he cut through layers of legal interpretations of high-level financial wrangling to reveal yet another political and economic deception by the BC government. He disclosed that 40 percent of Indigenous peoples in British Columbia are not willing to negotiate away their Aboriginal rights and title. In contrast, when filling in the forms to establish their credit rating, the BC government was using only the Nisga'a treaty,[17] formally called the Nisga'a Final Agreement Act, as an indicator for political certainty. The Nisga'a comprise only one of approximately 200 Indigenous nations in British Columbia, with over thirty distinct languages; thus it became apparent that the information used to determine the province's credit rating was sorely lacking in facts, if not an outright lie (Manuel and Derrickson 2015, 155–59).

Manuel discusses the political and financial certainty of Canada in terms of the nation-state's political and legal relationship to Indigenous peoples. He shows how the international capitalist market system relates to the extraction of resources and profit making on Indigenous lands in Canada. He said that, in fact, it is the Crown title that is a burden on Aboriginal title and rights, not the reverse. He made this statement to fellow activist Rita Wong at a political rally in Vancouver (R. Wong, personal communication, June 2017).

So, is it not time for the Canadian state to institute a paradigm shift in the colonial narrative in terms of how it relates to Indigenous peoples and their ancestral lands? A paradigm shift by the federal and provincial governments would include a substantive revenue sharing process, which would be a step toward true reconciliation between Indigenous peoples and their settler colonizers. A paradigm shift in the economic domain that is based on decisions that would benefit all Canadians by moving toward perpetuating life on the lands and waters, rather than leaving a path of destruction. Given the state of global climate change, Indigenous and non-Indigenous allies recognize that the political actions of many Indigenous people and leaders are for the benefit of all peoples (Ducklow 2019), including the children and grandchildren of the politicians who seem oblivious to the environmental consequences of their actions. Faced with Canada's military actions against Indigenous peoples in January 2019, however, is it possible to conceive of a new narrative of relationship building in an environment that does not truly recognize diversity or the distinct place that Indigenous peoples have on these lands?

On September 30, 2021, colonial Canada exposed more of its real face when the man sitting in the highest political office showed his disrespect and disregard for the Indigenous peoples of this country by not attending the first-ever National Reconciliation Day proceedings at Tk'emlúps te Secwepemc. This Secwepemc community is where 215 unmarked graves of Indigenous children lie on the grounds of a former residential school. That day, Prime Minister Justin Trudeau destroyed any meaningful reconciliation efforts when he chose instead to take his family on vacation to a beachfront recreation property near Tofino, BC. His actions spoke louder than his empty words on the campaign trail announcing that reconciliation with Indigenous peoples was a priority for the Liberal Party. He truly is the white man with forked tongue!

Since the 215 graves were revealed, hundreds, some say thousands, of unmarked graves of Indigenous children have been uncovered at residential schools across these lands. Canadians rallied in Tk'emlúps (Kamloops) when this news was released on May 27, 2021. I was touched by the actions of many Canadians who illustrated that they have finally heard our truth as Indigenous peoples on these lands. I had heard the stories of kids being buried at residential schools since I was a child. A number of political actions brought me to tears, but it was a convoy of 215 truckers (Klassen 2021) who drove into Tk'emlúps that was so visible and touched my heart deeply. I have to be optimistic and believe that these Canadians who were moved to action will stand up to the deception of colonial Canada's story on these lands. This horrific reality of Indigenous peoples has shifted the dialogue between Indigenous and settler peoples. Now, it may be possible to co-create a new narrative for these lands known as Canada – one that is fair and equitable for Indigenous peoples.

A New Narrative for a Different Relationship

In a global world where "deceptive utopias, political cynicism, and public apathy" (CBC Radio 2017) exist and where we are all "in search of a better world," a realistic new model of relating between Indigenous peoples and settler colonists is the next step. Regan's (2010) new path of coexistence, Barker and Battell-Lowman's (2015) new approach to settler identity, and Manuel and Derrickson's (2015) proposal for Canada to share revenue provide the cornerstones of the framework of a new model of relationship. This model moves away from the very tired old binary system of colonialism that privileges Euro-Western epistemologies and upholds whiteness at the top of the pyramid in the hierarchy of race.

It is essential that the issue of land and its resources be a central component of any new framework because it is the most crucial concern that stands between Indigenous and settler peoples. For Indigenous peoples, land holds cultural knowledge through their place-based stories, while for settler peoples, their colonial narrative legitimizes their place on the land through centuries of political skulduggery. Settlers erased Indigenous peoples and their place-based stories from their history books and did not include the place of Indigenous peoples in their education curriculums. I suggest that Indigenous place-based stories and settler colonial stories are competing narratives that are at the core of social and political tensions that exist in Canada's very colonial political landscape.

Practical and real changes that would be effective include implementation of policies and practices that recognize that the Indigenous knowledge that shapes the place-based stories of Indigenous communities and nations is very different from the Euro-Western knowledge system, particularly when it comes to land. When looking for common ground that could possibly lead to solutions, Edward Chamberlin (2004) asked years ago: "If this is your land, where are your stories?" A truthful answer to this question would reflect a substantial change, which could ease tensions and bring clarity to the confusions that arise when Euro-Western knowledge and Indigenous knowledge(s) meet at the cultural interface.

Recently, I met a man who grew up in my traditional homelands. He told a story about his grandfather being one of the first settler men in the region and how his grandfather had a solid relationship with the local Indigenous peoples. During the Spanish flu pandemic, his grandfather was treated by the medicines of our lands, and he lived. I daresay, there are intergenerational relationships between Indigenous/Secwepemc/Syilx and early settlers that remain strong today. We never hear the voices of those early settlers who have grown to love the land like their Indigenous landlords. But we do hear the voices of the settler politicians, which are based on their actions.

British Columbia became the first jurisdiction in Canada to make a substantive step toward what could be considered a real reconciliation on November 28, 2019. On that date, the Legislative Assembly of British Columbia unanimously adopted the Declaration on the Rights of Indigenous Peoples Act, 2019, thus enshrining the United Nations Declaration on the Rights of Indigenous Peoples (UNDRIP) into law. The province issued an action plan with eighty-four specific actions, which will require the immense patience and understanding from both sides of the colonial fence to achieve any real trickle-down change in our communities.[18] The visionary politicians who brought it forward obviously understand the need for a different relationship with Indigenous peoples; however, do the bureaucrats who have the power to initiate a paradigm shift in policies and procedures understand what that will entail? Or will they continue to work behind the scenes to thwart any positive steps toward change?

Two years later, on June 21, 2021, Canada's federal political body gave royal assent to the United Nations Declaration on the Rights of Indigenous Peoples Act in their legislative chambers, which came into force immediately.[19] Both these political actions are new to both the province of British Columbia and the nation-state of Canada. A shift to a truthful colonial narrative, one that moves beyond centuries of political and economic deceptions and acknowledges the foundations of a white supremacist ideology as the way settler colonial governments engage with Indigenous peoples, would indeed be a meaningful first step to an authentic reconciliation. It remains to be seen whether there will truly be an authentic reconciled relationship established between Indigenous peoples and the settler governments – one that brings political and economic reconciliation – or whether the political skulduggery will continue. The question remains: What stories will these lands perpetuate seven generations from now?

Notes

Epigraph: Adam Joseph Barker and Emma Battell-Lowman, *Settler Identity and Colonialism in 21st Century Canada* (Halifax: Fernwood, 2015): 48.

1 "Turtle Island" is a term commonly used among Indigenous peoples to describe what settler peoples know as "North America."

2 I was on the front lines of both the 1990 Oka Crisis and the 1995 Gustafsen Lake standoff, offering my skills in communications to get the Indigenous side of the story out to the world.

3 https://www.justice.gc.ca/eng/declaration/index.html.

4 https://laws-lois.justice.gc.ca/eng/acts/J-0.8/.

5 Historically for Indigenous peoples, a "runner" is one who literally runs from community to community to deliver news. In this case, Beaucage was delivering a message from the Indigenous arts communities to the arts sector agencies in Canada.

6 Lee Maracle has written over thirty books of fiction, non-fiction, and poetry, and has edited numerous anthologies.

7 https://iso-bea.ca/news-events/2024/03/14/statement-by-kerry-swanson-ceo-of-indigenous-screen-office-in-response-to-ongoing-funding-confirmation-by-the-government-of-canada/#:~:text=Today%2C%20the%20Honourable%20Pascale%20St,%2413%20million%20per%20year%20ongoing.

8 I originally made this statement in 2002, when my thirteenth-generation settler-ally-friend Victoria Freeman and I were invited to Caux, Switzerland, to speak at a UNESCO-sponsored peace conference, where I stated that the colonization process is brutal and that both sides of the colonial coin have healing work to do.

9 This phrase is most often attributed to Duncan Campbell Scott, but in 2013 Mark Abley's *Conversations with a Dead Man: The Legacy of Duncan Campbell Scott*, disputed that fact. See the *Maclean's* book review by Andrew Stobo Sniderman (2013).

10 The title of this section is Malissa Phung's (2011) question in her chapter of the same title in *Cultivating Canada*.

11 The novel was made into a TV mini-series in 2015.

12 I was told this oral history while researching Native-Chinese relations in the 1990s.

13 See Sanders (2017) for coverage by the Winnipeg *Free Press*.

14 *Delgamuukw v British Columbia*, [1997] 3 SCR 1010.

15 *Indian Act*, RSC, 1985, c I-5.

16 See, for example, Facebook postings from this period that are no longer accessible, such as Gidimt'en Checkpoint dated November 23, 2021. https://www.facebook.com/photo.php?fbid=2251145481604934&set=a.674286982624133&type=3&eid=ARDq11ahZ5TA_0KNKyDQSWfBFQCaY-stTH7Inr5TFvRo2OELgio_o6dQh1-llQKVwMihBzAd-pjmJMK1 (accessed June 10, 2020).

17 https://www.bclaws.gov.bc.ca/civix/document/id/complete/statreg/99002_01#:~:text=Treaty%20and%20land%20claims%20agreement,of%20the%20Constitution%20Act%2C%201982.

18 https://news.gov.bc.ca/releases/2022IRR0018-000457#:~:text=British%20Columbia%20made%20history%20on,(Declaration%20Act)%20became%20law.

19 https://www.justice.gc.ca/eng/declaration/about-apropos.html#:~:text=On%20June%202021%2C%202021%2C%20the,Canada's%20relationship%20with%20Indigenous%20peoples.

References

Alfred, Taiaiake. 2016a. *Reconciliation as Recolonization Talk*. Video, 47:48. https://www.youtube.com/watch?v=LEiNu7UL7TM.

— 2016b. *T Alfred 20sept 2016*. Audio recording of excerpts of Dr. Taiaiake Alfred's public lecture "Reconciliation as Recolonization." Internet Archive, https://archive.org/details/TAlfred20sept2016.

Archibald, Jo-Ann. 2008. *Indigenous Storywork: Educating the Heart, Mind, Body, and Spirit*. Vancouver: UBC Press.

Barclay, Barry. 1990. *Our Own Image*. Auckland, NZ: Longman Paul.

— 1999. "The Vibrant Shimmer." *Contemporary Pacific* 11 (2): 390–413.

— 2003a. "Celebrating Fourth Cinema." Lecture presented at the Film and Media Studies Department, Auckland University, New Zealand, July 2003. *Illusions Magazine*, 1–11. http://www.maoricinema.com/wp-content/uploads/2014/02/BarclayCelebratingFourthCinema.pdf. https://www.academia.edu/4905111/Printed_in_Illusions_Magazine_NZ_July_2003_CELEBRATING_FOURTH_CINEMA.

— 2003b. "Exploring Fourth Cinema." Lecture presented at the Re-imagining Indigenous Cultures: The Pacific Islands Summer Institute, National Endowment for the Humanities, University of Hawai'i, Honolulu, September 2003.

Barghout, Caroline, and Bryce Hoye. 2017. "Point Douglas Man Spews 'White Power' Rhetoric through Neighbourhood." *CBC News*, August 28. https://www.cbc.ca/news/canada/manitoba/racism-eritrea-winnipeg-newcomer-family-1.4264988.

Barker, Adam Joseph, and Emma Battell-Lowman. 2015. *Settler Identity and Colonialism in 21st Century Canada*. Halifax: Fernwood.

Barrera, Jorge. 2015. "Harper's 2008 Residential School Apology Was 'Attempt to Kill the Story,' Says Ex-PMO Speechwriter." *APTN National News*, September 10. http://aptnnews.ca/2015/09/10/harpers-2008-residential-school-apology-was-attempt-to-kill-the-story-says-ex-pmo-speechwriter/.

Brown, Wendy. 2006. *Regulating Aversion: Tolerance in an Age of Identity and Empire*. Princeton, NJ: Princeton University Press.

CBC News. 2014. "Tsilhqot'in First Nation Granted B.C. Title Claim in Supreme Court Ruling." June 26. https://www.cbc.ca/news/politics/tsilhqot-in-first-nation-granted-b-c-title-claim-in-supreme-court-ruling-1.2688332.

CBC Radio. 2017. "The 2017 CBC Massey Lectures – In Search of a Better World." August 11. https://www.cbc.ca/radio/ideas/the-2017-cbc-massey-lectures-in-search-of-a-better-world-1.4222812.

Chamberlin, J. Edward. 2004. *If This Is Your Land, Where Are Your Stories?* New York: Penguin Random House.

Christian, Dorothy. 2017. "Gathering Knowledge: Indigenous Methodologies of Land/Place-Based Visual Storytelling/Filmmaking and Visual Sovereignty." PhD diss., University of British Columbia. https://open.library.ubc.ca/cIRcle/collections/ubctheses/24/items/1.0343529.

Columpar, Corrin. 2010. *Unsettling Sights: The Fourth World on Film*. Carbondale, IL: Southern Illinois University Press.

Dawson, Tyler. 2019. "Pipeline Spat Pitting Hereditary Leaders against Elected Band Councils Reveals Intricacies of B.C. Indigenous Governance." *National Post*, January 10. https://nationalpost.com/news/canada/pipeline-controversy -pitting-hereditary-leaders-against-elected-band-councils-reveals -intricacies-of-b-c-indigenous-governance.

de Bruin, Tabitha. 2019. "Ipperwash Crisis." Canadian Encyclopedia, February 6. https://www.thecanadianencyclopedia.ca/en/article/ipperwash-crisis.

Democracy Now! 2019. "First Nations Pipeline Protest: 14 Land Protectors Arrested as Canadian Police Raid Indigenous Camp." January 8. https://www.democracynow. org/2019/1/8/protesters_resist_as_police_raid_protected?fbclid=IwAR2d4eG T8qrLdZN6-ykbLVqSiJyjKTA_UkjBNmqgzPordO1EsI88IGqaA9E.

DiAngelo, Robin. 2018. *White Fragility: Why It's So Hard for White People to Talk about Racism*. Boston: Beacon Press.

Ducklow, Zoë. 2019. "Judy Wilson's Message for Canadians: 'The Land Defenders Are Doing This for Everybody." *Tyee*, January 10. https://thetyee.ca/ Analysis/2019/01/10/Not-What-Reconciliation-Looks-Like/.

Final Report of the Truth and Reconciliation Commission of Canada. 2015. Volume One: Summary. Honouring The Truth, Reconciling For The Future. Toronto: James Lorimer.

Fong, Anthony, and Zamir Saar. 2022. "Canada Needs to Be as Welcoming to Afghan Refugees as It Is to Ukrainians." *The Conversation*, May 25. https:// theconversation.com/canada-needs-to-be-as-welcoming-to-afghan-refugees -as-it-is-to-ukrainians-182363.

Godelmann, Iker Reyes. 2014. "The Zapatista Movement: The First for Indigenous Rights in Mexico." Australian Institute for International Affairs, https://www. internationalaffairs.org.au/news-item/the-zapatista-movement-the-fight-for -indigenous-rights-in-mexico/.

Greenhill, Pauline, and Diane Tye, eds. 1997. *Undisciplined Women: Tradition and Culture in Canada*. Montreal and Kingston: McGill University Press.

Hassannia, Tina. 2017. "The Story of How a New Era of Indigenous Filmmaking Began in Canada." *CBC Arts*, February 24. https://www.cbc.ca/arts/the-story -of-how-a-new-era-of-indigenous-filmmaking-began-in-canada-1.3997754.

Hill, Lawrence. 2007. *The Book of Negroes*. Toronto: HarperCollins Canada.

Idle No More. n.d. "About the Movement." https://idlenomore.ca/about-the -movement/.

Ignace, Ronald E. 2008. "Our Oral Histories Are Our Iron Posts: Secwepemc Stories and Historical Consciousness." PhD diss., Simon Fraser University. https://docs2.cer-rec.gc.ca/lleng/llisapi.dll/fetch/2000/90464/90552/5483 11/956726/2392873/3614457/3615225/3635142/3718931/A96444%2D8_ Appendix_4_%2D_Ronald_Ignace%2C_Our_Oral_Histories_are_our_Iron_ Posts_%2D_A6L6D2.pdf?nodeid=3718520&vernum=-2.

Klassen, Chad. 2021. "VIDEO: More than 215 Trucks Roll Past Former Kamloops Residential School to Show Support for Indigenous Community." *CFJC Today*, June 5. https://cfjctoday.com/2021/06/05/video-more-than-215-trucks-roll -past-former-kamloops-residential-school-to-show-support-for-indigenous -community/.

Kunuk, Zacharias, and Puhipau. 2005. "Dialogue: Puhipau in Conversation with Zacharias Kunuk." In *Transference, Tradition, Technology: Native New Media Exploring Visual and Digital Culture*, edited by Dana Claxton, Stephen Loft, and Melanie Townsend, 42–59. Banff, Alberta: Banff Centre Press.

Lightfoot, Sheryl. 2016. *Global Indigenous Politics: A Subtle Revolution*. London: Routledge.

Lupick, Travis. 2019. "Vancouver among 30 Cities with Rallies Planned in Support of Unist'ot'en Camp and Wet'suwet'en People." *Georgia Straight*, January 7. https://www.straight.com/news/1184711/vancouver-among-30-cities-rallies -planned-support-unistoten-camp-and-wetsuweten-people.

Mackey, Eva. 2016. *Unsettled Expectations: Uncertainty, Land and Settler Decolonization*. Winnipeg: Fernwood.

Manuel, Arthur, and Ronald Derrickson. 2015. *Unsettling Canada: A National Wake-up Call*. Toronto: Between the Lines.

– 2017. *The Reconciliation Manifesto: Recovering the Land, Rebuilding The Economy*. Toronto: James Lorimer.

Masayesva, V. Jr. 2005. "Indigenous Experimentation." In *Transference, Tradition, Technology: Native New Media Exploring Visual and Digital Culture*, edited by D. Claxton, S. Loft, and M. Townsend, 164–77. Banff, AB: Banff Press.

McNeil, Kent. 2013. "Editorial Opinion: Idle No More Deserves Our Thanks." *Toronto Star*, January 27. https://www.thestar.com/opinion/editorialopinion/ 2013/01/27/idle_no_more_deserves_our_thanks.html.

Michel, Katheryn A. 2012. "Trickster's Path to Language Transformation: Stories of Secwepemc Immersion from Chief Atahm School." PhD diss., University of British Columbia.

Monk, Katherine. 2001. *Weird Sex and Snowshoes and Other Canadian Film Phenomena*. Richmond, BC: Raincoast Press.

Morgan, Geoffrey. 2018. "Canada Buys Kinder Morgan's Trans Mountain Pipeline for $4.5 Billion – But Can We Sell It?" *Financial Post*, May 29. https://business. financialpost.com/commodities/energy/ottawa-buys-trans-mountain -pipeline-for-4-5-billion-but-can-it-sell-it.

NFB (National Film Board of Canada). 2017. *Indigenous Filmmaking at the NFB: An Overview*. Toronto: National Film Board of Canada. http://onf-nfb.gc.ca/wp -content/uploads/2017/06/Backgrounder-NFB-IndigenousFilmmaking.pdf. Accessed October 4, 2016.

O'Keefe, Derrick. 2009 "Harper in Denial at G20: Canada Has 'No History of Colonialism.'" *Rabble.ca*, September 28. http://rabble.ca/blogs/bloggers/ derrick/2009/09/harper-denial-g20-canada-has-no-history-colonialism.

Phung, Malissa. 2011. "Are People of Colour Settlers Too?" In *Cultivating Canada: Reconciliation through the Lens of Cultural Diversity*, edited by Ashok Mathur, Jonathan Dewar, and Mike DeGagne, 289–98. Ottawa: Aboriginal Healing Foundation. https://www.ahf.ca/files/cultivating-canada-pdf.pdf.

Raheja, Michelle. 2010. *Reservation Reelism: Redfacing, Visual Sovereignty, and Representations of Native Americans in Film*. Lincoln: University of Nebraska Press.

Regan, Paulette. 2010. *Unsettling the Settler Within: Indian Residential Schools, Truth Telling, and Reconciliation in Canada.* Vancouver: UBC Press.

Roth, Lorna. 2005. *Something New in the Air: The Story of First Peoples Television Broadcasting in Canada.* Montreal and Kingston: McGill-Queen's University Press.

Sanders, Carol. 2017. "Hate Lives Close to Home for Eritrean Family." Winnipeg *Free Press*, August 28. https://www.winnipegfreepress.com/local/hate-lives-close -to-home-for-eritrean-family-441952753.html.

Sehdev, Robinder. 2001. "Anti-Racism and Public Spheres: An Examination of the Politicization of Anti-Racism at the Writing Thru Race Conference, 1994." MA thesis, University of Calgary.

Simpson, Leanne. 2014. "Land as Pedagogy: Nishnaabeg Intelligence and Rebellious Transformation, Decolonization: Indigeneity." *Education and Society* 3 (3): 1–25.

Sniderman, Andrew Stobo. 2013. "The Man Wrongly Attributed with Uttering 'Kill the Indian in the Child': *Conversations with a Dead Man: The Legacy of Duncan Campbell Scott* by Mark Abley." *Maclean's*, November 8. https://macleans.ca/culture/books/conversations-with-a-dead-man-the -legacy-of-duncan-campbell-scott/.

Tator, Carol, Frances Henry, and Winston Mattis, eds. 1998. *Challenging Racism in the Arts: Case Studies of Controversy and Conflict.* Toronto: University of Toronto Press.

Tuck, Eve, and K. Wayne Yang. 2012. "Decolonization Is Not a Metaphor." *Decolonization: Indigeneity, Education and Society* 1 (1): 1–40.

Unist'ot'en Camp. 2019. "Gidimt'en Checkpoint Breached by Armed RCMP and Military, Communications Cut, Moving in to Unist'ot'en." January 7. http:// unistoten.camp/gidimten-checkpoint-breached-by-armed-rcmp-and -military-communications-cut-moving-in-to-unistoten/.

Welch, Mary Agnes. 2019. "Gustafsen Lake Standoff." *Canadian Encyclopedia*, February 4. https://www.thecanadianencyclopedia.ca/en/article/gustafsen- lake-standoff.

Writers' Union of Canada. n.d. "History." https://writersunion.ca/about.

4

Whither Redress?: Interrogating Liberal Multicultural Accounts of Japanese Canadian History

R. Tod Duncan

As a mixed-race Japanese Canadian Sansei/Yonsei,[1] my life has been situated at a curious and confusing intersection in Canadian history. On the one hand, I was raised and educated during a time when Canadian identity has been almost entirely defined by the seemingly uncomplicated idea of multiculturalism. On the other hand, my family history includes a period wherein my mother and her family were interned during the Second World War as well as a period in 1988 that was framed by redress for this injustice against the Japanese Canadian community. I recall the day my mother picked me up from a soccer game holding a simple cardboard tube with red plastic end plugs, containing documents representing the hard-won acknowledgment of the injustice of the internment and announcing some of the government's redress measures. What is peculiar is that a period of ascendant multiculturalism in Canada and the redress of wrongs done to Japanese Canadians have produced within me – shaping my identity – the desire to appropriate those parts of an imagined Japanese-ness that were accepted by my mostly white peers. As a child, I took karate classes and watched *many* ninja movies while simultaneously desiring to reject the Japanese Canadian culture of my mother's family for fear of being different (i.e., I hated Japanese food and feared my grandfather who didn't speak a lot of English). In other words, I developed an innate sense of what level of Japanese Canadian difference would be acceptable to my friends, who were themselves steeped in multiculturalism. When I reflect on these childhood experiences today, it feels impossible to fully analyze the effects multiculturalism and the internment/ redress of Japanese Canadians have had on me.[2]

The impossible task of parsing the emergence of Canadian multicultural- ism and the country's reckoning with the internment of Japanese Canadians suggests that the two are not only closely connected in history but have also produced comparable effects in me. My carefully curated and contra- dictory sense of Japanese Canadian-ness is symptomatic of how Canadian multiculturalism simultaneously praises and prohibits different features of an imagined group identity. I was free to choose characteristics of Japanese- ness that could give me standing and allow me to be accepted among my peers, but I was always careful to avoid those other characteristics that might make this acceptance less certain. In much the same way, the effects of internment/redress have been to make implicit to Japanese Canadians a degree of acceptable and unacceptable difference. Many Japanese Can- adians,[3] for instance, lost their Japanese language skills or were never taught them to begin with. Like many Japanese Canadians, I was never presented with the option of learning Japanese. I was, however, acutely aware that pos- sessing language skills beyond English and French ran the risk of appearing too un-Canadian. The similar effects that multiculturalism and internment/ redress have had in producing liberal subjects provides a framework for understanding the complex relationship between history and identity in the Canadian nation-building context.

The goal of this chapter is to analyze the connection between the emer- gence of Canadian multiculturalism and the internment/redress of Japanese Canadians. Whereas these subjects are commonly considered historically separate, I argue they should instead be examined together as manifesta- tions of specific techniques of liberal governance and, more revealingly, as a site of tension. Multiculturalism and the internment/redress of Japanese Canadians are both forces that have shaped the identity of Japanese Can- adians, in addition to being discursive sites where Japanese Canadians have resisted the ways in which their identities have been shaped by the tech- niques of liberal governance. These techniques have articulated the primacy of the autonomous sovereign subject and have made certain the view of the inevitable march of historical progress. They have continuously reinforced the supremacy of whiteness in Canada by constructing a Canadian national identity rooted in history that has gradually evolved away from the racism of early colonialism and nation building toward a society of equality. Here, racism is located in the past and not something that continues to exist in everyday Canadian society both as an intergenerational effect and as a structural reality for racialized communities. The result is a failure to recognize that past racism lingers as a traumatic effect and lays the groundwork for systemic discrimination in the present. By focusing on multiculturalism and the internment/redress as a site of tension, we can begin to better appreciate how past racism and, often, resistance to it shape the relationship between Japanese Canadians and the broader definition of Canada as a multicultural liberal democracy. This relationship broadly separates Japanese Canadians from Canadians by making internment/redress trauma a uniquely Japanese Canadian experience, which the rest of Canada has no connection to. In effect, the relationship transforms redress into a financial transaction and not an enduring relationship based on a common history.

Multiculturalism, Ideological State Apparatuses, and Liberal Governance

As a starting point for my definition of "multiculturalism," I look to build on the theoretical work of Louis Althusser. His work on ideology and ideological state apparatuses is particularly relevant here. Himani Bannerji (2000) has previously recognized the importance of Althusser's theory of ideological state apparatuses in her work on multiculturalism, which influences the approach I take here. Referring to multiculturalism in Canada, Bannerji (2000, 27) writes that

> multiculturalism is a state sanctioned, state organized ideological affair in Canada. Not just in Orwell's ideologically constructed communist dystopia, but in actual mundane granting/funding, in electoral policies and outcomes, in ethnic fairs and religious celebrations, in court legal defences, this particular variant of multiculturalism organizes the socio-cultural, legal-economic space of Canada.

What I find to be particularly important about her comment is that as an ideology, multiculturalism *organizes*. In effect, multiculturalism structures all of the spaces (both literal and figurative) that we move through. We should be careful, however, not to impose a cause-and-effect relationship between multiculturalism and its organizational impetus. Instead, Bannerji's characterization might be better understood as positing multiculturalism's ability to organize as evidence of its materiality.

In this short section, I will not provide a lengthy genealogy of Althusser's use of "ideology."[4] What makes his examination of the concept useful for an understanding of multiculturalism is that, for him, "an ideology always exists in an apparatus, and its practice, or practices. The existence is material" (Althusser 1971, 166). "Ideology" in this regard is not "ideas." For Althusser, Warren Montag (1995, 62) writes, "ideology, even as it could be said to be imaginary, did not consist of false or illusory ideas 'contained' in the minds of individuals (and still less in some collective mind or spirit) that would then cause them to act in certain ways." Which is to say, ideology is not separate from the material world. Instead, ideology should be understood as necessarily having a materiality: it "is immanent in its apparatuses and their practices, it has no existence apart from these apparatuses and is entirely coincident with them" (63).

That ideology exists only "in its apparatuses and their practices" is essential to understanding multiculturalism. Multiculturalism is not an "idea" per se. Multiculturalism exists at the level of ideological state apparatuses and the practices therein. Specifically, you find multiculturalism manifested in apparatuses such as schools, media, government institutions, the family, and so on. Ideological state apparatuses reproduce the dominant relations in society, more or less, non-violently.[5] Within the ideological state apparatus, ideology organizes space through the interpellation of subjects. Subjects are imbued with an imagined sense of their own autonomy and the social space that they inhabit is reordered accordingly.[6] But because there is no *before* ideology when we consider ideological state apparatuses, "*individuals are always-already subjects*" (Althusser 1971, 176; emphasis in original). Multiculturalism, as an ideology, is not only an inescapable substance reproducing Canadians as liberal subjects but is also the mechanism through which liberal-capitalist power relations are reproduced. By organizing "the socio-cultural, legal-economic space of Canada" (Bannerji 2000, 27), multiculturalism does not exist prior to these ideological state apparatuses. Ideology, instead, is manifested in them by both reproducing subjects and establishing the limits within which these subjects exist. Such limits are structured around the dominant power relations, which in this case are predominantly colonial, white supremacist, and liberal-capitalist in nature. In other words, ideological state apparatuses are the primary techniques of liberal governance and the mechanism through which its subjects are reproduced.

The connectedness between multiculturalism and the internment/redress of Japanese Canadians is no more apparent than in the way a specific group of historians – whom, drawing inspiration from Ian McKay (2000, 632), I will call "liberal-revisionist historians"[7] – have evaluated Japanese

Canadian efforts to write the history of internment/redress from the perspective of their perceived objectivity. While the actual internment of Japanese Canadians demonstrates specific techniques of liberal governance that are worthy of study, I will consider them only briefly here. Instead, my focus is directed more squarely on how multiculturalism and its techniques of liberal governance are apparent in the research and writing on the internment and redress themselves.[8] The ways in which the history of Japanese Canadians has been told are an important ground on which a tension within multiculturalism appears.

Liberal-revisionist historians, through the belief in their own objectivity, have tended to separate themselves from the historical events they are writing about. But like me, they too are writing their histories from *within* the context of Canadian multiculturalism. By claiming objectivity in their histories, they mistakenly ignore the continuum linking the internment to redress, and then again linking internment/redress to multiculturalism. In this chapter, I will show that the ways in which liberal-revisionist and Japanese Canadian historians have written about the internment/redress are a symptom of the tension surrounding the techniques whereby the liberal subject is reproduced within Canadian multiculturalism. Without effectively resolving this tension, Canadians will fail in their attempts to redress the injustices of the past as they relate to Japanese Canadians. What is at stake in the analysis that I am putting forth is not only the need to posit redress as an ongoing relationship that appreciates how history shapes the present, but also the fact that acceptance of this relationship is fundamental to realizing what Bannerji (2000, 2003) has called a "multiculturalism from below."[9]

A productive starting point for interrogating multiculturalism and liberal governance is to look at McKay's work on the topic. Specifically, McKay's (2000, 621) central argument – that we ought to understand Canada's historical development as being characterized by the gradual entrenchment of a liberal order – should be brought into conversation with the tension within multiculturalism and, correspondingly, the writing of internment/redress history. McKay's "liberal-order framework" is meant to read "Canada" anew by recognizing the nation as a "project of rule" that has seen a liberal order established over a specific time and space (621). His reading proposes "to imagine a 'Canada' simultaneously as an *extensive* projection of liberal rule across a large territory and an *intensive* process of subjectification, whereby liberal assumptions are internalized and normalized within the dominion's subjects" (624; emphasis in original). As Mona Oikawa (2012) points out, what McKay's work implores us to do is to view the historical development of Canadian liberal democracy, including the internment and other injustices, as a coherent whole. These events were not "abnormalities, crimes, and mistakes" (McKay 2000, 632), but instead ways through which the liberal order came to be entrenched in the production and reproduction of liberal subjects (Oikawa 2012, 39).

While McKay acknowledges that some might view his historical analysis, or "liberal-order framework," as being susceptible to collapse under the weight of being too state-centric, he stresses that his focus on the development of a liberal order is not meant to appear as a top-down relationship. Instead, for him, the liberal order has developed through the tension between the liberal core and its "resistors" on the periphery (McKay 2000, 641). My analysis takes McKay's argument a step further. Though useful for illuminating the diffuseness of power relations, the core-and-periphery analogy may yet conceal and homogenize the more complicated relationships between individuals and groups found in contemporary Canadian multiculturalism. This is to say, the liberal order may be so pervasive that in the context of multiculturalism, distinguishing between core and periphery becomes a more challenging matter.

While fleshing out the liberal-order framework, McKay cites Fernande Roy, who observes that "the term 'liberalism' simultaneously suffers from semantic overabundance and poverty" (Roy 1988, 45; McKay 2000, 624). Roy (1988, 45) suggests that there is no shortage of scholars who have defined "liberalism" in terms of an attitude of tolerance, openness, and progress, and who have conflated it with capitalism and democracy. Capitalism, for instance, is no doubt connected to liberalism in many ways, but as McKay suggests, it is important to keep these "analytically separate" insofar as it is possible (McKay 2000, 631, note 24).[10] As such, analytically, the liberal order should be viewed as connected to a fundamental process of subjectification: "A liberal order is one that encourages and seeks to extend across time and space a belief in the epistemological and ontological primacy of the category 'individual'" (624).[11] In the tradition of C.B. Macpherson's (1962) "possessive liberalism," McKay contends that the liberal order reproduces the belief that the foundations of knowledge and being are rooted in the notion of the individual. Through the rule of law and property, the liberal order elevates the "individual" by endowing it with rights, to such an extent that it has largely replaced "society" as a socio-political category. The various rights of the individual have come to eclipse the rights of society or groups.

McKay's liberal-order framework provides a lens for understanding not only the national project in Canada but also the role of multiculturalism within it. His concept also illuminates how we might interpret the effects of the incarceration and the breaking apart of Japanese Canadian communities and families, as well as their later expulsion from the west coast of British Columbia. Specifically, the internment dismantled Japanese Canadian communities by dispersing individual families to new spaces. These families were more often than not fractured further when men were sent to road camps elsewhere in British Columbia or to prisoner-of-war camps in Ontario, or when family members were "repatriated" to Japan.[12] The process of breaking apart Japanese Canadian communities would continue well after the formal end of the internment into the redress movement and even now. The processes are, however, more subtle and less recognizable compared with the more overt violence of the internment. Whether through physical separations or through the denial of lived histories, what these processes have in common are the breaking apart of communities and identities in a way that favours the reproduction of a liberal multicultural citizenry.

The liberal-order framework remains visible in the way Canadian multiculturalism functions today. For instance, this framework is apparent in liberal-revisionist historians' assessments of Japanese Canadian attempts to write their own internment/redress histories, coinciding with and following the fight for redress. While this fight has given a voice to a community and brought a history of injustice in Canada to bear on Canadians, liberal-revisionist historians have relegated this voice to a narrow expression that separates Japanese Canadian identity and history from Canadian identity and history as a whole. As such, Japanese Canadians have been shaped as liberal multicultural subjects by and through the work of liberal-revisionist historians. First, the unrecognized transgenerational traumatic effects of internment on Japanese Canadian communities are placed at odds with the ability of Japanese Canadians to document their own histories. Indeed, efforts by Japanese Canadians to think through the trauma of the internment have been dismissed as too emotional or biased to be considered of historical value. Second, multiculturalism as a feature of the modern liberal-order framework disrupts any historical continuity between Japanese Canadians and non-Japanese Canadians because it requires the former to exist within specifically defined limits. Here, multiculturalism, as a function of the liberal-order framework, is at odds with the ability to appreciate the lasting traumatic effects of the internment and, as such, to appreciate the true nature of redress.

While my approach may be somewhat unconventional, my analysis of multiculturalism contributes to existing work critiquing its features and functions (Bannerji 2000; Day 2002; Dhamoon 2009; Haque 2012; Kerner-man 2005; Mackey 2002). However, what my work focuses on is a tension within multiculturalism that is often signalled but not clearly characterized historically. Bannerji (2000, 120) elaborates on the tension that exists within multiculturalism when she writes that "multiculturalism … is not a 'thing.' It is not a cultural object, all inert, waiting on the shelf to be bought or not." Instead, "it is a mode of the workings of the state, an expression of an interaction of social relations in dynamic tension with each other, los-ing and gaining its political form with fluidity" (120). Multiculturalism is not a commodity; instead, it is intimately tied to the historical formation of the Canadian state and to social relations that exist therein. Specifically, as manifested within the ideological state apparatuses, multiculturalism is a symptom of the simultaneous individualizing pressures of the liberal order and the collective efforts of communities like those wherein Japanese Can-adians have been situated.

The notion that ideological state apparatuses are a site of tension is not foreign to Althusser's theoretical analysis. While his investigation of ideol-ogy and ideological state apparatuses implies that for individuals there is effectively no escaping how ideology reproduces them as subjects, it is not meant to suggest that individuals have no means of resistance. In fact, he points out that the basis for understanding ideologies is possible only from the starting point of class struggle (Althusser 1971, 185). Class struggle and resistance are alive within the ideological state apparatuses, and as such within multiculturalism. Ideological state apparatuses are the site where lib-eral governance and resistance meet. They are the site where a state multi-culturalism from above conflicts with a multiculturalism from below.

Canadian multiculturalism has been shaped by the tension between the liberal order and the groups that have sought to resist it. While in some ways multiculturalism is indeed determined by the state, it is often shaped by a resistance to state policies. As Bannerji (2000, 118) writes, we should not forget "that what multiculturalism … gives us was not 'given' voluntarily but 'taken' by our continual demands and struggles." Roy Miki (1998, 106) points to a similar tension where in the early 1980s multicultural policy lacked the ability to manage the systemic racism faced by racialized Canadians. As a function of how the liberal order has developed in Canada, multicultural-ism captures the way the state has sought to manage conflicts and includes, simultaneously, the ways in which diverse social relations have acted within the context of the nation-state in both sanctioned and unsanctioned ways (see Mackey 2002). There is an obvious connection here between McKay's liberal-order framework perspective, which sees a tension between the liberal core and its peripheral resistors, and Bannerji's characterization of the tension within Canadian multiculturalism. Like the liberal-order framework, multiculturalism is not something that can be thought of in purely repressive terms because it has been shaped by the demands, agitation, and protest of those who are often on the fringes of the status quo. It was within this conflicted nature of early multiculturalism that the Japanese Canadian redress movement began to take shape, and "perhaps even thrived on the changes going on" (Miki 1998, 106).

This chapter expands on the critiques of multiculturalism of McKay, Miki, Bannerji, and others by considering the ways in which a response to redress activism can be seen in the work of liberal-revisionist historians. In the same way that the activism of Japanese Canadians fighting for redress should be understood as belonging to the tension within multiculturalism, the liberal-revisionist histories of the internment (and even redress) – written between the early 1980s and now – are instances where the hegemonic Anglo-European culture itself demonstrates a resistance to such changes from below. The work of liberal-revisionist historians on internment and redress demonstrates techniques of liberal governance that reproduce the idea of Canada as a successful multicultural project. It does this by requiring that Japanese Canadians step outside their individual and collective trauma of the internment, thereby denying the impact and effects of this history on the community. In effect, liberal-revisionist historians are active in defining the identity of the Japanese Canadian community in a way that continues to break up and disperse the community. In this instance, the dispersal is not so much spatial as it is socio-historical.

The Multicultural Context of Redress

Multiculturalism, as we know it, did not emerge suddenly with the pronouncements of Prime Minister Pierre Elliott Trudeau in the House of Commons on October 8, 1971 (Canada 1971). And though we might ordinarily trace the rise of multiculturalism to federal government policies in the 1970s and 1980s, it has been shown that an early bureaucracy of multiculturalism – through funding, memoranda, and the creation of government departments – appeared during the Second World War, paving the way for its entrenchment as national policy (Day 2002, 9; see also Abu-Laban and Gabriel 2008, Blanding 2013, Dreisziger 1988, and Meister 2021). Thus, albeit in a slightly different form, some Canadians began to "think" in terms of multiculturalism as far back as the 1940s. This long view of Canadian multiculturalism contrasts with the belief that it was an invention of the 1970s and it helps to reveal some of the mechanisms of diversity that have been present throughout its historical development. Multiculturalism is embedded in the historical development of the Canadian nation-state and its apparatuses, and has always been a way of managing difference, often through processes of exclusion.

From the early 1960s, with the Royal Commission on Bilingualism and Biculturalism, to the July 21, 1988, Canadian Multiculturalism Act,[13] there was an intensification of multiculturalism characterized by both increased presence in government discourse and greater activism on the part of minority groups. I use the word "intensification" not only to challenge the perception that multiculturalism in Canada developed progressively but also to emphasize the transformation in the techniques of governing diversity, which moved from direct (i.e., internment) to more subtle forms (i.e., through the ideological state apparatuses and, more specifically, through the governing of historical narratives).[14] While such a notion of gradual progress – dialectical or otherwise – may seem like an obvious way to characterize the development of multiculturalism, this is not my intention. In characterizing a tension within the liberal-order framework of multiculturalism, I am not suggesting that its inherent conflicts will lead to its gradual perfection. To suggest so would only reinforce the notion that Canadian multiculturalism has been an intentional project, the culmination of which we are still moving toward. As Étienne Balibar (1991a, 86) argues, the perception of a "project" being fulfilled over time is integral to the "illusion of national identity":

> The illusion is twofold. It consists in believing that the generations which succeed one another over centuries on a reasonably stable territory, under a reasonably univocal designation, have handed down to each other an invariant substance. And it consists in believing that the process of development from which we select aspects retrospectively, so as to see ourselves as the culmination of that process, was the only one possible, that is, it represented a destiny.

National identity is presented as the project and destiny of a national people, and appears to its subjects as a narrative of struggle and the overcoming of this struggle. Since the 1960s, multiculturalism has become the defining characteristic of national identity in Canada. Multiculturalism – read as progress – becomes an essential substance moving throughout the entirety of Canadian history, and its realization in the present is its destiny. Indeed, the notion of "progress" only reproduces liberal ideals of individual, social, political, and economic perfection, and disguises the role peripheral subjects have had in resisting and transforming the dominant narrative.[15] Applied analytically to an interrogation of racist power relations, the idea of multicultural progress would suggest that racism is gradually disappearing. Canadian multiculturalism, in contrast, is not an example of the disappearance of racism, but it demonstrates instead the ways in which racism is changing.

In her study of the 1963–70 Royal Commission on Bilingualism and Biculturalism, Eve Haque (2012) shows how the commission encountered resistance from Indigenous and ethnic minority groups to the government's efforts to envision a bilingual and bicultural Canada based on the nation-building roles of the English and French. Acknowledging some of these protests, the commission's final report proposed that Canada adopt a form of multiculturalism. In 1971, Prime Minister Trudeau presented a compromise on the recommendations of the commission by declaring a policy of "Multiculturalism within a Bilingual Framework" (Canada 1971, 8545). By announcing that Canada was composed of no one single culture, and yet framing the national identity as having two official languages, this policy would only institutionalize a tension between the officially recognized French and English group rights, and fractured and unrecognized minority interests. In other words, within multiculturalism's "bilingual framework," minority groups were without political standing and would only have political status as individuals (Mackey 2002, 66). According to Haque (2012, 225), "the end result was that the individualization of ethnic identity, in contrast to the official-language collectivities, effectively denied any collectively based third-force or third-element claims once and for all." While responding to the resistance of communities, multiculturalism within a bilingual framework reinforces the liberal order that affirms the primacy of the individual *within* multiculturalism.

Throughout the 1970s and 1980s, multiculturalism would only continue to reinforce the status of the individual while still facing activism on the part of communities. During this period, government rhetoric around multicultural policies increasingly revolved around the notion of "rights" (Mackey 2002, 67). In contrast to the period of "Multiculturalism within a Bilingual Framework," the move toward legislating multiculturalism was no longer focused on helping "cultural groups to overcome cultural barriers" (Canada 1971, 8545) that might prevent them from contributing to life in Canada.

This new phase of multiculturalism, instead, sought to facilitate "race relations" where all Canadians have equal rights, combined with a responsibility to improve Canadian society (Mackey 2002, 66–67).

The shift in the discourse around Canadian multiculturalism is usefully understood through the lens of what Balibar has called "neo-racism." He writes that "[neo-racism] is a racism whose dominant theme is not biological heredity but the insurmountability of cultural differences, a racism which, at first sight, does not postulate the superiority of certain groups or peoples in relation to others but 'only' the harmfulness of abolishing frontiers, the incompatibility of life-styles and traditions" (Balibar 1991b, 21).[16] While Balibar's concept attempts to capture the shift in racism (particularly in France) after decolonization, it nevertheless provides insight into the discursive shift described by Mackey. "Race relations," as a form of neo-racism, signals the impossibility or danger of "overcoming cultural barriers" and places the onus on minority communities to find ways to assimilate into the hegemonic white-European culture or, instead, to remain outside it.[17] As I will explain in the next section, this shift toward neo-racism corresponds to the way Japanese Canadians have been required to *overcome* the trauma of the internment in order to be accepted into broader Canadian society. In so doing, this overcoming has meant that the Japanese Canadian traumatic experience has been separated from the broader social conditions that caused it (Oikawa 2012, 88). Being required to overcome this trauma has become a primary condition for gaining legitimacy as someone capable of telling the stories of the internment and redress. This legitimized subject, however, is someone who must deny the collective experience of historical trauma and, as such, is someone who disfigures the collective identity of many Japanese Canadian communities.

The Multicultural Subsumption of Japanese Canadian Redress Activism

It was in 1977 that the Japanese Canadian fight for redress began to take hold. In that year, the Japanese Canadian Centennial Project presented a photo exhibit celebrating 100 years of Japanese immigration to Canada, called *A Dream of Riches: Japanese Canadians, 1877–1977* (Japanese Canadian Centennial Project 1978; Miki 2005, 144). The project gained momentum through the 1980s following the publication of a book version of *A Dream of Riches* in 1978.[18] According to Roy Miki (2005, 317), the multicultural context of the fight for redress was a well-understood reality: redress activists "recognized the power of multiculturalism discourse in bringing to prominence the issue of redress for Japanese Canadians." To push Miki's historical insight further, not only was the redress movement shaped by existing multicultural policies but Japanese Canadians' redress activism had the effect of shaping multiculturalism. There was, in a sense, both a pushing and pulling that characterized the fight for redress that is analogous to the tension from above and below that shapes Canadian multiculturalism.

For instance, within the Japanese Canadian community, the desire for redress took hold in a very specific way: the internment was largely couched in the language of being a violation of the *individual* rights of Japanese Canadians. As Audrey Kobayashi (1992, 2) wrote only a few years after redress: "Between 8 December 1941 and 31 March 1949, Japanese Canadians were uprooted from their homes, deprived of property, possessions, dignity and civil rights, including the rights to work, to travel freely, to vote and, in the case of those who were subsequently 'deported' to Japan, to their status as Canadians." While the loss of all of the above is unquestionably an injustice, notably missing from Kobayashi's initial reflections are the many collective "rights" that were lost by the community: the right to maintain a language identity other than English or French, or the right to not have one's family torn apart. While authors like Miki and Kobayashi have correctly situated redress within the early development of multiculturalism, what they don't examine is how through redress activism and resistances, Japanese Canadians both produced and reproduced individual rights-based, "liberal-order multiculturalism." The redress movement both belonged to and was shaped by a multicultural fervour: their activism was subsumed within multiculturalism. Nevertheless, the Japanese Canadian fight for redress should be understood as a period when Japanese Canadians began to think through their history *as* Canadians. During this period, they were able to engage with their history and community, and to write about Japanese Canadian experiences in their own words.

Despite this earlier period of mostly successful activism, in the aftermath of formal redress on September 22, 1988, liberal-order multiculturalism would become an antagonistic environment for Japanese Canadians and their histories. Multiculturalism, as conveyed in the Canadian Multiculturalism Act, mobilized diversity in merely symbolic and not political ways. As Mackey argues, the act was largely seen as symbolic by the politicians who crafted it. It was designed as a way for Canada to send the signal of diversity and openness to the rest of the world, and to reap the global economic benefits of its inherent multicultural resource (Mackey, 2002, 68–69). Cultural diversity would be mobilized as Canada's competitive advantage within the global economy.

Not only was Japanese Canadian redress won by the activism of Japanese Canadians but it could also be positioned symbolically as evidence of the multicultural resources Canada could offer global capitalism. Being Japanese Canadian came to be *symbolically* acceptable. But as Mackey (2002, 70; emphasis in original) notes, "despite the proliferation of cultural difference, the power to define, limit and tolerate differences still lies in the hands of the dominant group. Further, the degree and forms of *tolerable* differences are defined by the ever-changing needs of the project of nation-building."

Nowhere is this symbolic nature more apparent than in the need for Japanese Canadian culture – which is to say, history – to conform to dominant discourse. Much of the historiography of internment/redress demonstrates how Japanese Canadian researchers and the histories they have written have been given a mostly symbolic status by liberal-revisionist historians. These historians, who represent a core ideological state apparatus,[19] have often and troublingly distinguished their own perceived impartial and objective analyses of the internment from what they believe to be the emotional or narrative accounts that have been written by members of the Japanese Canadian community. Though Japanese Canadians may have the right to produce such histories, their work is often deemed purely narrative. But these historians who have critiqued Japanese Canadian accounts of internment history under the guise of their own "objectivity" reveal a tension within multiculturalism between the symbolic status of "race" as a legitimate category and the collective experience of groups that experience "race" as it has been historically constructed.

In being reduced to symbolic status, Japanese Canadians have been separated from their history, having been both individualized and, effectively, depoliticized. In the context of internment/redress, the autonomous individuals affected by injustice must *overcome* the emotional effect of their historical experience to gain recognition and legitimacy. In other words, the multicultural compromise requires that in order for racialized individuals to gain recognition, they must first disavow any emotional or traumatic attachment to a collective experience of racialization. The liberal-revisionist historians' need for objectivity runs up against the lived experience of Japanese Canadians and leads the latter to raise questions about whether they should be able to participate in shaping their own historical identity.

There is no doubt that the way I am framing my argument in terms of the tension between objective and subjective accounts of history may only exacerbate the perceived difference between liberal-revisionist historians and Japanese Canadian researchers. Nevertheless, this rift as I am outlining it clearly depicts the power relations within multiculturalism. The liberal-revisionist historians' control over internment/redress history has had a profound impact on those Japanese Canadians at the heart of this history, and has also permeated the wider Canadian perception of redress. Through the lens of multiculturalism, the objective separation of Japanese Canadians from their traumatic history has posited the effects of internment/redress as discontinuous.

Objectivity as a Technique of Liberal-Order Multiculturalism

In his pamphlet for the Canadian Historical Association series "Canada's Ethnic Groups," titled *The Japanese in Canada*, historian Peter Ward (1982) draws a distinction between rigorous scholarly research and more "popular" accounts of the internment. While Ward's short essay may not be rigorous scholarship itself, it is one of the first post-internment accounts of this history written by a white liberal-revisionist historian. *The Japanese in Canada* is important for another reason: by equating historical rigour with objectivity, his text explicitly reveals the power relations that existed at a time when Canadian multiculturalism was at its most intense period of debate. Ward situates historical authority among those whose work demonstrates objectivity, while giving only symbolic status to those whose work does not.

This construction of historical authority is revealed in the appendix to *The Japanese in Canada*. Included there are annotated suggestions for further reading that construct difference between the liberal-revisionist historian's so-called objective accounts and the emotional bias of Japanese Canadian authors. Books and articles written by historians like Ward (1978) himself, or social scientists such as C.H. Young and H.R.Y. Reid (1978), and F.E. LaViolette (1948), "argue," "carefully examine," or use "objective description or analysis." In contrast, works emerging from the Japanese Canadian community are discounted as being "largely narrative and descriptive" in the case of Ken Adachi ([1976] 1991), or as "contentious and superficial" in the case of Ann Gomer Sunahara (1981). An exception to this is Takeo Ujo Nakano's (1980) book *Within the Barbed Wire Fence*, which is described as "sensitive and thought-provoking." Nevertheless, for Ward, Nakano's book – a memoir of his time spent in a prisoner-of-war camp in Ontario during the internment – remains merely "description" (Ward 1982, 21).

Ward directs a particularly pointed criticism at Adachi, whose book *The Enemy That Never Was* (1976) is seen to have problems resulting from the author's failure "to consult available Japanese language sources and major archival collections, relying instead on newspapers and other published materials" (Ward 1982, 21). The two alleged deficiencies of Adachi's work should be unpacked. One problem noted by Ward is that Adachi's work failed to use major archival collections. While it may be the case that Adachi could have had access to certain relevant archives, the major government archives containing materials related to the internment were inaccessible at the time of his research. As Sunahara (1981, 2) herself points out, "Adachi could only draw upon published memoirs, the proceedings of inquiries and royal commissions, and other documents in the public domain." The second problem cited by Ward is that Adachi should have consulted Japanese-language sources. Ward does not say why this was necessary. Adachi, who, in his own words, was "born in Canada, brought up on big-band jazz, Fred Astaire and the novels of Rider Haggard," considered himself "to be as Canadian as the beaver" (Adachi 1988). It should not be assumed that for him to be able to write history, he should have to conduct research in what was, for many Nisei, or second-generation Japanese Canadians, like him, effectively a foreign language. This criticism situates Adachi as "Japanese" rather than "Japanese *Canadian*." Ward normalizes the unequal power relations that exist between white academics and Japanese Canadian community researchers and writers. Like liberal-order multiculturalism, Ward sees Adachi's individual "race," but he will do so only in symbolic terms. This is to say, Adachi's "race" is uniform, and not a product of Canada's history and the processes of racialization therein. Ward does the work of liberal-order multiculturalism by constructing Adachi among a group of very carefully imagined Japanese.

A co-authored work by historians Jack Granatstein and Gregory Johnson demonstrates a similar propensity to diminish the work of authors close to the Japanese Canadian community because of a perceived lack of objectivity. In 1986, Granatstein and Johnson presented a "realist" critique of the "received version" of the Japanese Canadian internment story.[20] In developing this critique, they position themselves as realist historians analyzing the proliferation of what they call a "received version" of the events of the internment. They characterize the received version as the dominant narrative through which Japanese Canadian history is told. They name the work of Hugh L. Keenleyside (1982), the aforementioned Adachi and Sunahara, and the National Association of Japanese Canadians (1984) as accounts that have helped to constitute the "received version" (Granatstein and Johnson 1988, 102).

While the term "received version" might be considered a red herring, its use reveals something of the tension in multiculturalism. More specifically, the authors' unqualified use of the descriptor "received" obfuscates the power relations inherent in multiculturalism and their role in reproducing them. By highlighting the problem of the "received version," they shift the critical gaze away from the dangers of the process of differentiating between accounts connected to the Japanese Canadian community and those of liberal-revisionist historians. In deploying the word "received," Granatstein and Johnson reify the idea of a coherent group of writers that has taken up the defence of a particular version of the internment story and who posit Japanese Canadians as the victims of racism. In their own, albeit abbreviated, words (Granatstein and Johnson 1988, 102):

> The popularly accepted version of the evacuation of the Japanese Canadians from the Pacific Coast in 1941–1942 and the background to it runs roughly like this. The white population of British Columbia had long cherished resentments against the Asians who lived among them, and most particularly against the Japanese Canadians ... After 7 December 1941 and the beginning of the Pacific War, public and political pressures upon the Japanese Canadians increased exponentially. Suspected subversives were rounded up by the RCMP in the first hours of the war ... and then escalated through the evacuation from the coast of male Japanese nationals between the ages of 18 and 45 to the removal of all Japanese, whether Canadian citizens by birth or naturalization and regardless of age or sex, into the interior ... These events occurred despite the facts that the RCMP and Canada's senior military officers considered the removal of the Japanese unnecessary, there being no credible military or security threat; that the responsible politicians in Ottawa ... knew that the Japanese Canadians posed no threat to national security and acted out of a desire to pander to the bigotry of some whites or for political motives relating to the conduct of war at home.

Granatstein and Johnson admit this to be a "bald" summary (102), but its "baldness" is not what I take issue with. More important is reflecting on the effects whereby a particular narrative is posited as "popularly accepted" despite its having been contested for over fifty years, until the time Granatstein and Johnson wrote their "realist critique."[21]

With the exception of the personal memoir of the former assistant under-secretary in charge of the American and Far Eastern Divisions within the Department of External Affairs, Hugh L. Keenleyside,[22] it was accounts that came from within the Japanese Canadian community prior to and during the fight for redress that Granatstein and Johnson labelled as the "received" or "popularly accepted" versions. Given the public support that the Japanese Canadian redress movement was beginning to gain at that time, Granatstein and Johnson may have been right about the reception of these narratives. But it is significant that these historians, "whose trade obliges them to rummage with more or less science through the past" (Granatstein and Johnson 1988, 102), believed they had a responsibility to correct these authors. That these narratives are described as "received" or "popular" hides the fact that Granatstein and Johnson's argument presupposes bias in the work of Japanese Canadians and redress activists. Their "realist" critique distinguishes between their own accounts, which use "more or less science," and the "received" accounts of those affected directly by the internment or who, at the time, were actively fighting for redress. The work of those individuals or groups was, as a consequence, "allegedly lacking" this objectivity. Here, participation in a particular history – especially when one's participation is already so constrained by existing power relations – results in one's disqualification from its proper narration.

Granatstein and Johnson's passing remark on the historian's "objectivity" serves a more tactical purpose. In this case, what is at stake in this debate is not necessarily the "facts" that make up these histories (though these, too, are important) but rather the *effects* of these interventions. To that end, the publication of Granatstein and Johnson's intervention coincided with several significant events in Canada in 1988. This was not only the year in which Canadian multicultural policy culminated in the Canadian Multiculturalism Act but also an election year in Canada when the most debated issue was the North American Free Trade Agreement. Most obviously, it was also the year the redress settlement was announced and the Canadian government acknowledged the injustice of the internment of Japanese Canadians during the war. Thus, in 1988 a number of significant historical tensions related to diversity, globalization, and Canadian identity came to prominence (Miki 2005, 10). Granatstein and Johnson's intervention cannot be read outside of this, its own Canadian history. Indeed, some of Granatstein's work can be read as a critique of liberal-order multiculturalism. For instance, he has advocated for Canada's military history to be used to buttress Canadian identity "against an increasingly globalized and homogenized cultural world" (Granatstein 2004, 6). His elevation of the country's military history can be seen as a critique of the political attempts to mobilize multiculturalism for Canada's competitive advantage within an increasingly globalized economy.

Granatstein and Johnson's (1988) article reveals how historical objectivity emerged as a technique of liberal-order multiculturalism. Their

work is reinforced by the long-held belief that "history," as a specific discipline, should be governed by clear rules. Canadian historians debated the
demands placed on the discipline by emerging group identities in the late
1960s and early 1970s, and the debate continues today. Even so, by the time
Granatstein and Johnson's article was published, many prominent historians had already lamented the destruction of Canadian identity resulting
from the proliferation of social, regional, feminist, class, race, and ethnic
histories. These were the so-called limited identities (Careless 1969, 1981),
a set of histories that had been "specialized, fragmented, and ... privatized"
(Bliss 1991–92, 9). Under the guise of historical objectivity, Granatstein and
Johnson's (1988) article is an intervention on behalf of this concern.

Despite their willingness and desire to present their perspectives and
experiences, as well as to carefully analyze the internment and redress,
members of the Japanese Canadian community are perceived to lack objectivity. The process of constructing objectivity thus involves the careful
articulation of historical boundaries. This can be seen as a twofold pressure:
1) Japanese Canadians can have authority writing the history of the internment only if they too become "objective"; and 2) the internment becomes
a Japanese Canadian history and not part of the history of Canadians or
British Columbians. The second boundary is particularly revealing since by
claiming impartiality, the objectivity of liberal-revisionist historians presupposes the idea that white Canadians were not participants in Japanese
Canadian internment history, when in fact they were. This is not to say that
Ward and Granatstein and Johnson have been affected in the same way by
the internment and redress as Japanese Canadians. Instead, however, I think
it's important that we think differently about what it means to be affected
by historical events. For instance, the internment was accompanied by a
significant social and economic upheaval with clear material and structural
consequences that benefited non-Japanese Canadians (Oikawa 2012, 175).
It should be assumed that the effects of internment apply to both Japanese
Canadians *and* non-Japanese Canadians.

Multicultural Objectivity and the Need to Overcome

Such claims to objectivity are not confined to history books published
during the 1980s, in the midst of redress activism. No, the critique of Japanese
Canadian authority in the writing of their own history is still taking place
today. More recent reviews of Mona Oikawa's *Cartographies of Violence*
by Patricia Roy (2014) and Greg Robinson (2013) are examples of the

durability of this strategy. In her study, Oikawa uses interviews with two generations of Japanese Canadian women in order to analyze the long-term and transgenerational effects of the internment: women who had survived the internment and their daughters. In each of their critiques, Roy (2014) and Robinson (2013) make claims about Oikawa's emotional bias, and in doing so delimit the boundaries of so-called scholarly objectivity. While Roy's rebuttal of the work focuses on how Oikawa's attachment to her subject matter detracts from her intended message, Robinson's review is more an attempt to convince the reader of the benefits of the objectivity he brings to writing on Japanese Canadian history as a non-Japanese Canadian.

Robinson, who at the time was the historian-in-residence of the Japanese Canadian community newspaper *Nikkei Voice*, focuses on the following question Oikawa asks of non-Japanese Canadian writers who are studying this history: "Why are you writing about Japanese Canadians?" (Oikawa 2012, 250). He writes that while he "sympathizes" with what he perceives as "Oikawa's irritation" regarding misappropriation of this history, he nevertheless has "a certain feeling of wariness over her injunctions regarding the Japanese Canadian subject" (Robinson 2013, 7). His wariness comes from Oikawa's hope that Japanese Canadian authors recognize how they represent "the Internment and Japanese Canadians," while non-Japanese Canadians think through "their relationship to the Internment and to the people they claim to be re-presenting" (Oikawa 2012, 250). Each – Japanese Canadians and non-Japanese Canadians – has a responsibility to the internment and, I would argue, to a relationship of redress with the Japanese Canadian community. Oikawa's is an essential vision of historical research in a multicultural context. Indeed, her entreaty may be the key to resuscitating a form of critical activism that helped achieve redress for Japanese Canadians, but repurposed for the community's efforts to continuously reshape multiculturalism.

Robinson, in contrast, sees himself as having a responsibility only to the "truth." Indeed, he feels that what he calls "accountability" to the community can be a hindrance and that his scholarship benefits from his distance (Robinson 2013, 7). For Oikawa, however, one's responsibility to the internment and to Japanese Canadians does not mean that we elevate fiction over fact. Instead, she implores authors and historians to understand their own subject positions when creating "re-presentations" of the Japanese Canadian community. Put differently, Oikawa's question might be understood as imploring writers and historians to recognize the history of the internment and redress as *both* a Japanese Canadian *and* a Canadian history. The effects of these histories are myriad and are not specific to Japanese Canadians.

Non-Japanese Canadians and their "re-presentations" of Japanese Canadians are equally implicated in these events and their impacts.

In a similar fashion, Patricia Roy notes Oikawa's personal investment in her research on Japanese Canadians. This leads her to criticize Oikawa for what she calls her "bitterness" and "anger," and to suggest that these emotions "may turn off some readers" (Roy 2014, 223). It is interesting that Oikawa herself analyzed how the words "despair" and "bitterness" in the Canadian War Museum's "forced relocation" display were applied to Muriel Kitagawa's (1985) writings during the internment. That same astute insight works here. While Oikawa (2012, 69) notes how "despair" and "bitterness" evoke a sense of "resignation and even pathology," the word "anger," one might add, suggests a lack of control and the absence of clear thinking. Oikawa's analysis of how Kitagawa has been "re-presented" as a speaking subject within a community constructed as silent can be slightly altered to apply here: the liberal-revisionist historian's critique of Oikawa, the speaking subject, is being used to silence other Japanese Canadian subjects (69). Unless Japanese Canadians are able to speak without bitterness or anger, they should remain silent.

Both Roy and Robinson perpetuate the tendency within the discipline of history to construct the work of Japanese Canadian community members as being too personal to be considered serious scholarship. But unlike the arguments of Ward and of Granatstein and Johnson, whose critiques are directed (for the most part) at Japanese Canadian authors who experienced the internment "directly," in critiquing Oikawa, Roy and Robinson are assessing a study written by a researcher one generation removed from the internment, but who was still involved in the redress movement. For Roy, this makes Oikawa's anger baffling, if not completely misplaced. She writes: "Although Oikawa is much too young to have been directly affected by the 'expulsion' of the Japanese Canadians from the Pacific Coast, her anger at the treatment they endured during and immediately after the Second World War is apparent in the very use of the word 'Violence' in the title" (Roy 2014, 222). That Roy is unable to accept that someone one generation away from being interned could feel anger about these events only betrays a mistaken understanding of history (let alone the effects of psychological trauma), as well as the intent of Oikawa's project in examining the transgenerational effects of these injustices. It also reveals something important about the status of Japanese Canadians within liberal-order multiculturalism.

The fact that Roy places little stock in the fight for redress in her own book *The Triumph of Citizenship* (2007) may be an indication of her motivation. For Roy, the "triumph" affecting Japanese Canadians culminated in the transformation of Canadian immigration policies in 1967, and not in their successful fight for redress (Roy 2007, 309). She argues that it was not the fact that Japanese Canadians were granted the right to vote that allowed them to become "first class citizens" (231), but instead, the moment of their "triumph" was when a policy regarding immigration from Japan to Canada was introduced. Her thesis implies that there was one continuous and amorphous Japanese population made incomplete by a policy that prevented immigration from Japan. It also hides the fact that many Japanese in Canada were in fact Japanese Canadians. Here, Canadian politicians and bureaucrats brought about "triumph," not the resistance and activism of Japanese Canadians.

Roy is unable to locate the originality of Oikawa's accomplishments in *Cartographies of Violence*. According to her, what is new in Oikawa's work is her analysis of the "loss of important intangibles such as the destruction of networks of families and friends, educational opportunities, and language" (Roy 2014, 22). I would suggest that this is not particularly "new" research, since several scholars and authors before Oikawa (most of whom are Japanese Canadian) have written about these losses (Adachi [1976] 1991; Kogawa 1994; Makabe 1998; McAllister 2010; Miki 2005; Sunahara 1981). What Roy misses is how Oikawa, as well as a number of other researchers, demonstrates that these "intangibles" are actually quite *tangible* from the perspective of many Japanese Canadians. You *can* measure how families, friends, education, and language are all lost. These losses are not measured precisely in economic figures, but they are still tangible material losses. The originality of Oikawa's research is that it points to a real intangible: the emotional and transgenerational psychological effect of the internment. In other words, what's new is not the account of the measurable losses themselves, but the long-term effect of these losses on subsequent generations. Unfortunately, these losses are obscured by the elevation of individual rights over those of social groups within liberal-order multiculturalism. The result is bitterness and anger, which for many Japanese Canadians is the key symptom of these losses.

Roy seems unable to appreciate that the effects of the internment did not diminish with the end of the internment or with the successful fight for redress. The intangibility of the internment (and redress) is due to the fact that the psychic and emotional effects of these events are both present *and* immeasurable. That Oikawa, according to Roy, "judges historical actions by the standards of her own time" (Roy 2014, 222) is not a problem; it only demonstrates that the effects of this history are still present today. The effects lived not only by the surviving members of the community who were forcibly removed from their homes but also by those who fought for redress, and by the later generations of children post-redress. For many Japanese Canadians, the internment and redress are part of the *present* and are not simply confined to history (see Kogawa 1994; McAllister 2010; Miki 2005; Oikawa 2012).

History in the Present, or the Emotions of Political Agency

The efforts of certain historians to promote historical objectivity while delegitimizing accounts of the internment that come from the Japanese Canadian community are a symptom of the tension that exists within liberal-order multiculturalism. In his study of the colonial context of Canadian multiculturalism, Dene political scientist Glen Coulthard (2014), writing from the perspective of an Indigenous critique of settler colonialism, argues that the state-sanctioned process of reconciliation for past injustice often requires that survivors of the injustice relegate the events in question to the past. These survivors are expected to *overcome* their histories (22). Under these circumstances, according to Coulthard, "those who refuse to forgive or reconcile are typically represented ... as suffering from this [past injustice], unable or unwilling to 'move on' because of their simmering anger and resentment" (22). Those who have anger and who are "unable" to overcome are characterized as irrational and their work deemed to lack scholarly rigour. While recognizing its theoretical specificity, Coulthard's analysis corresponds with the progress-oriented nature of liberal-order multiculturalism identified by Oikawa and Miki. Specifically, the work of liberal-revisionist historians like Ward[23] and, I would argue, Roy characterizes the racism of the internment as an irrational and temporary breakdown in the development of Canadian democracy. But thinking about Canadian history in such a teleological way obfuscates the effects of the events deemed "temporary." Oikawa cites Bain Attwood, writing: "When past/present historicist temporality presents the Internment as an unusual blip on the Canadian horizon of progress and tolerance, it 'creates a sense of distance between the past and the present that tends to deny the presence of the past'" (Attwood 2005, 248, quoted in Oikawa 2012, 42). Whether it is articulating the need for historical objectivity or writing about injustice as fleeting in the context of the progressive march of the liberal order, the effect is the same: there is a failure to understand that history actually exists in the present.

By establishing such a clear contrast between objective and subjective histories, liberal-revisionist historians like Granatstein, Johnson, Ward, Roy, and Robinson actively exclude the voices of those who know the scope of injustice best. The belief that history should be purged of emotion reveals how such processes are connected to the way national identity is defined. As Carol Schick (2002, 108) has argued, when individuals make claims to strict rationality, reason, and self-control, these act as "markers of civility and the right to govern. Their claims create a distinction between 'us' and 'them' around the ownership and distribution of emotions and intellect." In other words, these claims are used "to secure white entitlement" (108). A national identity emanates from history, but in this case, the history is carefully curated. Because insight into the long-term and transgenerational effects of periods of injustice is often banished from official discourse, we fail to recognize the extent to which such effects of racism continue to shape both multiculturalism and national identity. Instead, historians frame the history of Japanese Canadians as "the triumph of citizenship" or encapsulate the history of British Columbia as moving from "exclusion to inclusion."[24] These liberal notions of gradual historical progress also hide the fact of continuously existing racism.

In much the same way that the history of injustice continues to exist in the present, so too does the need for acknowledgment and redress. Both involve recognizing that the internment continues to have lasting effects on Japanese Canadians and non-Japanese Canadians alike. We should acknowledge that the writing of history can benefit from inclusion of the voices of the so-called angry. On this issue we can learn from Coulthard's (2014) aforementioned study and his theoretical interventions. In his theorization of the emotional responses of Indigenous people to state-guided reconciliation efforts, he provides a potent critique of the techniques of liberal governance associated with Canadian settler colonialism. And while his work, drawing on Frantz Fanon, is specific to the colonial experiences of Indigenous peoples, the theoretical framework that he develops can be used to effectively understand how techniques of liberal governance, rooted in a history of settler colonialism, have been resisted by Japanese Canadians' emotional response to the internment and their activism around redress. As he argues, emotions such as anger and bitterness exist at the foundation of resentment and can play a positive role in strengthening community.

In contrast to Nietzschean *ressentiment,* which is disempowering and impotent, *resentment,* as rooted in the work of Fanon and Jean Améry, is anger as a political expression against structures that reproduce violence

(Coulthard 2014, 109) in the form of racism, inequality, and forgetting. This is not to deny that anger can, at times, be unproductive, but rather to suggest that authors interrogate how they represent anger and recognize the effects this label has. As Coulthard (2014, 22) suggests, anger can be a sign of a "critical consciousness." I would argue that this critical consciousness is a necessary component of political agency. Anger is what brought about the acknowledgment of the injustice of the internment in the form of redress. In that sense, multiculturalism can be further shaped by recognizing that political agency is the creative embodiment of emotion.[25] Likewise, multiculturalism is strengthened by appreciating the immanence of history in subject identities. The failure to appreciate this only reproduces a gulf between what are constituted as Canadian and Japanese Canadian identities.

To think through why a Japanese Canadian who did not live through the internment would become so "bitter," as Roy puts it, we must think about the intangible effects of the internment. The problem with many liberal-revisionist historian accounts of the internment, with their insistence on differentiating between objective history and narrative bias, is that they do not acknowledge that the internment has had lasting effects on Japanese Canadians, and, I would insist, on Canada more generally. More cynically – and we should hope that this is not the case – it could be perceived that these historians are arguing that anger and bitterness, what I've equated with the transgenerational effects of the internment, should disqualify Japanese Canadians from attempting to analyze their own histories. Canadian history as a whole will not benefit from such exclusions. The internment would become merely a Japanese Canadian history, but one that Japanese Canadians are unable to write themselves. Historical objectivity does not bring us closer to "truth," but only obfuscates how the identities of some are limited by others within liberal-order multiculturalism.

In a speech presented in 2004, sixteen years after he and Johnson had their intervention published, Granatstein announced that at the Canadian War Museum – where he was director and CEO from 1998 to 2000 – history that gets the "right things right" (Granatstein 2004, 7) had finally "turned a corner" (11).[26] In the aftermath of formal redress, we should see his feeling of relief as a warning. His vision of Canadian history has largely succeeded. Patricia Roy is one of the most prominent scholars of Asian Canadian history and Greg Robinson writes for a Japanese Canadian community newspaper and is an invited speaker at community events.[27] More recently, a significant federal research grant (from 2014 to 2021) was awarded to a group of largely white scholars studying Japanese Canadian dispossession during the internment. The funded research project, called "Landscapes of Injustice," involved few Japanese Canadian scholars.[28]

For Japanese Canadians and their allies contemplating research on internment, redress, and/or multiculturalism, the aforementioned interventions should not be taken for granted. Insofar as they continue to proliferate, they will continue to influence Canada's multicultural identity and will work to discipline groups that exist outside the status quo. The research and writing on internment/redress is an example of the terrain on which multiculturalism is fought over and influenced. It is, likewise, a site of knowledge production that will lead to either domination or liberation. Rather than reproduce the racism that for Japanese Canadians denies the connection between their present and their past, anti-racist researchers and writers should use the past to liberate their present. Granatstein – of all historians – provides an insight that can be used to guide activist researchers who wish to produce histories that challenge the work of the historians who reproduce liberal-order multiculturalism: "History is memory, inspiration and commonality and a nation without memory is every bit as adrift as an amnesiac wandering the streets. History matters, and we forget this truth at our peril ... If *we* have no past, then surely it must follow that *we* have no future" (Granatstein 1998, xviii; emphasis added). We should certainly heed Granatstein's words but with the caveat that remembering history should not necessitate obscuring or obfuscating the emotion embodied in that past.

Notes

1 I define myself as a Sansei/Yonsei, or third-/fourth-generation Japanese Canadian, on account of the fact that my grandfather was Issei (first-generation), while my grandmother was Nisei (second-generation).
2 While I recognize the problematic nature of conflating "internment" and "redress" as "internment/redress," I will do this throughout this chapter because in doing so, I'm signalling a history that is "bookended" by the events of the internment and redress. In the same way others have argued that the internment was connected to a broader anti-Asian sentiment in Canada (among others, Roy 2007; Sunahara 1981; Ward 1978), I argue here that redress and racism continue from this history. Neither the internment nor redress can be properly understood as mere isolated "events."
3 I should specify that I'm using a fairly narrow definition of "Japanese Canadians" here. For my argument, I am, not unproblematically, referring to Japanese Canadians as those whose families experienced the internment. The Japanese Canadian community as a whole is more diverse than this and includes a number of people who have had no experience of the internment or redress.

4 Other authors have done excellent work tracing Althusser's definition of "ideology" and the "ideological state apparatuses." For instance, readers can look to the work of Judith Butler (1997a), Terry Eagleton (1991), and Warren Montag (1995, 2013), among others.

5 In Althusser's work, ideological state apparatuses are contrasted with the repressive state apparatuses such as the police or military. Althusser (1971, 145) indicates that the repressive state apparatuses function primarily by repression and secondarily by ideology, whereas the ideological state apparatuses function primarily by ideology and secondarily by repression. We might contrast this "double functioning" with the dualism of coercion and consent of Antonio Gramsci's analysis of "hegemony" (Montag 1995, 69).

6 Althusser (1971, 173) writes "all ideology ... interpellates concrete individuals as concrete subjects." There is an entire history associated with defining the concept of "interpellation," not to mention debate about what it means. Suffice to say, I subscribe to Althusser's view (1976, 135 and 1997, 7) that a complete theory of ideology (and, in turn, a theory of interpellation) can be found in Baruch Spinoza's *Ethics* (1992). Ideology in this regard produces a subject who imagines himself as an autonomous actor who affects the reality around them rather than being affected by it. As Judith Butler (1997b, 33) notes, "[t]he mark interpellation makes is not descriptive, but inaugurative. It seeks to introduce a reality rather than report on an existing one; it accomplishes this introduction through a citation of existing convention." In the context of liberal capitalism, ideology interpellates individuals as, among other things, autonomous liberal subjects who then see their lived reality as one that is naturally ordered according to their independent beliefs and needs.

7 Ian McKay (2000, 632) makes a brief reference to the tendencies of "revisionist Canadian history" and its tendency to discount past injustices as anomalous in the development of the Canadian liberal nation-state. Following McKay, I use the term "liberal-revisionist historians" to characterize a group of historians who have questioned the objectivity of Japanese Canadians in the writing of internment/redress history. The work of these liberal-revisionist historians is "liberal" in the sense that it attempts to perpetuate the notion of liberal progress in Canadian history. Their work generally characterizes the gradual perfection of the Canadian state, which moved away from past injustices toward a nation-state that values above all else human rights and freedom. At the same time, these historians are "revisionist" insofar as the progress and gradual perfection of the nation-state require that the internment and other periods of injustice be treated as anomalies or exceptions in the liberal nation-building project.

8 Importantly, other authors have made note of how the use of specific euphemistic language and discourse around the "rules" of writing Japanese Canadian history have been used to reproduce particular Japanese Canadian subjects. See Audrey Kobayashi (1992, 1992–93) and Mona Oikawa (2012), in particular.

9 Himani Bannerji (2000, 2003) has made the distinction between "multiculturalism from above" and "multiculturalism from below." The theoretical framework for the former is based on Louis Althusser's (1971) formulation of the ideological state apparatuses, while the framework for the latter is based on Antonio Gramsci's (1971) discussion of civil society. As I suggest later in this chapter, "multiculturalism

from below" can be rooted in Althusser's (1971, 185) work entirely insofar as the ideological state apparatuses are sites of conflict between ruling ideology and the ideologies of repressed classes. The implicit notion of power that develops from Bannerji's framing of multiculturalism, as some have argued, has parallels to Michel Foucault's work (Bakan and Dua 2014, 123; see Foucault 1990).

10 This is another instance where making a clean separation between the ideological and the material proves difficult, since liberalism and capitalism mutually reproduce one another. The existence of autonomous individuals who possess the right to sell their labour power is a necessary foundation to capitalism. And yet, the structure of capitalism constantly reproduces the idea that individuals are autonomous in their everyday existence. The need for an analytical separation, however, is to avoid confounding it with capitalism (McKay 2000, 624).

11 The need to analytically separate liberalism (with its elevation of the autonomous individual, freedom, and progress) from capitalism overlaps with the study of the reproduction of the individual within capitalism. A fruitful theoretical architecture for this endeavour can be found in the marriage between the ethical system developed by Baruch Spinoza (1992) and the political economy work of Karl Marx in *Capital* (1990). In particular, Althusser (1971), and his study of ideology, is vital here. For further insight see works by Warren Montag (2013), Jason Read (2024), and Hasana Sharp (2007).

12 See works by Adachi (1976), Kobayashi (1992), Miki (2005), Nakano (1980), Oikawa (2012), and Sunahara (1981), among others.

13 *Canadian Multiculturalism Act*, RSC 1985, c 24. https://laws-lois.justice.gc.ca/eng/acts/C-18.7/index.html.

14 Jeffrey Nealon's (2008) work looking at Michel Foucault's conception of power and its "intensifications" has influenced my thinking on multiculturalism here.

15 Matt James (2013) has taken this further, arguing that in redressing past racism and exclusions, the government has reframed these injustices within a discourse of "contributions to building Canada." These past events are thus reinscribed "as signposts of national progress and triumph" (37–38).

16 Several other authors have made note of the development of a "new racism" (Barker 1981; Foucault 2003; Goldberg 1993). My dissertation (forthcoming) expands on this idea by looking at the internment of Japanese Canadians as an exemplary and formative moment for the development of "new racism" in Canada. Liberal-order multiculturalism, as one can begin to see here, is intimately entwined with this "new racism."

17 Audrey Kobayashi has developed an insightful critique of the notion of "race relations" in her assessment of the Japanese Canadian redress settlement and the creation of the Canadian Race Relations Foundation. She writes that "by legitimizing rather than challenging the concepts of 'race' and 'race relations,' even among those who do not practice overt racial discrimination, it has the potential of actually producing the very social relations of racism that are meant to be eliminated" (Kobayashi 1992, 8).

18 A clearer picture of how the activism around redress developed among Japanese Canadians can be found in Roy Miki's important book *Redress: Inside the Japanese Canadian Call for Justice.*

19 For more on the special significance of the educational ideological apparatus, see Althusser (1971, 152).

20 According to the editors of the anthology, all the chapters, including Granatstein and Johnson's article, were first presented at a symposium called "Ethnicity, the State, and War: Canada and Its Ethnic Minorities, 1934–1945," held at Queen's University in September 1986 (Hillmer et al. 1988, ix).

21 It is interesting to note that Peter Ward's overall thesis – that a racist psychology among white citizens of British Columbia and politicians in Ottawa led to the internment of Japanese Canadians during the war – was not named by Granatstein and Johnson as they interrogated the "received" version, even though this text would have been available to them at the time. Also important, Granatstein and Johnson (1988, 102) admit that the conflation of these works as the "received version" does gloss over "the variations of emphasis of these accounts."

22 Keenleyside has an important status within Japanese Canadian history, as "the Japanese Canadians' chief defender" during the early 1940s (Sunahara 1981, 39).

23 Roy Miki notes how Peter Ward describes racism in British Columbia as a "deeply irrational yearning." He argues that Ward's wording "obscures the power relations maintained through race discourse" (Miki 2005, 19).

24 According to Roy (2015–16), she originally proposed as the title of her book "From Exclusion to Inclusion." And, indeed, she writes in the conclusion to her book that "inclusion replaced exclusion as Canada's policy toward its citizens and people of Chinese and Japanese ancestry" (Roy 2007, 309). An early version of my chapter was presented at the 2015 BC Studies Conference at Kwantlen Polytechnic University, May 7–9. The theme of the conference was "From Exclusion to Inclusion: Forging a Multicultural Identity in British Columbia." Patricia Roy was both my co-panelist and the keynote speaker. Her keynote was titled "From Exclusion to Inclusion: An Informal Historiographical Memoir of East Asians in British Columbia."

25 Roy Miki differentiates between "abstract" and "concrete" unities. The former are created through the declarations of authorities, while the latter develop through community engagement and participation (Miki 2005, 196). Importantly, Kirsten McAllister (2010, 16) warns that even when communities are mobilized to fight injustice, there is always the risk that social and political differences can be homogenized.

26 History that gets the "right things right" could mean any number of things for Granatstein. Most likely, he is referring to Canada's military history, which he hopes to have "front and center in our consciousness" (Granatstein 2004, 10) while having its depiction avoid "pandering to political correctness and victimology" (6–7).

27 One such instance was as a keynote speaker for the Japanese Canadian Cultural Centre's Japanese Canadian Post War Experience conference on April 6–7, 2013. Robinson's talk was called "After Camp, Canadian Style: the Japanese Canadian Post War Experience Conference."

28 See "Landscapes of Injustice" at https://www.landscapesofinjustice.com. One unfortunate feature of the project that is being dealt with by the Japanese Canadian community is its efforts to digitize and publish online correspondences and other information about families during the internment. None of this information has been published with the consent of the families affected despite the fact that it is both deeply personal/private and traumatic/retraumatizing. My own experience with information published by Landscapes of Injustice in this archive is troubling in that I've been forced to question whether or how to speak to my mother about

information I found there. For instance, some of the information pertains to debts owed for hospital visits. Again, this is an instance where historians can look at these documents while claiming "objectivity," without recognizing that this information is not mere "data." Two events organized by the Japanese Canadian community have touched on the problems associated with studies that have researched the Japanese Canadian community in this way, stressing the need for meaningful community consultation and awareness of the possibility of traumatizing or retraumatizing people whose families' personal histories are exposed by the publication of this work (see McAllister et al. 2021; Kovach et al. 2022).

References

Abu-Laban, Yasmeen, and Christina Gabriel. 2008. *Selling Diversity: Immigration, Multiculturalism, Employment.* Toronto: University of Toronto Press.

Adachi, Ken. (1976) 1991. *The Enemy That Never Was: A History of the Japanese Canadians.* Toronto: McClelland and Stewart.

– 1988. "Internment Scars Run Deep." *Toronto Star,* September 24.

Althusser, Louis. 1971. "Ideology and Ideological State Apparatuses." In *Lenin and Philosophy.* New York: Monthly Review Press.

– 1976. *Essays in Self-Criticism.* London: New Left Books.

– 1997. "The Only Materialist Tradition, Part I: Spinoza." In *The New Spinoza,* edited by Warren Montag and Ted Stolze. Minneapolis, MN: University of Minnesota Press.

Attwood, Bain. 2005. "Unsettling Pasts: Reconciliation and History in Settler Australia." *Postcolonial Studies* 8 (3): 243–59.

Bakan, Abigail, and Enakshi Dua. 2014. "Introduction to Chapter 6: Marxism and Anti-Racism: Reflections and Interpretations." In *Theorizing Anti-Racism: Linkages in Marxism and Critical Race Theories,* edited by Abigail Bakan and Enakshi Dua. Toronto: University of Toronto Press.

Balibar, Étienne. 1991a. "The Nation Form: History and Ideology." In *Race, Nation, Class,* edited by Étienne Balibar and Immanuel Wallerstein. New York: Verso.

– 1991b. "Is There a 'Neo-Racism'?" In *Race, Nation, Class,* edited by Étienne Balibar and Immanuel Wallerstein. New York: Verso.

Bannerji, Himani. 2000. *The Dark Side of the Nation: Essays on Multiculturalism, Nationalism and Gender.* Toronto: Canadian Scholars.

– 2003. "Multiple Multiculturalisms and Charles Taylor's Politics of Recognition." In *Whither Multiculturalism? A Politics of Dissensus,* edited by Barbara Saunders and David Haljan. Leuven, Belgium: Leuven University Press.

Barker, Martin. 1981. *The New Racism: Conservatives and the Ideology of the Tribe.* London: Junction Books.

Blanding, Lee. 2013. "Re-branding Canada: The Origins of Canadian Multiculturalism Policy, 1945–1974." PhD diss., University of Victoria.

Bliss, Michael. 1991–92. "Privatizing the Mind: The Sundering of Canadian History, the Sundering of Canada." *Journal of Canadian Studies/Revue d'études canadiennes* 26 (4): 5–17.

Butler, Judith. 1997a. *The Psychic Life of Power: Theories in Subjection*. Stanford, CA: Stanford University Press.

– 1997b. *Excitable Speech: A Politics of the Performative*. New York/London: Routledge.

Canada. 1971. *House of Commons Debates*. 28th Parliament, 3rd Session, Volume 8 (October 8): 8545–48.

Careless, J.M.S. 1969. "'Limited Identities' in Canada." *Canadian Historical Review* 50 (1): 1–10.

– 1981. "Limited Identities – Ten Years Later." *Manitoba History* 1: 3–9.

Coulthard, Glen Sean. 2014. *Red Skin, White Masks: Rejecting the Colonial Politics of Recognition*. Minneapolis: University of Minnesota Press.

Day, Richard. 2002. *Multiculturalism and the History of Canadian Diversity*. Toronto: University of Toronto Press.

Dhamoon, Rita. 2009. *Identity/Difference Politics*. Vancouver: UBC Press.

Dreisziger, N.F. 1988. "The Rise of a Bureaucracy for Multiculturalism: The Origins of the Nationalities Branch, 1939–1941." In *On Guard for Thee: War, Ethnicity, and the Canadian State, 1939–1945*, edited by Norman Hillmer, Bohdan Kordan, and Lubomyr Luciuk. Ottawa: Canadian Committee for the History of the Second World War.

Eagleton, Terry. 1991. *Ideology: An Introduction*. New York: Verso.

Foucault, Michel. 1990. *The History of Sexuality: An Introduction*, vol. 1. New York: Vintage Books.

– 2003. *"Society Must Be Defended": Lectures at the Collège de France, 1975–1976*. New York: Picador.

Goldberg, David Theo. 1993. *Racist Culture: Philosophy and the Politics of Meaning*. Oxford: Blackwell.

Gramsci, Antonio. 1971. *Selections from the Prison Notebooks*. Edited by Quentin Hoare and Geoffrey Smith. New York: International.

Granatstein, Jack L. 1998. *Who Killed Canadian History?* Toronto: HarperCollins.

– 2004. "At Play in the Fields of the Museologists." *Journal of Military and Strategic Studies* 6 (3): 1–11.

Granatstein, Jack L., and Gregory A. Johnson. 1988. "The Evacuation of the Japanese Canadians, 1942: A Realist Critique of the Received Version." In *On Guard for Thee: War, Ethnicity, and the Canadian State, 1939–1945*, edited by Norman Hillmer, Bohdan Kordan, and Lubomyr Luciuk. Ottawa: Canadian Committee for the History of the Second World War.

Haque, Eve. 2012. *Multiculturalism within a Bilingual Framework*. Toronto: University of Toronto Press.

Hillmer, Norman, Bohdan Kordan, and Lubomyr Luciuk. 1988. "Preface." In *On Guard for Thee: War, Ethnicity, and the Canadian State, 1939–1945*, edited by Norman Hillmer, Bohdan Kordan, and Lubomyr Luciuk. Ottawa: Canadian Committee for the History of the Second World War.

James, Matt. 2013. "Neoliberal Heritage Redress." In *Reconciling Canada: Critical Perspectives on the Culture of Redress*, edited by Jennifer Henderson and Pauline Wakeham. Toronto: University of Toronto Press.

Japanese Canadian Centennial Project. 1978. *A Dream of Riches: The Japanese Canadians, 1877–1977*. Vancouver: Japanese Canadian Centennial Project.

Keenleyside, Hugh L. 1982. *Memoirs of Hugh L. Keenleyside*. Vol. 2, *On the Bridge of Time*. Toronto: McClelland and Stewart.

Kernerman, Gerald P. 2005. *Multicultural Nationalism: Civilizing Difference, Constituting Community*. Vancouver: UBC Press.

Kitigawa, Muriel. 1985. *This Is My Own: Letters to Wes and Other Writings on Japanese Canadians, 1941–1948*, edited by Roy Miki. Vancouver: Talonbooks.

Kobayashi, Audrey. 1992. "The Japanese-Canadian Redress Settlement and Its Implications for 'Race Relations.'" *Canadian Ethnic Studies* 24 (1): 1–19.

– 1992–93. "Review of *Mutual Hostages*: Canadians and Japanese during the Second World War, by Patricia Roy, J.L. Granatstein, Masako Iino, and Hiroko Takamura." *BC Studies* 96: 117–21.

Kogawa, Joy. 1994. *Obasan*. New York: Anchor Books.

Kovach, Margaret (keynoter speaker and panellist), Jennifer Matsunaga (moderator), Kirsten Emiko McAllister (discussant), Laura Ishiguro, Mona Oikawa, Pamela Sugiman, Bailey Irene Midori Hoy, Henry Yu, and Tod Duncan (panellists). 2022. "Ours to Tell: Ethics of Research in Indigenous and Japanese Canadian Communities." Symposium sponsored by Dr. David Chu Program in Asia-Pacific Studies, University of Toronto, the Canadian Race Relations Foundation, and the Greater Toronto Chapter of the National Association of Japanese Canadians, March 25.

LaViolette, F.E. 1948. *The Canadian Japanese and World War II: A Sociological and Psychological Account*. Toronto: University of Toronto Press.

Mackey, Eva. 2002. *The House of Difference: Cultural Politics and National Identity in Canada*. Toronto: University of Toronto Press.

Macpherson, C.B. 1962. *The Political Theory of Possessive Individualism: Hobbes to Locke*. London: Oxford University Press.

Makabe, Tomoko. 1998. *The Canadian Sansei*. Toronto: University of Toronto Press.

Marx, Karl. 1990. *Capital*, vol. 1. Translated by B. Fowkes. New York: Penguin Books.

McAllister, Kirsten. 2010. *Terrain of Memory: A Japanese Canadian Memorial Project*. Vancouver: UBC Press.

McAllister, Kirsten Emiko (moderator), Laura Ishiguro, Jennifer Matsunaga, and Nicole Yakashiro. 2021. "Ethics of Representing Asian Communities in Research." Panel discussion for National Forum on Anti-Asian Racism, Toronto Metropolitan University, Toronto, November 9.

McKay, Ian. 2000. "The Liberal Order Framework: A Prospectus for a Reconnaissance of Canadian History." *Canadian Historical Review* 81 (4): 616–45.

Meister, Daniel. 2021. *The Racial Mosaic: A Pre-History of Canadian Multiculturalism*. Montreal/Kingston: McGill-Queen's University Press.

Miki, Roy. 1998. *Broken Entries: Race, Subjectivity, Writing*. Toronto: Mercury Press.

– 2005. *Redress: Inside the Japanese Canadian Call for Justice*. Vancouver: Raincoast Books.

Montag, Warren. 1995. "'The Soul Is the Prison of the Body': Althusser and Foucault, 1970–1975." *Yale French Studies* 88: 53–77.

– 2013. *Althusser and His Contemporaries: Philosophy's Perpetual War*. Durham, NC: Duke University Press.

Nakano, Takeo Ujo. 1980. *Within the Barbed Wire Fence: A Japanese Man's Account of His Internment in Canada*. Toronto: University of Toronto Press.

National Association of Japanese Canadians. 1984. *Democracy Betrayed: The Case for Redress*. Ottawa: National Association of Japanese Canadians.

Nealon, Jeffrey. 2008. *Foucault beyond Foucault: Power and its Intensifications since 1984*. Stanford, CA: Stanford University Press.

Oikawa, Mona. 2012. *Cartographies of Violence: Japanese Canadian Women, Memory, and the Subject of the Internment*. Toronto: University of Toronto Press.

Read, Jason. 2024. *The Double Shift: Spinoza and Marx on the Politics of Work*. New York: Verso.

Robinson, Greg. 2013. "On Mona Oikawa's Landscapes of Injustice [sic]." *Nikkei Voice*, Holiday Edition, 7.

Roy, Fernande. 1988. *Progrès, harmonie, liberté: Le libéralisme des milieux d'affaires francophones de Montréal au tournant du siècle*. Montréal: Boréal.

Roy, Patricia. 2007. *The Triumph of Citizenship: The Japanese and Chinese in Canada, 1941–67*. Vancouver: UBC Press.

– 2014. "Review of *Cartographies of Violence: Japanese Canadian Women, Memory, and the Subjects of the Internment* by Mona Oikawa." *Canadian Ethnic Studies* 46 (1): 221–23.

– 2015–16. "From Exclusion to Inclusion: An Informal Historiographical Memoir about East Asians in British Columbia." *BC Studies* 188 (Winter): 91–106.

Schick, Carol. 2002. "Keeping the Ivory Tower White." In *Race, Space, and the Law: Unmapping a White Settler Society*, edited by Sherene H. Razack. Toronto: Between the Lines.

Sharp, Hasana. 2007. "The Force of Ideas in Spinoza." *Political Theory* 35 (6): 732–55.

Spinoza, Baruch. 1992. *Ethics*. Translated by Samuel Shirley. Indianapolis, IN: Hackett.

Sunahara, Ann Gomer. 1981. *The Politics of Racism: The Uprooting of Japanese Canadians during the Second World War*. Toronto: J. Lorimer.

Ward, Peter. 1978. *White Canada Forever: Popular Attitudes and Public Policy toward Orientals in British Columbia*. Montreal and Kingston: McGill-Queen's University Press.

– 1982. *The Japanese in Canada*. Canada's Ethnic Groups, No. 3. Ottawa: Canadian Historical Association.

Young, C.H., and H.R.Y. Reid. 1978. *The Japanese Canadians*. New York: Arno Press.

5

Narrating the After of the Moment of Redress: Fred Kelly's "Confession of a Born Again Pagan" and Roy Miki's *Redress: Inside the Japanese Canadian Call for Justice*

Smaro Kamboureli

Roy Miki concludes *Redress: Inside the Japanese Canadian Call for Justice* with a short section titled "The Moment of Acknowledgment: Dissonance and Harmony." The moment to which he refers is the culmination of "the singular event" (Miki 2004, 325) of the 1988 settlement the National Association of Japanese Canadians (NAJC) reached with the Government of Canada. This "brief moment" took place in the House of Commons: against parliamentary convention, the NAJC members in the guest gallery stood up to applaud when Prime Minister Brian Mulroney offered the official acknowledgment. This double gesture of rising and applauding, signalling at once defiance and celebration, bears witness to their "historical transfiguration":

> When they rose to clap their hands, they were no longer the same "Japanese Canadians" who had sat down in the guest gallery ... When Japanese Canadians achieved their settlement ... they gave their wartime experience as a gift to the official history of the nation ... [I]n the singular event of redress, that history had to be surrendered. From that time on, "Japanese Canadian" entered a post-redress condition of new transformations and limitations. (325)

Miki narrativizes what constitutes the Japanese Canadians' entry into an unprecedented exchange with the Canadian nation-state, unprecedented because this moment marks a crucial turning point in this community's place in Canada, but also because it inaugurates a period of formal apologies and restitution offered to other Canadians and Indigenous peoples who suffered injustices as a result of the Canadian state's racist policies.[1]

Enabled by the constitutional developments in the 1980s that necessitated a reconsideration of the past, the new Canadian Charter of Rights and Freedoms, and the Canadian Multiculturalism Act, but also emboldened by the NAJC's success, redress movements began to gain momentum in the 1980s. Dak Leon Mark and Shack Yee are credited with initiating the Chinese Canadians' redress movement in 1983,[2] but it was not until the Japanese Canadian Redress Agreement (JCRA) in 1988 that the government signed its first collective redress negotiation. This momentum may have faltered as a consequence of shifts in government and different policies regarding redress,[3] but the JCRA stands as a landmark event that ushered in a paradigm shift in what Jennifer Henderson and Pauline Wakeham (2013, 4) identify as "the heterogeneous culture of redress in Canada."

If the significance of this moment reaches beyond the JCRA, it is because it does not simply concern a specific point in history. It is characterized by different temporal and spatial dynamics. Temporalities, Sarah Sharma (2014, 8) writes, "are not times"; rather, "like continually broken clocks, they must be reset again and again," for the particular experience of time they evince "depends on where they are positioned within a larger economy of temporal worth." With this in mind, I see the JCRA not as a unified moment but as one that signifies differentially in that how it is understood by the nation-state is not coincident with the understanding it bears for Japanese Canadians. From the government's perspective, the JCRA constitutes a moment of reckoning: coming to terms, after considerable pressure, with a particular chapter of Canada's haunting history, but doing so by reproducing the nation-state's liberal script. Yet, against the nation-state's intention to see the JCRA as a moment of closure, the import of this redress moment resonates synecdochically, for it gestures toward the other state-sanctioned histories of inequity and injustice that remain to be addressed. In this context, I consider the JCRA as a moment that exceeds its singularity because it interrupts the unfolding of homogeneous empty time so that something different emerges from within that rupture, a new understanding of things that have passed but the brunt of which endures.

" 'The 'moment,'" writes Heidrun Friese (2001, 1), "is a word that addresses particular relations to time and temporality." From the Gnostic tradition to the King James Bible to existentialism, the moment as an atom of time has been valorized as that which signals an unexpected, often violent, irruption of the other that goes against the flow of time, that announces a radical break from it. For Søren Kierkegaard, a moment is what creates space for the past, present, and future in a way that allows us to relate to all these aspects of temporality. "The future," he wrote, "is the whole of which the past is a part ... The moment and the future *in turn* posit the past ... the future *in turn* is the eternal's (freedom's) possibility" (Kierkegaard 1980, 89–91; emphasis added). Kierkegaard's repetition of "in turn" highlights the successive processes that a moment generates. It commences new serial, though not necessarily linear, action that makes it possible to actualize agency. The moment may be a point of contemporaneity but its relations with the past and the future hold the possibility of the advent of a different temporality that builds on conditions relying on the materiality of historical experience. Hence the moment as a "decisive caesura, which bids its farewell to the irrevocable past and opens up towards that which is to come, to the not-yet of the future" (Friese 2001, 2). Because the moment is both of the now and of the not-yet future, it has the potential to alter the course of history.

It is in this sense of the moment that I consider the official apology the Japanese Canadians received to operate as what I have called elsewhere an emergent event, an event that initiates disruption and triggers a process that has the potential to reconfigure the ideological apparatus of the state's field of action. Emergent events constitute turning points: they re-script normative paradigms; they disturb the status quo; from the perspective of dominant discourses, they may even cause havoc (Kamboureli 2012, 8–18). But it is this release of forces, which have been contained or rendered invisible until a given moment, that brings about a new and different movement, a movement that reveals the "immediate presence of the true in which that which is invisible discloses itself" (Friese 2001, 11).

This is the reason why I wish to take a close look at both Miki's narrativization of the Japanese Canadian moment of redress and Anishinaabe Fred Kelly's essay "Confession of a Born Again Pagan" in order to offer a reading at a micro level that will, nevertheless, draw up to scale a macro view of the process of redress. Paying attention to how redress is narrativized does not disclose only its differential temporalities; it also reveals that not every redress is of the same order. If "the microscope is an epistemological telescope, a *meaning-making machine*," as Christian Moraru (2015) argues, then its ability to magnify can "[decompress] meaning" and divulge how the big picture is "folded inside the little picture" (222). In what follows, then, I first reach toward the macro level in order to consider the larger context of official apologies, in particular how their recurring tropes of confession and transference operate as iterations of liberalism; I then turn to Kelly's narrative as an exemplary case that deploys these same tropes but does so in a manner that recants their liberal function, thus unmasking the contradictions underlying redress as a process and an event; finally, I return to Miki to examine his use of narrative tactics that invite us to regard the moment of the JCRA as one whose promise of transformation lies in what comes after redress.

Redress as a Liberal Script

Situating the Japanese Canadian moment of redress as a key event that has animated a range of political and cultural redress initiatives by other communities does not mean that this settlement has served as a wake-up call for the Indigenous peoples seeking recognition and reparation or for other marginalized Canadians. In their own ways and at their own pace, these communities had already been calling for similar official acknowledgment for the wrongs they had endured long before 1988. Instead of positing it as a foundational narrative of redress, I see the JCRA moment as belonging to the genealogy of truth commissions and public apologies across the globe – from Argentina to Algeria, from South Africa and Rwanda to Germany – a phenomenon characteristic of liberal states with a colonial history and/or a history of human rights abuses, the frequency of which continues to generate many and often contradictory arguments as to what propels the double call for recognition of and apology for injustices and reparation since the latter part of the twentieth century.

Although these events address what Danielle Celermajer (2009) refers to as the "sins of the nation," they remain decidedly embedded within liberalism. Far from positing this as an original observation, my point is that this is a condition that we must remain alert to, lest we allow liberalism, as Anna Carastathis (2010, 95) puts it, "to tell its own story." Placing redress exclusively within a liberal script is a strategy that not only acquiesces to the liberal and settler states' own terms of executing justice but also confines the meaning of justice within a singular ideological paradigm. Henderson and Wakeham (2013, 7) articulate this criticism succinctly:

> The strategic depiction of reconciliation as a coherent social paradigm in
> Canada ... is motivated by more than the desire to preserve a reputation as
> a supposed multicultural beacon; it is prompted by a pragmatic attention
> to a global context of shifting expectations of modern liberal-democratic

nation-states, a context that requires demonstrations of historical reckoning ... as a criterion of admission to the international civil society of free-trade zones and corporate investment.

Liberalism may be the chief political ideology driving these state apologies but, as attested by the fact that such apologies come about only after intense pressure is applied to the state apparatus from the outside, redress is not necessarily triggered by desire for justice; nor do the apologies of liberal states always manifest themselves in the same fashion. What grants the admission of guilt its particularity is that it does not necessarily bring to light previously hidden acts. Since the admission of wrongdoing concerns acts that were officially sanctioned and executed by a government, what is at stake is the public nature of the acknowledgment. Public acknowledgments and apologies resemble speech acts in that they set out to perform what they enunciate – divulge guilt and promise restitution – but they do not automatically transform or eliminate the values entrenched in liberal states, often the very same values employed to justify the deracination of undesirable others. They may mimic confession, but they turn the Christian trope of confession from a private sacramental act that is mediated by a single witness into a ritual of repentance that is enacted publicly. In this respect, public apologies are only approximations of conversion narratives, for conversion narratives are meant to express a "sense of transformation constituted by those asserting a public, deep, fundamental change from one state of being, knowing, and acting to another" (Waisanen 2018, 11), what a sincere apology ought to convey. The problem is that, more often than not, even when official apologies are accompanied by verbal and bodily signs of penitence, such as tears, no fundamental change occurs, so that the redress that follows does not undo systemic issues.

In addressing the implications of deploying religious tropes in secular politics, Celermajer (2009, 5) reminds us that, if we look at the history of Judaism and Christianity, one of "the principal means for addressing systematic wrongdoing in the past was public, ritualized repentance." The public sphere is crucial because it involves collectivities: the speaker apologizing does so "in a representative capacity" (15), while the apology addresses the collective wronged. This public process, usually carefully staged, raises the stakes of accountability, for the apology constitutes a social contract that creates binding expectations. For Michel-Rolph Trouillot (2000, 173), public apologies issued by nation-states reflect the "transfer[ence] of attributes from individual to collective subjects testif[ying] to the changes in historical perception." In contrast, Jeffrey K. Olick and Brenda Coughlin (2003, 56), taking a strong stance against Trouillot, argue that he "has the order of logic reversed: the confessional individual mimics the regretful state, not the other way around – or at the least they are codetermined phenomena." Girma Negash (2006, 5–6), who finds their respective arguments to be credible yet problematic because of "their seductively parsimonious but sweeping conclusions," stands somewhere between them. For him, the increased number of public apologies is the result of "a convergence" of different philosophical and political traditions shaped by "the accumulated wisdom of liberalism" whereby modern liberal states may "[imitate] the liberal individual," but may also exercise their own initiative to "[display] their remorse publicly," and thus accept accountability and "promote rapprochement."[4]

My aim here is not to engage with these approaches in detail, but rather to tease out some of their implications regarding the ways in which the culture of apology remains embedded within, and thus circumscribed by, liberalism. The tropes of confession and its transference, namely recasting confession's private scene as a public stage whereby the confessing party represents a government, rely on a notion of subject formation that is decidedly installed in the humanistic tradition that has shaped as much liberalism as Christianity. Both tropes are relevant to understanding the culture of apology, but employing them as a universal paradigm that can account for the complex particularities of redress culture situates redressed subjects exclusively within the Western mould of subject formation, when in fact these subjects have been typically those whose difference Western liberal states have tried to eradicate or contain. As Marina Warner (2002) notes, "public apologies made by leaders of world affairs cast them in priestly roles ... Their verbal retractions are ... designed to ease and soothe and purge hatred and grudge." When the role of the penitent-apologizer converges with that of the priest-absolver, however, the affectivity and political efficacy of the confession-apology is compromised. Confession continues to operate, to echo Foucault, as a discourse of power that facilitates the normalization of transgressive acts.[5] In this scenario of public apologies, the redressed subjects remain framed within a hegemonic system that is complicit with the power structures that subjugated them in the first place.

Decolonizing the Liberal Script of Apology:
From Confession to Conversion

In his essay "Confession of a Born Again Pagan," Fred Kelly, a member of the Anishinaabe Nation in Treaty Number Three, situates the official apology the Canadian government issued to residential school survivors in 2008

(Government of Canada 2008) in the interstices of colonialism and liberalism. Kelly's essay is the opening chapter in *From Truth to Reconciliation: Transforming the Legacy of Residential Schools*, the first of a set of three volumes published in the Aboriginal Healing Foundation Research Series (Kelly 2008).[6] The Aboriginal Healing Foundation, the non-profit private corporation established in 1998 with a $350 million federal grant,[7] was part of *Gathering Strength: Canada's Aboriginal Action Plan* (Indian and Northern Affairs Canada 1997), the federal Liberal government's formal response to the 1996 *Report of the Royal Commission on Aboriginal Peoples* (RCAP 1996). Such policy documents recognize grievances but their agenda pivots on a restrictive and self-sustained logic. *Gathering Strength*, for example, which promises to pursue "a Renewed Partnership ... with Aboriginal people," refers to "historic injustices" as events of an "ostensibly exceptional" nature (Wakeham 2012, 220), thus eliding the reality of Canada as a settler state. Consequently, the dramatic irony with which this document's positivist and recuperative rhetoric is infused – what "renewed partnership" and on whose terms? – helps to further Canada's neoliberal agenda while maintaining colonial asymmetries.[8] Prime Minister Stephen Harper's official apology in 2008 exemplifies this kind of double-speak in that, as has already been noted by others (e.g., Henderson and Wakeham 2009; Corry 2020), it is marked by its lack of any direct reference to colonialism.[9] This speaks to what Lisa S. Villadsen and Jason A. Edwards (2020) identify as the "symbolic nature" (5) of the genre of apologies – in other words, how their rhetoric of regret can easily "degenerat[e] into self-preserving, self-congratulatory, and nonvictim-centered apologies that do more harm than good" (11). In contrast to the affirming yet often disingenuous elements of official apologies, Kelly's essay is composed and is placed in *From Truth to Reconciliation* as a counter-discourse that both echoes and unsettles the empty rhetoric characterizing the genre of such apologies.

Having Kelly's voice open *From Truth to Reconciliation* is an astute editorial act that simultaneously administers respect and healing. Coming right after the opening section's subtitle, "Truth-Telling," "Confession" enacts via its genre the act of truth-telling, and so it materializes the "truth telling" mandate of the Truth and Reconciliation process.[10] But it is not only the genre of this essay that is important. As the opening piece, and along with its formal elements, as I discuss below, Kelly's "Confession" also takes on the role of the prayer an Indigenous Elder offers at the start of a ceremony to help prepare the ground for healing. The biographical information included in the editorial note that prefaces Kelly's essay explains why the honour of opening the collection is granted to him. Kelly is introduced as a "distinguished Elder": he "is a member of *Midewewin*, the Sacred Law and Medicine Society of the Anishinaabe" and has "served as chief of his own community, grand chief of the Anishinaabe nation in Treaty Number Three, and Ontario regional director of Indian and Northern Affairs Canada" (Kelly 2008, 14). A residential school survivor and a Drum Keeper and Pipe Carrier in his community, Kelly was at the forefront of the Indigenous civil rights movement in Canada. He played a key role in, among other things, the "recognition of Aboriginal and Treaty rights in the Canadian Constitution," and has been invited to administer "healing therapies" and conduct "sacred ceremonies" among many Indigenous communities on Turtle Island, the United States, Mexico, Japan, Argentina, and Israel (First Peoples Group). More recently, he accompanied the 180-member Indigenous delegation to Rome as a spiritual adviser, and led "a traditional Anishinaabe ceremony" at a private meeting with Pope Francis (Grant, Fiddler, and Reguly 2022).[11] "Confession," then, as the editors write in the "Introduction," animates the path the readers of this volume are invited to follow, from "truth-telling" about "the legacy of residential schools," through "formal actions and informal developments" like those Kelly's text performs, to the "pursuit of justice and reconciliation" and, ultimately, to "spiritual renewal" and the "ethical obligation to take concrete action" (Castellano, Archibald, and DeGagné 2008, 4).[12]

A hybrid of memoir, historical narrative, ideological critique, and Anishinaabe world view and cosmology, Kelly's essay comprises a confession that, italicized and interspersed throughout the text, offers an account of his traumatic experience addressed to the very God in whose name he was brutally treated time and again at St. Mary's Residential School in Kenora, Ontario, which he was "thrown into" at the age of four (Kelly 2008, 16). It is through this simultaneous deployment and recasting of the confessional mode that he subverts the ideology and politics of the liberal script of apologies.

Kelly's narrative begins with the conventional apostrophe to a confessor: "Father, forgive me for I have sinned." Although he "*more or less, follows the old protocol*" of confession (emphasis in original, 13), he does so with critical difference, for the present tense of his confession immediately breaks open and takes Kelly to a different temporal plain: the first time he went to confession "at the age of fourteen, the experience of which is clearly etched in memory. It was an acrimonious and a deeply traumatic event in my life in residential school. I swore I would never go back" (15). Yet, he does go back, so that the now of his narration constitutes an intersection of the present tense of his confession and the past tense of his residential school experience, the crossing of which instantiates a complex temporality whereby each moment of the past claims space in the moment of the present, in effect neutralizing their distinctness and inscribing in his narrative the non-progressive temporality of trauma.

"Confession is now the Sacrament of Reconciliation," Kelly says. But in the now of Reconciliation time, confession is recast as a "new rite"; no longer a "recitation" of "prepared sins" whispered "through a little screened window," it is now "revamped" as a public and collective performance. He is referring to "group reconciliation where a general confession is performed," but he also signals that his narrative's composition performs a similar function (15).

> Because I came to hate everyone connected to the school and the religion ... I committed a sin. For that, I repent. And for the times I blamed God for the pain and anguish that we were going through and allowed myself to think in anger that he was mean and wicked, I sinned against him. I am deeply remorseful. For all the things that I personally saw and experienced and knew were wrong but did not report to the authorities, I committed an act of complicity. (27)

A tactical inversion of colonial mimicry, the "sins" he seeks penance for are "symptom[atic]" of the "sinfulness" of colonialism, the "disease" that he and his people have endured (15) for generations. The fact that Kelly feels guilty for the violations committed on behalf of the settler state by those in positions of authority – *"the nuns, priests, brothers"* (27) – signals the complex ethos of his decolonizing discourse. That it is not *"the nuns, priests, brothers"* who repent but Kelly himself turns his confession into an indictment of the common assumption that the Canadian state's formal admission of guilt and public apology exonerates everyone involved in the residential schools, thus revealing that official apologies are not tantamount to reconciliation.

Kelly's ironic use of Christian rhetoric plays an instrumental role, for it is precisely what allows him to deconstruct and decolonize the Christian tropes employed in public apologies. He does not only tell a story that has long been denied narration – being "denied narration is not just a metaphor," as David Carroll writes, "it is already a form of injustice itself" (Carroll 1989, 59) – thus converting himself from a subject without a voice to one who speaks (up). His story also directly references the residential schools' goal to "kill the Indian in the child,"[13] a project of violent conversion that both prevailed and failed. It prevailed, hence the cultural genocide suffered by Indigenous peoples, but it has also failed, as evidenced by Kelly's conversion back to his "pagan" ways. To put this otherwise, what he posits as a confession largely functions as conversion – conversion understood as a gesture characterized by the action of turning away from or toward a particular condition, a movement that, be it singular or ongoing, is transformative. That this shift in genre still entails Kelly's adoption of a discourse that has decidedly Christian origins (see, for example, Shinn 2018) grants greater subversive force to the politics and aesthetics of his text.

By exposing that what was presented as an educational agenda was in reality a colonial program of assimilation and physical abuse, Kelly's narrative unmasks the liberal ideology of the state that has systematically obscured colonial violence. *"Father,"* he says, *"I tried to rationalize what I saw and experienced. The treatment of children, as horrific as it was, must have been our normal lot for having been the pagan sinners that we had been. Was everything all right?"* (Kelly 2008, 27). The question Kelly asks incriminates the priest-confessor, thus casting him as a witness to both what happened in the past and to Kelly's act of unmasking in the present, but also as the reader's proxy, thus granting the confession the function of a testimony addressed to his readers. This results in a canny reversal of Kelly's own narratorial position as a (presumed) complicit sinner to that of a critical witness, a reversal amplified by the fact that he is also one of the children victimized. Being a first-person narrator who simultaneously occupies different locations dramatizes Susan David Bernstein's (1997, 33) description of the difference between confession and testimony:

> Embedded within confession is at least the potential of testimony whereby the confessional subject describes vaster social inequities as well as the transgressions of others, those in positions of authority whose violations are most often construed as prerogative. In the discourse of confession, typically the speaker is the transgressor; in the discourse of testimony, usually the speaker is an onlooker, sometimes a witness to a crime committed against oneself or against those sharing the speaker's social identity.

As confession-testimony, Kelly's narrative breaks the silence and secrecy that normally characterize confession by manifesting the repression of the truth behind residential schools. As Shoshana Felman and Dori Laub

(1992, xix) write, because testimony "decanonize[s] the [confession's] silence ... [and] desacralize[s] the witness," testimony *"liberat[es]"* the unspeakable. In this context, the text's modal shifts from confession to conversion and then to testimony flag the political and spiritual work carried out by Kelly's decolonial turns, thus embodying his desire to unsettle the monologism of the liberal script.

When Elder Dave Courchene asked the Truth and Reconciliation Commission, "When you talk about truth, whose truth are you talking about?" the commission's answer was that "by *truth,* we mean not only the truth revealed in government and church residential school documents, but also the truth of lived experiences as told to us by Survivors ... Together, these public testimonies constitute a new oral history record, one based on Indigenous legal traditions and the practice of witnessing" (Truth and Reconciliation Commission of Canada 2015, 12). Kelly's narrative may be marked by a self-reflexive aesthetics not usually found in testimonies but, like (Nlaka'pamux) Shirley Sterling's novel *My Name Is Seepeetza* (1992), written in the form of a fictionalized diary, it undoubtedly belongs to the archive of residential school survivors' testimonies. The formal and narrative transitions from confessing sinner to indicter to witness actualize temporality as a palimpsestic moment where the past and present remain interwoven.

Kelly does not challenge only the epistemological authority of Christian confession. He also overturns the epistemic authority of the eyewitness, specifically an eyewitness who represents the legal system. *"Even the crown attorney from town was in the chapel for Mass every Sunday,"* he says, *"So things must have been all right"* (Kelly 2008, 27). The devoutness of the crown attorney makes a travesty of both his faith and the justice system he represents. Figured as a witness who remains blind or indifferent to what he witnesses, he operates at once as a proxy of God and the state. His regular attendance at the residential school's church draws attention to the vicissitudes of bearing witness, thus inviting the reader to bear witness "to the witness's inability to witness" (Felman and Laub 1992, 200). The layers of complicity that are inscribed in Kelly's narrative (as cited above, he admits to his own complicity for not speaking out sooner) ultimately implicate all settlers. Like the crown attorney, settlers have displayed an astounding inability to take notice of the injustices suffered by Indigenous people. Pointing to the complicity of an entire settler culture serves to convert Kelly's confession-testimony into a self-reflexive encounter through which the settler reader, via the figure of the crown attorney, experiences the interplay of and tension between identification and distance, complicity and recognition, with regard to the ethical and interpretive limits that the temporal gap between then and now both hides and discloses.

In his confession, Kelly performs the double role of survivor-witness but also draws attention to the role of God as witness. If the priest who listens to Kelly's confession has the power to absolve sin or administer penance, it is because he is God's proxy in the moment when the sacrament of confession is enacted. God as a figure who is at once present and invisible does not simply complete the triangular structure of the confessional script; as an all-seeing and omnipresent being, he allegorizes the pervasive force of the settler state, the visible and invisible mechanisms through which it claims the legitimacy of the power it exercises. This becomes apparent in Kelly's (2008, 39) supplication that both appeals to and disavows God: "*Father ... I am not seeking penance and far be it for me to deny hell. I have seen it ... Through the kindness of the Creator, I am at peace with myself. I have returned to Midewewin, the principal spirituality of the Anishinaabe.*" As a gesture that approximates reconciliation without conciliation, this apostrophe resituates the confessional script outside the structural and ideological confines of Christianity and liberalism. Kelly may accept the belief of others in the Christian God but he does not submit to Christian dogma: he confesses without seeking penance; he acknowledges that Christians believe in hell but he makes it abundantly clear that the hell he has experienced is of a different order. Moreover, Kelly's apostrophe to God as a silent, and thus complicit, witness of what he has suffered is tantamount to a farewell, for God is addressed not by a "born again" Christian but from the perspective of an Indigenous subject who, against all odds, has claimed back his own spiritual tradition.

"*How did I get here?*" he asks more than once (16, 20), the *here* referring to both the residential schools where he was sent and the present moment he inhabits. His process of being born again further discloses the web of complicities that shape Indigenous-settler relations. He may have "memorized the catechism dutifully" (17) but, being a child with an "inquisitive mind," he resisted blind faith and "*sneaked out*" searching for answers (18). He "*sinned*" by discovering and reading books like Bertrand Russell's *Why I Am Not a Christian* in the local town's library (18–19), but his sin was his salvation. Significantly, Kelly does not reject Christianity outright nor is he interested in polarizing the Christian God and the Anishinaabe Creator. Indeed, he reiterates this sentiment, that there is "no conflict between Anishinaabe ways and Christianity," and that "the Creator respects and understands the intention of each religion and spirituality," when he was interviewed while in Rome (Grant, Fiddler, and Reguly 2022). Shunning the dualism and binarism that form the ground of political liberalism, he constitutes Turtle Island as a space where the Western and Indigenous spiritual traditions can coexist. As he says: "Neither side believes that the other is going anywhere. This is home. So, how do we live side-by-side and build a future of prosperity together?" (Kelly 2008, 29). He thus practises decolonization via what Audra Simpson (Mohawk) and Andrea Smith (2014, 9) call "theoretical" or "intellectual promiscuity," an integral aspect of the methodology they advocate whereby Indigenous epistemologies exist side by side with or employ multiple forms of theory (19), including certain Western modes of knowledge production.

"Father," Kelly (2008, 16) avows, *"given the chance, we will come to accept what we have in common and learn to respect our differences."* The inclusiveness of the first-person-plural pronoun triggers a redress and reconciliation process that transforms the oppressiveness of his past experience into a dynamic relationship that holds the potential to be all-encompassing. An instance of what Shari Goldberg (2013, 14) calls "quiet testimony," a testimony that involves "an encounter that does not register as a confrontation but that serves as the catalyst for a new approach to the world," Kelly's statement posits agential and differential relationships as the prerequisite for reconciliation. This process depends on an understanding of subjectivity that both recognizes and circumvents the presumed autonomy of liberal subjects as well as the coercion and culpability that characterize their relations with the liberal state. Subjectivity may not exist outside the discursive regimes and their coercive practices that produce it, but the subjectification of Indigenous subjects differs radically from that of settlers. Indigenous people are at once subjectified by and subjected to the colonialism underlying settler cultures precisely because they have been constituted as subordinate subjects.

Founded on Anishinaabe philosophy, Kelly's (2008) position advances a redress process that starts *"at the personal level"* (29) and involves *"reclaiming one's identity"* as an embodied and relational subjectivity, one *"reconciled to traditional spirituality"* (39), and thus a process that is "intrinsically connected to Mother Earth" (22), Turtle Island. Crucially, this process of redressing colonial wounds takes place outside the liberal state's regulatory regime. It does not seek *"penance"* (39), nor does it demand apologies as such; rather, it relies on healing and calls for recognition, respect, and accountability. Enunciated in the future tense and thus occurring subsequent to the present moment – *"Given the chance, we will ..."* – Kelly's statement envisages a settler state that accepts *"responsibility for inflicting the horror of the residential school system"* and is committed to respecting the *"enforcement of Aboriginal rights and treaties as the basis for a reconciled future"* (40). His narrative, then, ultimately functions as a scene of instruction that reverses and subverts the colonial instruction he received in residential school. The *"condensed* version" (20) of colonial history and Anishinaabe philosophy and spirituality that he offers is addressed at once to the *Father,* who hears his confession, and to the reader, who receives that confession as testimony. *"The sound of pain in any narrative on the legacy left of residential schools is not merely the incessant whining of hypochondriacs seeking pity. Father, we do not need pity. Your people and our people both need the healing that comes with reconciliation"* (29). That both the Father and the reader inhabit the same now of the narrative's present tense, with the former cast as the residential school priest and as a proxy of God and state, exposes the limits and incommensurability of public apologies and redress. The settler state may acknowledge its sins, but redressing these sins in terms that honour Indigenous rights and spirituality is still a thing to come because of the state's deferral practices.

The Canadian liberal state may be a long way from demonstrating in practice the kind of recognition and accountability envisaged by Kelly, but his deconstruction of the confessional trope operates within a temporal structure of the present moment that is shaped as much by the before as well as the after of his residential school experience. I am referring specifically to the fact that Kelly's healing process does not rely on the settler state's apology and redress mechanisms; instead, it is launched by the decolonization tactics employed in his narrative of confession, that is, his embrace of Indigenous epistemologies.

I read his confession, then, as a decolonizing speech act that enacts the healing necessary to move forward. Kelly is able to move forward in a personal and relational way because he already inhabits the temporal moment of the after. As head of the "Nimishonis-Nokomis Healing Group, a consortium of traditional healers" (First Peoples Group), he works with residential school survivors to heal the "lingering aftershocks" of their experience that "require a comprehensive approach," one that "addresses the individual, the family, the community, and indeed the nation" (Kelly 2008, 30). In effect, Kelly has long been involved in a genuine redress process, despite the fact that the liberal state lags behind. Redress, in this instance, is not carried out by the state, but by those who must be redressed. It is precisely this time lag that stresses the importance of the afterness of redress. A moment of apology cannot by itself heal the aftershocks of trauma, nor is it constitutive of redress. What comes after can be equally traumatic; as Gerhard Richter (2011, 11) reminds us, "for those who undergo trauma, it is not only the moment of the event, but of the passing out of it that is traumatic ... The trauma of afterness and the afterness of trauma are ... a crisis." An apology and the redress it promises stand at the crossroads of the before and after of injustice. This afterness, as Kelly's narrative shows, constitutes a call for and a practice of redress that require the settler state to convert its apology from a public speech act to active engagement, "politically and epistemically," with decolonizing projects that "[build] communal futures" (Mignolo 2011, xxvii).

The importance of the after of apology is inscribed in similarly complex ways in Roy Miki's (2004) *Redress*. It is the shift from how Japanese Canadians had been constructed in the internment years to who they become after the Canadian state apologized to them that assigns to the Japanese Canadian redress moment its paradigmatic value in the context of official apologies in Canada. This conversion reveals, as I hope to show, an uncanny limit situation that exposes the ways in which the articulation of official regret by the Canadian liberal settler state both bears witness to the remembrance of a traumatic past and relies on a strategy of repressing precisely what is remembered. It is what comes after the state's apology, specifically how this after is inscribed in Miki's narrative of the Japanese Canadian inaugural moment of redress, that intimates why we should be wary of succumbing to the euphoria of public apologies.

Redress Interrupted: The Present Tense of Exceptionalism

Like Kelly, Miki does not render collective trauma and its redress in the past tense; he may employ the past tense to refer to the actual 1988 event, but his narrativization reveals the same time lag characterizing Kelly's decolonizing tactics, namely, an asymmetry between the response to the call for justice and the realization of justice. For both Indigenous people and the Japanese Canadians, redress is not a finished event, nor is it a thing contained by the temporal frame of the moment of apology. Unlike Kelly's narrative, though, Miki's narrative of the Japanese Canadian redress does not rely on a different epistemology or spiritual ontology; instead, it introduces and problematizes a different temporality through his tactical repetition of the same event. The ways in which Miki's narration of the moment of redress is woven into his text manifest the durational temporality of redress.

Miki's *Redress* does not just end with an account of the actual moment of redress, as I indicate in the opening of this chapter; it also begins with it:

> I had been anxiously anticipating this moment for years. Here I was, with my older brother, Art Miki, the other members of the ... [NAJC], and a handful of Japanese Canadians from Ottawa. All of us were lined up outside the door to the section of the House of Commons gallery reserved for "special guests." We were present to witness the official announcement by Prime Minister Brian Mulroney that a "redress agreement" had been reached with the NAJC. (Miki 2004, 1–2)

> The young government aide who directed us to enter the gallery from the dark hallway advised us of parliamentary protocol – that "guests" were not to stand or applaud. We were to remain seated in silence. To the left and right of us, the seats were unoccupied. The whole upper gallery was almost empty but for a handful of Japanese Canadians, far on the opposite side, who were "spectators," not "guests" ... It was hardly a full house – though the cameras, as we saw later in the news reports, framed only the occupied seats, presenting the illusion of fullness to the TV audience. (3–4)

Miki's narrativization of the same event in both the beginning and end of his book frames his chronicle, but this does not mean that this scene is granted the teleological weight of a moment of closure. "Relief, relief and more relief" (7) certainly marks what he justly calls "that moment of euphoria" (8), but what follows is not exactly a narrative of progress.

Indeed, the interplay between silence and speech, guests and spectators, empty seats and the illusion of fullness, casts a cloud of ambivalence, if not suspicion, on what he refers to as a "moment forward" (80). Employing the same narrative strategy that suspends and then resumes Kelly's confession, Miki interrupts the representation of the moment of official apology both times that it occurs. In the opening chapter, he discontinues its representation by recounting personal memories and offering historical context (1–2, 3–4, 7–8); he does so again in the last chapter, this time through a recourse to memory that is accompanied by a brief but highly nuanced critical analysis calling the reader's attention not to the past but to "a post-redress condition" (320–21, 325–26), the after of redress. These narrative breaks are not only symptomatic of the episodic nature of reparation procedures; they echo the political deferrals and delays both inside and outside the Japanese

Canadian community that mark the long and arduous process of its redress movement, a process that triggers a shift in consciousness. As Christopher Lee (2012, 131) puts it, by "interrupting the time of redress ... Miki imagines an ethics of commemoration that exceeds the mechanisms of exchange, both symbolic and material." Accordingly, what is supposed to be a moment of closure opens up a fold that destabilizes the temporality of events *Redress* chronicles to reveal political, cultural, and affective ambivalences, what is implied in Miki's (2004, 325) comment that the post-redress condition is accompanied by "transformations *and* limitations" (emphasis added). Thus, the moment that is re-narrated at the conclusion of *Redress* is identical to but not exactly the same as that which we encounter at its beginning, for it is the same but also the other that it has become by the time we re-encounter it at the end of the book.

Miki's story of the history of the redress movement lies between these two iterations. It is the now to the then this moment delineates, but the now's temporal logic encompasses an inassimilable residual situation, one of the reasons why the second staging of the moment of redress is different. The dual trope of iteration and interruption that constitutes this moment's representation reflects the negotiations that take place between history and narration, thus pointing to a time that is not as yet actualized in the present. It announces, instead, other temporalities – different relations and avenues of action to be pursued – that occur within the ambiguous space created when the histories of the hegemonic state and of the Japanese Canadians' internment are reconfigured as the afterlife of a past that is overcome but that continues to reverberate in the now. The systemic and discursive dimensions that his memoir lays bare regarding the Canadian nation-state that Japanese Canadians are so happy to now be part of on their own and rightful terms suspend a narrative emplotment of emancipation. The pauses and returns in Miki's text, the hiatus created when the narration of the moment of redress is interrupted and re-narrated, generate an instance of dislocation that the reader experiences at once as an aperture signalling the gaps in the process of effecting justice and as a traversal, a crossing into a different temporality that resists the resolution of any monologic interpretation of the injustices committed and redressed. Hence the moment's "dissonance and harmony," the fact that this euphoric moment is also referred to in Prime Minister Mulroney's (1988, 19499) redress speech as a "solemn occasion." Singular yet iterative, it is a moment that both encloses the narrative and resists narrative containment.

This repetition with critical difference is precisely what inscribes in the event of redress its afterlife. From within the intervals that constitute what has been and the now, there emerge the spectres of the past that demand we "think," as Richter (2011, 4) writes, "in a nonsychronist, nonpresentist manner," a manner in which our understanding of what has passed as we recognize it in its afterlife – the after of redress – involves continuously re-encountering and reinterpreting history. As Mona Oikawa (2012, 309) writes, "just as the Internment lives on in our [Japanese Canadian] memories and in its material and social effects, the effects of the process of redress are ongoing and are informed by and inform the memories of Japanese Canadians and other citizens." In other words, the understanding afforded by the moment of redress as it is exemplified in Miki's narrative, its paradigmatic significance, is not lodged in its presentness; it is performed by the after of redress and remains elusive in that it belongs to a temporality that is not yet.

The difference this narrative structure introduces is reflected in the disappearance of the scare quotes around the moniker "Japanese Canadians": "from this moment forward," Miki (2004, 8) writes, "'Japanese Canadians' – 'citizens of Japanese ancestry,' in the prime minister's acknowledgement – were no longer lacking redress but were now 'redressed.'" To be redressed here signals that they are no longer othered, no longer apostrophized as "enemy aliens." Still, they are the same – the citizens they have always been – *and* other, the afterlife of their redressed otherness as victims of injustice, precisely what is conveyed by Kelly's (2008) ironic use of the trope of confession. In both Kelly's and Miki's narratives, redress reveals an asymmetry between the response to the call for justice and the realization of justice. It is because the justice redressed subjects deserve remains incommensurable that the representation of the moment of redress in Miki's (2004) book is narratively augmented and deferred by being at once suspended and repeated.

That justice remains incommensurable is evident in Mulroney's formal apology and the protocols of its delivery. The prime minister's speech must apostrophize the Speaker of the House of Commons and refer to the Japanese Canadians present in the third person, further reinforcing the irony that Miki and the other Japanese Canadian "guests" and "spectators" must bear witness while remaining silent. Mulroney's speech acknowledges and apologizes for the injustices suffered by the Japanese Canadian community but does so in a way that redeems the nation. "Mr. Speaker," he says, "not only *was* the treatment inflicted on Japanese-Canadians during the War both morally and legally unjustified, it went against the very nature of our country, Canada. We *are* a pluralistic society. We each respect the language, opinions and religious convictions of our neighbor" (Mulroney 1988, 19499; emphasis added). The shift from the past tense to the present tense executes an uncanny maneuver that renders the internment of the Japanese Canadians as a moment of aberration in Canadian history, an exception to "the Canada our ancestors worked to build," a country of "tolerant people," one that "at all times and in all circumstances works hard to eliminate racial discrimination at home and abroad" (19450). Mulroney's iteration of the pernicious myth of Canadian benevolence recuperates Canadian history in a way that makes it possible for the state to inter the spectre of injustice haunting national discourse. His apology does not set out to undo – indeed, cannot undo – the syntax of the nation's settler history. The interplay between his use of past and present tenses speaks to the liberalism of the Canadian nation-state, namely, its intention to single out the unjust treatment of Japanese Canadians not as a symptom of a nation-state (and its society at the time) that was unmistakably invested in its racist ideology but as an anomaly to the unerring itinerary of the state that the apology speech constructs, one blemished only by a single exception. In Mulroney's speech, the moment of acknowledgment becomes indeed a moment of closure.

Mulroney's official apology, then, exemplifies the problem of remaining attached to the accumulated wisdom of liberalism. Presenting the Japanese Canadians' internment as an aberration in Canadian history not only exonerates the Canadian state but also cancels out the redress movements of the Chinese, Ukrainian, Italian, and German Canadians, not to mention Canada's ongoing process of reconciliation with Indigenous peoples, thus pre-empting the possibility of coalition politics. The exceptionalism that the Canadian state's various apologies[14] evoke acknowledges isolated misdeeds that belong to a distant past, meanwhile failing to recognize that they belong to the same discursive field, that they have been caused by the same ideological and historical contingencies. In this instance, exceptionalism operates as a habitual instrument of regret, one that speaks to the epistemic and political violence that is entrenched in the foundations of Canada as a liberal settler state.

There is another interesting rhetorical shift in Mulroney's speech that demonstrates what Pauline Wakeham (2012, 215) calls "the cunning of reconciliation," namely "the strategic co-optation of the ethical project of offering recompense for injustices by the political program of silencing resistance and manufacturing premature closure." Mulroney (1988, 19500) concludes his speech by establishing an analogy between the state and persons: "Most of us in our own lives have had occasion to regret certain things that we have done. Error is an ingredient of humanity, so too is [sic] apology and forgiveness. We all have learned from personal experience that as inadequate as apologies are they are the only way we can cleanse the past." Echoing the complicities that tie together in Kelly's "Confession" the entire cast of human and divine characters responsible for the atrocities committed in residential schools, the parallelism Mulroney draws between individuals and the nation-state belongs to the naturalist tradition of juridical philosophy, forcefully articulated by John Hobbes in *Leviathan* (1651, 16), where nature and nations share the same law.[15] But, as Alia Somani (2011, 2) notes in her essay about Stephen Harper's apology for the *Komagata Maru* incident, the "qualities of sincerity and authenticity that we might attribute to the personal apology might be difficult to discern in a national apology." Mulroney's person-state analogy further naturalizes the state's wrongdoing, thus encouraging forgiveness of the state, that is, inviting us to conceive it as "analogous to a rights-bearing natural individual," an approach that has "clear affinities to liberal theory" (Whelan 2015, 17).

This particular aspect of the state's reckoning also admits, in a paradoxically candid way, that forgiveness of the nation-state is equivalent to forgetting. Recalling Ernest Renan's ([1882] 1990, 11) notion that "forgetting ... historical error[s] ... is a crucial factor in the creation of a nation," that "deeds of violence" are "at the origin of all political formations," the prime minister's redress speech manages at once to reference and normalize violence, and apologize for injustice yet bypass the systemic issues that gave rise to it. Reminiscent of God and the crown attorney in Kelly's (2008) text as witnesses who see but who fail to bear witness, the state's narrative strategy produces a performative speech act that fails to perform what it enunciates. Sara Ahmed (2006) calls performative acts that do not produce what they name "nonperformatives." Such statements still function as performative utterances, but their failure to do what they say "is not a failure of intent or even circumstance, but it is actually what the speech act is doing. In other words, the nonperformative does not 'fail to act' because of conditions that are external to the speech act; it 'works' *because* it fails to bring about what it names" (105, emphasis in original). The nonperformative aspect of Mulroney's (1988) speech, along with the simultaneity of the tropes he deploys, effects an inversion of the moment of redress. This is evident in the language employed in Hansard, where, under "Routine Proceedings" and right before Mulroney's redress speech is recorded, the Japanese Canadians are referred to as "Visible Minorities," a term that signals that the hegemonic status quo, far from being destabilized, let alone excised, remains entrenched. Mulroney's speech pledges that the Japanese Canadians' citizenship will be fully restored, yet they are officially scripted in minoritized terms. From the perspective of the settler nation-state, the redress project is predicated on the assumption that the injustices of the past are forgivable errors, a kind of routine, if not banal, approach that impairs the authenticity of the redressed subjects' material experience and its lingering impact. Performing redress in this fashion may vindicate those wronged by offering them formal recognition of the injustices they have suffered, but also reproduces the terms that it sets out to critique; it thus situates victims within a critical outside that upholds the state's epistemic structures.

The "Re-" of Redress and Chronic Time

The Japanese Canadian moment of redress, as Miki (2004, xii) rightly observes, may have "become a national story," but it is not a story that has launched a radical epistemological shift as far as the state is concerned. My focus on the narrative contingencies of the moment of redress has shown, I hope, that the state's project of redress cultivates a presentism that keeps echoing the past. Consequently, the state's apology and recuperative measures undo the bare life relegated to the Japanese Canadians as "enemy aliens" who had been reduced, as per Giorgio Agamben's (1998) trope, to *bios,* but its configuration of the internment as an exceptionalist event does not cause a changeover in how it views and manages biopolitics; it does not quite transform *bios* to *zoe.* The fact that this kind of exception is, as I argue above, structurally integral to the nature of the liberal nation-state as inscribed in Mulroney's speech and other government documents, such as *Gathering Strength,* suggests that redress does not constitute a radical intervention, a moment that might interrupt the continuum of time. The nation-state's redress mode produces homogeneous spatialized time, time that is quantified and regulated, unfolding through successive presents that depersonalize persons, thus reproducing the state's chronic conditions of colonization and racism.

The dominance of the prefix "re-" (meaning "again" *and* "back") in discourses of redress – redress, recuperation, reparation, recognition, reconciliation, restitution, and so on – points to a temporality that is directed, unfailingly so, backward, to a past that is nevertheless attached to the presentism of the now. This iterative action is not by default palindromic, for it does not always reproduce what it returns to. Still, the non-coincidence between what lies on either side of this movement, and thus the difference it points to, announces what Eric Cazdyn (2012, 13) calls a "new chronic mode, a mode of time that cares little for terminality and acuteness ... A solid remission, yes, but always with the droning threat of relapse ... echoing back to us from a far-off future or from the memory of a distant past." Cazdyn derives his notion of the new chronic mode from medical advances that have changed terminal illnesses into chronic conditions, but his study, *The Already Dead: The New Time of Politics, Culture, and Illness*, sheds light on how the "re-" of the state's redress of biopolitics operates. Situating the culture of apology as a practice designed to cure the body politic of its historical abuses within the now of the Canadian settler state's time does not make it possible to address, let alone heal, the chronic condition of systemic injustice. A viable culture of apology must outpace the state's continuous "retooling" of the reconciliation processes that emphasizes "history and the imperative of 'moving on,'" and insists on conceptualizing "harm ... in relation to liberal individuals and property" (Henderson and Wakeham 2013, 13). Synchronized with the new chronic mode of time, this kind of retooling offers only Band-Aid solutions to injustice.

For Cazdyn (2012, 6), the "desire to cure" in the new chronic mode "is displaced by the practical need to manage and stabilize"; even though this shift is posited as progress, "there is also a reactionary dimension that effectively colonizes the future by naturalizing and eternalizing the brutal logic of the present." Seen from the perspective of this new chronic modality of time, the exceptionalist status of redress as practised by the liberal state is rendered as a habitual condition that seals off – forgets, as it were – the past. In doing so, it reifies the time of the now as a temporal mode that has fulfilled itself, that fails to recognize the "anachronism" that Agamben (2009, 40) assigns to the "contemporary" person. Contemporary persons have an anachronistic relationship with "their own time" because they "are more capable than others of perceiving and grasping" the problems of their own moment. They perceive, as Agamben puts it, not the light of their contemporary moment but "rather its darkness" (44). This is indeed what Kelly's (2008) narrative dramatizes through its deconstructive recitation of the liberal and Christian scripts that brings to light the nonperformative nature of the official apology Indigenous people received. By refusing to forget the presentness of the past and the not-yet future, the contemporaneity of Kelly's and Miki's (2004) narratives resists the completeness of the present that the settler state's apology enacts. Their shared tactic of interruption, repetition's twin strategy, both re-presents redress and de-spatializes it from its new chronic mode, thus unsettling the Canadian nation-state's dominant discourse.

Undoing the New Chronic Time of Injustice

The last section in *Redress* (Miki 2004), "The Moment of Acknowledgment: Dissonance and Harmony," opens with a poignant reference to Kirsten Emiko McAllister that addresses precisely the question of how Japanese Canadians can rejoin the nation-state as redressed subjects without capitulating to the limits of the liberal state. To effect this political necessity, Japanese Canadians had, in McAllister's (1999) words, "to write themselves into the nation's public sphere. They needed *to be seen* as Canadian citizens whose parents and grandparents were also Canadian as opposed to new immigrants, Asians, Japanese, or the Yellow Peril" (88; quoted in Miki 2004, 322; emphasis added). Miki cites this passage because it articulates what he calls the "reciprocal nature" of the redress movement and settlement: namely, the need to align the process of redress – deracializing and including Japanese Canadians into the Canadian "family" from which they had been expunged – with the liberal discourse of Canadian citizenship. He does not mention, however, that, at the same time that McAllister argues for the important role narrative representations by Japanese Canadians have played in "mak[ing] practical and moral claims" about their internment experience, she is primarily concerned with the "damaging effects" (1999, 80) of the realist mode of these representations.

Indeed, McAllister's argument offers an incisive critique of the realist tradition, demonstrating, on the one hand, its "instrumental political power" to give voice to "a group's 'reality'" (81) and, on the other, its complicity with "the linear narrative of Western progress" (88). Linear narratives, such as Gordon G. Nakayama's *Issei* (1984) and Toyo Takata's *Nikkei Legacy: The Story of Japanese Canadians from Settlement to Today* (1983), were the dominant mode through which the community began to construct its personal and collective experiences. Such accounts represented Japanese Canadians' trajectory in Canada through "'evolutionary' stages" that reproduced the "'pioneer'" master narrative of the settler culture (McAllister 1999, 88). Their self-identification as pioneers helped dispel their characterization as "enemy aliens," thus proving the "violation of their civil and human rights" (McAllister 1999, 88–89) and, consequently, advancing the cause of redress. The consonance that emerges between the Japanese Canadians' self-image as pioneers and the settler state's master narrative of hard labour that rationalizes its claims to the settled land casts these narratives as an ambivalent legitimizing discourse, precisely the "cost" of realism (91) that McAllister sets out to question. Relying on the tradition of realism,

according to which "there is one concrete reality" (80), texts like those referenced above embrace the state's chronic time as the new chronic mode that
manages their representation of violence.

Miki (2004, 322) recognizes this when he writes that "there needed to be
a congruency in the language of redress between a general liberal discourse
founded on citizenship status and the Japanese Canadian subjects whose
social and political identity had been founded on the[ir] racialized exclusion from this discourse," but he does not fully register McAllister's critique
of realism. As she states, this realist discourse "requires the erasure of not
only traits denoting cultural and historical specificity, but traits that 'can not
be shed': bone structure, hair texture, skin pigmentation, the way an eye-
lid folds. These traits become reified as immutable differences" (McAllister
1999, 91). Miki's (2004, 323) own emphasis, instead, is on "the power of language," the importance of "speak[ing] through a collective voice." Inscribed
in this statement is not only the Japanese Canadian collectivity but also the
commonality inherent in employing language as a tool of communication,
an attribute shared with the settler state that accounts for the inescapable
complicity that marks this telling. The redress process unsettles the linear
temporality of the settler culture's colonial time but also traverses its path,
thus remaining lodged within its chronic mode.

Yet the congruence that Miki identifies does not comply with the state's
master narrative. In fact, if we pay attention to the language McAllister
(1999) uses, there is actually a lack of congruence between the compulsion
to take action, and thus reclaim agency, and the passive voice in which this
action is enunciated – "they needed to be seen as Canadian citizens" (88;
quoted in Miki 2004, 322) – a grammatical mode that makes subjectivity
the recipient of the actions of others. McAllister's (1999) use of passive voice
draws attention to the condensed narrative of different temporalities that
are entangled in the process of redress at once as an act of seeing and an
act of being seen, a moment of critical reckoning and of re-visioning, what
Kelly (2008) also dramatizes through the silence shared by the omniscient
and omnipresent Christian God and the ever-present crown attorney. The
grammar of McAllister's salient formulation thus contains the possibility of
transformation whereby subject and object exchange positions: the passive
mode at once evokes and overrides the curtailment of Japanese Canadians'
agency in the internment years, while putting the Canadian public in the
dual position of both having its racist practices called out being summoned
to re-view those practices and, in the process, also look at Japanese Canadians through different eyes. So, what appears to be a single act of Japanese

Canadians writing themselves into the public sphere actually materializes the particular tactic of *re*dress as a moment that turns the Althusserian doctrine of interpellation inside-out. While as the tellers of their national story the Japanese Canadians change their status as objects in spatialized time, the materiality of the history narrated both reproduces and disassembles their subjected subjectivities. The Canadian state is similarly put in a position whereby its power is critiqued yet at the same time it is called on to respond to this national story and, above all, renounce and re-form its exercise of power.

If there is reciprocity in this exchange of positions, it is a paradoxical one. This overlaying of temporalities and discourses can be understood through Judith Butler's (1997, 83) Foucauldian notion of subjectivation, a concept that "denotes both the becoming of the subject and the process of subjection – one inhabits the figure of autonomy only by becoming subjected to a power." The telling of this national story, then, simultaneously destabilizes and upholds power, drawing attention to Foucault's (1990) notion of it as a force that emanates from diverse sources. As an act of redress, the storying of trauma hails the Canadian state to make itself accountable but it also depends on the state's goodwill to effect change. The acts of seeing and "re-cognition" that constitute this story are not reducible to each other, nor do they occur simultaneously even though they inhabit the same moment. They may be bound together by a certain reciprocity, but reciprocity here evokes a historical relationality that has been breached – the forsaken Canadian citizenship rights – and the desire for restitution. What holds them together within the moment of the redress is the reciprocal act of re-cognition, and the hope that this coincident moment may not be limited to an isolated event but may also encompass the responses of those embedded within it. The moment of the redress is thus simultaneously historical and temporal, of what has passed and what is passing.

The doubleness of this act of seeing is not a matter of synchronicity; rather, it affirms the importance of sequencing. Before the Japanese Canadians wrote themselves into the public sphere, they had to claim back, as Miki (2004, 322) says, their "dislocated memories," they had to form a collective identity. The moment that made this possible entailed a double apostrophe: they had to "re-dress" themselves and, in turn, address the public sphere. Miki encapsulates this process cogently (323):

Japanese Canadians were themselves formed by the call for redress. They shaped their unredressed identity out of the racialized national boundaries that had disenfranchised them since the issei first arrived in Canada, and that had led to their incarceration during the war as the "enemy" within. To read themselves into that nation as "citizens," they had to situate themselves in the narrative of nation building as a collective of "citizens" to which they belonged through the rights and responsibilities of citizenship.

That this dual act occurs in the public sphere is crucial. The public sphere was the space within which the Japanese Canadians were racialized and disenfranchised. Moreover, it constitutes the domain where the Canadian polity and the Canadian public meet, a spatial as well as ideological realm reflecting the complicity between the two. After all, it was in the name of the Canadian state's security and the public's safety that the federal government, in collaboration with the provincial government of British Columbia, enacted its policy of incarceration and internment, a policy in which the white public participated with a vengeance. The public sphere was the stage where the national pedagogy of that era was performed, hence the need to redress that history in a similarly public fashion.

Miki's emphasis on reading does not propose a tactic that is different from McAllister's own emphasis on writing. Reading about and storying one's experience of injustice are equally instrumental as tactics, for they complement and unsettle the trope of redress occurring in the now. Because this now encompasses the dual moment of re-cognition and redress, it announces a crisis point, a moment of reckoning that fails to materialize, namely, the moment when the settler state must begin rereading its past through the Japanese Canadians' self-reading and writing acts but fails to do so because it operates within the new chronic mode of its liberal script. In Kelly's (2008) confession, this crisis is inscribed through his declaration of being a "born again pagan," a conversion that serves both as a castigation of the settler state and a challenge to it to recast its old ways. In Miki's (2004, 7) narrative, this turning point occurs at the moment when the Japanese Canadians in the House of Commons defy their instructions by "spontaneously r[ising] and clap[ping]," thus breaking official protocol and the silence imposed on them. In this instance, crisis signals Kelly's and Miki's respective transformation in their narratives' present moment into undisciplined subjects, subjects who re-dress themselves and who, in doing so, reside outside the settler state's new chronic time. The temporal content of this narrativized turning point is the current moment, a moment that is of the now but that also pushes against the margins of the settler state's temporal order. In both Kelly's and Miki's narratives, this moment of re-dress unfolds via the materiality and present form of their writing, which hold together the accumulated trau-matic experience of residential schools and the internment, along with their surrounding discourses and practices. It is shaped by the retention of experience, its durability, and its continuous impact. Because this now is of the present moment but also the site that memory inhabits, it encompasses different temporalities and tells a story that exposes the homogeneity and monologism of the settler state's liberal script.

If Kelly (2008) overrides the nonperformative aspects of the settler state's redress by claiming back his Indigenous spiritual tradition, Miki (2004, 325) incurs the breakdown of the state's new chronic mode by performing a remarkable act of generosity on behalf of the redressed Japanese Canadians. In the penultimate paragraph of "The Moment of Acknowledgement" he writes:

> In receiving the gift of redress from a nation that had stripped them of their rights in the 1940s, they also gave the gift of redress to a nation that had acknowledged the injustices they suffered as a consequence of that action. The receivers had become the givers ... they gave their wartime experience as a gift to the official history of the nation ... The 20th-century history that had been carried in the living bodies of Japanese Canadians for over many decades had to be resolved – it was one of the givens in their negotiations with the nation – but in the singular event of redress, that history had to be surrendered. From that point on, "Japanese Canadian" entered a post-redress condition of new transformations and limitations.

Far from not recognizing the limits of the nation-state's apology, Miki is fully aware of what Lee (2012, 131) calls the "irony of redress ... that it was both a moment of loss as well as of gain." This is abundantly evident in Miki's (2004) use of the term "surrender." Also the title of his third collection of poetry (Miki 2001), which won the Governor General's Award for Poetry, "surrender" signals neither defeat nor capitulation. Rather, it speaks of an ethical approach to justice that sets out to realign the Japanese Canadians' relationship with the state. Although the moment of redress is constructed as a ceremony, gift-giving in this instance does not carry the same obliga-tion of reciprocation that accompanies ritual gift-giving in public and offi-cial contexts. Redress here is certainly the result of an exchange, but the reciprocity that normally joins the giver and the receiver in gift exchanges is asymmetrical in this instance. For, while the Japanese Canadians accept the apology and its attendant settlement agreement as a gift, the gift Canada receives from Japanese Canadians "is far more difficult to quantify" (Lee 2012, 130). This may be so, but I read the surrender of their history to the official history of the Canadian state as an act of subversion, for it functions as a supplement to the state's liberal script. Not a mere gesture of amplification, the coexistence in that history of both the "Japanese Canadians" who had been deracinated and the Japanese Canadians who are now redressed mirrors the iterative narration of the moment of redress, thus signaling the beginning of a transformation process. Significantly, this transformation does not occur in the present moment; instead, it belongs to the temporal economy of "post-redress." Justice – justice not only for the Japanese Canadians – would be the ultimate reciprocal gift that the Canadian state could offer, but its realization lies beyond the now of redress, in the after of redress.

The After of Redress

The after of redress speaks of an uncanny temporality in that any shifts it might open room for are mediated by the temporal closure embodied in the moment preceding it that spatializes – territorializes – the differential dynamics between the before and the after. What comes after the formal process of redress does not necessarily signal that the state as well as those who have been redressed have entered a triumphalist phase. Nor can it be synonymous with the end of history, which is predicated on the displacement of the before and thus on a discourse of deliverance that often relies on mechanisms of acquiescence and their coercive results. The before, to appropriate a phrase by Agamben (2005), is a time that remains.

The after of redress may start in the now of time, but this doesn't perforce mean that it has sublimated the particularities of what has preceded it, nor does it guarantee the beginning of an ethically re-envisioned relationship between the liberal state and the redressed subjects. The after of redress encompasses the limits of justice; it may even signal a political or ethical impasse. Indeed, as Denise Ferreira da Silva (2014, 527) writes, "knowing at the limits of justice is both a kind of knowing and a kind of doing; it is a praxis, one that unsettles what has become but offers no guidance for what has yet to become." Because redress sought in the context of liberal politics of recognition, apologies, and compensation requires rendering the violence redressed legible in terms that are consonant with the state's juridical scripts, it can never wholly exceed the limits of the state. As ceremony that has to follow the form of the parliamentary environment where it takes place, it is constituted as a moment that both enunciates and annunciates justice, thus creating expectations of ethical transformation, but cannot be held accountable for what comes after it. Redress is not lawmaking; it is an ethical response to the catachrestic use of the state's legal force. It is therefore important to be reminded of the fact that an apology in the House of Commons has no legal status, even though it may involve a legally binding settlement, as has been the case with the Japanese Canadian Redress Agreement. Because of its non-legal status, it remains complicit with the very state apparatus that the process of redress sets out to redress. In this sense, the after of redress occurs within a temporal zone whose fulfillment is held in perpetual abeyance.

Knowing the limits of redress, and thus of justice, involves a praxis of vigilance, an approach that resists assimilation into the order of politics and law. The after of redress, then, cannot afford to be wholly reduced to legal measures such as settlements. It must be experienced, instead, as an ongoing agonistic relationship with the state. It is best seen as an aporetic moment whose indeterminacy resists the state's desire to seek closure. Far from pointing to a distant horizon, the after of redress remains embedded in the now – not the present moment of the new chronic mode but the incommensurable now – because justice cannot wait.

Notes

1 According to the document *Evaluation of the Historical Recognition Programs*, issued in January 2013 under Stephen Harper's Conservative government, the Japanese Canadian Redress Agreement is presented not only as an instance that "demonstrated the government's commitment to historical redress" (3.1.3) but also as the event that "spurred ... a number of ethno-cultural groups in Canada, including the Chinese, Italian, Ukrainian, Jewish and Indo-Canadian communities" into action (3.1.1) (Citizenship and Immigration Canada 2013).

2 See "The Road to Justice: The Legal Struggle for Equal Rights of Chinese Canadians," http://www.roadtojustice.ca/redress-campaign. See also James (2004).

3 For an analytical account of the different Canadian governments' approach to redress, see James (2008, 2013).

4 Richard Vernon (2012) makes a similar argument in *Historical Redress: Must We Pay for the Past?* See especially the chapter "What Memory Calls For" (64–87).

5 See Foucault (1990), especially the chapter "Scientia Sexualis" (51–73).

6 Gathered together in a beautifully designed and produced boxed set, the second and third volumes of the set are *Response, Responsibility, and Renewal: Canada's Truth and Reconciliation Journey*, edited by Gregory Younging, Jonathan Dewar, and Mike DeGagné (2009), and *Cultivating Canada: Reconciliation through the Lens of Cultural Diversity*, edited by Ashok Mathur, Jonathan Dewar, and Mike DeGagné (2011).

7 Though the Aboriginal Healing Foundation (https://www.ahf.ca) had an eleven-year mandate, it shut down in 2014. Its history, board membership, activity reports, financial statements, and diverse activities remain available via its archived website, with many of the files being downloadable.

8 Pauline Wakeham (2012, 209–33) makes a persuasive argument along these lines. For further discussion of Canada's neoliberal agenda with regard to policies about redress and reconciliation, see also James (2013, 31–46).

9 Harper did refer to colonialism a year after his official apology, but only to disavow its reality. His statement at the G7 meeting in the United States that Canada "has no history of colonialism" was a shocking incident that attracted a lot of media attention. See, for example, https://www.youtube.com/watch?v=gqTMbSrAnxQ&ab_channel=CanuckPolitics. In contrast, when in 2017 Prime Minister Justin Trudeau offered an official apology to the Indigenous students of Newfoundland and Labrador left out of Harper's apology, he directly referred to "colonialism" and "colonial ways of thinking" a total of four times (Trudeau 2017).

10 As the Truth and Reconciliation Commission's (2015, 12) report states: "Without truth, justice, and healing, there can be no genuine reconciliation ... truth telling ... restores the human dignity of victims of violence and calls governments and citizens to account."

11 Following the private meetings of different groups of Indigenous delegates with the Pope at the Vatican, Pope Francis offered an apology and also promised to visit with Indigenous people in Canada in the coming summer (see Hager 2022). For the full text of the Pope's apology in translation see "Address of His Holiness Pope Francis, Maskwacis," https://www.rcaanc-cirnac.gc.ca/eng/1689777364741/1689777394126. While the papal apology fulfilled in principle the purpose of the delegation's meetings at the Vatican, some Indigenous leaders and communities found it lacking partly because it would have no legal standing due to the Vatican's diplomatic immunity (Fine 2022).

12 Though the table of contents does not list any authors under "Introduction," I assume it was authored by the collection's three editors.

13 The phrase is commonly attributed to Duncan Campbell Scott, who was associated with the expansion of the residential school system in the 1920s and 1930s, but Mark Abley (2013, 36–37) attributes it to Richard Henry Pratt, a high-ranking officer in the American army.

14 See, for example, Stephen Harper's (2006) apology to Chinese Canadians.

15 For an analysis and critique of Hobbes's person-state analogy, see Ben Holland (2017), especially his "Introduction" (4–13) and "Conclusion" (208–17).

References

Abley, Mark. 2013. *Conversations with a Dead Man: The Legacy of Duncan Campbell Scott*. Vancouver: Douglas and McIntyre.

Agamben, Giorgio. 1998. *Homo Sacer: Sovereign Power and Bare Life*. Translated by Daniel Heller-Roazen. Palo Alto, CA: Stanford University Press.

– 2005. *The Time That Remains: A Commentary on the Letter to the Romans.* Translated by Patricia Daley. Stanford, CA: Stanford University Press.

– 2009. *What Is an Apparatus? and Other Essays.* Translated by David Kishik and Stefan Pedatella. Redwood City, CA: Stanford University Press.

Ahmed, Sara. 2006. "The Nonperformativity of Antiracism." *Meridians: Feminism, Race, Transnationalism* 7 (1): 104–26.

Bernstein, Susan David. 1997. *Confessional Subjects: Revelations of Gender and Power in Victorian Literature and Culture.* Chapel Hill: University of North Carolina Press.

Butler, Judith. 1997. *The Psychic Life of Power.* Redwood City, CA: Stanford University Press.

Carastathis, Anna. 2010. "Fanon on Turtle Island: Revisiting the Question of Violence." In *Fanon and the Decolonization of Philosophy,* edited by Elizabeth A. Hope and Tracey Nicholls, with a Foreword by Mireille Fanon-Mendès France, 77–102. Lanham, MD: Lexington Books.

Carroll, David. 1989. *Paraesthetics: Foucault, Lyotard, Derrida.* London: Routledge.

– 2006. "The Aesthetic and the Political: Lyotard." In *Jean François Lyotard: Aesthetics,* edited by Victor E. Taylor and Gregg Lambert, 39–71. London: Routledge.

Castellano, Marlene Brant, Linda Archibald, and Mike DeGagné. 2008. "Introduction." In *From Truth to Reconciliation: Transforming the Legacy of Residential Schools,* edited by Marlene Brant Castellano, Linda Archibald, and Mike DeGagné, 1–8. Ottawa: Aboriginal Healing Foundation.

Cazdyn, Eric. 2012. *The Already Dead: The New Time of Politics, Culture, and Illness.* Durham, NC: Duke University Press.

Celermajer, Danielle. 2009. *The Sins of the Nation and the Ritual of Apologies.* Cambridge: Cambridge University Press.

Citizenship and Immigration Canada. 2013. *Evaluation of the Historical Recognition Programs.* https://www.canada.ca/content/dam/ircc/migration/ircc/english/pdf/pub/historical_recognition.pdf.

Corry, M. Shivaum. 2020. "Apology Ad Infinitum: Colonialism and the Need for Repeated Apologies for Canadian Aboriginal Boarding Schools." In *The Rhetoric of Official Apologies: Critical Essays,* edited by Lisa S. Villadsen and Jason A. Edwards, 117–37. Lanham, MD: Lexington Books.

Felman, Shoshana, and Dori Laub. 1992. *Testimony: Crises of Witnessing in Literature, Psychoanalysis, and History.* London: Routledge.

Ferreira da Silva, Denise. 2014. "Radical Praxis or Knowing (at) the Limits of Justice." In *At the Limits of Justice: Women of Colour on Terror,* edited by Suvendrini Perera and Sherene H. Razack, 526–37. Toronto: University of Toronto Press.

Fine, Sean. 2022. "Pope Francis's Apology for Abuses at Church-Run Residential Schools Unlikely to Have Legal Ramifications, Experts Say." *Globe and Mail,* April 1. https://www.theglobeandmail.com/canada/article-pope-residential-schools-apology/.

First Peoples Group. n.d. "Fred Kelly, First Nations Elder." https://firstpeoplesgroup.com/team-member/fred-kelly/.

Foucault, Michel. 1990. *The History of Sexuality,* vol. 1. Translated by Robert Hurley. New York: Vintage Books.

Friese, Heidrun. 2001. "Introduction." In *The Moment: Time and Rupture in Modern Thought*, edited by Heidrun Friese, 1–15. Liverpool: Liverpool University Press.

Goldberg, Shari. 2013. *Quiet Testimony: A Theory of Witnessing from Nineteenth-Century American Literature*. New York: Fordham University Press.

Government of Canada. 2008. "Statement of Apology to Former Students of Indian Residential Schools." https://www.rcaanc-cirnac.gc.ca/eng/1100100015644/1571589171655.

Grant, Tavia, Willow Fiddler, and Eric Reguly. 2022. "Indigenous Delegation Arrives in Rome for Historic Meetings with Pope Francis." *Globe and Mail*, March 27. https://www.theglobeandmail.com/canada/article-pope-francis-vatican-indigenous-reconciliation/.

Hager, Mike. 2022. "Pope Francis's Apology Elicits Mixed Reactions from Members of Tk'emlúps te Secwépemc First Nation." *Globe and Mail*, April 2. https://www.theglobeandmail.com/canada/british-columbia/article-pope-residential-schools-apology-reaction/.

Harper, Stephen. 2006. "Chinese Canadians." *House of Commons Debates*, 39th Parliament, 1st Session, June 22, 141: 1515. House of Commons, https://www.ourcommons.ca/DocumentViewer/en/39-1/house/sitting-46/hansard#OOB-1619175.

Henderson, Jennifer, and Pauline Wakeham. 2009. "Colonial Reckoning, National Reconciliation? Aboriginal Peoples and the Culture of Redress in Canada." *English Studies in Canada* 35 (1): 1–26.

– 2013. "Introduction." In *Reconciling Canada: Critical Perspectives on the Culture of Redress*, edited by Jennifer Henderson and Pauline Wakeham, 3–27. Toronto: University of Toronto Press.

Hobbes, Thomas. 1651. *Leviathan: The English and Latin Texts*, edited by Noel Malcolm. Oxford: Oxford University Press.

Holland, Ben. 2017. *The Moral Person of the State: Pufendorf, Sovereignty and Composite Polities*. Cambridge: Cambridge University Press.

Indian and Northern Affairs Canada. 1997. *Gathering Strength: Canada's Aboriginal Action Plan*. Ottawa: Minister of Indian Affairs and Northern Development. https://publications.gc.ca/site/eng/9.696357/publication.html.

James, Matt. 2004. "Recognition, Redistribution and Redress: The Case of the 'Chinese Head Tax.'" *Canadian Journal of Political Science* 37 (4): 883–902.

– 2008. "Wrestling with the Past: Apologies, Quasi-Apologies, and Non-Apologies in Canada." In *The Age of Apology: Facing Up to the Past*, edited by Mark Gibney, Rhoda F. Howard-Hassmann, Jean-Marc Coicaud, and Niklaus Steiner, 137–53. Philadelphia: University of Pennsylvania Press.

– 2013. "Neoliberal Heritage Redress." In *Reconciling Canada: Critical Perspectives on the Culture of Redress*, edited by Jennifer Henderson and Pauline Wakeham, 31–46. Toronto: University of Toronto Press.

Kamboureli, Smaro. 2012. "Introduction. Shifting the Ground of a Discipline: Emergence and Canadian Literary Studies in English." In *Shifting the Ground of Canadian Literary Studies*, edited by Smaro Kamboureli and Robert Zacharias, 1–36. Waterloo, ON: Wilfrid Laurier University Press.

Kelly, Fred. 2008. "Confession of a Born Again Pagan." In *From Truth to Reconciliation: Transforming the Legacy of Residential Schools,* edited by Marlene Brant Castellano, Linda Archibald, and Mike DeGagné, 13–41. Ottawa: Aboriginal Healing Foundation.

Kierkegaard, Søren. 1980. *The Concept of Anxiety: A Simple Psychological Orienting Deliberation on the Dogmatic Issue of Hereditary Sin,* edited and translated by Reidar Thomte in collaboration with Albert B. Anderson. Princeton, NJ: Princeton University Press.

Lee, Christopher. 2012. "Asian Canadian Critical Practice in Commemoration." In *Cultural Grammars of Nation, Diaspora, and Indigeneity in Canada,* edited by Christine Kim, Sophie McCall, and Melina Baum Singer, 119–33. Waterloo, ON: Wilfrid Laurier University Press.

Mathur, Ashok, Jonathan Dewar, and Mike DeGagné, eds. 2011. *Cultivating Canada: Reconciliation through the Lens of Cultural Diversity.* Ottawa: Aboriginal Healing Foundation.

McAllister, Kirsten Emiko. 1999. "Narrating Japanese Canadians In and Out of the Canadian Nation: A Critique of Realist Forms of Representation." *Canadian Journal of Communication* 24 (1): 79–103.

Mignolo, Walter. 2011. *The Darker Side of Western Modernity: Global Futures, Decolonial Options.* Durham, NC: Duke University Press.

Miki, Roy. 2001. *Surrender.* Toronto: Mercury Press.

– 2004. *Redress: Inside the Japanese Canadian Call for Justice.* Vancouver: Raincoast Books.

Moraru, Christian. 2015. "Decompressing Culture: Three Steps toward a Geomethodology." In *The Planetary Turn: Relationality and Geoaesthetics in the Twenty-First Century,* edited by Amy J. Elias and Christian Moraru, 211–44. Evanston, IL: Northwestern University Press.

Mulroney, Brian. 1988. "Japanese Canadians Interned during World War II – National Redress." *House of Commons Debates,* 33rd Parliament, 2nd Session, September 22, 15: 19499–500. Library of Parliament, http://parl.canadiana.ca/view/oop.debates_HOC3302_15/1037?r=0&s=3.

Nakayama, Gordon G. 1984. *Issei.* Toronto: NC Press.

Negash, Girma. 2006. *Apologia Politica: States and Their Apologies by Proxy.* Lanham, MD: Lexington Books.

Oikawa, Mona. 2012. *Cartographies of Violence: Japanese Canadian Women, Memory, and the Subjects of the Internment.* Toronto: University of Toronto Press.

Olick, Jeffrey K., and Brenda Coughlin. 2003. "The Politics of Regret: Analytical Frames." In *Politics and the Past: On Repairing Historical Injustices,* edited by John Torpey, 37–62. Lanham, MD: Rowman and Littlefield.

RCAP (Royal Commission on Aboriginal Peoples). 1996. *Report of the Royal Commission on Aboriginal Peoples.* https://www.bac-lac.gc.ca/eng/discover/aboriginal-heritage/royal-commission-aboriginal-peoples/Pages/final-report.aspx.

Renan, Ernest. (1882) 1990. "What Is a Nation?" In *Nation and Narration,* edited by Homi K. Bhabha; translated and annotated by Martin Thom, 8–22. London: Routledge.

Richter, Gerhard. 2011. *Afterness: Figures of Following in Modern Thought and Aesthetics*. New York: Columbia University Press.

Sharma, Sarah. 2014. *Temporality and Cultural Politics*. Durham, NC: Duke University Press.

Shinn, Abigail. 2018. *Conversion Narratives in Early Modern England: Tales of Turning*. London: Palgrave.

Simpson, Audra, and Andrea Smith. 2014. "Introduction." In *Theorizing Native Studies*, edited by Audra Simpson and Andrea Smith, 1–30. Durham, NC: Duke University Press.

Somani, Alia. 2011. "The Apology and Its Aftermath: National Atonement or the Management of Minorities." *Postcolonial Text* 6 (1): 1–18.

Sterling, Shirley. 1992. *My Name is Seepeetza*. Toronto: Groundwood Books and House of Anansi.

Takata, Toyo. 1983. *Nikkei Legacy: The Story of Japanese Canadians from Settlement to Today*. Toronto: NC Press.

Trouillot, Michel-Rolph. 2000. "Abortive Rituals: Historical Apologies in the Global Era." *Interventions* 2 (2): 171–86.

Trudeau, Justin. 2017. "Statement of Apology on Behalf of the Government of Canada to Former Students of the Newfoundland and Labrador Residential Schools." https://www.pm.gc.ca/en/news/backgrounders/2017/11/24/statement-apology-behalf-government-canada-former-students.

Truth and Reconciliation Commission of Canada. 2015. *Honouring the Truth, Reconciling for the Future: Summary of the Final Report of the Truth and Reconciliation Commission of Canada*. Ottawa: Truth and Reconciliation Commission of Canada. https://www.deslibris.ca/ID/218849.

Vernon, Richard. 2012. *Historical Redress: Must We Pay for the Past?* London: Continuum.

Villadsen, Lisa S., and Jason A. Edwards. 2020. "Introduction." In *The Rhetoric of Official Apologies: Critical Essays*, edited by Lisa S. Villadsen and Jason A. Edwards, 1–19. Lanham, MD: Lexington Books.

Waisanen, Don. 2018. *Political Conversion: Personal Transformation as Strategic Public Communication*. Lanham, MD: Lexington Books.

Wakeham, Pauline. 2012. "The Cunning of Reconciliation: Reinventing White Civility in the 'Age of Apology.'" In *Shifting the Ground of Canadian Literary Studies*, edited by Smaro Kamboureli and Robert Zacharias, 209–33. Waterloo, ON: Wilfrid Laurier University Press.

Warner, Marina. 2002. "Sorry: The Present State of Apology." *openDemocracy*, November 7. https://www.opendemocracy.net/democracy-apologypolitics/article_603.jsp.

Whelan, Frederick G. 2015. *The Political Thought of Hume and His Contemporaries: Enlightenment Projects*, vol. 2. London: Routledge.

Younging, Gregory, Jonathan Dewar, and Mike DeGagné, eds. 2009. *Response, Responsibility, and Renewal: Canada's Truth and Reconciliation Journey*. Ottawa: Aboriginal Healing Foundation.

6

The Political Act of Defining Ourselves After Redress: Japanese Canadian Activism, Identity, and What Can Be Learned from the Principles of Indigenous Storytelling

Kirsten Emiko McAllister

Understanding who we are as Japanese Canadians has been an ongoing struggle in the aftermath of the government's racial elimination plan. Our stories, including research, have been essential for defining who we are, especially during the movement to demand redress from the Canadian government in the 1980s. To make a case for redress Japanese Canadian activists and artists had to challenge the racist work of white historians, sociologists, writers, and filmmakers who justified the government's treatment of our families as threats to national security (Oikawa 2012, 19–78). In terms of research, the government acted as gatekeeper, discrediting Japanese Canadian thinkers, for example, by describing them as "bitter" and "resentful" (see Roy 1978, 2014) and attempting to block their publication in academic presses (Chapter 4, this volume). More widely, Indigenous scholars have written extensively about the role of storytelling for their peoples. Cherokee Daniel Heath Justice (2018, 75) writes, "story makes meaning of the relationships that define who we are and what our place is in the world; it reminds us of our duties, our rights and responsibilities, and the consequences and transformative possibilities of our actions." As Secwepemc/Syilx Dorothy Cucw-la7 Christian (2017) explains, Indigenous peoples know that telling their stories in their terms, in accordance with their principles and practices, and refusing colonizers' attempts to control how they are defined, is essential for their survival and self-determination. Now, over thirty-five years after the 1988 Japanese Canadian Redress Agreement, drawing on

Indigenous scholars' work on storytelling, this chapter argues that Japanese Canadians need to critically rethink the stories we use to define ourselves today in what is a new political context.

Before the settler colony of Canada rounded up everyone along the Pacific coast in 1942, my mother's generation grew up in vibrant, tightly knit Japanese Canadian communities on the territories of the Songhees, Sḵwx̱wú7mesh (Squamish Nation), xʷməθkʷəy'əm (Musqueam), səlílwətaʔɬ (Tsleil-Waututh), Nuu-chah-nulth, Kwakwaḵa'wakw, and the many other sovereign Nations of this land. After the last restrictions imposed under the authority of the War Measures Act were lifted in 1949, little remained of these communities.

Before 1949, Canadian leaders believed that "only a racially homogeneous society could be stable ... [and] that the Asian was genetically incapable of commitment to the [country's] way of life and to British values and institutions" (Sunahara 1981, 7). Thus, to stop what anti-Asian leagues and politicians claimed was the "quiet insidious penetration" of British Columbia by an "aggressive, unassimilable" race (Ward 1990, 107), in 1942 the government uprooted Japanese Canadians from their homes in settlements along Pacific coast, sent them to internment, labour, and prisoner-of-war camps, liquidated their properties, and, when the war ended, forced them to leave the province, relocating the majority across the rest of the country and shipping over 4,000 to Japan.

Today, faced with assimilation, the loss of identity, high rates of "intermarriage," and increasing numbers of *hapa*[1] with little contact with other Japanese Canadians beyond a few family members, it would seem that the plan to remove all people of "Japanese racial origin" from Canada has been for the most part successful. But over the years, I have learned that members of each generation come to understand who they are as Japanese Canadians in their own way, confronting how we've been constituted through a history of exclusionary laws and racial elimination. This is challenging since Canadian history has at different times erased, vilified, discounted, and then paternalistically re-explained our existence to us through white settlers' perspectives and agendas (Oikawa 2012; see also Chapter 4 in this volume). To explore over 100 years of community life and activism, many of my generation turned to the words of other Japanese Canadians whose families were targeted by the War Measures Act during the 1940s, such as Ken Adachi ([1976] 1991), Ann Sunahara (1981), Toyo Takata (1983), Muriel Kitagawa (Miki 1985), and Mona Oikawa (1986). They brought to life the visions of both little-recognized community members and outspoken activists who challenged racist laws as far back as the early 1900s. For each of us, though, even within the same family, the process of understanding who we are is different. The majority will likely never identify as Japanese Canadian, and many others no longer feel a need to take part in community life. Then there are those who have returned to the community, seeking a way to give shape to what is not otherwise knowable, something unsettling that yearns for a voice for which none of us alone has the words. For myself, it was only when I returned in the late 1980s that I began to understand why my mere presence, even as a child, could provoke anxieties and aggression when I unknowingly crossed the invisible lines protecting whiteness and disturbed the secrets of its guilt. My return also made me realize all that was possible when you belonged to the larger collective of community, despite the divisions and difficulties.

For many of my generation, it was the Japanese Canadian redress movement that made the return possible. Building on decades of activism, redress activists mobilized thousands of Japanese Canadians across the country in the 1980s, reconnecting people and rebuilding community organizations[2] in a movement to demand redress from the federal government for its violation of their rights during the 1940s (Miki 2004). Building on Asian Canadian activism from the 1960s and 1970s, redress activists made clear that the act of defining who we are was a political act. Like Indigenous leaders, they understood that, faced with high rates of assimilation, to survive we had to assert control over the stories that defined us, and write our histories in our terms, according to our needs. As I explain below, demanding redress required challenging the government's story that defined Japanese Canadians as threats to national security. Thus, activists proposed a new story where Canadian citizenship defined the thousands the government rounded up, interned, and sent to work in road camps and on sugar beet farms as forced labourers, making the case that the Canadian government had violated the rights of its own citizens.

Over the last twenty years, there have been extensive criticisms of how states use apologies, reparations, reconciliation, and redress to repair governments' reputations and avoid making meaningful structural changes. In this context, I examine the strategy of using a national framework to define ourselves as citizens and conclude the chapter by reflecting on the disavowals it entails, including the failure to recognize our responsibilities to rework our settler colonial relations with the Indigenous peoples and confront our complex relations to Japan in the larger geopolitical arena of imperialism (see Day 2016; Fujitani 2011; Oikawa 2012; Yoneyama 2016).

While Asian American scholars have examined Japanese American redress (Inouye (2016) also examines Japanese Canadian redress), including how it has functioned to produce compliant model minorities (Fujitani 2011, 21, 31; Paik 2016, 23), there has been little critical research on Japanese Canadian redress from the perspectives of survivors and those intergenerationally affected by the government's use of the War Measures Act to remove all people of "Japanese racial origin" from Canada. Moreover, it isn't clear what recent generations know about the redress movement and how it shaped today's community, including what can be learned from its strategies and limitations. In keeping with the theme of the volume, this chapter examines the community "after" the conclusion of the redress movement with the 1988 Redress Agreement and how it shaped Japanese Canadian identity. To rethink how to conceptualize our identity without relying on national frameworks, I first turn to Indigenous theories of storytelling and defining identity. Scholars like Justice (2018) explain that a people are defined by their stories and the importance for Indigenous peoples to tell their own stories in accordance with their principles and practices, refusing colonizers' attempt to control how they are defined (Lawrence 2004, 2013). While I argue that Japanese Canadians need to critically question whose stories we now use to define ourselves, we also need to explore what we want to embrace as our guiding principles (both of which are beyond the scope of this chapter). This is challenging since many community organizations increasingly rely on non-Japanese Canadians (including other Asian Canadians, in addition to post–Second World War Japanese immigrants whose families were not directly targeted by the War Measures Act in the 1940s) to research our histories and use their frameworks to tell our stories, acquiescing to, and in many cases embracing, their authority to define who we are.

Given the limited amount of critical research on redress from Japanese Canadian perspectives, in the next section I draw on my own story of return in the late 1980s to recall how redress contributed to rebuilding the postwar community and how, in this period, the National Association of Japanese Canadians' (NAJC) vision of justice went beyond Japanese Canadians, recognizing the importance of solidarity with other groups. The third section examines Japanese Canadian redress in the broader context of the widespread criticisms of state redress, apologies, and reconciliation. This section discusses the Canadian state's use of redress to turn its violation of Japanese Canadians' rights into a humanitarian lesson while turning its back on its ongoing genocidal treatment of Indigenous peoples. The fourth section examines the activities of the NAJC following the Redress Agreement.

While the NAJC led the redress movement in the 1980s, I question whether it has continued to prioritize its social justice mandate, especially in relation to Indigenous and Black Lives Matter's (BLM) most recent calls for justice. And while there isn't space to analyze other major community organizations – which one would expect to prioritize the empowerment of Japanese Canadians while pursuing social justice more widely – much of the chapter is written with them in mind.[3]

The fifth section examines the national framework of the community's story of redress. I explore why this framework has been so appealing to many Nisei. But insofar as it sets up a national binary that positions being Canadian in opposition to being Japanese, I argue that it has restricted our ability to think beyond the script of being good multicultural Canadian citizens and critically examine our relations not only to Imperial and postwar Japan but also to the Indigenous peoples whose lands we illegally occupy as well as the ever-growing numbers of people globally, who, like Japanese Canadians, have been displaced, dispossessed, incarcerated, and hyper-exploited. This chapter concludes with an account of my family's visit to East Lillooet, where my mother was interned, and what Chief Michelle Edwards of the Cayoose Creek Band from the St'át'imc Nation taught us about storytelling and upholding our relations and reciprocal responsibilities to one another.

A Framework for Identity: What Can Be Learned from Principles of Indigenous Storytelling

After redress, understanding our identities as Japanese Canadians continues to be an ongoing struggle. During the grassroots activism of 1960s and 1970s, the redress movement in the 1980s, and the cultural politics of the 1990s, there were many lively forums to discuss and debate issues like identity, racism, and power, linking past and ongoing injustices. These forums were illuminating (and challenging) because they were embedded in larger political struggles that included Indigenous and other racialized and marginalized communities and pushed us to think beyond our own experiences and act more widely in solidarity with other groups wanting to build a more just world (Gilroy 2001). But today, how many Japanese Canadian forums critically explore identity beyond Japanese heritage, Canadian citizenship, and the community's story of internment and dispossession (which, I argue below, has been appropriated by the government)?[4] Moreover, over the last two decades, few community forums have critically examined or taken action to change our involvement in colonialism as racialized settlers or our complex relations to Imperial Japan, including in the context of war and the forced "deportation" of over 4,000 Japanese Canadians, most of whom were born in Canada and spoke little Japanese (Kage 2012). This raises questions about the stories that our national organizations, such as the NAJC, Nikkei Place, and the Nikkei National Museum, along with the new generation of artists and storytellers, use to define us.

During the 1980s, the NAJC primarily served Japanese Canadians whose families immigrated before 1942 and were targeted as threats to national security during the 1940s. At the time, there was no question that identity was a political issue (see Miki and Kobayashi 1991). However, following the 1988 agreement and the NAJC's disbursement of redress funds in the 1990s, participation of this demographic has significantly decreased, as noted by a number of NAJC staff and board members. Moreover, while there are Japanese immigrants, like those on Salt Spring Island, who have run projects on local Japanese Canadian history and are concerned with social justice, national organizations have noted that the Japanese immigrants and non-Japanese Canadians who predominantly use community centres such as Nikkei Place want programs that deliver Japanese social and cultural activities that conform to widely criticized multicultural definitions of ethnic identity and reduce our cultures to what can be easily commodified and consumed. Multicultural definitions of identity are categorically separated from the political (or reduce the political to palatable stories of victimhood). They typically do not consider widespread criticisms of multiculturalism's link to settler colonialism or how multiculturalism is used to manage racialized sectors of Canada's immigrant/settler population. In other words, these organizations are making political choices to align themselves with the settler colony of Canada's agenda (Abu-Laban and Gabriel 2002; Kamboureli 2000; Kobayashi 1993; Mackey 2002).

My conception of identity has been shaped by earlier generations of critical race, Black, and anti- and post-colonial scholars (for example, Baldwin 1955; Fanon [1952] 2008; Gilroy 2001; Hall 1990; Lorde 1984; Memmi 1965; Spivak 1988) who foreground questions of power, examining how racialized groups are constituted by, as well as in resistance to the structures and discourses of racism, colonialism, and transatlantic slavery (Jiwani and Dessner 2016; McKittrick 2013; Sharpe 2016). Of particular importance for my research has been their analyses of how power works at a subjective level, and thus the need to self-reflexively examine how we can internalize racist, heteronormative, nationalist, white supremacist, and colonial discourses and identify as "good ethnics" (model minorities for "Asians") complicit with the dominant order (Kawai 2005; Mamdani 2004; Ramadan 2010). In this chapter, I turn to what can be learned from the theories of Indigenous storytelling, on the one hand, to heed the call for settlers to decolonize our relations to Indigenous peoples and lands; and, on the other hand, to consider the way these theories (like Black and anti-colonial theories) foreground questions of power, resistance and self-reflexivity, in addition to how their epistemological starting point is a world of interdependence that calls on us to recognize our responsibilities as "good relatives" to humans and non-humans (Justice 2018, 84). I recognize that the work of scholars such as Stó:lō and St'at'imc Jo-Ann Archibald Q'um Q'um Xiiem (2006), Christian (2017), Nêhiyaw and Saulteaux Margaret Kovach (2009), and Justice (2018) concern Indigenous identity and self-determination. Yet as a racialized settler, their work has helped me think more deeply about how our stories define who we now are and could become as Japanese Canadians in relation to the worlds that make life possible (see Fujikane 2021). With a conception of the world as interdependent, these scholars explain how storytelling teaches their peoples that they are defined through their relations and the responsibilities these relations entail. Like Christian (2017) and Archibald, Lee-Morgan, and De Santolo (2019), Justice writes about these relations in terms of kinship. Kinship can be defined narrowly, legitimating "only certain kinds of relatedness ... based on ideas about race, blood and DNA that typically supports heteronormative patriarchal forms of kinship" (Justice 2018, 74). In contrast, kinship in Indigenous stories includes the land and non-human relatives to whom they are responsible, recognizing they can survive only through interdependence with these relatives (75).

As racialized settlers, it is important we recognize that our relations to the lands we illegally occupy are of a different ontological order than those of Indigenous peoples. Kovach (2009, 55–63) states that each Indigenous group's relation to their lands and kin have uniquely developed over thousands of years and are the basis for what she refers to as their "tribal knowledge." As such, settlers cannot "tell" or "use" their stories to guide us in our own relations. This would fail to understand how each story is specific to a particular Indigenous people (and often a lineage within that people) and is intrinsic to whom they are according to their unique and ongoing relations and responsibilities to their territories and kin. In contrast, as Japanese Canadians, we need to first recognize how our stories place us in extractive and genocidal relations to the lands and peoples where we live, and the need to learn how to respectfully build non-appropriative, non-destructive relations (see Fujikane 2021). What are these relations and responsibilities for us regarding the particular Indigenous peoples whose territories we illegally occupy as well as the other (exploited, displaced) peoples and the lands our lives depend on?

To understand how our stories define us, I turn to what Justice (2018, 34) writes about storytelling – namely, that stories are fundamental to the process of "how we learn to be human":

> [The] role of experience, of teaching, and of story – [is] to help us find ways of meaningful being in whatever worlds we inhabit, whatever contexts we've inherited ... Our lives are incarnations of the stories we tell, the stories told about us, and the stories we inherit ... even those not given voice are inextricably embraided into our sense of self.

He explains that stories necessarily involve relationships:

> In all cases, story makes meaning of the relationships that define who we are and what our place is in the world; it reminds us of our duties, our rights and responsibilities, and the consequences and transformative possibilities of our actions. It also highlights what we lose when those relationships are broken or denied to us, and what we might gain from even partial remembrance. (75)

As Christian (2017, 12) writes,

> Our cultural stories are at the core of our ways of knowing, being, doing, acting, listening and thinking ... Furthermore, our Sek'lep or Senklip7/ Coyote stories are intimately connected to the land and embed the customary laws and cultural protocols that give us our operating principles of how we as Secwepemc and Syilx peoples are to live with each other and all the other sentient beings on the land.

Colonization, she explains, has depended not just on laws and military force but also on colonizers' stories that attempt to sever Indigenous people from their land, from each other, and from their non-human kin (8, 171) and, as Justice (2018, 84) also argues, turn "these lands into exploitable resources and diverse people into memories." Justice further explains that "to be a good relative ... is to counter these exploitative forces and the stories that legitimate them, while at the same time affirming – or reaffirming – better, more generative, more generous ways to uphold our obligations and our commitment so our diverse and varied kin" (84).

Indigenous storytelling does not romanticize an ideal community embalmed in the misty past. These stories are not always happy. They chronicle the destructive forces of colonial devastation (84). They recognize the weakness of humans and how relations with non-humans are not all benevolent. "A truly respectful understanding of relationality also means respect for other people's capacity to cause each other harm" (96–97). Justice notes that "while many traditional peoples continue to practice lives of accountability and honour with the world, a great resource-consuming mass of humanity is busy ravaging these delicate threads of interdependence" (39).

Writing in "the contexts we've inherited" (34), including colonialism, Indigenous scholars make clear how Indigenous storytelling is political and involves power. As Mi'kmaw Bonita Lawrence (2004, 16) has so systematically explained:

Who is an Indian in North America begins with the colonial project of land theft and regulation of Native Identity ... through direct legislation such as the Indian Act ... At present formal regulation of Native identity in Canada and the United States [has an] overarching primary goal: to set the legal parameters by which Indigenousness can be said to be eliminated.

Likewise, in the wake of legislation that has regulated Japanese Canadian identities first as threats to national security and now as apolitical ethnics, if we are going to be more than ciphers of the state, our national organizations, like the NAJC and Nikkei Place, need to show leadership and question the repercussions of the stories we use to define ourselves as Japanese Canadians. As Justice (2018, 48) further states:

Settler colonialism isn't something one just gets over; it's woven into all aspects of your experience, and those strangling threads are too often invisible and all the more wounding as a result. What Indigenous texts do is make visible what's so often unseen, and suggests a much more complicated perspective to what is too often grossly simplified in popular culture ... And in considering the frayed edges of kinship that so many of us have worked to reweave in our own lives and those of so many of our communities, Indigenous writers have offered powerful provocative, and often quite deliberately "unsettling" visions that chronicle the challenges of rebuilding what settler colonialism has mangled.

Here I also call on generations of Japanese Canadian artists and activists to make visible the settler colonialism woven into what constitutes us as racialized settlers (see Yakashiro 2021). I ask: What provocative and unsettling visions do they offer that "chronicle the challenges of [building]" ways of being good relatives (May 2021; Matsunaga 2021)? Do they criticize or reproduce entrenched racist and white nationalist narratives about, for example, exotic Japan or the "silent" traumatized Japanese Canadian (Oikawa 2012)? Like their Indigenous and Black peers, does this new generation draw on the knowledge, political activism, and oppositional cultural practices of the generations preceding them or their contemporaries within and across other targeted communities – rather than relying on white researchers and a small group of easily accessible community experts whose voices have become institutionalized by white and other non-Japanese Canadian academics and hegemonic community institutions along with Japanese Canadian artists who uncritically use popular discourses about "Japanese/Canadian" identity? How do they/we find – never mind learn how to listen to – what can be learned from the experiences that white institutions and our own community have silenced? And how can we support and learn from newer generations of activists, artists and thinkers who are trying to collaboratively build new futures across communities and borders?

Archibald, Lee-Morgan, and De Santolo (2019) discuss how Indigenous peoples have developed "decolonizing research that aspires to re-cover, re-cognize, re-create, re-present and 're-search back' by using [their] own ontological and epistemological constructs," and how they understand the importance of intergenerational knowledge (6). Japanese Canadian artists and activists working in the political contexts from the 1960s to the early 2000s, such as Roy Kiyooka, Nobuo Kubota, Roy Miki, Aiko Suzuki, Jesse Nishihata, Midi Onodera, Denise Fujiwara, Louise Noguchi, and Cindy Mochizuki, have likewise explored methods to "re-cover, re-cognize … re-present and 're-search back.'" But as Japanese Canadians, where are the venues to more widely explore our shared ontological and epistemological constructs? Without this knowledge, how do we identify principles that can guide us that do not reproduce hegemonic theories of justice that reinforce colonialism and racial capitalism (Said 1979; Smith 2012)? We can't simply draw on the constructs guiding pre–Second World War Issei generations.

It is easy to romanticize their local village cultures, so if we turn to this generation, we need to be aware that by the late 1800s they were already affected by industrialization and the Meiji era's growing nationalism and militarization (Nakai 2018). Can we start by examining our relations to the lands we occupy now as racialized settlers? As Justice (2018, 75) asks, what stories make "meaning of the relationships that define who we are and what our place is in the world; [that remind] us of our duties, our rights and responsibilities, and the consequences and transformative possibilities of our actions ... what we lose when those relationships are broken or denied to us, and what we might gain from even partial remembrance"?

Again, it's "not enough to claim relations with other peoples – we must consider what those relations ask of us, and how we may learn to be kin in ways that make one another's lives better" (82). These relations can't be learned through abstract theorizing, reading, or decolonizing workshops alone. Nor can we decide what is "better" for other peoples. Rather, it involves a commitment to building relations over time; it is through these relations we enter the never-ending process of learning "our place in this world" as racialized settlers who seek to be good relatives (see Fujikane 2012, 2021; Matsunaga 2021; Okamura and Fujikane 2008; Suzuki and Knudtson 1992).

A Story of Return: Redress and Rebuilding the Community

As a *hapa* Sansei who grew up in the 1960s and 1970s on Snuneymuxw territory in the white working-class settler town of Nanaimo, it has taken me years to fathom the enormity of the government's plan to remove "all people of Japanese racial origin," and even more to recognize our role as racialized settlers in Canada. In contrast to many Sansei of my generation, my brothers and I learned about the internment camps as children from the stories of my mother's family, the Nakashimas. Family members spoke openly about their experiences of being forced to leave Vancouver in 1942 and their internment in East Lillooet, though everyone had different views, from "it was the end of my life!" to stories about ingenuity and survival (McAllister 2006). At home, my mother filled our bookshelves with publications by Japanese Canadians, with authors like Ken Adachi ([1976] 1991), Shizuye Takashima (1971), Takeo Uji Nakano (1980), Joy Kogawa (1981), and Toyo Takata (1983). Not only did their voices resonate with something familiar yet unarticulated within me, but the claim they made over our history was inspiring at a time when there were few published Japanese Canadian writers (and even fewer now). But it was only once I "returned" to the community in 1989 that, paradoxically, I began to comprehend the scale of the loss and the extent of all that had been destroyed. To begin registering the loss, I had to learn about the vibrant prewar community that lived on in the memories (and social relations) of surviving Issei and Nisei.

When I became involved in the Japanese Canadian community, it was 1989, one year after the NAJC negotiated a redress agreement with the Canadian government. With funding from the Redress Agreement, over the next decade the NAJC and its local branches (or centres) – Japanese Canadian Citizens' Associations in towns and cities across the country – embarked on an ambitious program for rebuilding and revitalizing the community.[5] When I returned, I was thus initially swept up in this excitement.[6]

It was a cold, grey day in November 1989 when I first walked into the office of the Japanese Canadian Citizens' Association on Powell Street in Vancouver. From approximately the 1920s to 1942, my mother's family, the Nakashimas, lived just two blocks away on Jackson Avenue and my great-grandfather, Eikichi Nakashima, owned a house on Cordova Street west of Princess Avenue. In the early 1900s, he and my great-grandmother, before she died of the Spanish flu following the First World War, had a store up the coast in Egmont where he also fished.

By November 1989, little remained of the vibrant, bustling nihonmachi *of my mother's childhood memories. Gone was the* ofuro *where my* Obaasan *(née, Miyuki Mukai) went in the evenings to soak in the hot steaming waters with the other neighbourhood ladies. According to my mother, my mischievous 7-year-old aunt was often scolded for disturbing their serenity with her splashing and attempts to swim. She also recalls my* Ojiisan *(Yatsumatsu Nakashima) bringing them freshly churned ice cream from the local Japanese Canadian confectionary and taking her next door to buy sensible Oxfords, dismissing her little girl's wish for shiny "Shirley Temple" shoes. As children they had a carefree life, whether taking the trolley to English Bay or chewing large mouthfuls of raw garlic in order to ward off the Sisters of Atonement who ran a daycare for "immigrant" children (and according to my mother, baptised their wards without their parents' permission, thus her own name, "Rosalie").*

My mother also talks about the "hobo tent city" near the railway tracks, which was near American Can Company's parking lot where local children would roller skate like speed-demons. My mother always reminds me it was the Depression, and men would knock on their door looking for odd jobs stacking wood or bringing coal to their cellar. In the 1980s, the house that my mother's family rented until 1942 was still there. It was second in a row of four surviving Edwardian houses, still standing tall overlooking Powell Street Grounds where the famous

Asahi baseball team once drew massive crowds in the 1930s and is now among the last witnesses of another era, watching over the changing neighbourhood.

When I returned on that November day in 1989, before I went to the JCCA, I stopped by Tonari Gumi, an elders' drop-in centre that grassroots activists established in the 1970s. I approached the man sitting at the front desk and asked about volunteering. Surrounded by stacks of paper, he asked if I spoke Japanese, and when I said no, he waved his hand as if to dismiss me. At least that is how I remembered the encounter. I didn't consider how overworked he looked in the poorly lit room full of the tired sofas and chairs. I would later learn he was the famous shakuhachi *master, Takeo Yamashiro, who immigrated to Canada in the 1970s and worked valiantly each year to find funding to keep Tonari Gumi's doors open.*

But as a recent university graduate at the time, I reacted full of youthful arrogance and retorted that most Japanese Canadians didn't speak Japanese. Citing the lessons I had learned about colonization from the Filipina and Filipino activists I met when in Zambales, just north of Manila in the Philippines, as a participant in Canada World Youth,[7] *I rhetorically asked: "Didn't you know? The government had attempted to get rid of Japanese Canadians and that stripping our ability to speak Japanese was part of the plan." At that point he stood up, looking extremely irritated. Taking this as a cue, I quickly scuttled out.*

With Tonari Gumi scratched off my list, I went next door to the JCCA. With ruffled feathers, I introduced myself to Fumiko Greenaway. She was the editor for the JCCA Bulletin, *who welcomed me in her quiet gentle way, "I know your Obasaan, Mrs. Nakashima." After chatting about my experience and interests, she paused, and then, getting up from her desk, said, "I have something I think that might interest you." She asked me to wait and brought in two nondescript filing boxes from the storage room. "This is the Oral History Project. Have a look."*

I soon found myself working as the JCCA's oral history coordinator, driving across the territories of the Coast Salish Nations in British Columbia's Lower Mainland in my rusty, broken-down Volkswagen Beetle with Mari-Jane Medenwaldt and Waylen Miki.[8] *We met with issei and nisei from Vancouver and Burnaby to Steveston, Maple Ridge, and Surrey whose accounts brought to life colonial British Columbia's fishing ports, coal-mining, and lumber towns; its agricultural settlements in the Fraser Valley; and urban centres from Vancouver to Nanaimo and Victoria.*

In an earlier version of this chapter, I had planned to build on this auto-ethnographic tale of return, arguing that the postwar community would be only a shadow of what it was today without the redress movement. With the drive to reconnect and unite the community across the country through the goal of seeking justice, there was an inclusive, welcoming intergenerational ethos. Every time you met another Japanese Canadian, there would be a flurry of questions about where your family lived before the war, where they were interned, and what happened after the war in order to discover our connections to each other and the places from which the community was erased. In this (mostly) welcoming context, the redress movement made it possible for me and others to return to the community.

Art Miki,[9] the NAJC president who led the negotiations with the federal government, explained that an "integral part of the redress agreement was the establishment of a $12 million community fund[10] to assist in the revitalization and rejuvenation of the Japanese Canadian community devastated by the Canadian government's wartime [and postwar] actions" (A. Miki 2003, 54–55).[11] The NAJC set up the Japanese Canadian Redress Foundation to implement the terms of the agreement in the period from 1988 to 2002, awarding funding to capital projects such as community centres, eldercare facilities, and historical centres, including Vancouver's Nikkei Place and the Nikkei National Museum. Funding was also available for projects and programming for public education, cultural events, historical commemoration, human rights workshops, research, literature, and the arts (A. Miki 2003).

I wanted to write about this exciting period of growth in part because over the last twenty years it has become increasingly unclear whether today's NAJC, its local JCCA branches across Canada (some, notably the Toronto NAJC, have shown more leadership than others), and national community organizations have remembered the political legacy of redress. I am not just referring to its role in rebuilding the community and the pursuit of justice. The redress movement also prioritized Japanese Canadian voices. It fostered an inclusive intergenerational ethos, welcoming those seeking to reconnect with the community, drawing on the expertise and experience of our many different members (rather than spotlighting the same individuals and excluding and undermining others), and building relations with other communities, aware that the pursuit of justice depends on recognizing our interdependence, as Justice (2018) explains.

But as I wrote this chapter, I kept circling back to the government's plan to remove all "people of Japanese racial origin" from Canada and its impact over the last eighty years. As I remembered the euphoria of my return and what felt like the embrace of a long-lost community, I kept remembering the fear many Nisei expressed about the disappearance of the community with the high rates of assimilation and "intermarriage"[12] to white Canadians.[13] And even as the oral accounts of the Issei and Nisei magically resurrected long-gone places and people whom the government sought to remove from within its borders, they also traced the uneasy, unspeakable terrain of erasure that continues to haunt the community today (McAllister 2010, 2011, 2018; Oikawa 2012).

Still etched into my memory are two Nisei I met when I returned to the community. They witnessed what happened to the community as young adults (in contrast, my mother's generation were children in 1942), when the government rounded them up, interned them, and then, in 1945, forced them to leave British Columbia. Deeply involved in the redress movement, they had a political understanding of the government's intent.

They asked me: "Why are you coming back, now?" underlining "it is too late." I couldn't understand what they meant. In response to my confusion they explained, "the community is ending; it is over. Now the redress movement has finished there is nothing to hold us together. The sansei who led redress will now go back to their lives and leave the rest of us behind."

Unable to comprehend what I considered to be their apocalyptic views, I tried to convince them that redress had opened the doors to a whole new generation of Sansei and Yonsei who, like myself, were discovering new meaning and purpose as we reconnected with the community.

Only years later did I began to realize what they meant (McAllister 2006, 2010, 2011). These Nisei recognized that the government's policies, in the bluntest terms, amounted to a racial elimination plan. The social bonds that once bound them together inter-subjectively as a community, regardless of their conflicts and their class and political differences, had, in their eyes, unravelled beyond repair, and the inexplicable centrifugal force that made them a community had been extinguished. From that moment of shock, over the years, I have come to recognize how the measures that the government implemented under the War Measures Act have continued to unfurrow across the generations long after the last policies and programs targeting people of "Japanese racial origin" were dismantled. As I began to reflect on the ongoing impact of the elimination plan, the earlier drafts of this chapter describing my autoethnographic return seemed too nostalgic and too celebratory. Importantly, the redress movement, as I learned from the Nisei who spoke of "the end of the community," was in part driven by anxieties about the survival of the community. Issues about survival have not gone away, but in contrast to the period from the 1970s to the 1990s, they are no longer topics in our meetings, publications, and workshops.

The leadership of the NAJC during the 1980s and the implementation of the agreement relied on research and consultation with a wide range of community members. They confronted difficult issues and brought a new vision of what the community could be (see Kobayashi 1992; A. Miki 2003). During the 1990s, the NAJC ran a series of conferences to bring Japanese Canadians together to discuss issues we faced and plan future growth. And while arguably their format replicated mainstream white corporate models for conferences, importantly, topics included forced assimilation and the loss of identity, high rates of "intermarriage," lack of facilities for elders, tensions between Nisei and postwar Japanese immigrants, and human rights (A. Miki 2003, 110–32). Artists, musicians, filmmakers, writers, dancers, playwrights, and researchers were part of these discussions (also see McAllister and Oikawa 1996). Like the generations before them, this group challenged mainstream discourses about Japanese Canadians (Oikawa 2012, 19–78) as well as problematic beliefs such as the internment being "a blessing in disguise" (Miki 2004; Oikawa 2012) while forging new ways to conceive what it meant to be Japanese Canadian, with the NAJC underlining that redress was only the beginning of the process of "healing" and "revitalizing" the postwar community (A. Miki 2003).

Today, as discussed above, it isn't clear how many of our organizations retain the political vision of redress[14] and instead rely on popular multicultural definitions where we are just another ethnocultural community and our duty regarding racism is to simply educate other Canadians about ourselves as so-called "model minorities" who came to Canada as "pioneers," contributed to the country's economic development (Kawai 2005; McAllister 1999; Miki 2004, 260–61; Ty 2017), supposedly overcame racism by demanding redress, and now have successfully assimilated into Canada with large numbers of doctors, lawyers, and business leaders. This story of Japanese Canadians is problematic. Here, the definition of racism is reduced to just a set of incorrect beliefs that can be changed with education, empathy, and information, ignoring how the racist structures remain intact. This narrative (which several Japanese Canadian organizations use in their exhibitions and historical timelines) also ignores the fact that we are racialized settlers profiting from the genocidal occupation of the unceded territories of hundreds of sovereign Nations whose rights Canada continues to violate. If indeed this is how community organizations, whether the Japanese Canadian Cultural Centre, Nikkei Place, the Nikkei Museum, or the NAJC, define us, some might argue that we have accepted the government's definition of how to be acceptable non-whites in Canada.

In contrast, the 1980s redress activists defined Japanese Canadians as "agents of change," citizens seeking justice that would serve both the community and future generations of Canadians (Kobayashi 1992; Miki 2004, 234). In the 1980s and 1990s, the NAJC's commitment to broader human rights was reflected in its support of Ukrainian, Chinese, and Italian Canadians' redress movements, in addition to Indigenous rights. Its support went beyond making public statements. It included action, such as the work the NAJC did with the Assembly of First Nations' Residential School Committee and its legal advice to the Stony Point First Nation on the latter's submission requesting the return of land the Canadian government expropriated to use as a military base under the authority of the War Measures Act (A. Miki 2003, 172–73). Regarding justice beyond our community, the NAJC's terms of redress included: 1) amending the War Measures Act so the government could not abuse its power and detain, intern, or imprison Canadian citizens or landed immigrants on the basis of race, national or ethnic origin, colour, religion, sex, age, or mental or physical disability; and 2) establishing a Race Relations Foundation to foster human rights, assist groups targeted by racism, and provide grants for research on "racism and prejudice" (Kobayashi 1992; Miki and Kobayashi 1991, 97). However, neither ended up achieving what the NAJC proposed (Miki and Kobayashi 1991, 97, 121). Before the Redress Agreement was finalized, in response to the NAJC's proposed amendments to the War Measures Act, the government abolished this act and introduced the Emergencies Act.[15] Further amendments were made following the NAJC's concerns that "the injustices of the past could be repeated under the new Act" (121) but as Sunahara argued, while the new act was an improvement over the War Measures Act, "perhaps its greatest flaw [was] that it [was] only an Act of Parliament. It [could] be revoked with something worse" (quoted in Miki and Kobayashi 1991, 121). Roy Miki and Cassandra Kobayashi explain that "the only way to ensure what happened to Japanese Canadians [could] not be repeated [was] to amend the Charter of Rights and Freedoms to ensure that human rights [could] never be eroded even in times of emergency" (121).

The NAJC did not pursue the amendments required, and just over a decade later, everything was swept away in the response to the September 11, 2001, attacks in the United States when Prime Minister Jean Chrétien introduced Bill C-36, which became the Anti-terrorism Act.[16] Oikawa (2012) describes the "effects of the emergency legislation in Canada post-September 11, 2001, and the forms of policing of immigrants and racialized people [in terms of a] ... carceral continuum," linking it to the incarceration of

Japanese Canadians. The protection of civil liberties was further eroded in 2015 when Prime Minister Stephen Harper's government introduced "Bill C-51, the Anti-terrorist Act, 2015."[17] This resulting act expanded what was defined as a threat to national security to include public speeches and protests, while increasing the state's discretionary power to detain and charge Canadians. Civil rights organizations criticized the act, arguing that it undermined the Canadian Charter of Rights and Freedoms.[18]

Despite initial hopes (see Kobayashi 1992), the impact of the Canadian Race Relations Foundation has been almost non-existent. With its $24 million endowment, which is supposed to fund conferences, workshops, and research, its goal is to contribute to "eliminating racism." But it has been almost completely absent from public debates and campaigns against racism and colonialism. Moreover, compared to the terms the NAJC proposed in 1986, which were considerably whittled down in the 1988 Redress Agreement, its mandate is now almost unrecognizable. Instead of the "Japanese Canadian Human Rights Foundation" proposed in 1986, which was mandated to assist groups that were targets of racism and whose rights had been violated (Miki and Kobayashi 1991, 97, 139), the mandate now lacks reference to the violation of rights and narrowly focuses on racism in education and employment, mirroring the neutered language of equity, diversity, and inclusion policies in the institutions it should be challenging.[19]

So why didn't the NAJC lobby the government to fully implement the two terms in the Redress Agreement aimed at eliminating racism: amendments to the Charter of Rights and Freedoms and ensuring the Race Relations Foundation was mandated to protect the rights of those targeted by racism? From what I understand, after the agreement was signed, many Nisei and Sansei who had led the redress movement began to step back from the community. Many were exhausted from years of mobilizing; the ongoing community divisions; the hostility and racism from the larger public; and the community's insatiable need to continue the process of bearing witness to the devastating losses, pain, and damage. While more research is needed, it seems that despite the NAJC's efforts to revitalize the community and mentor new leaders (again, it would be important to assess the models they used for mentorship and determine if they replicated mainstream white ideals), after 1988 it did not have the capacity or political will to further pressure the government to make amendments to the Charter of Rights and Freedoms (Miki and Kobayashi 1991, 121) or take decisive action and campaign against Bill C-36 or Bill C-51.[20] Nor did the NAJC (or other organizations) demand that the Race Relations Foundation fulfill the role the NAJC originally envisioned (97).

In pointing out that the central NAJC office did not campaign against the Anti-terrorism Act and other bills that have eroded human rights, such as the removal of Section 13 on hate speech from the Canadian Human Rights Act[21] in 2012 by Steven Harper's Conservative government (Saint-Cyr 2012), I am not dismissing what the NAJC achieved in the 1980s. Looking back, it is astounding that it succeeded in getting the government to replace the War Measures Act and establish the Race Relations Foundation. Yet the question remains – after the Redress Agreement, why didn't the NAJC continue demanding changes to legislation that threatened civil liberties or make the Race Relations Foundation more accountable to anti-racist groups and Indigenous peoples? Was this a sign that the organization that once represented our political interests was exhausted? Or did it indicate that we now accepted our place in the settler colony of Canada as apolitical ethnics? Did the process of negotiating redress, followed by fourteen years of working with the government to implement the terms of the settlement result in the NAJC's adoption of the government's bureaucratic logic (see Ng 1996; Ng, Walker and Muller 1990), redefining how we approach "solving" injustice and, importantly, how we define ourselves, which also defines what injustices concern us? Like liberal political theorists (see Miller 2009 and Rawls 1993), are we primarily concerned with the violation of "democratic" citizenship rights rather than the way these rights legitimize the stealing of Indigenous land, the hyper-exploitation of migrant workers, the political destabilization of countries where, for example, Canadian mining companies extract ores, which we depend on for everything from our communication networks to border surveillance? Beyond the need for research on why the NAJC did not continue its work to end systemic racism, there are the broader discussions about how redress and other types of state apologies and reparation have limited the efforts of persecuted groups to achieve justice, a topic rarely discussed in Japanese Canadian community forums.

State Redress: Making the Racial Elimination a Humanitarian Lesson

In the wake of over three decades of truth and reconciliation commissions in countries from Latin America and Asia to South Africa and now Canada, legal scholars have questioned the extent to which state apologies and reparations can change power structures or rectify the damages resulting from state persecution, whether forced assimilation, apartheid, or genocide. They also document how the process of reconciliation and implementing the terms of reparation can inflict further damage through the traumatizing testimonies survivors must give to apply for reparations, further institution-alizing discourses that construct survivors as damaged victims who need to be under the "care" of the state rather than, for instance, returning their appropriated land and reinstating their autonomous governments. These commissions also protect the interests of the states who agree to take part in reconciliation rather than holding them accountable for the atrocities (see Chapter 1; Henderson and Wakeham 2013; Lanegran 2005; Matsunaga 2016; Million 2014; Yoneyama 2016). Most scholars recognize that for per-secuted groups, demanding reparations and reconciliation can be part of the process of seeking justice, but maintain that states use them primarily to repair their international reputations and absolve themselves of further responsibility for the damage and losses they have inflicted. Moreover, as Lisa Yoneyama (2016, 168–69) has argued regarding Asian "immigrant-citizens" in the United States who seek redress from Japan for prewar and wartime imperial violence, these citizens can reproduce discourses that "nationalize" and "discipline" themselves as subjects, reinforcing their "normative subject positions in America's settler present." This, as I argue below, applies to Japanese Canadians' calls for redress.

The NAJC and other Japanese Canadian organizations have not critic-ally examined the redress framework in relation to the criticism of state apologies and reparations. Understandably, criticisms could be viewed as an attack. But critically assessing the redress framework should not preclude recognizing its significance and the contributions of redress activists to the community. Critical assessment should instead help us better understand the challenges of seeking justice and the need to continuously revise our approach. In the 1980s, the NAJC itself used a critical approach, question-ing how our identity was defined by both the government (as "Japanese" ver-sus Canadian citizens) and also those community members who sought the safety of assimilation (as model minorities) (Miki 2004, 129, 260). Activists strove to redefine our identity, as mentioned, in political terms as agents of change (234). Here, I am specifically interested in the redress movement's use of a national framework to mobilize Japanese Canadians in the 1980s (McAllister 1999). Using a national framework and arguing that the govern-ment should recognize Japanese Canadians as its citizens, as I argue, ended up reducing our political agency to terms that serve the national project of settler colonialism (Byrd 2011; Day 2016; Yoneyama 2016). Moreover, again, as critics have argued more broadly, state redress treats injustices as resolved, imposing closure and undermining persecuted groups' ongoing efforts to pursue justice and rebuild their communities.

Looking back, when the Redress Agreement was signed over thirty-five years ago in 1988, civil rights organizations across Canada saw it as an achievement. They thought it would strengthen protection against the abuse of others' rights in Canada. For instance, Alan Borovoy (quoted in Miki and Kobayashi 1991, 127) from the Canadian Civil Liberties Association stated that Japanese Canadians

> are working hard for the future. [They] are helping to create a precedent from which future governments would find it very hard to retreat. [They're] serving notice to whoever is going to be in government, that from now to the end of time, to whatever extent they are tempted, to depart so radically from the norms of civilized behaviour, at the very least there will be a price to pay. [Japanese Canadians have created] an obstacle and a deterrent against abuse of other people – of Blacks, of Native people, of Pakistanis, of East Indians, of refugees, and of all the vulnerable people whom I hope we will be welcoming to this country.

For the NAJC, the 1988 Redress Agreement meant that Canada finally recognized that racism was the primary reason for its wartime treatment of Japanese Canadians: the government's use of "race" to categorize Japanese Canadians as "Japanese" rather than recognize them as Canadian citizens meant it could treat them as enemy aliens and violate their civil rights (Government of Canada in Miki and Kobayashi 1991, 138). Here, Prime Minister Mulroney's statement (quoted in Miki and Kobayashi 1991, 144) is telling:

> I think that all Members of the House know that no amount of money can right the wrong, undo the harm, and heal the wounds ... [and] not only was the treatment inflicted on Japanese Canadians during the War morally and legally unjustified, it was against the very nature of our country, of Canada. We are a pluralistic society ... We are a tolerant people who live in freedom in a land of abundance. That is the Canada our ancestors worked to build. That is the kind of country we want to leave our children.

It is instructive to revisit the language used in Borovoy's and Mulroney's statements. Both illustrate how public discourses have shifted. Today, widespread critiques of Canada's treatment of racialized and Indigenous peoples make clear that "the treatment inflicted on Japanese Canadians" has been very much part of "the very nature of our country, of Canada ... that our ancestors worked to build." If we are "a tolerant people," at best we "tolerate" others if their "ethnicity" and "Aboriginal-ness" is made palatable as easily recognizable stereotyped cultural products or performances that can be consumed as benign forms of multicultural diversity (Abu-Laban and Gabriel 2002; Kamboureli 2000; Kobayashi 1993). I am not questioning the significance of the NAJC's criticism of the state's use of "race" to justify its violation of Japanese Canadians' citizenship rights. Nor am I dismissing the importance of the Redress Agreement for thousands of Japanese Canadians or the role of the Agreement in rebuilding a postwar community.[22] From the vantage point of the present, it is far too easy to dismiss redress and overlook its complexity and the fact it was also an anti-racist movement. Thus, while recognizing the criticisms of the state's use of apologies, this chapter goes further and, like Jennifer Matsunaga (2016), calls on us to re-examine the redress movement, the resulting Japanese Canadian Redress Agreement, and its implementation, while continuing the struggle for justice.

Following criticisms of Truth and Reconciliation Commissions, subsequent redress agreements, and state apologies, we need to ask if redress ends up undermining our community's efforts to fully pursue justice. In 1999, I asked if defining redress in terms that made sense to the Canadian state derailed more critical visions of justice from the 1970s and early 1980s which, as I suggest above, were still evident in early proposals for the Race Relations Foundation. Today, many of our community organizations reinforce a model minority story of redress. This story focuses on the state's recognition that it violated Japanese Canadians' citizenship rights rather than its efforts to work in solidarity to dismantle the structures of racism.

Before the 1988 Redress Agreement, the government either justified its use of the War Measures Act against Japanese Canadians as a necessary security measure or dismissed it as something in the distant past that wasn't the responsibility of the current government (Oikawa 2012, 4–42). Before 1988, at an everyday level, I remember how any reference to the camps would incite virulent defensiveness, hostility, and denial from white Canadians. This continues today, even in seemingly innocuous comments that defend the government's actions, such as comments like, "but since they weren't allowed to vote, they weren't citizens," (from this line of reasoning it follows that as they were not Canadian citizens, so she was implying that Japanese Canadian citizens' rights were not violated by the government). Or by dismissing us as model minority "sellouts," which in addition to making a broad generalization about Japanese Canadians, fails to recognize questions of power and how the internalization of white values is evidence of the chilling effectiveness of state violence.

It is true that once the government signed the Redress Agreement, it had to reposition itself. But admitting its own racism did not mean the government would subsequently dismantle the racist and colonial structures defining Canada. Following the grandiose recuperative language of Prime Minister Mulroney's statement above, Canada turned the more concrete images of its treatment of Japanese Canadians, such as the internment camps, into proof of its ability to recognize its wrongs, so ironically, the camps are now symbols of Canada's commitment to equality and democracy. As Oikawa (2012, 39) writes, "when heads of government (and few they have been) have publicly acknowledged the Internment ... [it] is often accompanied by a recuperation of liberal notions of Canada as a just and fair country." After the settlement, as Mulroney's speech indicates,[23] the government used the camps as a humanitarian lesson that Canadians have learned, hanging their heads low, their racist beliefs corrected, making Canada an example to other countries struggling with their own human rights violations, while ignoring its ongoing genocidal treatment of Indigenous people and exploitation and dispossession of people in the Global South (Million 2014; Regan 2010).

Indeed, federal and provincial governments have embarked on projects to memorialize sites of Japanese Canadian internment and dispossession. This does not mean that memorialization is always a tool for obfuscating state violence. Much depends on the aim and form of memorialization: does it turn the past into a neatly packaged eulogy in the service of government agendas, or does it allow multiple voices, irresolvable experiences, and radical forms of grieving and/or haunting that ignite new generations to pursue justice in solidarity with others (McAllister 2010; Radstone and Schwarz 2010; Sharpe 2016; Trouillot 2015)? Tellingly, as Matsunaga (2021) explains, the government had no intention of using the same model to redress subsequent groups calling for justice (with individual and community-level compensation). Arguably, the Canadian government attempted to compartmentalize its structural violence into a series of wrongs it could resolve by demonstrations of contrition and tokenistic reparation. It has used strategies that have exhausted communities' resources, created internal tensions and conflicts, and, in the case of residential school survivors, inflicted further harm (see Chapter 1). Once "redressed" and "reconciled," the state turned each violation into a dark chapter in the past that "we" as a country have supposedly resolved. The state subsequently has used these cases to instruct us about racism (James 2013)[24] and colonialism, while simultaneously still enforcing racist and colonial laws, as discussed above, through anti-terrorist and omnibus bills that undermine basic freedoms and civil liberties; and, for example, by requiring Indigenous peoples to use colonial forms of governance regulated by the Indian Act[25] that are designed to dismantle their traditional systems of governance (which they must use in order to receive the funds that Canada is required to annually disburse, in a context where the majority of their lands have been appropriated [and thus restricting their ability for self-sufficiency] and their sovereign rights, ignored) (Royal Commission on Aboriginal Peoples 1996, 237).

Understanding the state's use of redress, reconciliation, and state apologies to protect its reputation and discursively turn political violence into humanitarian lessons while avoiding structural changes should make us wary about celebrating Japanese Canadian redress as a triumph of justice. As Art Miki underlined in the early 1990s, the work of redress is incomplete and ongoing. And as Oikawa (2012, 309) argued regarding the Nisei women she interviewed in the 1990s, as subjects of internment they could not "be neatly contained by the discourse of the resolved 'redressed subject.'" What is clear is that the racism that was aimed at ridding Canada of "people of Japanese origin" continues today, targeting Indigenous peoples, Black Canadians, Muslim Canadians and many others.

After Redress: A Snapshot of the NAJC's Social Justice Activities

Above, I argued that the NAJC's pursuit of justice waned after the 1988 Redress Agreement. For a closer look at its activities after redress on the front lines of anti-racism and decolonization, I examine the ten-year period dating back from October 2020, drawing on the NAJC's reports about its activities found on its website.[26] Its National Office website includes statements that decry racist incidents in Canada and support other communities' calls for justice. The website also cites the NAJC's participation in panel discussions and workshops on racism and decolonization run by other groups, including forums run by the Truth and Reconciliation Commission of Canada (TRC). But in contrast to other community organizations with social justice mandates, such as the National Council of Canadian Muslims,[27] nothing indicates that the NAJC has developed a coordinated plan to address racism, or, given the opportunities following the TRC, made much effort to work in conjunction with local JCCA branches to decolonize our relations with the Indigenous peoples whose territories we occupy.[28]

For a closer look at the NAJC's social justice activities, I reviewed the reports posted on the website of the NAJC National Office from February to

October 2020. During this period, public interest in anti-racism rose significantly following media coverage of violence against Indigenous, Black, and Asian North American communities, especially following Black Lives Matter's cross-border mobilization in response to the police killing of George Floyd in Minneapolis on May 25 as well as the increased media coverage of pipeline blockades by Indigenous land protectors. This would have been an important moment for the NAJC to show leadership regarding anti-racist movements and solidarity with Indigenous peoples.[29] During this period, in addition to reports on the NAJC's negotiations with the BC government for Japanese Canadian redress, there were six news items on racism and Indigenous rights (compared with only five from June 2017 to January 2020): an announcement for an online anti-racism workshop; an anti-Black racism statement; an anti-Asian racism statement; information about the NAJC survey regarding anti-Asian racist incidents; an announcement for Freedom Day in Toronto; and a statement supporting the Wet'suwet'en Nation's protection of its territories against the Coastal GasLink pipeline. The majority of the approximately forty news items during this period are monthly reports from the NAJC president, announcements about cultural activities (book launches, festivals, sports, workshops, etc.), events on Japanese Canadian history, COVID-19 information, and funding opportunities.

Given the NAJC's commitment to "eliminating racism," I next examined the content of these news items. The hour-long anti-racism workshop (online due to COVID-19) covered four topics: COVID-related racism, how to respond to hate, the Asian Canadians Together Network, and anti-Black racism. It is not clear why there wasn't an entire workshop on anti-Black racism given the political mobilization of Black communities across Canada (and globally) and their calls for action against structural anti-Black racism (see Cole 2020; Maynard 2017). Moreover, what could be accomplished regarding anti-Black racism as the last of four topics in a one-hour online session? No one from the Black community was invited to speak (or run) the workshop. This was an opportunity for learning from, as well as building solidarity with Black communities. It was also an opportunity to draw on the leadership of the younger generations with their knowledge about intersectional politics, social media, and activism. This suggests, in Justice's (2018) terms, a lack of recognition of Japanese Canadians' relations with Black communities, in terms of both structural racism and the differences and intersections between our communities and the responsibilities those relations entail, which, as Justice indicates, can be understood only in discussion between the relevant groups.

Then there is the NAJC's Black Lives Matter "solidarity statement." Although it is just one post and doesn't necessarily characterize other posts, since it pertains to such a crucial political issue (and was the only other website item that referred to anti-Black racism during this period), as I explain below, it is troubling. One of the main points in the brief two-paragraph statement addresses people who dismiss Black Lives Matter with the response that "all lives matter": "For those who say 'all lives matter' open your hearts, recognize systemic racism, and know as we stand with the Black community in their time of need, this does not diminish the importance of any other groups of people" (NAJC, n.d.c).

"All lives matter" has been widely criticized as a statement by predominantly white people who refuse to recognize how racism devalues the lives of Black people, whose conditions of living are affected because they are not granted the same access that white people have to education, employment, health care, housing, finances, and legal services. They are also targets of racial profiling, exponentially higher rates of incarceration, police violence, and killing (Maynard 2017). So why did the NAJC include a compassionate plea to those who react to Black Lives Matter with "all lives matter" (as signalled by the phrases, "open your hearts," "stand with [them] in their time of need," and "this does not diminish the importance of other groups of people")? It is one thing to discuss the inherent racism in the statement "all lives matter" in a workshop but quite another to make it one of the main pleas in a solidarity statement (one-third of the statement). It suggests that the NAJC is making an appeal to racist white people. The compassionate, pleading language suggests anxiety about confronting white people. And if instead the NAJC assumes the audience is Japanese Canadian, it suggests that the denial of anti-Black racism is a major community issue.[30] If so, there is a need for more than fifteen minutes in one workshop that does not include Black community leaders.

The statement continues. After noting that the NAJC will continue to speak out against anti-Asian racism (no mention of anti-Black racism), the BLM statement then inexplicably turns to Indigenous peoples. "We know the suffering of Indigenous peoples since colonial white settlers first came to their traditional lands and the injustice which persists today." The sudden switch to Indigenous suffering suggests an inability to address anti-Black racism, reinforcing the troubling conclusion that the NAJC as an organization might be afflicted with the anti-Black racism epitomized in the statement "all lives matter." Furthermore, by focusing only on Indigenous "suffering," it uses a colonial framework that constructs them as victims rather than recognizing their leadership, savvy use of the legal system, and activism to force provincial and federal governments to recognize their sovereignty while running powerful movements nationally and internationally.

More generally, there are many Japanese Canadians knowledgeable about these issues (some of whom are on the NAJC board). Why weren't they consulted? But even if both the BLM solidarity statement and anti-racism workshop do not accurately represent the views of all NAJC board members (which they do not), the fact that the NAJC posted such a message on such a politically important issue without more oversight in a context where social media can quickly discredit organizations suggests, at best, serious issues with leadership (and limited followers, as one would have expected a torrent of criticism and questions about its lack of involvement in BLM, anti-racist movements, and the absence of any impactful allyship with Indigenous peoples).

The only other news item pertaining to the violation of rights in Canada during the period reviewed is a statement about Indigenous rights. It is notable that there is only one news item on Indigenous rights even though there were multiple and ongoing violations of Indigenous sovereignty in this period.[31] The statement focuses on the Wet'suwet'en Nation's protection of its territories against Coastal GasLink. The NAJC states that it is "alarmed by recent RCMP incursions into the sovereign and unceded territory of people. We affirm the right of the hereditary chiefs, who hold legal title to their land, to refuse to allow construction of the Coastal GasLink pipeline on their territory" (NAJC 2020). In contrast to the BLM statement, this shows an understanding of the colonial power dynamics that the Wet'suwet'en Nation is challenging and their political prowess and autonomy (by recognizing the hereditary chiefs and their sovereign rights over their territory). But like the BLM statement, beyond making a statement, it does not identify meaningful action that community members can take. This sharply contrasts organizations such as the National Council of Canadian Muslims (see note 27), which offers a range of different ways for people to inform themselves about issues and become involved in social justice campaigns.

More generally, the NAJC website has six times the number of announcements about cultural and historical events than about racism and social justice, suggesting a drift toward becoming an apolitical ethnic organization. Does this reflect a lack of resources and overworked, fatigued individuals who continue to take leadership positions because no one else will step forward? Community organizations cannot be effectively run alone by a handful of board members. Or do community members lack interest in social justice and think the Redress Agreement resolved the injustices past generations suffered? Or does this point to a leadership that excludes other community members who have much-needed expertise, vision, energy, and generational experience in favour of either the same handful of community members or white and·other non-Japanese Canadian experts? These are questions for both the leadership and, more widely, the many Japanese Canadians who believe in the idea of a community committed to the hard work of building a just, sustainable world. In fact, there are signs that a new leadership is gaining the consensus to re-embrace a social justice mandate that is inclusive, even if until recently many of these initiatives have been actively supported by only a small handful of board members.[32]

The Colonial Limits: Japanese Canadian Redress and Its Political Definition of Identity

I began this chapter by explaining how, in the aftermath of the Canadian government's racial elimination plan, understanding who we are as Japanese Canadians has been an ongoing struggle. Recounting my own story of return in the late 1980s, I discussed how the redress movement contributed to rebuilding the community, making it possible for my generation to return while showing us that the act of defining ourselves was a political act. Over thirty-five years after the 1988 Redress Agreement, I now ask if we still understand what is at stake in defining ourselves. Have we internalized what Canada defines as a "good" (apolitical) ethnic? Do most Japanese Canadians now subscribe to the pervasive image of the silent Japanese Canadian (reproduced even by younger generations of Japanese Canadian artists now performing and exhibiting their work, who seem unaware of over a hundred years of Japanese Canadian activism and resistance [Miki 2004; Oikawa 2012)]? Do our community organizations now replay the state's humanitarian story of redress, a story that makes the racial elimination of Japanese Canadians politically and emotional safe to memorialize as a dark chapter in the distant past rather than an obliterating force that continues to proliferate across the generations as it is connected to larger structures of racism and colonialism?

In terms of our stories, arguably, the last story that defined us was the story of redress. And even if the principles of this story are no longer remembered, key elements still shape our identity today. As I argued, this story originally emphasized our relations and responsibilities to our and other communities struggling against racism. But my assessment of the NAJC's social justice initiatives following the 1988 Redress Agreement suggest, and especially over the last two decades, it no longer maintains these relations and responsibilities (though this doesn't mean other Japanese Canadians do not).

Today, what possibilities and limitations can we learn from critically assessing Japanese Canadians' story of redress? As mentioned above, the hegemonic version relies on a national framework that defines us as Canadian citizens. Our investment in this story, I argue, has impeded our ability to recognize how the very premise of Canada is based on the violent attempt to eliminate over 630 Nations in order to appropriate their sovereign territories (see Coulthard 2014; Henderson 2013; Lawrence 2013; Tuck and Yang 2012). That said, there are critical writings by Japanese Canadian scholars such as Oikawa (2002, 2012), Matsunaga (2016, 2021), Yakashiro (2021) and Suzuki and Knudtson (1992), in addition to Japanese Hawai'ians Jonathan Okamura and Candace Fujikane (2008), who have critically examined Nikkei relations to Indigenous peoples. But as Justice (2018, 82) points out, it is important to hear what Indigenous scholars have to tell us about our relations. Chickasaw scholar Jodi Byrd (2011) writes about how Japanese American civil rights movements have ended up reproducing colonialism. She examines how their discourses about their experiences of racism ignore the larger colonial system and thus silo their experiences and relations to the state without considering how the United States is founded on the attempt to eradicate Native Americans. In focusing on how Japanese Americans are negatively viewed as either "immigrants" or model minorities, they fail to recognize how their incarceration by the United States was intrinsically linked (conceptually, legislatively, and through policies and plans) to the same violent logic applied to Native Americans (in contrast see Shimoda 2024). Moreover, as Byrd makes clear, in contrast to Japanese Americans, Native Americans are sovereign and have prior rights to the land now occupied by the United States and Japanese Americans (188–97).

Thus to critically assess what our stories can teach us about "how to be human" (Justice 2018, 34), we need to listen carefully to what Indigenous peoples tell us. Like Japanese Americans, in Canada our story of redress has prioritized our relation to the Canadian state, not Indigenous peoples. It is a story of finally becoming Canadian. To change this story, we need to question what it teaches us about our relations to the world; does it support or destroy the interdependence that makes life possible? As noted by Justice (2018, 82), "It's not enough to claim relations with other peoples – we must consider what those relations ask of us, and how we may learn to be kin in ways that make one another's lives better" (82). It is important to ask why we as Japanese Canadians have been so attached to the story of being Canadian. I argue that it is more complicated than just wanting to be model minorities, as some claim (Miki 2004).

In the 1980s, to challenge the government's classification of Japanese Canadians as "Japanese" nationals in the 1940s, the NAJC made clear to the government that they were Canadian citizens. Classified as Japanese, it was possible for the government to strip their rights, categorize them as enemy aliens, and, in 1945, begin "deporting" them to Japan. Many Nisei were shocked, outraged, and hurt when they realized the government did not recognize them as its citizens (Miki 2004). Miki (2004, 67) describes how Yukio (Bob) Shimoda and Tameo Kanbara wrote, "If 'we' are Canadians ... then why are we subjected to restrictions and the confiscation of personal belongings ... jailed, interned ... we are being denied every right and freedom of a so-called democracy." Forty years later, the redress movement's language of citizenship gave them the recognition they had been denied. This language recognized the Nisei's "common threads" of experience, which were the basis of what Miki (2004, 253) calls the collective "redress identity." This identity incorporated "the more inclusive language of 'citizenship' and 'human rights' that constitutes the liberal democratic values of the Canadian nation" (264).

The desire to be recognized as Canadian, however, wasn't simply about rights or challenging denigrating racist discourses. In the 1930s and '40s, Canadians linked those identified as Japanese to Imperial Japan's atrocities. More research is needed, but what I have heard over the years suggests that the anti-Japanese racism fuelled by wartime propaganda drove many Nisei to disassociate from Japan while at the same time being unable to shed their family's ties to their parents' homeland, creating ambivalent feelings. This affected Sansei brought up before the 1988 Redress Agreement. The fear and anger of being misidentified as Japanese by white people was passed down to me. While my *hapa* features no longer signify "Japanese," I still feel the sting of this racist classification system. I feel the anger at the legal apparatus that gave this nomenclature the power to construct my mother's family as enemy aliens while exoticizing Japan when, at the same time, in the eyes of white Canada, my grandparents were atavistic ethnics and my brothers and I illicit, impure "products" of a "mixed-race" marriage.

Yet, as mentioned above, as Yoneyama (2016, 156, 270) argues regarding Asian immigrant-citizens in the United States who have mobilized to demand redress from Japan, the national (American) frameworks they use can invoke amnesia regarding the United States' own imperial violence in their former homelands (and other states), averting attention from its ongoing neo-colonial agenda. She writes that there is a "tenacity of the habitual – and normative, in the sense that a historical discourse interpellates and disciplines subjects – ways of knowing the US wars in Asia and the Pacific Islands" (156–57). Further research about Japanese Canadians' amnesia and our resistance to exploring our ambivalent and troubling relations to Japan must address how our use of national and colonial frameworks to define ourselves occludes Canada's interests and involvement in maintaining US imperialism and (neo)colonialism in Asia and elsewhere.

In this context, paradoxically, by reasserting their Canadian (and rejecting their Japanese) identity, the redress story allowed Nisei and Sansei (many of whom grew up separated from the community, with little knowledge of what their families underwent during the 1940s) to continue to distance themselves from Japan, which for many Nisei was a negative signifier of wartime and postwar Japan, even as some tried to find ways to reconnect with their Japanese "roots." There continues to be a limited number of stories that recognize that our relations to Japan are multi-layered and complex, including our relations to Issei (great/grand)parents' prefectures with pre-Second World War kin networks that once criss-crossed the Pacific and knit together distant families and villages under the pressure of Meiji industrialization (and militarization plus imperialism that expanded in the Shōwa era) through steamships, *kika* Nisei,[33] the exchange of goods, telegraphs, and letters. At the same time, we have a relation to postwar Japan as the war-torn country where the Canadian government arranged with General Douglas MacArthur for the "repatriation" of thousands of Japanese Canadians after it revoked their Canadian citizenship. Tatsuo Kage's *Uprooted Again: Japanese Canadians Move to Japan After World War II* (2012) is the only book in English that documents the experiences of exiled community members. Then there are those who returned to Canada after years of exile, often bringing Japanese spouses who survived the Allied bombing, carrying their own experiences of wartime destruction and loss.

There have been few community forums to discuss what happened when family and other community members were shipped to Japan, which was a foreign country for most (Adachi [1976] 1991). There are the individual memories one hears about those who tried to save enough money to bring family members back to Canada while struggling to find enough work to feed and house children, younger siblings, and elderly relatives in unfamiliar, often hostile locations scattered across Canada (see Kage 2012; Oikawa 1986). Oikawa's

(1986) research is a sharp reminder of the reception that Japanese Canadians forcibly relocated across the country faced in the 1940s and after the end of the war. She refers to a government survey asking Canadians in June 1945 whether they would be willing to allow "Japanese" to settle in their communities. Sixty-nine percent of the "English" said no. Twenty-nine percent cited "distrust of Japanese on grounds of treachery"; 19 percent cited "difficulties with assimilation often associated with differing standards of living"; and 19 percent stated, "just don't like them," while 4 percent said "job and wage competition" and 2 percent said "to protect Japanese from persecution" (Government of Canada, quoted in Oikawa 1986, 109).

In addition to Kage (2012), a handful of Japanese Canadian artists and writers, including Midi Onodera, Cindy Mochizuki, Michael Fukushima, Hiromi Goto, and Kerri Sakamoto, have explored these broken, ambivalent, and disturbing relations, working against what Lisa Yoneyama (2016, 152) has called in the context of the United States "the amnesia" regarding "the entangled" relations between the state and Japan that fosters complicity in imperial violence. Some artists have explored the memoryscapes that link our geographies and ecologies, providing approaches that are "provocative and unsettling" (Justice 2018, 48). They show us that until we move beyond our national and colonial frameworks, and like Black Canadian writers and artists who, as Rinaldo Walcott (2003) so eloquently wrote in 2003, examine their Black Atlantic and diasporic relations (Antiwa and Chariandy 2017), we won't be able understand our complex, changing relations and responsibilities.

For Japanese Canadians, whether frozen in the national binary of "Canadian and not-Japanese" or what they assume is a safe multicultural version of being Japanese ethnics, our ability to work through our complex relations with wartime and postwar Japan is restricted by the stories we use to define ourselves. At another level, in this effort to disassociate from Canada's wartime vilification of Japan, we need to ask if in over-identifying with Canada and being good ethnics who are forever caught up in trying to prove our loyalty to Canada, we are unable to face Canada's foundations as a genocidal settler colony. Is this why, as a community, we haven't made more effort to build relations and learn what decolonial initiatives Indigenous peoples would view as meaningful? Or why we don't identify with others who have also undergone dispossession, displacement, incarceration, or deportation within and beyond Canada's borders? If we don't create new stories that problematize ethnonationalism, how can we dis"entangle" (Yoneyama 2016) ourselves from the destructive geopolitical structures of ongoing colonialism that constitutes us in relation to Canada, Japan, and other regions of the world? If we retreat to national ideas of Canadian identity, where our "Japaneseness" is reduced to an apolitical multicultural ethnic hyphen and we refuse to see how "Canadianness" is articulated with colonialism, war, military occupations, racial capitalism, environmental disasters, deportation, refugee camps, and internment, how can we be "good relatives" (Justice 2018, 84) and seek solidarity with those confronting a global reality of mutating forms of violence and environmental collapse (Gilroy 2001)? It may feel more comfortable to identify as Canadian with this country's mythic status as a democratic nation, but the psychic and political disavowals necessary to uphold this myth can only create more damaged and damaging subjects (Chow 2002; Eng 2001).

Here, from the story of the redress movement – while refusing its national narrative of settlers heroically overcoming racism – we can still learn from its practice of critically and self-reflectively examining how we have internalized the state's story about us being a suspect race. This has driven many of us to try to prove to white Canadians that we are not a threat and are in fact an "assimilable race." We can learn from the efforts of the redress movement to build relations of solidarity and implement its inclusive vision of justice. Both the possibilities and limitations of the redress movement can help us generate new ways to recognize and re-create ourselves in relations that entail responsibilities in alliance with others to create more just, sustainable worlds (Archibald, Lee-Morgan, and De Santolo 2019; Miki 2004; Young 2011). As Justice (2018, 84) states, "to be a good relative ... is to counter ... exploitative forces and the stories that legitimate them, while at the same time affirming – or reaffirming – better, more generative, more generous ways to uphold our obligations and our commitment to our diverse and varied kin."

Bridging Stories and Upholding Responsibilities: East Lillooet Japanese Canadians and the St'át'imc

It was May 2022, and snow still dusted the massive mountain range looming over Lillooet. We returned with my ninety-year-old mother, Rosalie Chitose McAllister (née Nakashima), for the opening of the East Lillooet Memorial Garden. Over the years, she has shared many stories about the internment camp. Her stories are from the perspective of a girl and then a teenager, speaking as a mother to her children. On this visit, she recounted the story about bicycling to school with her best friend Ritsu. Singing loudly and apparently tunelessly, she pedalled over the wooden bridge crossing the mighty Fraser River, which separated the camp from the town.

Standing on the bridge today, you can feel the river heaving and churning, full of life, as it gathers strength, moving southward toward the Pacific Ocean. On the bridge seventy-eight years ago, Ritsu turned, and with a grin exclaimed (in essence), "your singing is so bad you could make the Fraser River stop ... and flee in the opposite direction!" Mum always warmly laughs whenever she recalls Ritsu's playful sense of humour.

Hearing my mother recount this story in Lillooet in the presence of other Nisei who also returned for the opening of the memorial garden, and like her were children in the camp seventy-eight years ago, I then understood the story differently. This is a story about the friendship of two girls in an internment camp. The story recounts how Ritsu gave my mother an image of strength – that she could change the direction of even a mighty river. This image sustained her in the years to come. And my mother's story, in turn, forever captures the power of Ritsu's humour, where she playfully enacts jocularity in order to deliver an otherwise awkward truth (my mother's joyful singing was tuneless) which she then, as only a loving friend can, turns into something uniquely empowering.

We were in Lillooet because Ritsu's daughters, Laura and Debra Saimoto, had invited my mother and other surviving Nisei to the opening of the memorial garden. Mum's dear friend Ritsu was there too, though now quite frail. Under the direction of Louis Horii and Bruce Tasaka, the garden was built with a volunteer committee of East Lillooet Nisei and their families (including Laura and Debra) along with the District of Lillooet. By collaboratively working together to create a place of return, these sisters were rebuilding relations within families, between generations and with the region's communities and Nations.

Among the honorary guests at the opening ceremony, Chief Michelle Edwards of the Cayoose Creek Band from the St'át'imc Nation spoke to all present. I learned that the bridge from my mother's story was where St'át'imc have caught salmon for thousands of years. Chief Edwards recounted her Nation's story that teaches us it is a place where the life of salmon, the River, and the St'át'imc are linked together in larger cycles of reciprocity that provide sustenance for all.

The next day, Chief Edwards invited everyone to their Community Hall to show us the copper mural they were completing. It spanned the entire width of the spacious light-filled hall. The mural depicts the story of their people. Working with artists who understood the properties of copper, they gently hammered sheets of this pliable yet strong medium, embossing scenes depicting significant people, events, places and political agreements, which were all intertwined with the figure of the salmon egg with its multiplying cells of life. Chief Edwards explained that the salmon egg emblematically holds the life of generations, connecting their human and non-human worlds in the larger ecology of rivers, oceans, and human societies.

Chief Edwards explained that her Nation's story included our story as Japanese Canadians in East Lillooet. She gestured upwards to a scene depicting the camp and her great grandfather Moses Frank. Faced with the sudden arrival of all these strangers in rows of small squalid shacks on a site with no access to drinkable water he brought salmon and vegetables hidden from the RCMP in his horse-drawn cart. Following the teachings of his people, he was concerned with the well-being of these newcomers on St'át'imc land. Another scene included Dr. Miyazaki, who, as Chief Edwards explained, delivered many St'át'imc babies and provided the Nation with medical care long after the internment camp was closed, all part of the life-sustaining reciprocity the great river teaches us.

By linking our stories, Chief Edwards taught us about the relations between our people from past generations. We learned about the responsibilities that tied us together. And through the act of including these stories in their mural, stories dating back to when my mother and Ritsu were young girls, and passing them down to us, Chief Edwards, was now upholding the responsibility for maintaining these relations. Through her Nation's story, she thus opened the possibility for generating new relations that continue to draw on our strengths in reciprocal ways.

Notes

Acknowledgments: Many thanks to Mona Oikawa, Naomi Sawada, Smaro Kamboureli, and Cindy Mochizuki for their insightful suggestions. Their feedback helped me navigate all I continue to find unwieldy, politically difficult, and elusive about the Japanese Canadian community. Many thanks to Chief Michelle Edwards of the Cayoose Creek Band from the St'át'imc Nation for giving me permission to include my account of what I learned from her during our visit to her territories.

1 *Hapa* is a complex term. The story goes that it originated in Hawaii and referred to those with one parent with histories of migration from Japan and one non-Japanese, typically white, parent. Originally it had derogatory connotations associated with terms such as "mixed race," "racial impurity," and "miscegenation" but now is widely used in Canada without explicitly (even if inflected with) negative meanings.

2 Activists established Japanese Canadian Citizens' Associations (JCCAs) in centres with significant Japanese Canadian populations. The JCCAs are branches of the National Association of Japanese Canadians (NAJC).

3　While I critique our national organizations, I also acknowledge, their importance and contributions to the community as well as the challenges they have faced running their organizations, for example, because of limited funding. I also want to acknowledge that there are a number of organizations and individuals (including artists and activists) whose community service and/or creative and critical work continue to make powerful contributions to rebuilding the community and critically and innovatively confronting injustice more broadly.

4　As this chapter was undergoing review, a new generation of Japanese Canadian scholars began publishing their critical analyses and challenging previous Japanese Canadian frameworks. See Shelly Ikebuchi and Takara Ketchell (2020); Angela May (2021); and Nicole Yakashiro (2021).

5　The NAJC's main office is in Winnipeg. During the redress movement from 1986 to 1988, the NAJC National Council had an Executive Committee, a President's Committee, a Strategy Committee, legal advisers, and representatives from the following centres: Calgary, Edmonton, Hamilton, Kamloops, Kelowna, Lethbridge, Manitoba, Ottawa, Thunder Bay, Toronto, Quebec, Vancouver, Vancouver Island, and Vernon (Miki and Kobayashi 1991, 156). The political views and concerns of each centre were distinct, reflecting the local leadership, the impact of the government's elimination program in their region, members' interests, and what were at times tensions between the centres. Note that many of the Toronto NAJC's activities have had a strong human rights focus over the years.

6　The italicized paragraphs signal my autoethnographic account in contrast to other indented paragraphs with quotations from other writers and scholars.

7　Canada World Youth is a program established by the Canadian International Development Agency to teach youth from Canada and the Global South about the politics of underdevelopment.

8　I applied for a grant from the federal government's Unemployment Insurance program for three positions (for Irene Nemeth, myself, and Mari-Jane Medenwaldt who, like me, was a *hapa* Sansei, though of Steveston's Tasaka clan). The JCCA's BC student grant was used to hire Waylen Miki. After consulting with oral historians and sound artists across Vancouver, I ran the interviews so that they were aimed not just at collecting "data" but also building intergenerational relations and knowledge. Focusing on the process versus the products of interviewing, we had over thirty Japanese Canadian volunteers conducting, translating, and processing interviews.

9　In in-text citations, I use "A. Miki" for Art Miki and "Miki" for Roy Miki. They are brothers. Roy Miki was a member of the NAJC's Redress Strategy Committee and is a literary scholar, poet, editor, and activist whose anti-racist work has been recognized through multiple awards and honours, including a Governor General's Award.

10　"No less than $8 million [was] for capital projects ... [And] no more than $4 million for educational, social and cultural activities and programs that contribute to the well-being of the community or that promote human rights" (A. Miki 2003, 56).

11　This was in addition to $376,908,000 for individual compensation (17,948 Japanese Canadians received $21,000 each); $24,000,000 for the Canadian Race Relations Foundation; and $9,241,000 for the operating costs of the implementation, running local, regional, and national liaison offices. It included a $3 million implementation fund from the government for "community liaison" covering the costs of the Redress Advisory Committee and NAJC executive meetings, plus miscellaneous events and projects like Jesse Nishihata's film on redress activists, Audrey Kobayashi's demographic study, and Kokoro Dance's performances of "Rage" (A. Miki 2003, 35–37).

12 "Intermarriage" is the heteronormative term the community uses for families where one of the primary adults is Japanese Canadian and the other is non-Japanese Canadian who, until recently, was usually white; terminology for "mixed-race" households and children is ideologically loaded with assumptions about race, gender, sexuality, etc., as Mari-Jane Medenwaldt and I discussed in community newspapers and a number of intermarriage workshops in the 1990s.

13 In addition to forced assimilation, starting in the late 1950s there were concerns about the high rates of intermarriage. There are few studies on Japanese Canadian intermarriage other than the 1989 demographic study by Audrey Kobayashi, commissioned by the NAJC. She found that in 1986, 90.2 percent of women and 88.4 percent of men under thirty-seven years married non-Japanese Canadians (without Japanese ethnicity) (Kobayashi 1989, 33).

14 As the manuscript for this chapter was under review, Susanne Tabata successfully led the NAJC's call for redress from the Government of British Columbia. It differs from the 1980s redress movement in many ways, but the structures she set up to make a case for redress, nevertheless, like the earlier movement, relied on the involvement of and consultations with a wide range of different Japanese Canadian organizations, experts, and community representatives as well as accredited research consultants. The BC government agreed to provide $100 million for redress initiatives in areas such as senior health and wellness and education in acknowledgement of the injustices it committed against Japanese Canadians (a large proportion is for elder housing). It must be disbursed in five years by the Japanese Canadian BC Legacies Society (which Tabata set up to be independent of the NAJC). What will the impact of this redress initiative be, not just in terms of the funding but in terms of the inclusive and consultative process and structures she set up, first to make a case for redress and second, to disperse the funds through the advisory and adjudication committees in addition to the application process itself (all of which have been guided by the principles of redress)? By bringing together Japanese Canadian experts, organizations, and individuals across Canada to determine the terms of funding under the collective goal of redress, she has arguably also contributed to building the foundation (with new networks, collective knowledge, and practices rather than just infrastructure and short term projects) for envisioning what could be a renewed community.

15 *Emergencies Act*, RSC, 1985, c 22 (4th Supp).

16 *Anti-terrorism Act*, SC 2001, c 41.

17 See the Canadian Centre for Policy Alternatives' 2001 report on Bill-36 "An Act to Combat Terrorism" from November 1, 2001. See https://policyalternatives.ca/sites/default/files/uploads/publications/National_Office_Pubs/Terrorism_Act.pdf, accessed November 2018. In addition, the report points out that in contrast to the former War Measures Act, which gave Cabinet extraordinary powers, bypassing Parliament only during national emergencies, the Anti-terrorism Act could be used at any time so it would not be emergency legislation. Also see https://www.policyalternatives.ca/search/site/anti-terrorism%2520act%25202001%2520c-36.

Regarding the 2015 Bill C-51, see Ruby and Hasan (2015); also see Forcese and Roach (2015) and Patterson (2015).

18 *Canadian Charter of Rights and Freedoms,* Part 1 of the *Constitution Act, 1982,* being Schedule B to the *Canada Act 1982* (UK), 1982, c 11, s 6.

19 See the Government of Canada's (2023) description of the terms of the Canadian Race Relations Foundation.

20 The NAJC's website includes two news items in 2015 regarding Bill C-51. The first, "NAJC Rejects Bill C-51," was posted at the end of February (NAJC n.d.d). It criticizes Bill C-51, linking it to the government's use of the War Measures Act against Japanese Canadians in the 1940s and, in "1970[,] during the 'crisis' in Quebec." It calls on the prime minister (at the time it was Stephen Harper, though the NAJC interestingly did not name him) to consider the words of the previous prime minister, Brian Mulroney, regarding the redress settlement in 1988: "such violations will never again in this country be countenanced or repeated." There is no call to action in this post or announcement about organizing a wider campaign. The second news item, "Stop Bill C-51," was posted on April 15, 2015, a few weeks before the third and final vote on the bill (NAJC n.d.d.). It urges Japanese Canadians to write their MPs and local papers or organize an event. But with only a few weeks remaining before the final vote, it was too late to effectively intervene (especially through a post on a website viewed by a limited number of people); more generally, it illustrates the NAJC's lack of leadership on human rights issues.

At a local level, Vancouver's (used here as shorthand for Metro Vancouver) JCCA, which has a human rights committee, also responded to Bill C-51. In the June 2015 edition of *The Bulletin,* the community's primary newspaper, Lorene Oikawa, the president of Vancouver's JCCA at the time, noted that the Anti-terrorism Bill, C-51 had gone through three readings and was being reviewed in the Senate (Japanese Canadian Citizens' Association of Greater Vancouver 2015). There is no indication that Vancouver's JCCA (or the NAJC) had taken prior steps to organize a campaign to stop the bill. Interestingly, the first nine paragraphs (505 words) of the "President's Message" focused on historical plaques regarding the incarceration of Japanese Canadians in 1942; the next paragraph (129 words) focused on Asian Heritage Month, which Oikawa described as "another opportunity to share the history and celebrate the achievements of Asian Canadians," "fight for human rights," and "combat racism." Only two paragraphs (187 words) were on Bill C-51 and the last paragraph (193 words) was on fundraising and community events. The location of Bill C-51 (third of four topics) and the number of words devoted to it (only Asian Heritage Month had fewer words) indicates that Bill C-51 was less significant than historical plaques commemorating past injustices.

A more substantial article about Bill C-51 (which had passed in 2015, becoming the Anti-terrorist Act) was published in *The Bulletin* by Kathy Shimizu and Judy Hanazawa in 2016. They criticized the Act, reported what they learned from attending the Government of Canada Consultation on National Security's forum and urged Japanese Canadians to "send your thoughts to the Government of Canada by December 1, 2016." In addition, Vancouver's JCCA invited "Muslim speakers" to "share their perspectives of being Muslim in Canada" at the Legacy of Redress Forum on October 15, 2016, at Tonari Gumi. But while the article offers a more substantial critique and the forum offers solidarity with Muslim Canadians, there is no reference to organized action (beyond asking individuals to write letters) to revoke or amend the Act. Also see Patterson (2015) and Forcese and Roach (2015).

21 *Canadian Human Rights Act*, RSC, 1985, c H-6.

22 As Indigenous leaders have noted regarding the Truth and Reconciliation Commission of Canada for residential schools for Indigenous children, recognizing the commission's significance does not mean ignoring its problematic and damaging procedures or the ways the state has appropriated the Truth and Reconciliation process to rectify its reputation.

23 For the statements of other government officials, see Miki and Kobayashi (1991, 143–54).

24 Other than survivors of residential schools, who successfully launched a lawsuit against Canada and the churches running the schools, and the NAJC, which negotiated the terms of Japanese Canadian redress, there has been little opportunity for other groups to negotiate the terms of their redress settlements (Matsunaga 2016).

25 *Indian Act*, RSC, 1985, c I-5.

26 When I asked the NAJC for records about the disbursement of Japanese Canadian Redress Foundation funds it didn't seem to have easy access to these records so I used Art Miki's overview of the disbursement of these funds on his 2003 book. A forensic study of the NAJC's performance since 1988 is needed, using interviews and documents in the NAJC's Winnipeg office, public archives and personal records.

27 A comparison is useful here. My snapshot analysis of the NAJC's homepage below shows that its contributions to front-line work are considerably less than those of organizations like the National Council of Canadian Muslims (NCCM) that are also committed to social justice. I briefly compare each organization's homepage for social justice activities in October 2020. The NCCM states that it is an "independent, not-partisan, and non-profit organization that protects Canadian human rights and civil liberties, challenges discrimination and Islamophobia, builds mutual understanding, and advocates for the public concerns of Canadian Muslims." The navigation menu includes "Take Action" (Action Alerts, Hate Crimes Map, Community Resources, Report an Incident, and Volunteer); "Urgent Appeals" (which included a campaign to stop Bill 21 in Quebec, which aimed to prevent people who wear religious symbols from becoming teachers, prosecutors, or police officers); and "Donate" (National Council of Canadian Muslims n.d.). In October 2020, the first four posts on its homepage included two calls for the federal government to take action against white supremacists groups; a draft of a policy paper calling for oversight of the Canada Border Services Agency given its record of racial profiling and Islamophobia; and a report about two Federal Court decisions that show how "the Canadian Security Intelligence Service illegally gathered intelligence and then withheld evidence that would have assisted the accused on their case." See https://www.nccm.ca/?s=Canadian+Security+Intelligence+Service+illegally+&button=Search, accessed October 14, 2020. Like the NCCM, the NAJC is concerned with rights. According to the mission statement on its homepage, its purpose is "to strive for equal rights and liberties of all persons – in particular the rights of racial and ethnic minorities."

In contrast to the NCCM, the NAJC also aims "to promote and develop a strong Japanese Canadian identity and thereby to strengthen local communities and the national organization" (NAJC, n.d.b), likely combining services that in larger communities would be the domain of other organizations. In October 2020, of the six news items listed on the NAJC's homepage, none involved current human rights issues. Three refer to the NAJC (a message from the president; an update on its activities; and information about funding opportunities); there is an announcement about a Japanese (not Japanese Canadian) cultural festival; and announcements about a film and a book on Japanese Canadians' history of injustice. To analyze items about human rights issues, I thus extended my search back to February 2020 – which, in addition to more president's reports and funding announcements, include information about the COVID-19 pandemic, an interview with a Japanese Canadian athlete, and updates on the NAJC's redress negotiations with British Columbia. There were only three news items regarding current human rights issues in Canada, including anti-Black racism, anti-Asian racism, and Indigenous land rights (discussed in this chapter). And in the final stages of this volume's production in 2024, further indicating the NAJC's lack of commitment to human rights, it had not yet made any statements about the Israeli state's genocidal attacks and killing of over 44,000 Palestinian civilians in Gaza. This, despite the fact that in October 2023 over 500 Nikkei in the US, Canada, and elsewhere signed an open letter calling for Nikkei individuals and organizations to join the boycott of Israel since these organizations had not yet taken a position against the Israel's genocide against Palestinians in Gaza.

28 A number of Japanese Canadian individuals and organizations, including local JCCAs, have invited Indigenous speakers to their events. In 2017, the Japanese Cultural Association of Manitoba signed the city of Winnipeg's Indigenous Accord, but its commitment to reconciliation is not reflected on its webpage (in its headers, etc.) or more widely in its actions (see NAJC, n.d.a.).

29 During the decade after the 1988 Redress Agreement, the NAJC's National Executive Board and, notably, NAJC president Grace Eiko Thomson took a number of critical positions on injustice, for instance, criticizing and calling on the Japanese government to fully redress and apologize to the Korean women the Japanese Imperial Army forced into sexual slavery (Newmarket Era 2017). But over the last decade, the NAJC has taken a number of troubling positions that are arguably aligned with Japanese imperialism. For example, in 2016 NAJC president David R. Mitsui wrote Ontario premier Kathleen Wynne to oppose Bill 79, which proposed establishing Nanjing Massacre Commemorative Day; his letter was widely criticized by other Japanese Canadians, indicating that the NAJC at this time did not represent all members of the community (NAJC 2016; see Komori 2022).

30 In contrast, see *The Bulletin*'s May 13, 2020, publication of an article regarding COVID-19, racism, and anti-racist responses written by Kim Uyede-Kai (2020), a Minister for the United Church from the Shining Waters Regional Council. While the article was aimed at church-going Japanese Canadians, it asked readers to question their assumptions and respect the different forms of racism different communities face (here, the Black community).

31 During the period covered in the analysis, there was a surge of media coverage on police violence and killing of Indigenous peoples, and nationwide reports about the denigrating treatment and deaths of Indigenous people in Canada's health care system. See, for example, Bellrichard (2020), and the *Global News* coverage of the treatment of Joyce Echaquan of the Atikamekw Nation, who recorded her racist treatment by nurses while on her deathbed in a Quebec hospital in September 2020 (Canadian Press 2021).

32 There are a notable number of Japanese Canadians who have been board members of community organizations (including the NAJC) or work independently beyond the community who have dedicated themselves to building a sustainable, just world by inclusively bringing different community sectors together and drawing on the diverse strengths of community members rather than relying on the same inner circles.

33 Second generation Japanese Canadian children sent to Japan for education before returning to Canada.

References

Abu-Laban, Yasmeen, and Christina Gabriel. 2002. *Selling Diversity: Immigration, Multiculturalism, Employment Equity, and Globalization*. Peterborough, ON: Broadview Press.

Adachi, Ken. (1976) 1991. *The Enemy That Never Was: A History of the Japanese Canadians*. Toronto: McClelland and Stewart.

Antiwa, Phanuel, and David Chariandy. 2017. "The Ethics of Criticism: A Conversation with Rinaldo Walcott." *Transition: The Magazine of Africa and the Diaspora* 124: 51–61.

Archibald, Jo-Ann. 2006. *Indigenous Storywork: Educating the Heart, Mind, Body, and Spirit*. Vancouver: UBC Press.

Archibald, Jo-Ann Q'um Q'um Xiiem, Jenny Bol Jun Lee-Morgan, and Jason De Santolo, eds. 2019. *Decolonizing Research: Indigenous Storywork as Methodology*. London: Zed Books.

Baldwin, James. 1955. *Notes on a Native Son*. Boston: Beacon Press.

Bellrichard, Chantelle. 2020. "Investigation Finds Widespread Racism and Discrimination against Indigenous Peoples in B.C. Health-Care System." *CBC News*, November 30. https://www.cbc.ca/news/indigenous/bc-health-care-racism -report-1.5820306.

Byrd, Jodi. 2011. *The Transit Empire: Indigenous Critiques of Colonialism*. Minneapolis: University of Minnesota Press.

Canadian Press. 2021. "Two Quebec nurses Suspended after Allegedly Mocking Death of Indigenous Woman." *Global News*, March 15. https://globalnews. ca/news/7698720/two-quebec-nurses-suspended-after-allegedly-mocking -death-of-indigenous-woman/.

Chow, Rey. 2002. *The Protestant Ethnic and the Spirit of Capitalism*. New York: Columbia University Press.

Christian, Dorothy. 2017. "Gathering Knowledge: Indigenous Methodologies of Land/Place-Based Visual Storytelling/Filmmaking and Visual Sovereignty," PhD. thesis, University of British Columbia, 1–316.

Cole, Desmond. 2020. *The Skin We're In: A Year of Black Resistance and Power*. Toronto: Doubleday Canada.

Coulthard, Glen. 2014. *Red Skin, White Masks: Rejecting the Colonial Politics of Recognition*. Minneapolis: University of Minnesota Press.

Day, Iyko. 2016. *Alien Capital: Asian Racialization and the Logic of Settler Colonial Capitalism*. Durham, NC: Duke University Press.

Eng, David. 2001. *Racial Castration: Managing Masculinity in Asian America*. Durham, NC: Duke University Press.

Fanon, Frantz. (1952) 2008. *Black Skins, White Masks*. Translated by Richard Philcox. New York: Grove Press.

Forcese, Craig, and Kent Roach. 2015. "Why Can't Canada Get National-Security Law Right?" *Walrus*, June 9. https://thewalrus.ca/why-cant-canada-get-national-security-law-right/.

Fujikane, Candace. 2012. "Asian American Critique and Moana Nui 2011: Securing a Future beyond Empires, Militarized Capitalism and APEC." *Inter-Asia Cultural Studies* 13 (2): 189–210.

– 2021. *Mapping Abundance for a Planetary Future: Kanaka Maoli and Critical Settler Cartographies in Hawai'i*. Durham, NC: Duke University Press.

Fujitani, Takashi. 2011. *Race for Empire: Koreans as Japanese and Japanese as Americans during World War II*. Berkeley: University of California Press.

Gilroy, Paul. 2001. *Against Race: Imagining Political Culture Beyond the Color Line*. Cambridge, MA: Harvard University Press.

Government of Canada. 2023. "Organization Profile – Canadian Race Relations Foundation." https://federal-organizations.canada.ca/profil.php?OrgID=RRF&t=&lang=en.

Hall, Stuart. 1990. "Cultural Identity and Diaspora." In *Identity: Community, Culture, Difference*, edited by Stuart Jonathan Rutherford, 222–37. London: Lawrence and Wishart.

Henderson, James (Sa'ke'j) Youngblood. 2013. "Incomprehensible Canada." In *Reconciling Canada: Critical Perspectives on the Culture of Redress*, edited by Jennifer Henderson and Pauline Wakeman, 129–42. Toronto: University of Toronto Press.

Henderson, Jennifer, and Pauline Wakeham, eds. 2013. *Reconciling Canada: Critical Perspectives on the Culture of Redress*. Toronto: University of Toronto Press.

Ikebuchi, Shelly, and Takara Ketchell. 2020. "It Is Food That Calls Us Home: A Multigenerational Auto-Ethnography of Japanese Canadian Food and Culture." *BC Studies* 207: 11–33.

Inouye, Karen M. 2016. *The Long Afterlife of Nikkei Wartime Incarceration*. Redwood, CA: Stanford University Press.

James, Matt. 2013. "Neoliberal Heritage." In *Reconciling Canada: Critical Perspectives on the Culture of Redress*, edited by Jennifer Henderson and Pauline Wakeham, 31–46. Toronto: University of Toronto Press.

Japanese Canadian Citizens' Association of Greater Vancouver. 2015. "JCCA President's Message" https://jccabulletin-geppo.ca/jcca-presidents-message-2/.

Jiwani, Yasmin, with Matthew Dessner. 2016. "Barbarians in/of the Land: Representations of Muslim Youth in the Canadian Press." *Journal of Contemporary Issues in Education* 11 (1): 36–53.

Justice, Daniel Heath. 2018. *Why Indigenous Literatures Matter*. Waterloo, ON: Wilfrid Laurier University Press.

Kage, Tatsuo. 2012. *Uprooted Again: Japanese Canadians Move to Japan After World War II*. Victoria: TI-Jean Press.

Kamboureli, Smaro. 2000. *Scandalous Bodies: Diasporic Literature in English Canada*. Oxford: Oxford University Press.

Kawai, Yuko. 2005. "Stereotyping Asian Americans: The Dialectic of the Model Minority and the Yellow Peril." *Howard Journal of Communications* 16 (2): 109–30.

Kim, Jodi. 2010. *Ends of Empire: Asian American Critique and the Cold War*. Minneapolis: University of Minnesota Press.

Kim Uyede-Kai. 2020. "COVID-19 and the Racism Pandemic We Need to Talk About." *The Bulletin*, May 13. https://jccabulletin-geppo.ca/covid-19-and-the-racism -pandemic-we-need-to-talk-about/.

Kobayashi, Audrey. 1989. "A Demographic Profile of Japanese Canadians and Social Implications for the Future." Ottawa: Department of the Secretary of State, Canada.

– 1992. "The Japanese-Canadian Redress Agreement and Its Implications for 'Race Relations.'" *Canadian Ethnic Studies* 24 (1): 1–19.

– 1993. "Multiculturalism: Representing a Canadian Institution." In *Place/Culture/ Representation*, edited by James Duncan and David Ley, 205–31. London: Routledge.

Kogawa, Joy. 1981. *Obasan*. Toronto: Penguin Books.

Komori, Jane. 2022. "'Guilt by Association': Japanese Canadians and the Nanjing Massacre Commemorative Day." *Asia-Pacific Journal* 20 (16): 1–15.

Kovach, Margaret. 2009. *Indigenous Methodologies: Characteristics, Conversations, and Contexts*. Toronto: University of Toronto Press.

Lanegran, Kimberly. 2005. "Truth Commissions, Human Rights Trials and the Politics of Memory." *Comparative Studies of South Asia, Africa and the Middle East* 25 (1): 111–21.

Lawrence, Bonita. 2004. *"Real" Indians and Others: Mixed-Blood Urban Native Peoples and Indigenous Nationhood*. Vancouver: UBC Press.

– 2013. *Fractured Homeland: Federal Recognition and Algonquin Identity in Ontario*. Vancouver: UBC Press.

Lorde, Audre. 1984. *Sister Outsider: Essays and Speeches*. Berkeley, CA: Crossing Press.

Mackey, Eva. 2002. *The House of Difference: Cultural Politics and National Identity in Canada*. Toronto: University of Toronto Press.

Mamdani, Mahmood. 2004. *Good Muslim, Bad Muslim: America, the Cold War, and the Roots of Terror*. New York: Pantheon Books.

Matsunaga, Jennifer. 2016. "Two Faces of Transitional Justice: Theorizing the Incommensurability of Transitional Justice and Decolonization in Canada." *Decolonization: Indigeneity, Education and Society* 5 (1): 24–44.

– 2021. "Carefully Considered Words: The Influence of Government on Truth Telling about Japanese Canadian Internment and Indian Residential Schools." *Canadian Ethnic Studies* 53 (2): 91–113.

May, Angela. 2021. "Beyond Pain Narratives? Representing Loss and Practising Refusal at the Astoria Hotel." *Urban History Review* 48 (2): 76–96.

Maynard, Robyn. 2017. *Policing Black Lives: State Violence in Canada from Slavery to the Present*. Halifax: Fernwood.

McAllister, Kirsten. 1999. "Narrating Japanese Canadians In and Out of the Canadian Nation." *Canadian Journal of Communication* 24: 79–103.

– 2006. "Stories of Escape: Family Photographs from World War Two Internment Camps." In *Locating Memory: Photographic Acts*, edited by Annette Kuhn and Kirsten McAllister, 81–110. Oxford: Berghahn Books.

– 2010. *Terrain of Memory: A Japanese Canadian Memorial Project*. Vancouver: UBC Press.

– 2011. "Memoryscapes of Postwar British Columbia: A Look of Recognition." In *Cultivating Canada: Cultivating Canada through the Lens of Cultural Diversity*, edited by Ashok Mathur, Jonathan Dewar, and Mike DeGagné, 419–44. Ottawa: Aboriginal Healing Foundation.

– 2018. "Family Photography and Persecuted Communities: Methodological Challenges." *Canadian Review of Sociology/Revue canadienne de sociologie* 55 (2): 166–85.

McAllister, Kirsten, and Mona Oikawa. 1996. "Research: Re-search. Search. Searching, Sear-ch-ing." *Nikkei Voice: A National Forum for Japanese Canadians* 10 (2): 1, 11.

McKittrick, Katherine. 2013. "Plantation Futures." *Small Axe: A Caribbean Journal of Criticism* 17 (3): 1–15.

Memmi, Albert. 1965. *The Colonizer and the Colonized*. New York: Orion Press.

Miki, Arthur K. 2003. *The Japanese Canadian Redress Legacy: A Community Revitalized*. Winnipeg: National Association of Japanese Canadians.

Miki, Roy, ed. 1985. *This Is My Own: Letters to Wes and Other Writings on Japanese Canadians, 1941–1948 by Muriel Kitagawa*. Vancouver: Talonbooks.

– 2004. *Redress: Inside the Japanese Canadian Call for Redress*. Vancouver: Raincoast Books.

Miki, Roy, and Cassandra Kobayashi. 1991. *Justice in Our Time: The Japanese Canadian Redress Settlement*. Vancouver/Winnipeg: Talonbooks/National Association of Japanese Canadians.

Miller, David. 2009. "Social Justice versus Global Justice?" In *Social Justice in the Global Age*, edited by Olaf Cramme and Patrick Diamond, 23–37. Cambridge: Polity Press.

Million, Dian. 2014. *Therapeutic Nations: Healing in an Age of Indigenous Human Rights*. Tucson: University of Arizona Press.

NAJC (National Association of Japanese Canadians). n.d.a. "JCAM Signs the Indigenous Accord." https://najc.ca/jcam-signs-the-indigenous-accord/.

– n.d.b. "Mission Statement." https://najc.ca/about-us/.

– n.d.c. "NAJC Statement on Black Lives Matter." https://najc.ca/najc-statement-on-black-lives-matter/.

– n.d.d. "NAJC Rejects Bill C-51." https://najc.ca/najc-rejects-bill-c-51/.

– 2016. "Bill 79 Day to Commemorate the Nanjing Massacre." https://najc.ca/bill-79-day-to-commemorate-the-nanjing-massacre/.

– 2020. "NAJC Statement Regarding Wet'suwet'en Territory." https://najc.ca/najc-statement-regarding-wetsuweten-territory/.

Nakai, Kate Wildman. 2018. "State Shinto." In *Routledge Handbook of Modern Japanese History*, edited by Sven Saaler and Christopher W.A. Szpilman, 147–59. London, UK: Routledge.

Nakano, Takeo Ujo. 1980. *Within the Barbed Wire Fence: A Japanese Man's Account of his Internment in Canada*. Toronto: University of Toronto Press.

National Council of Canadian Muslims. n.d. https:www.nccm.ca.

Newmarket Era. 2017. "Apologize to Women: Coalition." *YorkRegion.com*, May 19. https://www.yorkregion.com/news/apologize-to-women-coalition/article_626f4c81–8896–535a-b8dc-aef620a8bc73.html.

Ng, Roxana. 1996. *The Politics of Community Services: Immigrant Women, Class and the State*. Toronto: Fernwood.

Ng, Roxana, Gillian Walker, and Jacob Muller, eds. 1990. *Community Organization and the Canadian State*. Toronto: Garamond Press.

Oikawa, Mona. 1986. "'Driven to Scatter Far and Wide': The Forced Resettlement of Japanese Canadians to Southern Ontario, 1944–1949." MA thesis, University of Toronto.

– 2002. "Connecting the Internment of Japanese Canadians to the Colonization of Aboriginal Peoples." In *Aboriginal Connections to Race, Environment, and Tradition*, edited by Jill Oakes and Rick Riewe, 17–25. Winnipeg: Aboriginal Issues Press.

– 2012. *Cartographies of Violence: Japanese Canadian Women, Memory, and the Subjects of Internment*. Toronto: University of Toronto Press.

Okamura, Jonathan Y., and Candace Fujikane, eds. 2008. *Asian Settler Colonialism: From Local Governance to the Habits of Everyday Life in Hawaii*. Honolulu: University of Hawai'i Press.

Paik, Naomi A. 2016. *Internment Remains: The 1988 Civil Liberties Act and Racism Re-formed*. Chapel Hill: University of North Carolina Press.

Patterson, Brett. 2015. "What's in Harper's Proposed Bill C-51 'Security of Canada' Legislation?" Council of Canadians, February 1. https://canadians.org/analysis/whats-harpers-proposed-bill-c-51-security-canada-legislation.

Radstone, Susannah, and Bill Schwarz. 2010. *Memory: Histories, Theories, Debates*. New York: Fordham University Press.

Ramadan, Tariq. 2010. "Good Muslim, Bad Muslim." *New Statesman*, February 12. https://www.newstatesman.com/religion/2010/02/muslim-religious-moderation, accessed November 4, 2020.

Rawls, John. 1993. "The Law of Peoples." *Critical Inquiry* 20: 36–68.

Regan, Paulette. 2010. *Unsettling the Settler Within: Indian Residential Schools, Truth Telling, and Reconciliation in Canada*. Vancouver: UBC Press.

Roy, Patricia. 1978. "*The Enemy That Never Was: A History of the Japanese Canadians* by Ken Adachi, and *Steveston Recollected: A Japanese-Canadian History* ed. by Daphne Marlatt." *Canadian Historical Review* 59 (2): 255–57.

– 2014. "*Cartographies of Violence: Japanese Canadian Women, Memory, and the Subjects of the Internment*: Review." *Canadian Ethnic Studies* 46 (1): 221–23.

Royal Commission on Aboriginal Peoples. 1996. *Report of the Royal Commission on Aboriginal Peoples,* vol. 1. Ottawa: Supply and Services Canada.

Ruby, Clayton, and Nader R. Hasan. 2015. "Bill C-51: A Legal Primer." Canadian Centre for Policy Alternatives, February 17. https://www.policyalternatives.ca/authors/nader-r-hasan.

Said, Edward. 1979. *Orientalism.* New York: Vintage.

Saint-Cyr, Marie-Yosie. 2012. "Section 13 of the Canadian Human Rights Act Repealed!?" *Slaw: Canada's Online Legal Magazine,* June 14. http://www.slaw.ca/2012/06/14/section-13-of-the-canadian-human-rights-act-repealed/.

Sharpe, Christina. 2016. *In the Wake: On Blackness and Being.* Durham, NC: Duke University Press.

Shimizu, Kathy, and Judy Hanazawa. 2016. "Repeal C-51, the Anti-terrorist [sic] Act." *The Bulletin,* November 14. http://jccabulletin-geppo.ca/repeal-c-51-the-anti-terrorist-act/.

Shimoda, Brendan. 2024. *The Afterlife is Letting Go.* San Francisco: City Lights Books.

Smith, Linda Tuhiwai. 2012. *Decolonizing Methodologies: Research and Indigenous Peoples.* 2nd ed. London: Zed Books.

Spivak, G.C. 1988. "Can the Subaltern Speak?" In *Marxism and the Interpretation of Culture,* edited by C. Nelson and L. Grossberg, 271–313. Champaign, IL: University of Illinois Press.

Sunahara, Ann Gomer. 1981. *The Politics of Racism: The Uprooting of Japanese Canadians during the Second World War.* Toronto: James Lorimer.

Suzuki, David, and Peter Knudtson. 1992. *The Wisdom of the Elders: Native and Scientific Ways of Knowing.* Vancouver: Greystone Books.

Takashima, Shizuye. 1971. *A Child in a Prison Camp.* Montreal: Tundra Books.

Takata, Toyo. 1983. *Nikkei Legacy: The Story of Japanese Canadians from Settlement to Today.* Toronto: NC Press.

Trouillot, Michel-Rolph. 2015. *Silencing the Past: Power and the Production of History.* Boston: Beacon Press.

Tuck, Eve, and K. Wayne Yang. 2012. "Decolonization is not a metaphor." *Decolonization: Indigeneity, Education & Society* 1 (1): 1–40.

Ty, Eleanor. 2017. *AsianFail.* Champaign: University of Illinois Press.

Uyede-Kai, Kim. 2020. "COVID-19 and the Racism Pandemic We Need to Talk About." *The Bulletin: a Journal of Japanese Canadian Community, History & Culture,* December 7.

Walcott, Rinaldo. 2003. *Black Like Who?* London, ON: Insomniac Press.

Ward, Peter W. White 1990. *Canada Forever: Popular Attitudes and Public Policy Towards Orientals in British Columbia.* Montreal and Kingston: McGill-Queen's University Press.

Yakashiro, Nicole. 2021. "Daffodils and Dispossession: Nikkei Settlers, White Possession, and Settler Colonial Property in Bradner, BC, 1914–51." *BC Studies* 211: 49–78.

Yoneyama, Lisa. 2016. *Cold War Ruins: Transpacific Critique of American Justice and Japanese War Crimes.* Durham, NC: Duke University Press.

Young, Iris Marion. 2011. *Responsibility for Justice.* Oxford, UK: Oxford University Press.

7
Post-Redress Japanese Canadian Scholar Activism

Audrey Kobayashi and Jeff Masuda

The redress campaign mobilized many of the Japanese Canadian community to become activists. Activist scholarship has been at the core of the redress movement from its inception. During the 1970s, there was a strong group of Nikkei, scholar activists, most of them students, who engaged in a number of activities, including the production of *A Dream of Riches* (Japanese Canadian Centennial Project 1978), a photo exhibit produced by a community collective, and *Inalienable Rice* (Powell Street Revue and the Chinese Canadian Writers Workshop 1979), the first anthology of Asian Canadian writing compiled by a collective of Japanese Canadian and Chinese Canadian students. It included the writings of many who were or who became well recognized authors, such as Joy Kogawa, Roy Miki, Roy Kiyooka, and Rick Shiomi.

By the late 1980s, the few Nikkei (along with other scholars of colour) who held university positions did not enjoy a welcoming environment for activism. There was still very little community-based research, either in the Japanese Canadian community or among social scientists generally. In most universities, community-based research was barely tolerated, and received almost no intellectual recognition or credibility. Since that time, however, participatory action research has come into its own, and is not only tolerated but actively encouraged by agencies such as the Social Sciences and Humanities Research Council of Canada (SSHRC) and the Canadian Institutes of Health Research (CIHR). Whereas we had few scholarly models to follow during the 1980s, reams of articles and books now advocate this "new" way of doing research. Post-structural paradigms have demolished the myth of objectivity, and it has become *de rigueur* to situate oneself, including one's political convictions, in relation to one's research subjects.

We are two *hapa* Sansei scholars, a generation apart in age. We have both spent virtually our entire careers doing community-based research, Audrey since becoming involved in the redress movement while a graduate student during the 1970s, and Jeff as a result of his initial training in community-based research during the late 1990s, which set the stage for a career emphasis on social geographies of health inequality in the Downtown Eastside (DTES) of Vancouver as well as other sites of urban socio-spatial injustice in Canada. Our collaborative work began in 2010 from a shared recognition that the fight for housing and social justice occurring in the DTES today, within the neoliberal city where housing prices have for some time been outpacing the ability of Vancouver's poorest residents to pay, is linked to a past history of dispossession that spans the entire colonial project, from dispossession of the Musqueam, Squamish, and Tsleil-Waututh peoples from their unceded lands, through the period of immigration, white supremacist subjugation, and ultimate dispossession of the Japanese Canadian community, to a post-Second World War period of increasing impoverishment, deterioration of the built environment, criminalization, and ongoing dispossession of precariously housed people over generations. At least one-third of the DTES population are Indigenous, and have sought in the DTES a sanctuary from a litany of twentieth-century colonial projects, from residential schools to psychiatric deinstitutionalization, the defunding of federal social housing, and, most recently, neoliberal urban revitalization (Masuda and Franks 2014). In this sense, the DTES continues to function as it did for the Japanese Canadian community as a racialized ghetto, albeit now in the context of multi-layered criminalization, systemic underinvestment, and heightened police violence against the unhoused. Despite these intense displacement pressures, the Indigenous community thrives in this neighbourhood, with numerous autonomous organizations we have had the privilege of working with over decades of supporting culture, health care, education, food sovereignty, and housing.

In this chapter, we aim to explain the inextricable relationships between our Japanese Canadian inheritance, political convictions, and lifelong research commitments in hopes of transmitting what we have learned to successive generations of Japanese Canadian scholar activists. We begin with two short autobiographical pieces, which situate us in the DTES. We do so with some care, bearing in mind that some scholars have been critical of the recent literature on positionality, as there is a risk that focusing on the positionality of the researcher – often invoking disclosure that the researcher is "privileged" – can ironically accentuate that privilege (Kobayashi 1994, 2017). We wish, therefore, to avoid the "me" syndrome, but at the same time we cannot escape the fact that our positioning as members of the Japanese Canadian community has given us a particular perspective on the DTES, filling a niche and giving us standing within the activist community. The stories that follow provide the starting point for unravelling the complex relationships involved in activist research. They speak to the legacy of redress in our own careers, and its ongoing relevance in our shared aspirations for justice in the DTES within our lifetimes.

Audrey

The *Powell Street Review* was my first introduction to community activism, and provided my first opportunity to publish my writing, which was very bad, but the sense of politicization that the experience provoked was profound and lasting. The collection was one of many initiatives that came out of the flurry of activities surrounding the Japanese Canadian celebration in 1977 of the arrival in 1877 of the first official Japanese immigrant, Manzo Nagano. The opportunity for members of the Nikkei community to come together to plan what turned out to be social events with a political twist was an important precondition for the redress movement that gained momentum over the next decade.

During the summer of 1977, I was excited to meet Gordon Hirabayashi, a sociologist at the University of Alberta but, more importantly, the plaintiff in one of the most important court cases in US civil rights history.[1] The occasion was the very first Powell Street Festival. Gordon met with a group of mostly Sansei students, and I recall him saying that to take on the redress battle was a serious proposition but would be worthwhile in the end. His call for commitment and determination was inspiring. He urged us to take the issues seriously and to stick with the battle.

I left Vancouver shortly afterwards to undertake a PhD at UCLA, and lost touch with the incipient Japanese Canadian redress movement. Over several years in Los Angeles (1978–80), I learned a great deal from some of the activists at the UCLA Asian American Studies Center, then spent two years in Japan (1980–82) researching the impact of emigration to Canada. By the mid-1980s, I had returned to Canada, taking up an assistant professorship at McGill, and was thoroughly focused on building a career that would document the lives of the Issei in great detail. I had – at least temporarily – pushed the political battle to the back burner.

In 1986, I received a telephone call from Roy Miki, who asked if I would join the team of people who by that time had made amazing progress in establishing the redress campaign. They were working on several fronts, negotiating with the federal government, documenting the impact of the uprooting and dispossession (which is where my demographic knowledge of the Japanese Canadian community was to play a role), and working tirelessly in Nikkei communities across Canada to raise awareness of their rights. I soon learned a lesson that would abide for a lifetime: that nothing can ever be achieved *for* communities without the collaboration and commitment *of* communities. Over the next two years, I worked with the powerful group of people who made up the negotiating team, but also with the wonderful people in the Nikkei community in Montreal. Like others across Canada, Montrealers played an important role in a process that could not have occurred had not the Nikkei in many places come together in a campaign that eventually achieved overwhelming support and culminated in the settlement of September 18, 1988 (see Miki and Kobayashi 1991).

The campaign changed not only my personal but also my academic life. At that time, participatory action research was vaguely understood and poorly recognized in the academy. It certainly was not part of my own discipline of geography. But I had emerged from the process of redress negotiation with two commitments that have been the foundation of my research ever since: First, if we are to overcome oppression of all kinds, we need to understand the fundamental social, institutional processes that create it. I shifted the focus of my research thereafter to understanding racialization, and how racialization has affected not only my own community but also other communities of colour, and in the part of Vancouver known as Powell Street, especially Indigenous people. Second, community research involves grassroots participation in community life and an understanding from the inside out of how social change can be achieved. The redress campaign was indeed a superb example of a community becoming politicized and organizing for a common goal.

The postscript to that activist transformation is that in 1989–90 I took my first sabbatical in London, England, where I was working with geographers studying racialization. I submitted my application for tenure before leaving Montreal, and in due course received a message from my dean informing me that the tenure committee was "tending" toward a negative decision but inviting me to return to Montreal to appear before them. It was a devastating blow. I returned and made my case before the committee. One committee member in particular informed me that what I had been doing within the redress movement was not scholarship, that spending time in the community and, even worse, writing things meant for community consumption, were inappropriate activities for an academic. I left the hearing emotionally drained, but received a phone call a couple of hours later to say that I would be granted tenure, but that in order to make a decision, the committee had removed from my curriculum vitae all those items considered to be community activism, then based their assessment on what was left. My dean subsequently wrote me a letter that meant a great deal to me, saying how much he admired the community work, notwithstanding the actions of the committee.

Meanwhile, I continued my work documenting Japanese immigration to Canada and the development of the segregated community known as Powell Street, or *Pauerugai,* through which more than 30,000 immigrants passed en route to their new lives in Canada. I tramped the streets, documenting each deteriorating building, trying to bring to life the past of those who had built them, inhabited them, made lives. It was not difficult to see that by the end of the twentieth century the very buildings that had been the boarding houses of Nikkei workers were now single-room occupancy homes to people who were precariously housed and living in deep poverty, but part of a new community marginalized within a white supremacist society. The streets of the Downtown Eastside, still unceded Indigenous territory, remain a testament to all of the colonial injustices that have taken place there, from its early seizure from Indigenous peoples to the erasure of Japanese Canadians whose ancestors had been imported across the Pacific to provide cheap labour for a burgeoning resource economy. It took me a long time to come to terms with the present-day reality of this place called Powell Street.

Ironically, we have come full circle as an academic community on the question of community/participatory research. It is now well established, even considered essential, for a large portion of social science. Participatory action research is now legitimately funded, students are attracted to it in growing numbers, and there is a large body of scholarship in most social science disciplines.[2] Reflecting on the nearly forty years of my career, however, I see that it is not the academic trajectory or the activist trajectory that seems most important, but the ways in which they are thoroughly fused in my own stubborn commitment to make a contribution to social change.

Jeff

By the late 1990s, when I had begun my graduate training, activist scholarship had become a generally accepted academic concept and practice,
and perhaps even dominant within particular disciplinary approaches in
social, environmental, and health studies. For example, in most universities, in the interdisciplinary field of health promotion, where I obtained my
master's degree, community-based research has become a core pedagogical
competency. Likewise, in human geography, activist researchers in Canada have become highly adept in scholarly approaches that support social
movements surrounding injustices related to structural racism, colonialism,
gender discrimination, and disableism, particularly as each takes specific
spatial forms, whether in urban, regional, or global contexts. This legacy,
now at least three decades in the making, is in no small part due to the pion-
eering work and boundary breaking led by feminist and anti-racist geographers in the 1980s and '90s, including my co-author.

At the time of my own graduate training, my motivations for beginning
a career as an activist scholar were drawn from a naïve environmental-
ism born out of childhood anxieties about Chernobyl, ozone depletion,
and other 1980s issues, combined with a vaguely defined antipathy toward
social injustice, the origins of which I had left largely unscrutinized thus
far in my life. With the benefit of hindsight, I have learned to attribute
a large part of my professional and personal commitment to social and
environmental justice to experiences related to coming of age in a sea
of whiteness in suburban Alberta. I had always known, of course, that
my personal geography – born in Southern Alberta and raised near
Edmonton – was inextricably linked to my Japanese Canadian heritage.
But at the incipient stage of my career, I had yet to attend to my own (late)
Sansei identity, including the intergenerational silence common among
many families in our community.

While Japanese Canadian legacies of injustice are not comparable to
Canada's genocidal policies spanning centuries and continuing to this day,
they nonetheless have sensitized me to the ways in which covert forms of
racism, from the personal to the institutional to the structural, have pene-
trated so deeply into the national psyche. But finding a coherent way to
articulate my positionality in ways that were not self-aggrandizing would
take years of training and no small amount of good fortune in connecting to
mentors along the way who subtly pointed me toward a career as an activist
scholar of urban social and environmental justice.

To the point: until 2010, I considered myself to be a non-racialized scholar, in the sense that I had yet to recognize how racism had influenced my personal or professional life; I had refused participation in what we now refer to as equity/diversity/inclusion (EDI) processes. Nor had I drawn from my experiences as a person racialized both within the community and academy to inform the direction of my scholarship. The late 1990s and early 2000s was a period where I felt very little affinity to my inheritance as a member of a dispersed Japanese Canadian diaspora, whether as part of my personal identity or, more significantly, with regard to my responsibility as an indirect beneficiary of redress. My own recollections of redress were mainly of the fleeting financial benefit of cash payments overheard as a mostly disinterested participant within casual conversations among my father and extended family. As a young teenager maturing at a distance from the heart of the redress movement in a pre-Internet society, I had little opportunity to connect with the significant events of the redress movement, especially the many years of struggle that preceded it. In fact, the specifics of my family history of racial banishment and postwar hardship were largely unknown to me, following the philosophy of *shigata ga nai* (it cannot be helped), so common among the Japanese Canadian diaspora (Suyemoto 2018), exacerbated by my father's young age (he was born in 1941) at the time of the uprooting relative to that of his older siblings and parents.

My own self-affirmation as a scholar whose work draws from and informs Japanese Canadian history and community came only by virtue of a coincidental series of events after 2007. At the time, I had chosen to shift my postdoctoral studies from the discipline of geography at McMaster University to critical health promotion studies at the UBC Centre for Health Promotion Research in order to revive my passion for community-based health research. It was during this time that I began to develop relationships with activist academic and community leaders working in and on behalf of the low-income community in Vancouver's Downtown Eastside. These relationships gradually led to a series of participatory action research projects involving new community relationships that would have me beginning to confront the deficit-oriented perceptions and approaches toward community intervention that prevail within research discourses on the DTES. From the outset, our aim was to focus more attention on the politically and historically relational modes of production of social and environmental injustice that are built into colonial urbanization processes and that consistently seemed to target low-income and racialized bodies within this highly dense, diverse, and historical community. To wit: the crux of my work has been

anti-racist and anti-colonial, exposing the systemic racial and colonial violence within contemporary institutions, including urban planning, housing,
and public health. The research approach we developed began to respond to
a largely unmet need within the community: to ensure that research capacity
remains with the community, activist researchers must stand in solidarity
with the community. This approach, inspired by a school of activist research
based on the original emancipatory pedagogy of Paulo Freire, requires that
we attend to the distinctions between those who do research and those who
are purported to receive its benefits. Such a stance means that participatory
action research practice must necessarily extend beyond the project. Our
role within the community is not only to produce knowledge for its own
sake but also to lend our institutional status and epistemic capacity to support and defend the community in whatever form is asked for.

Within this activist milieu, heated as it was in the lead-up to the 2010
Winter Olympics, I began to move down this trajectory of activist research
that forced a reconciliation between my own relatively unknown pre-1940s
family history, my recent affiliation with Vancouver's Japanese Canadian
community, and my growing solidarity with the struggle for justice in the
Downtown Eastside. All these things suddenly collided with such force as
to induce a permanent shift in my career orientation and research focus,
where, like Audrey, I began to see value in my work contributing more directly to the community than to my own disciplinary advancement.

Within this space, I began to encounter the links that scholars and activists had been drawing between other communities who have resisted state
oppression within the 150-year recent history of the city as a larger history
of systematic and cyclical colonial and capitalist dispossession and ensuing
struggle that seemed to be a hallmark of this tiny neighbourhood. Through
a series of preliminary interventions undertaken with my photographer and
filmmaker brother, we began to see ourselves as intimately connected to
the places and people of the neighbourhood. Gradually, through our in situ
experiences of doing research and volunteering within the community, we
began a process of discovery of our own intimate genealogical roots in that
place, including a twenty-five-year period during which our grandfather, his
father, and later the rest of the growing family dwelt in boarding houses in
and around Powell Street. We learned, through a combination of lay archival
research and family ethnography, of our family's entry into the resource
sector labour force, its experience of multi-generational inhabitation, of
distant memories of Powell Grounds (Oppenheimer Park), and ultimately
of uprooting curated in faded photographs of prewar family life, wartime

dispossession and banishment, and postwar rebuilding amid the sugar beet farming community in Southern Alberta.

Of course, there has been plenty of scholarship in this area to build on, and Audrey's efforts to "re-present" the DTES as a historical neighbourhood was notably influential, to the point that I (humbly) invited her to join a team I was building with my brother to do activist research that would explicitly tie together Japanese Canadian activists, young and senior, with activists in the DTES who had long been struggling to attend to issues of gentrification and dispossession in the neighbourhood (of course, we would quickly learn that many of these linkages already existed, albeit never previously formalized in the form of a participatory action research project!). Since 2010, we have directed our efforts toward connecting past and present struggles and achievements, meaningful not just symbolically but also practically; and toward using research as a means to equip present-day activists with a new way of articulating the systems of oppression that lie behind long-standing neoliberal prescriptions for the current housing and harm reduction crises. We aimed to create a space for old and new allies to consolidate efforts, not just to commemorate past struggles and achievements but to fight for social justice in our time.

In the ensuing decade, our small project has worked to strengthen relationships between Japanese Canadian and Indigenous movements and to connect the language of historical and cultural connection within a language of activist scholarship. Along the way, my success as a scholar owes a debt to those who struggled before me to build the edifice on which I have launched my career as well as to the small community of Japanese Canadian scholars who have embraced me and made me one of their own. Together, we have attempted to reassert the place of this small neighbourhood at the centre of the ongoing history of redress in such a way that a better future for its people will be connected to the legacy of our movement and vice versa.

In the remainder of this chapter, we describe our current collaborative work, highlighting some of the challenges and opportunities to help effect social change.

The Landscape That Was

The DTES is a particular relict landscape; it oozes the generations of dispossession and resistance that make it the paradox that it is today – a bastion of inclusion, social connectedness, and cultural diversity within a white supremacist city and society. Its historical geography is well documented, but we provide a very brief description here (for more details, see Kobayashi 1996). What is now the Downtown Eastside is often referred to as K'emk'emeláy̓, "Place where maples grow," in the language of the First Nation of the Sḵwx̱wú7mesh (Squamish) people on whose shared territory with the Musqueam and Tsleil-Waututh the neighbourhood exists. The colonial city of Vancouver originated with a few businesses in what is now Gastown along the northern waterfront, and a residential area emanating from the Hastings Sawmill at the foot of Dunlevy Street. Social class among the white settlers climbed the hill from Railway to Cordova Streets. Powell Street between 1885 and 1900 was the main corridor of the white middle class. By the 1890s, however, as the city grew quickly, its residents began moving, first to the West End, then to the Fairview Slopes. Powell Street and neighbouring Alexander Street began a brief period of physical decline. But within a decade, Japanese immigrants, who made up the largest (non-white) ethnocultural group employed in the sawmills, moved into houses abandoned by white residents. By the early twentieth century, they had created a thriving community, transforming the small one-and-a-half-storey homes, building on front and back and over the top to create the unique Japanese Canadian architecture known as the *naga-ya*, or long house, consisting of businesses facing the street front on the ground floor, family apartments above, and two-storey boarding houses in the back. By the 1920s, as the community grew and some members prospered, the *naga-ya* were interspersed with purpose-built, single-room occupancy residences that housed thousands of single men who worked the sawmills, or who lived on Powell Street between jobs in the interior logging, railway, or mining camps. Powell Street functioned as both a residence and an employment-staging area for Japanese immigrant workers.

By 1940, there were many fewer single Issei men inhabiting the boarding houses. Some had returned to Japan. Others had married and started families and moved to larger residences in the area surrounding Powell Street and in other parts of the Lower Mainland. The community had grown in neighbourhoods surrounding other mills, along the south shore of the Fairview Slopes, for example. There was a thriving community of fishers in nearby Steveston and in several locations on Vancouver Island and the Gulf Islands; and there were mining, sawmill, and agricultural communities along the Pacific coast and in the interior of the province. More and more families had made the transition from labour to farming and bought properties in the Fraser and Okanagan Valleys. But Powell Street still remained the largest and the most symbolic of Japanese Canadian communities, and was both a thriving business centre and residential enclave. For instance, by 1939, Japanese Canadians held nearly half of the 234 lodging house business licences in the area defined by the modern DTES boundaries.

Uprooting and the Emergence of a New Landscape

Everything changed after December 7, 1941. The story of the uprooting and dispossession of the Nikkei has been well documented and we shall not repeat it here (see, e.g., Adachi [1976] 1991). In early 1942, the Nikkei were brought from the island and coastal communities to Hastings Park to be processed for dispersal to one of the internment camps set up in the interior of the province. Smaller numbers went to farms in Alberta or Ontario. Many of the adult males were sent to prisoner-of-war or road camps. Powell Street was the last neighbourhood from which the Nikkei were removed. Their homes and businesses were abandoned, leaving a forlorn and empty landscape of storefronts, boarding houses, and *naga-ya*, which represented a distinctive architectural legacy. Unlike in other parts of the province, where homes and farms were soon scooped up by opportunistic buyers, many of the Powell Street properties lay more or less empty for many years, and buildings deteriorated. During the 1950s, two of the institutional properties, the Japanese Language School on Alexander Street, and the United Church, now the Buddhist Hall, at the corner of Powell and Jackson Streets, were returned to the community. A small number of businesses reopened on Powell Street, notably a restaurant and a fish store, and many Japanese Canadians returned to their former occupations and took up residence in single-room occupancy homes. But the wider arc of postwar history, and the geography of Japanese Canadian dispersal, rerouting, and rerooting, meant that a significant number of survivors would never rematerialize on Powell Street itself.

But while the gravitational pull of the old Powell Street had waned as a cultural hearth for Nikkei during their postwar re-establishment in the Lower Mainland, it would soon become the centre of gravity for a new community forced into motion during the postwar period of urban renewal and later neoliberal revitalization. The single-room occupancy landscape that the Nikkei had created had been custom-made for incorporation into the surrounding area known pejoratively as "Skid Road." The term "Skid Road" (also known as "Skid Row") comes from the temporary roads made of skids – logs laid side by side – on which timber destined for the sawmills were hauled out of the forests. The skid roads were lined with makeshift housing

for loggers, cooks, carpenters, sex workers, and others attached to the logging camps. When the term was transported to the city, it referred to the
single-room occupancy districts where largely single male workers (of all
ethnic backgrounds) from logging, mining, and railroad camps congregated
off-season or between jobs. Hence Japanese and Chinese immigrants were
also part of the "Skid Road" population.

After the 1940s, the DTES became a much more concentrated zone
of poverty, with virtually all of the Powell Street single-room occupancy
buildings occupied by the city's poorest residents: unemployed, precariously employed, retired, and disabled workers, and later, people who use
substances. The affordability of housing and acceptance of the community also made the neighbourhood a preferred destination for generations of
residential school and foster system survivors, as well as Indigenous people
seeking a better life beyond home communities. But the inclusiveness of
the community is also the basis of its exclusion from the white society just
beyond its borders. Just as Powell Street and nearby "China Town" had been
shunned by the white residents of the city for decades as a result of racism,
so too the DTES has continued to this day to be shunned, dismissed, and
derogated on the grounds of class and race, made all the more virulent by
criminalizing policies against sex work, drugs, and homelessness.

Until relatively recently, the DTES seemed immune to the actions of real
estate developers, who saw little potential for investment in its deteriorated
buildings. The 1986 Expo had begun a minor trend toward gentrification
to provide tourist housing by converting single-room occupancy dwellings,
but the 2010 Winter Olympics marked a major turning point when many
buildings were converted into more upscale hotels. The process of gentrification has intensified steadily since then, with several of the old buildings
torn down and replaced with condominium developments purpose-built
for short-term rentals and new urban migrants who populate the design
studios and other professional offices of a neoliberal city. These people are
increasingly impatient with this island of poverty so near its core. Recent
talk of "revitalization" takes little notice of the seemingly inevitable fate of
those who now live in the DTES, or at best ties their fate to weak incen-
tives of "social mix" given over to the private sector. Indeed, many residents
have already lost their homes to "renoviction" or been priced out of the
market, and have become homeless or forced to relocate to another muni-
cipality, such as Surrey. Such revitalization talk has also diminished, and
worse, romanticized the Japanese Canadian experience, rewriting the script
of community, rupture, and dispossession that is our legacy, substituting a

fanciful notion of a "Japantown" where cherry blossoms grow and paper lanterns sway, and where the streets look nothing like the largely working-class rooming house community that Powell Street was and is.

(Some) Nikkei Fight Back

Since the 1970s, a small number of Nikkei has steadfastly resisted contemporary forces of white supremacy in the Downtown Eastside. Prior to the 1977 centennial of the first Japanese immigration to Canada, there occurred a flurry of activities in Vancouver and elsewhere, which included both plans to celebrate the centennial and growing calls for redress. A few voices were also raised for a residential return to Powell Street. During the mid-1970s, there was a small but inspired movement of Japanese Canadians to the Powell Street area. They established Tonari Gumi, a drop-in cultural centre, and Sakura-So, a seniors' residence. But two decades later, these institutions moved to Burnaby (where many of the Nikkei now live), to new quarters financed partially by grants made possible through the Japanese Canadian Redress Agreement. By the 1990s, only a small handful of Nikkei were still living near the old Powell Street neighbourhood.

In 1977, the first Powell Street Festival (PSF) coincided with celebration of the centennial. The redress movement, until then only a few isolated voices, gained momentum from that time, growing in strength over a decade until the settlement in 1988. There was no discussion of gentrification in the movement but the festival has cemented the legacy of Powell Street as a spiritual homeland or, as many call it, *furusato* (place of origin). It draws people from all over the Greater Vancouver area and further, with its food, crafts, performance, and information booths. Many return year after year to rekindle memories and a sense of ethnocultural belonging. The festival is one of the many institutions that have flourished and grown since the redress settlement, largely sustained by the third generation (Sansei) as well as subsequent fourth (Yonsei) and fifth (Gosei) generations, and by more recent immigrants from Japan. For some, the festival – and Powell Street itself – has become both a symbol of past injustice and a beacon of identity for the future.

The Powell Street Festival brings past and present into stark contrast. Current residents of the DTES take a somewhat bemused view of the Japanese Canadians and the cultural tourists who descend for a few days each year. Some of them volunteer to help set up booths. There is a good-natured if guarded mingling of people from vastly different backgrounds. The visitors cannot help but notice the changes from year to year, however, as many buildings on Powell Street have materially deteriorated and the numbers of unhoused people have increased, even as the number of gentrified buildings dotting the landscape grows.

Some Nikkei recognize the ironic link between the past and present landscapes of Powell Street. Frankly, for most, Nikkei and non-Nikkei alike, the festival is a cultural tourism event, and both past and present are matters of social if not intellectual history. So, it is important not to exaggerate the small number of Nikkei for whom the Powell Street Festival, and Powell Street itself, represent a commitment to social justice in our time; but neither should we underestimate the difference that this small group of activists is making.

Redress as a Turning Point?

Insofar as the potential for the redress movement in the 1980s to make a difference on the ground in the Downtown Eastside, its timing could not have been worse. The area has figured prominently in Canada's long and lamentable war on drugs, going all the way back to Parliament's Opium Act (1908), prompted in large part by William Lyon Mackenzie King's observation of the largely white clientele of Chinatown's opium industry. But it wasn't until the launch of Nancy Reagan's "war on drugs" in 1986 and the simultaneous arrival of cocaine (later crack cocaine), and with it, HIV/AIDS, that the neighbourhood was utterly and finally transformed into the criminalized ghetto that it is today. While the DTES had been pivotal (a cauldron) to the formation of the redress movement, by the time the chips had fallen, there was nothing left of "value" in the devastated neighbourhood for the Japanese Canadian community to reclaim.

For many years, the Japanese Canadian community, including those institutions created by the redress movement itself, held a mostly ambivalent view of the DTES. The Powell Street Festival continued to take place, though always in uncomfortable juxtaposition with the surrounding environs. What is particularly ironic in hindsight is the epistemic dissonance between redress, one of Canada's most significant human rights achievements up to that point, and the massive human rights violations taking place before the very eyes of festival-goers, manifest in the racialized, unhoused, overpoliced, and generally undervalued people for whom the festival site is their proverbial "living room." Sadly, the majority of Nikkei want little to do with the DTES except for the annual celebration. Nor do they express a commitment to the ways in which communities of colour and Indigenous communities share important aspects of dispossession and the pursuit of repossession of rights historically denied to them.

Meanwhile, just as the neighbourhood gave birth to Japanese Canadian human rights five decades ago, the past three decades have seen a new human rights legacy born out of the DTES, expressed in the right to housing, to health, to harm reduction, and of course to self-determination on unceded Indigenous land. Amid increasing concern around housing affordability, land scarcity has grown. In the lead-up to the 2010 Olympics, the spectre of a new uprooting began to materialize in the DTES with the arrival of a strengthened municipal impetus for gentrification, euphemistically known as "revitalization." There have been a few successes: a needle exchange and safe injection site; the organization of advocates for sex workers' rights; the creation of organizations to advocate for decent housing and protection from unscrupulous landlords; resources put in place to address rising cases of opioid poisoning; and finally a modicum of reinvestment in housing. Perhaps most significantly, after decades of pressure on officials to address the hundreds of cases of missing and murdered Indigenous women and girls, a (controversial) commission of inquiry was established in 2016. This backdrop became the setting for our own affiliation with the DTES – for Audrey, a "return" of sorts, although she had never really left, and for Jeff a career-setting immersion. Through the lens of social geographers and with Audrey's encyclopedic record of Japanese Canadian legacy memory in the fabric of the neighbourhood and Jeff's activist connections, we began making common cause with those few Nikkei who saw Powell Street as a site not of nostalgia but of injustice.

The current triple crisis of housing inadequacy, mental health disinvestment, and drug criminalization is epitomized by the much-vaunted (by urban planners) and highly criticized (by DTES housing activists) Woodward's housing project, which opened its doors in 2009, paving the way for the rapid transformation of the neighbourhood under the guise of social-mix neighbourhood planning (Sutherland, Swanson, and Herman 2013), a "gentrification bomb" in the words of a local activist (Ball 2015). Within a couple of years, as we began our research, we observed the potential for cultural appropriation repeating itself in an impetus to manufacture a new "Japantown" out of a faux Japanese aesthetic, selectively drawing from the historical record when it suited the theme: Shinto arches (*torii*), lanterns, kimonos, and so on, but never working-class, labour aspirations for western lifestyle or embrace of contemporary western architecture, never challenging the complicity of a city administration in anti-Japanese racialization and human rights violations of the uprooting in the 1940s.

Our project, which began in 2012, introduced a giant question mark (literally, figuratively) into the idea of "Revitalizing Japantown?" that had taken hold in the planning processes. We proceeded to excavate the historical record of Japanese Canadian presence in the neighbourhood, actively tying our community's experiences to those of other past and present communities around a common sense of political inhabitation, human rights struggle, and the Right to Remain. Witnessing first-hand the inherent activism within the Nikkei community, often integral to social justice issues that surrounded them, we sought to activate and consolidate – to push back against the revitalization plan that many have worried is contributing to the uprooting of the low-income community. Refusing to allow our history to be co-opted into this agenda, we worked in tandem with DTES residents of all walks of life to critique the planning process, hopefully influencing it toward a more inclusive (rather than tokenistically consultative) approach that would pay far more attention to the historical antecedents of the traumas being felt in the neighbourhood. We were convinced that efforts to revitalize rather than "redress" past wrongs would only result in the worsening of human rights and lives disrupted.

In the summer of 2014, as our project was gathering steam, a tent city was erected in Oppenheimer Park, on the exact spot where the Nisei men's baseball team, the Asahi, played its home games. The Powell Street Festival was challenged to consider its social and political place (Cheung 2014), and the organizers made a decision to move the festival onto adjacent streets. That summer, for the first time, the Nikkei community showed explicit common cause with the current residents of Powell Street.

Shortly thereafter, our research project exhibited the works of activist artists with whom we had collaborated (Franks, Masuda, and Kobayashi 2017). There were two well-attended installations, one at Gallery Gachet in the Downtown Eastside, the other at the Nikkei National Museum in Burnaby (Carter 2015). We also undertook a range of informal street art projects that allowed dozens of people to express their feelings through art. Creative work both inspires the artists to articulate their human rights message and reaches out to the public, including city officials and members of the media, in a way that catches their imagination.

Drawing on the success of the first collaborative project, in 2017 we began a second project that continues to build on the theme of "The Right to Remain." This participatory project has had two major elements: 1) extending the creative aspects of the first project to a range of activities that include art, poetry (including Japanese-inspired haiku), and sharing circles overseen by Indigenous elders, poets, and Japanese Canadian haiku scholars, where Japanese and Indigenous cultural practices meet; and 2) working in collaboration with local tenant organizers to advocate for improved housing conditions. We have relied on the oft-stated concept of "nothing about us without us" to identify and document housing needs and to record the experiences of DTES residents. Our partnership is built on the firm commitment that trust matters. Deep partnerships with numerous DTES organizations, including the DTES Single-Room Occupancy Collaborative, a tenant organizing group, always ensure that we are part of, not observers of, the struggle. Most recently, this work has centred on supporting the emergence of the Uya'am Gaak Non-Profit Society, an Indigenous-led group dedicated to creating community and advocating for the rights of Indigenous single-room occupancy tenants in the DTES.

We hope that in the ongoing struggle our project is a catalyst for change. With our partners, we embody the hope that the redress settlement provided a clarion call for social justice. Notwithstanding the fact that one of us was among the crafters of the redress settlement and the other a distinct beneficiary (inspired toward activism and critical inquiry by the redress "seed"), we do not wish to romanticize the redress settlement or to make outrageous claims for its precedents. Indeed, we maintain a significant degree of ambivalence, given that the human rights issues surrounding the DTES have been taken up by so few in our community. Nonetheless, we observe a potential legacy for redress, mainly among Yonsei and Gosei activists, including a small but dedicated new generation of graduate students who find themselves advocating as Japanese Canadians for improved conditions for the low-income community, working in collaboration with allied activist groups in the DTES. The collaboration between scholars and community activists, and especially local Indigenous leaders, has led to a strong alliance for justice and a common understanding that the quest for justice involves all of us.

The Right to Remain Research Collective, of which we are a part, finds us in a privileged place to work with some of those students, and to take part in their growth as activist scholars. In addition to helping raise awareness of the dire need for improved housing and reduced persecution in the DTES, therefore, we can envision a future in which genuine and effective participatory, collaborative research action remains important. The campaign for the Right to Remain is not the same as the redress campaign, but it carries some of the same spirit and commitment to social change, which is ultimately what scholar activism is all about.

Notes

1 Gordon Hirabayashi refused internment and was convicted of curfew violation in
   1942. His case went to the US Supreme Court but was eventually overturned in 1987
   (*Hirabayashi v United States* 1987, 828 F.2d 591) when new evidence of misconduct
   of the part of the US government was discovered.
2 Indeed, a more cynical interpretation would say that participatory action research
   has for many become a matter of grants personship, a tick box in the research funding industry, which often brings little benefit to or involvement with local people.

References

Adachi, Ken. (1976) 1991. *The Enemy That Never Was: A History of the Japanese
   Canadians.* Toronto: McClelland and Stewart.
Ball, David P. 2015. "Inside Woodward's, a Still Contentious Social Housing Experi-
   ment." *The Tyee*, February 15, 2015, https://thetyee.ca/News/2015/02/25/
   Woodwards-Social-Housing/.
Carter, Beth, ed. 2015. *Revitalizing Japantown? A Unifying Exploration of Human
   Rights, Branding, and Place.* Burnaby, BC: Nikkei National Museum and Cul-
   tural Centre. https://www.righttoremain.ca/wp-content/uploads/2015/12/
   20151102.1856_rjcatalogue_web.pdf.
Cheung, Christopher. 2014. "UGM and Powell Street Festival Move Events from Oppen-
   heimer Park." *Vancouver Courier*, July 24. https://www.vancourier.com/news/
   ugm-and-powell-street-festival-move-events-from-oppenheimer-park-1.1259416.
Franks, Aaron, Jeff R. Masuda, and Audrey Kobayashi. 2017. "Mobilizing the Right
   to Remain." In *Public Art Encounters*, edited by Martin Zabrecki and Joni M.
   Palmer. Farnham, Surrey, UK: Ashgate.
Japanese Canadian Centennial Project. 1978. *A Dream of Riches: The Japanese Cana-
   dians 1877–1977.* Toronto: Gilchrist Wright.
Kobayashi, Audrey. 1994. "Coloring the Field: Gender, 'Race,' and the Politics of
   Fieldwork." *Professional Geographer* 45 (1): 73–80.
– 1996. *Memories of Our Past: A Brief History and Walking Tour of Powell Street.*
   Vancouver: NRC.
– 2017. "Situated Knowledge, Reflexivity." In *International Encyclopedia of Human
   Geography*, vol. 10, edited by Rob Kitchin and Nigel Thrift, 138–43. Oxford:
   Elsevier.
Masuda, Jeff R., and Aaron Franks. 2014. "The Right to Remain in Vancouver's Nihon-
   machi/Downtown Eastside." *The Bulletin: A Journal of Japanese-Canadian
   Community, History, and Culture.* https://jccabulletin-geppo.ca/the-right-to
   -remain-in-vancouvers-nihonmachidowntown-eastside/.
Miki, Roy, and Cassandra Kobayashi. 1991. *Justice in Our Time: The Japanese
   Canadian Redress Settlement.* Vancouver/Winnipeg: Talonbooks/National
   Association of Japanese Canadians.
Powell Street Revue and the Chinese Canadian Writers Workshop, eds. 1979.
   Inalienable Rice: A Chinese and Japanese Canadian Anthology. Vancouver:
   Intermedia Press.

Sutherland, Rory, Jean Swanson, and Tamara Herman. 2013. *No Place to Go: Losing Affordable Housing and Community; Carnegie Community Action Project's 2013 Hotel Survey and Housing Report.* Vancouver (unceded Coast Salish Territories): Carnegie Community Action Project.

Suyemoto, Karen L. 2018. "Ethnic and Racial Identity in Multiracial Sansei: Intergenerational Effects of the World War II Mass Incarceration of Japanese Americans." *Genealogy* 2 (3): 26. https://doi.org/10.3390/genealogy2030026.

Contributors

Dorothy Cucw-la7 Christian is of the Secwepemc and Syilx Nations from the interior of British Columbia. Her home community of Splatsin, is one of seventeen communities that comprise the Secwepemc Nation. She is the eldest of ten and has one daughter and more than seventy nieces, nephews, great nieces and nephews, and great-great nieces. She is the matriarch of her family. Dr. Christian currently serves in the Faculty of Graduate Studies at Simon Fraser University (SFU) as the Associate Director of Indigenous Policy and Pedagogy. Her research and work in academia has consistently centralized Indigenous knowledge long before those terms were recognized in the academy. Her academic work is juxtaposed with the latest buzzwords "decolonizing and indigenizing," and is reflected in her institutional engagement. She is Auntie Advisor to the SFU Advisory for Equity, Diversity and Inclusion.

R. Tod Duncan is a Sansei/Yonsei Japanese Canadian and a PhD candidate in Social and Political Thought at York University, where his dissertation research focuses on the development of Canadian multiculturalism, and the internment and redress of Japanese Canadians. This research is as much a personal history as it is an academic project, since several members of his family were interned during the Second World War. Tod currently lives in Toronto, where he works as a researcher for a municipal social services association, exploring issues around housing and homelessness, social assistance, and children's services.

Smaro Kamboureli is the Avie Bennett Chair in the Department of English at the University of Toronto. The author of *On the Edge of Genre: The Contemporary Canadian Long Poem* and *Scandalous Bodies: Diasporic Literatures in English Canada*, which won the Gabrielle Roy Prize for Canadian criticism, she has edited and co-edited many volumes, including her anthology *Making a Difference: Canadian Multicultural Literatures;* Lee Maracle's *Memory Serves: Oratories; Shifting the Ground of Canadian Literary Studies*, co-edited with Robert Zacharias; and more recently *Land/Relations: Possibilities of Justice in Canadian Literatures*, co-edited with Larissa Lai.

Audrey Kobayashi is a Fellow of the Royal Society of Canada and Professor Emeritus and former Queen's Research Chair in the Department of Geography and Planning, Queen's University. She has published extensively in the areas of human rights and activism, anti-racism, immigration, human geography theories, and the historical geographies of Japanese Canadian communities.

Bonita Lawrence teaches in the Indigenous Studies Program at York University. Her books include *"Real" Indians and Others: Mixed-Blood Urban Native Peoples and Indigenous Nationhood* (University of Nebraska Press, 2004); *Fractured Homeland: Federal Recognition and Algonquin Identity in Ontario* (UBC Press, 2012); and the historical novel *N'in D'la Owey Innklan: Mi'kmaq Sojourns in England* (Austin Macauley, 2020). Of Mi'kmaw ancestry, she co-authored "Decolonizing Anti-Racism" with Enakshi Dua in 2005, and "Indigenous People and Black People: Settlers or Allies" with Zainab Amadahy in 2006. She has focused on relations between Indigenous peoples and other peoples of colour for the past decade.

Jeff Masuda is a professor in the School of Public Health and Social Policy, University of Victoria. He is a Fellow of the Canadian Academy of Health Sciences and former Canada Research Chair in Environmental Health Equity. His research interests are in the historical geographies of racial dispossession, community organizing, health geography theory and method, anti-racism and decolonizing research, housing, public health, and urban inequality.

Kirsten Emiko McAllister grew up in Snuneymuxw territories in what is now known as Nanaimo in the colonial jurisdiction of British Columbia. A professor at Simon Fraser University's School of Communication, her publications include *Locating Memory: Photographic Acts* (Berghahn 2006); *Terrain of Memory: A Japanese Canadian Memorial Project* (UBC Press, 2010); *Migration and the Politics of Fieldwork: Reimagining Trans/national Spaces from the Perspectives of Migrants* (Routledge, forthcoming 2025); *Asylum and Art: Reconfiguring the Social Geography of Glasgow* (Palgrave Macmillan, forthcoming 2025). She has also published in areas that include Memory Studies, Visual Studies, and Refugee Studies, and has used creative non-fiction, including in her writing on her family's relations as settlers to the Indigenous Nations where they have lived and/or been interned.

Mona Oikawa lives on the territory care taken by the Anishinabek Nation; the Haudenosaunee Confederacy; the Wendat; and the current treaty holders, the Mississaugas of the Credit First Nation. This territory is subject of the Dish with One Spoon Wampum Belt Covenant. Mona is a faculty member in York University's School of Gender, Sexuality and Women's Studies, and is the author of *Cartographies of Violence: Japanese Canadian Women, Memory, and the Subjects of the Internment* (University of Toronto Press, 2012), the first book to analyse relational and gendered subject formation through the internment. Her academic publications situate the history of Japanese Canadians in relation to settler colonialism and Indigenous peoples. Her literary publications include poetry (forthcoming in Brynn Saito and Brandon Shimoda, eds., *The Gate of Memory: Poems by Descendants of Nikkei Wartime Incarceration* published by Haymarket Books) and creative nonfiction that address issues of racism, gender, and sexuality.

Index

Note: The following abbreviations are used in headings and subheadings: "DTES" for Downtown Eastside, "IRSSA" for Indian Residential Schools Settlement Agreement, "JCCA" for Japanese Canadian Citizens' Associations, "NAJC" for National Association of Japanese Canadians, "TRC" for Truth and Reconciliation Commission of Canada, and "UNDRIP" for United Nations Declaration on the Rights of Indigenous Peoples.

Printed and bound in Canada

Set in Segoe and Warnock Pro by Apex CoVantage, LLC

Copy editor: Frank Chow

Proofreader: Sophie Pouyanne

Indexer: Marnie Lamb

Cover designer: Gabi Proctor

Cover images: "Takao Tanabe, Cook Channel, Nootka Sound, 1996, lithograph on paper, 47/50, 48.9 × 57.2 cm. Gift of the artist, 2023. Courtesy of Takao Tanabe and the Art Gallery of Guelph. The land depicted in the cover art by Takao Tanabe is the "unceded and never surrendered territory" of the Mowachaht/Muchalaht First Nation (https://www.mmfn.ca/, 2023)."

Authorized Representative: Easy Access System Europe – Mustamäe tee 50, 10621 Tallinn, Estonia, gpsr.requests@easproject.com